PETER SMITH

MINING CAMP TALES OF THE SILVERY SLOCAN

A HISTORY OF BRITISH COLUMBIA'S SILVER RUSH

For Lochlan, Alex, Vignette, and Oswald

Heritage House Publishing Company Ltd.
heritagehouse.ca

Cataloguing information available from Library and Archives Canada

978-1-77203-539-1 (paperback)
978-1-77203-540-7 (e-book)

Copyedited by Alexis Anderson
Proofread by Jess Klaassen-Wright
Index by Alexis Anderson
Cover and interior design by Jacqui Thomas
Cover photo: Rambler-Cariboo mine, c. 1900. Photographer unknown.
Image courtesy of the Royal BC Museum and Archives.
Interior photographs as attributed.

The interior of this book was produced on 100% post-consumer recycled paper, processed chlorine free, and printed with vegetable-based inks.

Heritage House gratefully acknowledges that the land on which we live and work is within the traditional territories of the lək̓ʷəŋən (Esquimalt and Songhees), Malahat, Pacheedaht, Scia'new, T'Sou-ke, and W̱SÁNEĆ (Pauquachin, Tsartlip, Tsawout, Tseycum) Peoples.

We acknowledge the financial support of the Government of Canada through the Canada Book Fund (CBF) and the Canada Council for the Arts, and the Province of British Columbia through the British Columbia Arts Council and the Book Publishing Tax Credit.

29 28 27 26 25   1 2 3 4 5

Printed in Canada

CONTENTS

Shorn of its rough edges, the life of a prospector is a poem . . .
What a grand persevering life of struggle and privation and poverty!
With hope deferred from year to year, but always hopeful . . .

—"The Prospector," *The Miner*, April 11, 1891

Slocan Lake looking north, c. 1897. Artist: Lindley Crease.
IMAGE COURTESY OF THE ROYAL BC MUSEUM AND ARCHIVES

INTRODUCTION

THIS IS THE STORY OF a silver rush, and the mining camps it spawned, but the history of British Columbia (BC) in the nineteenth century is largely the story of two gold rushes: the Fraser River gold rush in 1858 and the Cariboo gold rush in the following years. The California gold rush of 1849 had established a pattern—riches aplenty for those willing to venture into the vast wilderness of western North America. There were plenty who were willing. Fortune seekers and adventurers set out in droves from the eastern United States and points further afield. California was followed by Fraser River and Cariboo, and other lesser bonanzas along the western cordillera.

Gold was king, but there were silver rushes too: the Comstock Lode in Nevada in 1860, followed by discoveries in Leadville and other Colorado sites; Tombstone, Arizona; and the immediate precursor to silver discoveries in BC's West Kootenay region—Idaho's Coeur d'Alene silver rush of the late 1880s. From 1891 to 1900, West Kootenay's Slocan district pushed its way into the spotlight. Almost completely unpopulated by settlers in early 1891, the Slocan attracted thousands of pilgrims over the following years, lured by some of the richest silver deposits ever discovered. Despite several setbacks, the Slocan was by 1897 the most important and productive mining district in all BC.[1]

The mining camps and boom towns of the west were a puzzle to easterners. Mining camps with names like Slocan City and Kaslo City taxed the minds of most easterners, who had come from cities with populations in the thousands and sometimes millions. Some of the "cities" on the western mining frontier had more horses and mules than people. But these were "boom times," and boomers expected populations to multiply and prosperity to reign. A contemporary source described a "boom" as "a rush of people to any region offering new and enhanced possibilities of improvement in condition or estate."[2] This is certainly what the people who rushed to the Slocan in the 1890s were counting on.

From the start, when prospectors began staking mineral claims, some were also staking townsites. This followed the pattern familiar from dozens of other western mining rushes. Following the laws of BC, mining camps started out as Crown grants for townsites. Once they were staked, prospective grantees would follow the basic requirements—having the land surveyed, for example—and then patiently await approval. If the lands were granted, then streets and lots would be laid out in grids, and promoters would soon be advertising the newest metropolis of the mining district. As historian Cole Harris has aptly described it, "the location of the future was up for grabs."[3] In the boom economy of the frontier, every so-called city expected to become one in fact as well as in name.

In the west, these "cities" were almost universally referred to as "mining camps." In 1898, the *Rossland Weekly Miner* weighed in on use of the term: "Miners applied thc name to the collection of tents and rudely constructed houses in which they resided while conducting their first mining operations." It could also apply to the larger, urbanized "town" that might grow from the mining camp, provided that its existence was reliant on the mines that had given the camp its start. The line between "mining camp" and "town" was hazy, and the terms were sometimes used interchangeably, but when referred to as a "mining camp . . . not a mining man in the west . . . would fail to understand its use."[4]

West Kootenay was just the latest extension of the western mining frontier. Wherever there was a mineral discovery, a mining camp would spring up. As early as May 1892, the *Vancouver Daily World* noted there were "no less than 16 townsites in West Kootenay district south of Revelstoke."[5] The *Inland Sentinel* of Kamloops complained that it was hard to keep track of all the new townsites, "they multiply so fast."[6] Of course, not all townsites prospered. Many were little more than a name on a surveyor's map—if they were on the map at all.

Annie Girdwood, a correspondent for the *Guelph Daily Mercury* and *Advertiser*, landed in the Slocan in 1897 to take on a teaching position. She described a typical mining camp for her eastern readers:

> A mining camp in its first boom presents a medley conglomeration of tents, hotels, restaurants, stores, log cabins, cedar shakes [*sic*] all

> huddled together . . . During the first boom land goes up to fabulous prices . . . A house that in Ontario would not be considered a first class wood-shed will rent for fifty dollars per month.[7]

Mining rushes are all about speculation. Not just the speculation of how rich a single claim might be, but speculation on the success of the whole district. Townsite speculators gambled on the prospects ahead. When newspaper correspondent R.E. Gosnell visited West Kootenay in 1892, he described the real estate situation as a "lottery."[8] There were many willing to take a chance, convinced that their numbers would come up.

The bishop of New Westminster saw it all on an early visit to West Kootenay. Clearly, he was not a gambling man:

> The real estate fiend had blocked out town sites every few miles without regard to anything but his own aggrandizement, a feat in which he is only too successful, for it is not exaggeration to say that one-tenth of the money sunk by the unwary investor in those embryo cities that will never be born could have accomplished such a development of mineral resources of the district as would have advanced by many years the prosperity both of the country and the investors themselves. There are, for example, largely advertised "towns" on the lake which consist of a shack and a tent or two. There are "towns" where instead of new buildings going up, the existing buildings are being torn down to be moved elsewhere. And yet the maps of these "towns" are to be seen posted in every real estate office throughout the land, and lots are being sold at prices which will certainly never be warranted during the present century.[9]

Throughout the mining districts of western North America, there was a common language of development and enterprise that made little sense to most easterners. The bishop of New Westminster had heard the language of boomers and was as baffled as others. Many westerners learned it but were not so naïve as to swallow it whole. Some even called for the abandonment of all "inflated and hifalutin' terms." In 1892 a writer for Nelson's *Tribune* tried to make this case after visiting a Montana mining camp that had recently proclaimed itself a "city." A minister there—recently arrived from the east—in one of his sermons made the mistake of referring to his new home as a "village":

> Let us drop our foolish notion that we can make things big by calling them by big names. A place of one, two or three thousand inhabitants is no city; why call it so? A creek does not become a river by naming it a river, nor does a school become a university by the same process. How ridiculous to call a little second-class tavern the "Grand Central Hotel," or a tailor shop a "merchant tailoring establishment," or a millinery shop an "emporium of fashion," or a barber shop a "tonsorial parlor."[10]

The author noted with approval a hotel in Idaho that billed itself as "the only second-class hotel in the Coeur d'Alene country." In the coming years, there would be plenty of "tonsorial parlors" and at least one "Grand Central Hotel" in the Slocan.

English author Rudyard Kipling travelled the western slope of North America in 1892. With his eye for detail, he vividly described the pervasive boom town culture. Of all the excitements of life, "there are few to be compared with the whirl of a red-hot boom." He described the scene: "the sweating, jostling mob at the sale of town-lots"; "the packed real-estate offices" filled with agents—"lost novelists of prodigious imagination"; and "the sleep of utterly worn-out men, three in each room of the shanty hotel." All of this rang true of the Slocan. As Kipling said, "There is a contagion in a boom as irresistible as that of a panic in a theatre."[11]

One of Kipling's schoolmates at the United Services College in North Devon was Charles Hugonin. Hugonin later emigrated to Canada and by 1892 was deeply involved in townsite promotion. Kipling visited Vancouver in early April 1892 on his way to India. Hugonin was there too, on his way from Victoria to the Slocan. Perhaps the two schoolmates renewed old acquaintances. If they did, it's likely the topic of western boom towns came up.

Revelstoke, Nelson, and Ainsworth—which started as Farwell, Stanley, and Hot Springs Camp, respectively—were the principal West Kootenay camps in 1890. Revelstoke, on the Canadian Pacific Railway (CPR) mainline at the northern margin of West Kootenay, was removed from the silver mining districts but did serve as an important transshipment centre. It was also a transition point for veterans of the CPR camps who would take up the prospecting life in West Kootenay. Nelson was sustained by the silver mines on Toad Mountain, first discovered by the Hall brothers in 1886.

Ainsworth got its start earlier, about the time an American prospector named Robert Sproule staked several claims on the eastern shore of

Kootenay Lake in 1882. The most promising was the Blue Bell. The Blue Bell's lead deposits were well known to Indigenous Peoples and a few trappers, but the district was so remote in the early 1880s that it was impractical for development. This would change. Sproule's claim attracted other adventurers. In October 1882, when Sproule left his claim briefly, an Englishman named Thomas Hammill, relying on some restrictive regulations in the mining law, re-staked the claim and called it the Silver Queen. Sproule was incensed. The dispute went to court, and while Sproule won at trial and appeal, he was forced to sell an interest in his claim to cover his court costs. This interest eventually ended up in the hands of Thomas Hammill. Sproule was outraged and sought revenge. In the spring of 1885, he tracked Hammill down and murdered him with a well-placed rifle shot. Sproule was hanged the following year.[12]

Despite a sensational murder, the "wild west" of legend and lore was waning in the years leading up to the Slocan rush, but the porous border and the chance to explore new territories lured many characters who loomed large in the tales told of pioneer days in the west. By the time that Robert Sproule dangled at the end of a hangman's rope, steamboats were plying the waters of the upper Columbia River, and the possibility of shipping ore out from West Kootenay was coming closer to reality. Wilbur "W.A." Hendryx, a physician and capitalist from Grand Rapids, Michigan, had taken over Sproule's interest in the Blue Bell and was putting money into development work. However, the location of the mine on the largely unpopulated eastern shore of Kootenay Lake hindered progress. Across Kootenay Lake, Ainsworth, dominated by Charles Olsen's saloon and Cariboo pioneer Gustavus Blin "G.B." Wright's store, served as the region's de facto commercial centre and became a jumping-off point for prospectors eager to explore regions even more remote.

Slocan Lake and valley are set in the Selkirk Mountains in the narrow cleavage between Kootenay Lake and the Purcell Mountains to the east, and the Monashee Mountains and Arrow Lakes to the west. The area was little explored by fur traders and Europeans before 1891, but it was inevitable that the inexorable expansion of the western mining frontier would eventually reach the mountainous divide and thickly forested slopes between Slocan and Kootenay Lakes. The Slocan wasn't a complete mystery, though. In 1884, BC pioneer Gilbert Malcolm "G.M." Sproat mentioned the lake in his official "Report on Kootenay" produced for the provincial government.[13]

At the time of the Slocan discoveries, BC had been part of Canada for just twenty years. The legacies of the earlier Crown colonies of Vancouver Island and British Columbia lingered on. Many of the politicians, judges, and civil administrators were part of that legacy. The new province's settler population was concentrated in Victoria and lower Vancouver Island, and on the mainland around New Westminster and upstart Vancouver. There were settlements in the goldfields of Cariboo and the Okanagan Valley, but the northern and southeastern portions of the province were sparsely populated, with vast tracts of territory largely unknown to outsiders. This was starting to change, however, as men and women looked to tap unexploited resource riches.

As Judge Howay, an early historian of BC, put it, "the land was infected with prospectors."[14] Thick forests of fir, pine, and cedar, and rumours of rich galena ore—a potent amalgam of silver and lead—drew adventurers to West Kootenay. The completion of the CPR in 1885 gave ready access to the Columbia River and its Arrow Lakes to the south. Prospectors were trickling in too from south of the border in Washington and Idaho Territories.

While the geographical area covered by this book is centred around Slocan Lake and the mountains that rise above it to the east, the story of the Slocan rush cannot be told without wandering a bit beyond these confines. Noted Slocan newspaperman Robert Thornton "R.T." Lowery, who would go on to finance and edit several Kaslo and Slocan newspapers, was adamant that anything on the Kootenay Lake divide, sloping down to Kootenay Lake—mines and camps—was not properly in the Slocan. This might strictly be true if the respective watersheds of Slocan and Kootenay Lakes were the only criteria used to define the area. But these criteria do not suffice. Nor do the artificial boundaries imposed on the landscape by the provincial government when, for administrative purposes, it created mining districts. The boundaries of the Slocan must not be drawn so narrowly. People who worked at the Whitewater mine on the Kaslo slope in the 1890s would have considered themselves residents of the Slocan—despite the fact that the waters of Whitewater Creek were destined for Kootenay Lake.

Kaslo and Nakusp, on Kootenay and Arrow Lakes respectively, clearly did not fit within Lowery's geographical construct. However, both were critically important to the early development of the Slocan. They were the principal gateways to the new district. The early history of Kaslo is inextricably linked to the Slocan. Most of the women and men who came looking for riches in the early 1890s did so by way of Kaslo, and many Slocan miners and mine owners took up permanent residence in the camp at the mouth of Kaslo Creek.

We will venture further afield too. The population of West Kootenay throughout the 1890s was highly mobile. It was common to find prospectors, miners, merchants, and capitalists moving from one camp to another, always looking for opportunities to get ahead. Nelson, Revelstoke, and Rossland will figure in our journey, but our central focus will always be the Slocan heartland of New Denver, Sandon, Three Forks, Slocan City, and their adjacent hinterlands.

For all its renown, the Slocan mining rush was contained in a relatively brief window of time. There is mining activity there today, but the story included in these pages fades to black by 1900—though, truth be told, the decline began in 1897. A precipitous drop in the price of silver, a unionized workforce at odds with stubborn mine owners, inept government management of the mining industry, and the strong pull of the Klondike gold rush all contributed to the decline and denouement of the Slocan silver "rush." There was a brief glimmer of hope in early 1900 when the labour troubles that had plagued the district for the better part of a year were resolved, but within weeks a devastating fire put an end to most hopes. The mining industry would recover from time to time over the next hundred plus years, but the glory days of the 1890s would never return.

Mining rushes present something of a challenge for historians and population analysts. In 1890 there were likely fewer than a dozen people living in the area where Kaslo and the Slocan mining camps first sprang up. As John Douglas Belshaw has noted in his study of population growth in BC, "a large Kootenay silver town might exist for fewer than ten years and thus fall completely between the cracks of decennial censuses." This was largely true of the Slocan. In 1890 there was likely no one living permanently along the banks of what would become Carpenter, Seaton, and Sandon Creeks. Sandon, which Belshaw described as a "shooting star" in terms of population growth, had a population of between two and five thousand in 1898, but the numbers plummeted by the time of the 1901 census and fell steadily thereafter. To present day readers, it might seem like the Slocan silver rush has fallen through the cracks of BC history.[15]

The last decade of the nineteenth century was a time of great change across North America and Europe. There had been a depression in 1873, but in the years that followed, wealth, technological innovation, and invention advanced on all fronts, leading to what became known as the Gilded Age. Historian Barbara Tuchman has noted that "the relative invention rate reached the highest point in history" during the 1890s.[16] Electrification and telephone networks became commonplace, electric and gasoline cars began to replace horse-drawn carriages, and the technology for sound recordings and moving pictures spread. No one would suggest that the Slocan was at the forefront of any of these developments, but residents were not unaware of them either. Though grounded in the nineteenth century, many looked forward to the twentieth.

But while the waning years of the nineteenth century were marked by great advances in science and technology, the racist attitudes and discriminatory practices that clouded much of the century lived on. The Slocan was not immune to the tenor of the times. There were few interactions between prospectors and Indigenous Peoples during the silver rush, but a significant number of Black people were present, and they often suffered from ingrained prejudices. Many Slocan residents prided themselves on being bastions of "anti-Chinese" sentiment, where Chinese men and women were not welcome. Various European groups, including the Irish, Italians, and Swedes, were treated poorly at one time or another, and Canadians and Americans sometimes butted heads. Women were often marginalized, and like Indigenous People, they could not vote. Their opportunities were limited by convention. Some of these attitudes are reflected in the pages that follow. Discriminatory behaviour was wrong then, just as it is wrong today, but we only learn from history by acknowledging it.

We should not downplay the threads of intolerance that ran through the western mining frontier, but the multi-ethnic and racial context of most mining camps, and the confined spaces they occupied, meant that the public face of intolerance was often more muted than it might have been in less diverse settings. Closely rubbed shoulders sometimes led to abrasions, but on the whole, people got along reasonably well. An 1895 account described one of the Slocan camps as "a cosmopolitan, Babalonian [*sic*] town."[17] There were Japanese, Black, and white people—including Canadians, Americans, and people from England, Scotland, France, and Italy. In private, people likely clung to the societal prejudices they had grown up with. In general, though—excepting the endemic prejudice against Indigenous and Chinese people—residents usually kept their prejudices to themselves. All were united in the pursuit of wealth.

As the Slocan mining camps grew, they had dreams of grandeur. Why couldn't the wealth of the silver mines transform one or more of the camps into a city to rival Chicago, Denver—or at least Spokane? Those with a stake in the Slocan believed in these dreams. In the gravy days of 1897 and 1898, so did visitors. Business leaders and industrialists paid attention too. The trade of the new mining district was eagerly sought by merchants on both sides of the border. Capital flowed in from all over the United States and Britain. There were calls to build a railway from Vancouver or New Westminster to the mines. Then, during the mid-1890s, the Slocan proved a key battleground in the war for North American railway dominance between the CPR's William Cornelius Van Horne and the Great Northern Railway's (GNR) James Jerome Hill.

Today, the Slocan seems a relative backwater, producing a few colourful and respected politicians but, as a district, not really drawing much attention. This was not the case in the 1890s, when the wealth of the Slocan and West Kootenay, and the growing population, could not be ignored by the more populous centres on the coast. The Slocan silver ores were fabulously rich and easily worked, leading to the district's reputation as a "poor man's country."

By 1897, the Slocan was an important economic driver and major influence in both politics and finance. Entrepreneurs from Victoria, Vancouver, and New Westminster pulled up their coastal stakes to profit from the interior silver mines. Local issues took centre stage in provincial election campaigns. Premiers and would-be premiers regularly trekked to the Slocan to promote their visions of prosperity for the people of BC.

Rossland, with its vast stores of copper and gold ore, is better remembered and lauded today. In the 1890s, it revelled in the riches extracted from the LeRoi and War Eagle. But even then, the much vaunted LeRoi did not pay out as much in dividends as the Slocan Star, and more miners were working in the Slocan mines than in those of Rossland. However, the "magic" of gold attracted investment to Rossland from Britain and beyond. Newspapers in the 1890s shifted their focus from the Slocan to the gold mines of Rossland, but the Slocan mines, at least up until 1899, quietly and consistently shipped out thousands of tons of silver-rich ore. As one Slocan capitalist remarked in 1897: "We do not make as much noise as the people of Rossland, but we get there all the same."[18]

Parts of the Slocan story have been told before in numerous histories, some of which are listed in the select bibliography at the back of this book. However, most of these histories are extremely local in focus and do not cover the entire ground. There is more to tell. I had the good fortune to interview several Slocan pioneers in the late 1970s and early 1980s. It was a pleasure talking with them, and their stories were fascinating, but the early days that form the focus here were before their time. They had tales passed down to them from those who were there at the beginning, but those stories inevitably reflected the bias of the original tellers. They were often misremembered or embellished with each retelling.

When I researched the early days of the Slocan rush through contemporary newspaper accounts—a resource not easily available to those long-time residents I interviewed—I found people and stories largely unknown to succeeding generations. Ed Vipond, one of the pioneers I interviewed, was well aware of the inconstancy of memory. His advice to another researcher has served as a guidepost to me: "I would still place most reliance on the printed records of the times, memories fade, as I find mine are . . . "[19] I am not so naïve, however, as to think newspaper accounts are entirely reliable either. They, too, are largely dependent on oral sources, and the diligence of reporters, and often mirror the political and social biases of their editors. Nevertheless, they allow us to at least get closer to versions of the truth.

I believe that we need to remember and celebrate the achievements of the silver rush pioneers in the same way that we do for veterans of BC's gold rushes. They played a critical role in the history of BC when the Slocan silver mines were lauded around the world. In a pioneering essay first published in 1985, Cole Harris described the "industry and the good life around Idaho Peak." He noted that in the 1890s, all the adult settlers in the Slocan "lived with memories of somewhere else."[20] Some of those memories stretched back to the middle of the nineteenth century and would influence the twentieth.

A NOTE ABOUT MEASUREMENTS:

Canada had not yet converted to the metric system in the 1890s. I have left the original weights and measures as they would have appeared in contemporary historical sources. To assist present day readers who are more familiar with the metric system, I have included conversions below:

WEIGHTS	MEASURES
1 ounce = 28.4 grams	1 inch = 2.5 centimetres
1 pound = 0.45 kilograms	1 foot = 30.5 centimetres
1 ton = 907.2 kilograms	1 mile = 1.6 kilometres
	1 acre = .40 hectares

1

DISCOVERIES

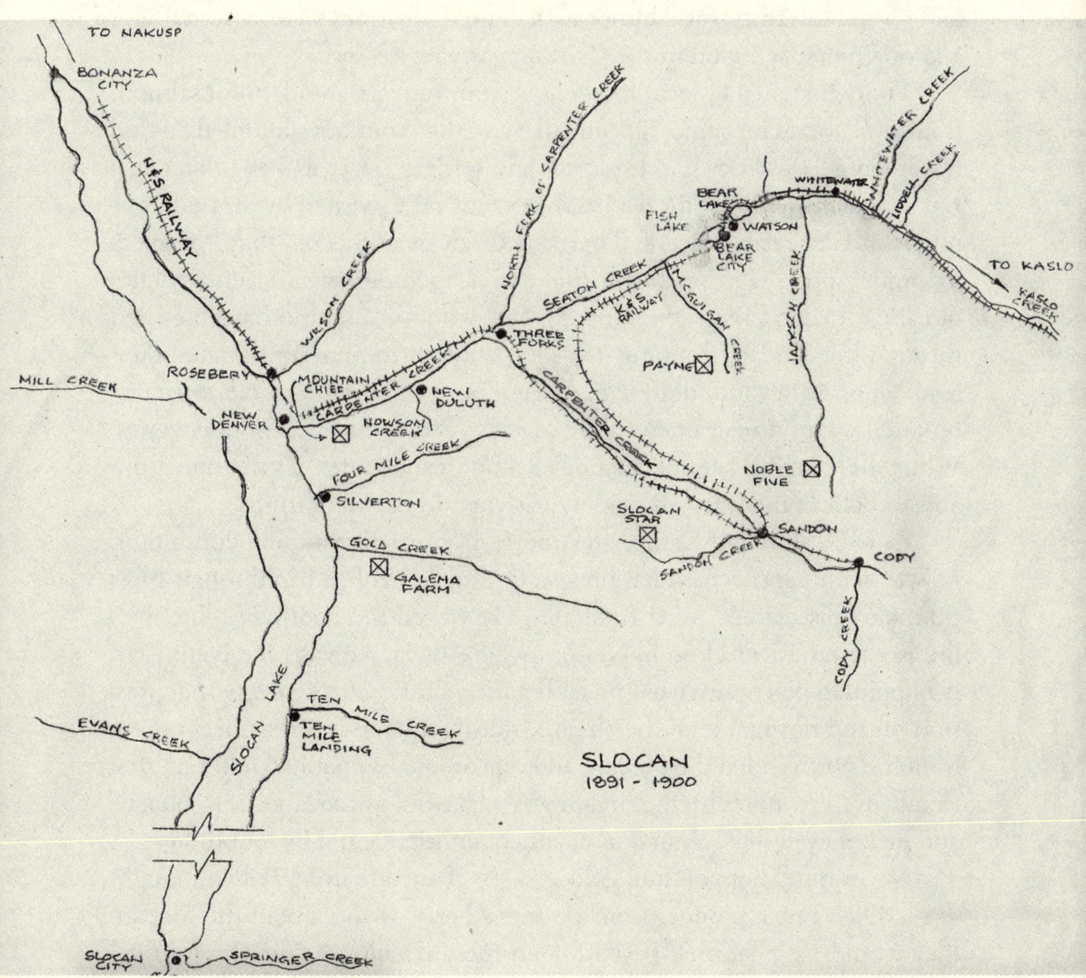

The Slocan, 1891–1900. IAN MCKAY

IN 1884, ROBERT "HAROLD" BAIRD, a Montana liquor salesman who supplied the CPR construction camps with whisky, did a little prospecting around Slocan Lake. Baird and his Indigenous companion were said to have found placer gold, but not enough to pay. However, Baird would not be around to corroborate the story. In November 1884, he was robbed and murdered north of the Slocan, allegedly by American badman "Bulldog" Kelly. Then in 1885, an unnamed prospector arrived in Farwell on the upper Columbia River. He had come from Kootenay Lake by way of Slocan Lake and River and was packing some fine specimens of galena ore—likely gathered in the Slocan. He also claimed to have found gold on Slocan River and vowed to return for a closer look. The discoveries were reported in a Victoria newspaper and in the *Canadian Mining Review*.

Though known to local Indigenous communities for plentiful salmon, trout, and abundant game, Slocan Lake and the mountains huddled around it were largely unknown to explorers and settlers as late as 1891. The lake was mapped by at least the 1840s, but it was rarely visited by fur traders or others of European descent. There are a few accounts of "stray" prospectors and trappers viewing the pristine waters, including near-legendary tales of early Hudson's Bay Company trappers who were said to have travelled through the Slocan, stopping just long enough to plunder the abundant lead deposits they found there to make their own bullets. An old forge was reportedly found near one of the Slocan's earliest and richest discoveries. While there is little other evidence to support such tales, it's not unreasonable to believe that they contain at least a grain or two of truth.

In 1889, Randall Kemp, an American journalist, mining consultant, railway scout, and occasional prospector, made his first trip through BC's Boundary district and West Kootenay. He visited the Poorman mine near the Kootenay River close to Nelson, where he spoke with Ike Nail: "Mr. Nail pointed down the river and called my attention to the deepest depression on the north side of the stream, stating a large creek came in there from the north called the Slocan, and that an old trapper had told him that twenty or thirty miles up the stream was a lake but not so large as Kootenay, and he believed that mineral in paying quantities would be found there."[1]

Never mind trappers and gold seekers. If anyone in 1891 had thought to ask Dick Fry, a pioneer from Bonner's Ferry, Idaho, about the Slocan, they would have learned he had been there decades before the Johnny-come-lately prospectors. In 1892, Fry told a reporter that he had been "all over that country and fished in the lake 30 years ago."[2] Indigenous Peoples, whether Ktunaxa or Sinixt, who had roamed West Kootenay for hundreds, perhaps thousands of years, told him he was the first white man into the country.[3] For Fry, there was probably nothing remarkable about the Slocan. A cursory search for gold yielded nothing of interest, and there were more than enough fish in other lakes and rivers closer to his home. Fry returned to Bonner's Ferry, and Slocan Lake and the surrounding mountains slipped back into obscurity. The years passed by one after another.

In 1890, George Kane applied for a Crown grant for land at the mouth of Kaslo Creek on Kootenay Lake. He got the grant, but for the first year the population of "Kaslo City" consisted only of his brother David and a semi-domesticated black bear. In the following summer, there was a minor silver rush up into the mountains sloping west above Kane's land, but by late August 1891, the Kaslo Creek excitement was in decline. The discoveries were not insignificant, but they were not as rich or as extensive as had first been hoped. Many prospectors, disillusioned and restless, packed out for new districts. However, there were at least two prospectors more venturesome than the rest. Former circus performer Eli Carpenter—known as "Frenchy" to some of his contemporaries—and John L. Seaton—sometimes known as "Tennessee Jack"—were both experienced prospectors who had been lingering in West Kootenay for at least a few months, perhaps longer.

The two partners followed Kaslo Creek up the mountain slopes until they reached Bear and Fish Lakes, two small bodies of water named by earlier visitors. This marked the divide between the Kootenay and Slocan Lake watersheds. Rather than turning back at the mountainous divide, the two men kept pushing west, into the thick forests and jutting mountains that bordered the two lakes. According to Seaton, "We decided to strike out for ourselves . . . we kept right up the north fork of the Kaslo and dropped down on the Slocan side into a basin."[4]

For several days the two men wandered the thickly forested mountainsides looking for mineralized outcroppings, or "ledges." While veins of silver and lead were often buried deep in the mountains, there was a saying that "whales always come up to spout." It was believed that silver veins would almost always at some point be visible on the ground. They were also looking for "float"—detached pieces of ore sucked up and spit out by ancient glaciers. The prospector's challenge was to trace the float back to its point of origin and so locate the ledge. This was made more difficult in the Slocan because of the forest and thick undergrowth.

The steep slopes were studded with a mixed coniferous forest. Fir, spruce, cedar, hemlock, pine, and tamarack grew to great heights. The biggest trees grew where the creeks ran. In the valleys, the undergrowth was thick with black huckleberry, white-flowering rhododendron, and red osier dogwood. Devil's club was especially troublesome: "The points of the spines break off in the flesh, causing it to fester and become very painful."[5] Giant cottonwoods, swollen with water, towered above small patches of wetland. Isolated pockets of coastal yellow cedar emphasized the wet, west-coast-like climate. In 1888, years before he ascended to the presidency of the United States, Theodore Roosevelt camped on the shore of Kootenay Lake and hiked the slopes rising above in search of grizzly bears. He vividly described the "tangled, brush-choked forest" he encountered.[6]

Carpenter and Seaton were never alone in the forest. Black bears, grizzly bears, wolves, cougars, caribou, lynx—one could expect to encounter any of them at any time. In the skies high above, ravens kept a watchful eye, while northern flickers flitted from tree to tree in the forest. Closer to Slocan Lake, ospreys soared over the water looking for prey. Canadian grouse, known locally as "fool hens," were easy to kill and tasty to eat. Prospectors were not fussy. They would eat pretty much anything they could get their hands on, including an apparent staple—porcupine.

Carpenter and Seaton were running low on provisions and patience. According to Carpenter, Seaton was sickly and reluctant to climb the steeper slopes. This likely frustrated the agile and energetic Carpenter. After tramping through the wilderness for a few days, Carpenter admitted that the two men were lost. They argued about the way back, and as they couldn't agree, they divided their meagre provisions and went their separate ways. Carpenter hadn't got very far when he came across a trail of float. As he was following it, Seaton overtook him. Together the two men traced the float to its source. According to Seaton, "We found no end of float and finally found a ledge, but we were running out of grub and we had only time to make one location, which we named the Payne. With a small sack of supplies we got out as quickly as possible."[7]

When they got back to Ainsworth, the ore samples they had gathered were assayed. There is confusion as to what happened next, but ultimately, the ore was found to be very rich. However, the partnership between Seaton and Carpenter dissolved in a cloud of accusations and mistrust.

When veteran prospector Bill Hennessy got wind of Carpenter and Seaton's discovery, he quit his job at the Blackhawk mine in Ainsworth.

"View from the divide between Kaslo and Slocan," c. 1899. Dept. of Mines. Photographer unknown. Looking west with Bear and Fish Lakes in the distance. This is the view that Carpenter and Seaton would have surveyed crossing over from Kaslo. "Had they been educated men, possessing intellectual ideas, they might have felt like stout Cortez when, with eagle eye, he gazed at the Pacific."[8] IMAGE COURTESY OF THE ROYAL BC MUSEUM AND ARCHIVES

Hennessy got hold of Seaton and convinced him that he had been double-crossed by Carpenter. According to Seaton:

> The Hennessey [*sic*] boys got on to it and came over to see me about it. Just to satisfy myself I took a sample over to the assayer and got a return of $600 to the ton. As soon as I knew my partner was trying to do me up, I made an agreement with Bill Hennessey his brother Jack, J.F. McGuigan and F.H. [*sic*] Flint to steer them in provided I got half of all we found.[9]

Whatever the circumstances of his dispute with Seaton, Carpenter was soon looking for a new partner. The man he hooked up with was Ernest "E.A." Bielenberg, known locally as "The Count." On Monday, September 21, Carpenter and Bielenberg left Ainsworth. The Nelson *Miner* reported that they "quietly packed up their blankets and left for the Slocan River, by way of Nelson."[10] But their departure did not go unnoticed. By Monday evening, Bill Hennessy had gathered together Seaton and New Englander Frank Flint. They decided on a partnership.

Seaton claimed he was the leader of this group, but it's clear that Bill Hennessy was in charge. Despite Seaton's own account, Seaton was offered three dollars a day and the opportunity to stake his own claims if he would guide Hennessy and the others back to the Payne.

When Jack Hennessy learned of his brother Bill's plans, he asked if he could join in on the expedition. Bill adamantly refused, citing the agreement he had with Seaton and Flint. Not to be denied, Jack decided to make the journey with or without Bill. He approached another prospector, Ontario-born Jack McGuigan, who agreed to partner with him. Bill Hennessy wasn't pleased but couldn't stop his brother from mounting his own prospecting expedition.

At about ten thirty or eleven o'clock in the evening on September 21, on a night with a waning moon, Bill Hennessy, Jack Seaton, and Frank Flint, accompanied by a few Indigenous packers, set out for Kaslo Creek in two boats. To Bill Hennessy's chagrin, he was beaten out of the gate by his brother and McGuigan, who had slipped out of Ainsworth about an hour and a half earlier. Also worrying—a number of other Ainsworth prospectors were preparing to paddle north. Jack Hennessy and Jack McGuigan were already camped at the mouth of Kaslo Creek when Seaton, Flint, and Bill Hennessy arrived at about 2 AM. They all met up later in the morning. Bill once again protested the presence of his brother and McGuigan. He got the two to agree they wouldn't stake any claims until Bill and Jack Seaton had staked extensions to the Payne. After that, according to Bill Hennessy, "it was to be every man for himself."[11]

It took the Hennessy expeditions two days to reach the site of the Payne and the two main creeks in the area, now named after Carpenter and Seaton. They arrived on September 24 and stayed on the ground for about eight days. During the whole time, they saw no sign of Carpenter or Bielenberg. They did see a few other prospectors, however, men who had followed them from Ainsworth. While on the ground at the Payne and more or less as agreed,

Bill Hennessy and Frank Flint staked the Mountain Chief, an extension of the Payne. In the meantime, McGuigan and Jack Hennessy discovered a ledge running crosswise to the Payne and staked the Maid of Erin. They also staked another claim, the Two Jacks, nearby. These discoveries put the "Two Jacks"—McGuigan and Jack Hennessy—on a more equal footing with Seaton, Flint, and Bill Hennessy. On September 26, the Northern Belle was staked. That night the five prospectors decided they would share equally in all the claims. Pleased with their claims near to or adjoining the Payne, the Hennessy party decided to start back for Kootenay Lake.

Meanwhile, Carpenter and Bielenberg had paddled to Nelson, where they stocked up on provisions. They loaded their canoe on to a railcar and unloaded at Slocan River. They reported no difficulty ascending the river but had trouble getting to the site of the Payne, "the brush being almost impenetrable."[12] Once there, they saw no sign of Seaton or Hennessy, their strikes, nor any signs of silver. They returned, empty-handed, to Ainsworth. Carpenter later claimed to have arrived two days after Seaton's new strikes near the Payne. By then, Seaton and the others would likely have been on their way back to Ainsworth.

Ainsworth, c. 1891. Photographer: Neelands Brothers. From Fred Mountain's photo album. IMAGE COURTESY OF THE UNIVERSITY OF CALGARY DIGITAL COLLECTIONS

When the Hennessy parties left the Payne, they kept prospecting as they made their way out. There was so much rich float along the way that they weren't always willing to make the effort to stake the ground. However, about a mile and a half past the Payne, they came across a ledge of silver "that made every one of the party imagine himself at once a millionaire."[13] The first claim they staked was the Bonanza King. Then they traced the ledge north and south. On the north, going up the mountain, they staked the World's Fair and Maud E. On the downward slope to the south, they staked the Knoxville, Blue Jay, and—in recognition of their newly formed partnership—the Noble Five. Most of the claims were staked under one or another of their names, but the Last Chance, adjoining the World's Fair, was recorded under George Hayward's name, though he wasn't on the ground with them.

Having staked what they believed were the most promising claims in the area, the Noble Five partners hurried back to Ainsworth to record their claims. They arrived triumphantly on October 1, 1891. News of the discoveries "set the town wild with excitement." Even the venerable G.B. Wright, almost sixty years old, "felt as if he was young enough to pack his blankets over the range to the new find." The news quickly spread that the Noble Five party had uncovered a silver ledge that, as Bill Hennessy claimed, was as "big and as plain as a wagon road . . . hundreds of tons of ore are in sight."[14]

Amid all the excitement, Carpenter and Bielenberg slipped back into camp, tails between their legs. They must have been discouraged by the news that greeted them. One of them ruefully complained that the first they heard of Seaton's new strike was when they were returning to Nelson, and someone threw them a copy of the most recent *Hot Springs News* from the train. Carpenter was sore about Seaton's actions but could do nothing about it.

Word travelled fast. Saloons and hotels in Ainsworth and Nelson emptied as prospectors raced into the new district. Newly installed telephone lines linking the two Kootenay Lake communities were "kept hot . . . transmitting messages regarding the wonderful finds."[15] Campbell Sweeny, who had established the first Bank of Montreal branch in Vancouver in 1887, was in Nelson when news of the strike came in. He called it the "most marvelous discovery ever made in the west."[16] On October 3, the Nelson *Miner* reported that Ainsworth was almost depopulated, with only one woman left in the town: "All the others, men and women, have gone to Kaslo City, 12 miles up the lake from Ainsworth and the place at which prospectors debark for the new district."[17] Dr. E.C. Kilbourne, a Seattle dentist and entrepreneur who was in Ainsworth at the time, described a chaotic scene: "Men were seen running along the street with bacon in one hand and a pick in the other."[18]

A week after the exodus from Ainsworth, the *Hot Springs News* noted: "The excitement continues, and probably a hundred men are now on the ground or on their way in."[19] News of the discoveries soon travelled across the border. The *Spokane Review* reported: "Not a boat or a siwash is obtainable for love or money; every able-bodied man who thinks he knows galena from country rock is away; and capitalists now looking after their interests in this vicinity are with difficulty restrained from offering themselves as a sacrifice to Mammon."[20] By October 13, the news had reached Victoria. The *Colonist* spoke of a "stampede" to the new discoveries.[21] Editorial hyperbole reached a peak two weeks later when Nelson's *Miner* exclaimed that "if the excitement lasts another month there will not be a poor man in the Kootenay Lake Country."[22] The only downside noted by some of the American newspapers was that the strike was on the wrong side of the border.

LARGELY UNKNOWN ONLY WEEKS BEFORE, the Slocan was now under intense scrutiny. Like the ripples in a pond when a stone is thrown in, news of the great silver strikes washed across North America as far as Florida, and across the Atlantic and Pacific Oceans to the United Kingdom, Australia, and New Zealand. The further the news travelled, the more likely facts would be sacrificed to fancy. In December 1891, the *Chicago Herald* printed a tale told by B.T. Rogers, who in 1890 founded the Rogers Sugar Company in Vancouver. Rogers added his own embellishments and took liberties with local geography.

> I have heard of towns springing up in a day, but I believe British Columbia can show the only instance on record of a town completely shrinking away in that space of time. One morning about a month ago a man came into my office and gave me an order for a carload of sugar to be shipped to Nelson, a town which had 5000 people when he left the day before. The sugar was started on the road at once, and when it arrived at Nelson there was no town there. All the houses were standing, but the people had deserted the place and there were not 10 persons left. Mining excitement had caused the hegira. Nelson . . . is in the region where the recent great discovery of silver was made.

> Nelson was at the south end of the lake, and on a certain morning, the strike was made at the north end. Before nightfall, the entire population of 5000 had packed up bag and baggage and moved to the north end of the lake and started up a new town.[23]

MANY PROSPECTORS IN WEST KOOTENAY were grubstaked by men and women who were willing to provide supplies on credit for a share of profits on paying claims. Merchants, saloon keepers, and others were almost always willing to invest in a prospector who knew his business and had a record of success. It was a gamble, but riches could be won for very little capital investment. Grubstaking also allowed men and women who, perhaps, weren't fit for tramping up the Slocan mountains to get in on the action. G.B. Wright grubstaked several Slocan prospectors. Despite his enthusiasm, he wasn't up for the physical hardships he would gladly have endured as a younger man. Wright was in Victoria when his name was entered into the record book for the Stonewall claim.

Of the crowd who scrambled into the Slocan following Carpenter, Seaton, and the Noble Five, the most successful prospectors were probably Bruce White, John Sandon, and Charlie Chambers. In October 1891, White and a group of prospectors set out for the Slocan. Once they reached the divide, White and Sandon decided to head off on their own. While most prospectors staked ground near the Payne and Noble Five claims, White and Sandon crossed the valley below and explored the slope opposite. They found a rich mineral vein thirteen feet wide in the bed of a small creek, later named after Sandon. The other prospectors, including Charlie Chambers, caught up to White and Sandon. In a thick stand of timber, they found more rich outcroppings and staked several claims. The Slocan Star was recorded under Sandon's name, the Slocan King under White's, and the Silversmith under Chambers's.

Bruce White later recalled the hardships that he and Sandon endured on their trip into the Slocan. It was, he said, the hardest trip of his life. He described fallen trees as big as houses. With their heavy packs, it took all their strength to climb over the toppled trees and through the dense, tangled forest. Almost out of supplies on their way back to Ainsworth, they were reduced to meals of sour cornmeal when the last of their salt pork was gone. Bruce tried fishing with a torn piece of his red flannel shirt as bait: "When

I lost a fish I was so hungry that I nearly cried."[24] White later recounted his early journey into the Slocan:

> That was a terrible trip. There were no paths. It was 7,000 feet down a mountain so steep every stop was a jolt, enough to shake your head off. In the valley the undergrowth was tangled, deep, and thick. It took us from daylight to go, well, I suppose about eleven miles. Pretty late one afternoon we found bits of mineralized rock, galena float, in the stream. It lay quite thick along the bed of the fork, and we kept following it up. Just at dusk we struck a ledge of some sort. We were both too hungry and tired to be much elated. It was too late to stake the claim off; and if we left it, some one might be slipping after us and get in first on our find. Then in dense forest it's very hard to find an exact spot. So we stretched out, hungry, cold, heart-sick. Every bone in my body was aching. My joints stiffened and pained at every move. I never put in a more wretched night. The sky was clear and cold. The rocks round seemed like ice, and the moist ground gave one a chill in the very marrow.[25]

Somehow, White, Sandon, Chambers, and the others made it safely back to Kootenay Lake.

THERE WAS NO REST FOR Chambers. He was soon back in the tangled wilderness of the Slocan. On one of his trips, he climbed up and crossed over the divide between Sandon Creek and a larger creek that ran parallel to it to the east. Coming closer to the larger creek, he found himself at the bottom of a slide, where birch and cottonwood saplings reached for the sunlight that would sustain them until the winter snow slides came to sweep them away. Chambers would have paid little attention to these scrub plants; his focus was on the ground. At the bottom of the slide closer to the creek, he picked up a promising piece of float. He broke it open to reveal a rich streak of galena, but because it was float, he didn't look the ground over too carefully. He probably reasoned that it had been washed down the creek and the lode was somewhere up in the mountains. He threw the rocks down and moved on.

Along with Ed Becker, Tom Shearer, and Charley Kent, Chambers staked several very rich claims, including the Chambers, Mattie B, and

"25." The next day, Chambers and the others located the Governor and Monarch claims. News of the "Chambers" group of claims caused a sensation when word reached Spokane. John Hardee, who had been on the ground at the same time as the Noble Five party, was in Nelson when Chambers and his partners brought in their ore samples: "I saw all four of them and they were wild about it when they got their returns from the assayer. They could hardly believe it."[26] Dr. Campbell of Revelstoke told the *Spokane Review* that before he left Ainsworth for Spokane, he had talked with Chambers and his partners and inspected some of their samples. If their claims were "only a tenth of what they expect it is one of the biggest mining discoveries ever made in America."[27]

Other prospectors who were scouring the mountains in the waning months of 1891 included Jack Buchanan, Jack Evans, William Hunter, William "Billy" McKinnon, Billy Simcox, Lorenzo Alexander, Billy Lynch, and "Toughnut" Jack Clunan. Buchanan, sometimes known as "Red Jack," because of a birthmark he wore, had prospected at Trail Creek and just before the Slocan strikes, in August 1891, was prospecting south of Toad Mountain. It didn't take him long to make the journey to the Slocan once he heard news of the strike. He went in with Jack Evans, Billy Simcox, William Hunter, and Billy McKinnon.

Jack Evans had been exploring West Kootenay since quitting CPR construction in 1885. Evans was known for his strength and endurance. According to one of his partners, Ike Lougheed, "he was an awful man to follow in the mountains. He could pack 100 pounds seemingly without tiring."[28] Buchanan, Evans, and the rest were soon in the thick of things. Buchanan staked several promising claims, including the Black Bear, Alaska, and Climax. Evans was busy too. A telephone call from Ainsworth to Nelson in late October carried the news that he had made the "biggest strike" ever in the Slocan, not far from Charlie Chambers's camp.

Billy Simcox located the Derby, Lady Jane, and Blue Jay (not to be confused with the Noble Five's Blue Jay) down by Sandon Creek. Lorenzo Alexander staked the R.E. Lee close to the Noble Five claims. Despite his claim's name, Alexander was born in Dublin in 1853, into a landed Anglo-Irish family. His father, John Alexander, was for a time the member of Parliament for Carlow. As the third son, Lorenzo likely believed his prospects would be brighter in the western mining camps than in his Irish homeland. Hunter and McKinnon likely did a bit of prospecting too, but they were more interested in starting a store at the mouth of Carpenter Creek.

"Toughnut" Jack Clunan lived up to his moniker. He was one tough Irishman who had cut a swath across the western mining frontier, prospecting in the Dakotas, Arizona, Colorado, and Utah. In 1876, he participated in the Black Hills gold rush, rubbing shoulders with Calamity Jane, Bronco Nell, Billy Goose-eye, and Kettle Belly Brown. He got his nickname in 1878, when he was involved in the discovery of the Toughnut, one of the mines that proved a catalyst for Tombstone, Arizona. Almost ten years after a perilous journey over desert and sea from Tombstone to Baja, California, and back, led by pioneering mining woman Nellie Cashman, Toughnut was clambering up the Slocan's slopes. Toughnut and Jack Buchanan were hired by Victoria assayer William "Billy" McCulloch to prospect in the Slocan. Toughnut had a hand in staking several claims, but he didn't make his fortune in the Slocan. Like so many others, he found it hard to hang on to money: "He drank it; he gambled it; it went like the wind."[29]

Billy Lynch, a pioneer in BC's Cariboo region, was once described as a "veteran of the sluice-boxes and other dicta of placer mining."[30] He was a veteran American prospector who partnered with several Slocan prospectors. His most promising claim was probably the Washington, near the Payne, staked with Martin Kinney.

ALL THE NOBLE FIVE PARTNERS were in Spokane in early November. Some—like the Hennessy brothers—were on their way to places further afield, others were simply looking for a bit of rest and relaxation before heading back to the Slocan. While in Spokane, the Noble Five hired a railway car, decked it out with streamers, and offered free liquor to the curious throngs looking to view the ore samples. They were treated like triumphant heroes by Spokane citizens eager to hear about the new mining district across the border.

The stories of the Slocan discoveries seemed to grow richer with each retelling. However, in some cases, members of the Noble Five found themselves downplaying the riches. They had arrived in Spokane at about the same time that news was received of the great strike made by Charlie Chambers and his partners. Jack Hennessy was asked if it was true they had a silver vein 150 feet in width: "I do not believe it. I met Mr. Frank W. Flint when he returned from the camp after the discovery, and he told me that they struck a vein about eighty feet wide, but not more. Even that . . . will fix the discoverers for life."[31]

The tales told by the Noble Five and other Slocan pioneers on their Spokane visits, even when tempered of excess exaggeration, spurred more fortune seekers to head to the Slocan. Jack Seaton returned, followed in late November by a large party of adventurers from Spokane. Eli Carpenter returned too, this time with Bruce White. Carpenter's bad luck continued. He and White had their outfits plundered by someone's dog. Seeking food and shelter, they came across an old trapper's cabin. Inside, they found a long-dead wild swan suspended from the roof. Bruce was reluctant to eat any of it, fearing it might have been poisoned. Carpenter had no such qualms: "Bruce, if we have got to die, we might as well died [*sic*] with our belly full."[32]

E.A. Bielenberg decided to try a new way into the Slocan by way of the Skyline mine west of Ainsworth. The *Hot Springs News* sounded the alarm when Bielenberg and his partner, William Moulse, had not been heard from for three weeks. After leaving Ainsworth, Bielenberg and Moulse eventually found themselves at the head of Coffee Creek, above Kootenay Lake, where an immense sheet of ice straddled the ground between the jutting, jagged mountain spurs. Almost out of food but not about to give up, they started to trek the four miles across the glacier. The ground and weather were harsh. At one point they were snowed in for three days.

Bielenberg and Moulse had stumbled across a glacier. If not the first white men to cross it, they were certainly in the vanguard. But once was enough. At last, they reached Slocan Lake at the outlet of what was later named Ten Mile Creek. They returned to Ainsworth after a lesson hard learned. "The Count" rued his attempt at a shortcut, unhappy that he had run so low on provisions. He would not make the same mistake again. When he returned to the Slocan with his new partner, Billy Lynch, the two men packed in 750 pounds of supplies over the Kaslo route.

Late arrivals faced daunting challenges. By November, prospecting was becoming increasingly difficult. Included in this late crowd were Billy McCulloch, Tom McGovern, Jasper "Jap" King, W.R. "Billy" Will, and the recently returned Jack Seaton. Jap King, originally from Ohio, was a Coeur d'Alene pioneer but had staked a few claims in West Kootenay. He was well known in local mining circles and celebrated as the discoverer of the Alice mine in the Goat River district. New arrivals like King and Tom McGovern were eager to get stakes into the snow. McGovern was clambering up a rock slope when he dislodged some moss, revealing a rich vein of galena. He staked the Iron Hand, while King staked the Blue Bird and

Side Issue. Diehards continued to explore the snow-covered ground near the Noble Five claims, but their efforts were becoming a matter of guesswork as the snow thickened. Prospectors moved down the mountains as the snow line descended. Despite the snow, more than fifty claims were staked in November alone.

Fred Franks, a well-known mining man from Wardner, Idaho, trekked into the Slocan in December. He was particularly impressed with the Washington claim but was taken with the whole district. He spread the word in Helena, Montana:

> The Kaslo-Slocan find is, I firmly believe, the greatest mineral discovery of the century. It beats the first finds at Leadville, at Butte, in the Coeur d'Alenes and everywhere else I have ever heard of or seen.[33]

Dick Fry's brother Martin was working a small claim near Nelson when he heard news of the Slocan strike. In late November, he and his friend and partner Alonzo "A.D." Coplen set out from Nelson in a canoe with about three weeks provisions. It was heavy going. Exhausted and hungry, they managed to get up the Slocan River and landed at the mouth of Carpenter Creek. They rested briefly, then set out for the mineralized area. It took them three days to fight their way up the thickly forested slopes. They spent a few days prospecting, staking at least one claim—the Excelsior. Then one evening Coplen found a promising piece of float at the bottom of a slide. They knew right away that someone else had found it before them, since it had the unmistakable marks of a prospector's pick. This was the rock discarded by Charlie Chambers earlier. Fry and Coplen retired for the night, intending to look for the float trail the next morning. When they awoke, it was snowing hard. They decided to return to the camp at Carpenter Creek.

By the close of 1891, a substantial camp was taking shape at the mouth of Carpenter Creek. But with the claims largely shut off to them by layers of snow, most of the men turned to other pursuits. They spent time hunting and trapping, whipsawing lumber for cabins, and sharing bottles and stories around the hot coals of campfires. E.A. Bielenberg, however, couldn't seem to put his prospector's pick down. In late December and early January, he and George Cleveland located fifteen claims south of Carpenter Creek. The snow was six to ten feet deep.

There was a floating population of about twenty over Christmas and the New Year at the mouth of Carpenter Creek, with a few others camped up and down the lake. Billy McKinnon later recalled the first Christmas in the Slocan, celebrated with Neil Gething:

> They took dinner with George Long, Jap King and Ben Anderson, who occupied one of the adjoining tents that went to make up the canvas town. The principal dish was plum duff, but, while both gentlemen were willing to admit that it was good, neither was ready to assert positively what it was made of. They were certain that there were no plums in the camp but knew that there were plenty of beans, and it was the general practice to substitute the latter for anything of which they happened to be short. However it was good, and they were ready to pronounce their first Christmas dinner in the Slocan a success.[34]

"Kokanee Glacier National Park" [though never a national park], c.1920. Photographer: Ray Goodwin. This is the forbidding terrain that would have confronted Bielenberg and Moulse on their "shortcut" to the Slocan in the winter of 1891/92. IMAGE COURTESY OF THE ROYAL BC MUSEUM AND ARCHIVES

2

THE RUSH

LONG BEFORE THE PROSPECTORS ARRIVED, Indigenous Peoples had explored, exploited, and inhabited Slocan Lake and the surrounding rivers and valleys. The whole area is part of the overlapping frontier between two ancient Peoples. To the west of Slocan Lake were the Interior Salish First Nations. One of these, the Sinixt Nation or "Lakes" People, historically occupied territory up and down the Arrow Lakes. To the east of Slocan Lake were the Ktunaxa, who, though linguistically unique, shared some cultural traits with Plains Indigenous Peoples. The Sinixt claim the Slocan as their traditional territory but so do the Ktunaxa. Indigenous Peoples—likely Ktunaxa—were there with Jack Seaton, Bill Hennessy, and others when they made their richest strikes. They packed in supplies for many of the prospecting parties but left few records of their presence.

For their part, some prospectors naïvely imagined themselves the first humans to view Slocan Lake and the majestic glacier that rose above it. If they had only looked carefully around them, they would have seen the abandoned campsites, the pictographs on some of the rock outcroppings, and the stone weights that had been used to anchor fishing nets lying strewn along the shore of Slocan Lake. Both the Sinixt and the Ktunaxa had been devastated by the smallpox epidemics of the late eighteenth and early nineteenth centuries. Slocan Lake was largely abandoned and most of the surviving Sinixt retreated to a reservation across the border in Colville, Washington. By early 1892, there were more than three hundred "Lake Indians"[1] there.

The Sinixt did not suddenly disappear from West Kootenay. They were there in 1889, travelling well-worn trails from the Slocan to the Arrow and Kootenay Lakes. There was an encampment at the mouth of Nakusp Creek

Sturgeon-nosed canoe, Nakusp, 1893. Artist: A.P. Coleman. IMAGE COURTESY OF THE VICTORIA UNIVERSITY LIBRARY (TORONTO)

in the summer of 1892, and seasonal camps dotted the lower reaches of the Arrow Lakes and perhaps the Slocan River and southern shores of Slocan Lake too. The prospectors that first headed to the Slocan from Nelson followed a Sinixt trail partway up the Slocan River. A few Sinixt continued to eke out meagre livings on their traditional lands during the late nineteenth and early twentieth centuries, and throughout the 1890s, their sturgeon-nosed canoes travelled up and down the Columbia and Slocan Rivers. There is even one account of an Indigenous man living at the mouth of Carpenter Creek when the first prospectors arrived.

Most Ktunaxa were located on a reserve at the south end of Kootenay Lake, and some travelled to the mouth of Kaslo Creek. A few worked as packers for prospectors; others were just curious to see the "white men." However, despite a bit of packing, Indigenous Peoples were largely on the sidelines for the Slocan rush. Some earned cash, liquor, or guns for packing work, but they couldn't have been too pleased to see hordes of prospectors slashing through their traditional territories.

There were three main routes into the Slocan. From Nelson, the favoured route was along the Slocan River by foot or boat and then up

Slocan Lake by boat or raft. From Ainsworth and other points along the northern shores of Kootenay Lake, the shortest route was up Kaslo Creek. A third route, from the Arrow Lakes to the north end of Slocan Lake, was less used in the early days but did prove useful to prospectors coming in from the CPR at Revelstoke. From the beginning of the rush, there were debates over which route was more practicable. Nelson, Ainsworth, and other communities competed in promoting the route most likely to win them a share of the Slocan trade. At a well-attended meeting in Nelson in early November 1891, a committee of prominent businessmen was charged with raising money to build the trail up Slocan River.

Brothers Wilson and Alfred Hill were placed in charge of trail construction. Each worker was paid two dollars a day plus board. Gorman West set up a camp at the foot of the lake and cooked meals for the trail crew. Averaging about a mile a day, by mid-December 1891, the crew reached a point four miles south of Slocan Lake. From there to the lake, the river was navigable by small boat, but they pushed on and reached the lake itself a few days later. From there, incomers could buy transport up the lake in one of Palma Angrignon's flat-bottomed bateaux. Born in Quebec, "French Pete" was coining money ferrying incomers up Slocan Lake. M.C. "Mickey" Monaghan, a man Angrignon knew from Nelson, was soon in the boating business too.

While work was under way on the trail up Slocan River, rival interests were clearing a trail from Kootenay Lake. They argued that the Slocan River route was impractical without a steamship service on Slocan Lake. Proponents of the Slocan River route countered that "the route up Slocan River is so much earlier that it will be an old-traveled route long before the snow is off the divide on the Kaslo Creek route."[2] Undaunted, men worked on the Kaslo Creek route through November and December. On Boxing Day, the *Hot Springs News* noted that the Kaslo trail builders were "in snow up to their waists but swear they will get through to the mines even if they have to tunnel their way in."[3]

In January 1892, Bruce White and Mike Gray, a mining man representing Seattle interests, travelled from Nelson to Spokane. It was a rough trip, with telegraph lines down and deep snow everywhere. Still, nothing could dampen White's enthusiasm. Interviewed by a reporter for the *Spokane Review*, he said "the excitement is keeping up."[4] By this time there were about fifty fortune seekers camped on the shores of Slocan Lake. About six feet of snow blocked the route from Kootenay Lake, but pilgrims were coming in every day by way of Slocan River. The rush was on. While a flood of fortune seekers arrived in the Slocan from the Coeur d'Alenes, others came from all over the United States and Canada. Young single men predominated, but all ages and types were represented. Women, however, were "as scarce as blue roses."[5] According to the 1891 census figures for Lower Kootenay, there were 1,099 men in the area and only 121 females, 58 of whom were under the age of 18.

While prospecting activity was reduced during the early months of 1892, it did not come to a stop. A few enthusiasts were determined to stake claims despite the snow. Often these were "wildcats," staked on guesswork and hope. When Ike Lougheed reached the Slocan early in the spring of 1892, he complained that "you need a ladder" to read the notices for "snow locations" nailed on trees when the snow was at its deepest.[6] Some of these "snow-claims"—when they were put on the market—would sour the taste for investors. Ainsworth's *Hot Springs News* had advice for prospectors:

Yes! Slocan is a roaring camp, boys,
The best camp in our day,
So just turn up that lamp, boys,
And listen to what I say.

Let us start in right and straight, boys,
Give all men a fair, square show,
But stick to it early and late, boys,
That "stakes in the snow don't go."[7]

The Kaslo Creek and Slocan River trails that were hastily cut in late 1891 served the immediate need but were wholly inadequate for the hundreds of adventurers who flocked into the area in early 1892. The spring melt created havoc, flooding out or washing away many sections of both the Kaslo and the Slocan River trails. In early April 1892, a crew under Tom Mulvey was hired to repair and improve the Slocan River trail. They built dozens of small bridges, and at Lemon Creek a more substantial structure took shape. This big bridge was 102 feet long, spanning the creek on three diamond shaped crib piers.

Repairs were made during the spring to the Kaslo trail too, and work was begun on a trail into the Slocan from Nakusp. Like the repairs to the Slocan trail, the Nakusp trail was financed by the provincial government. A crew of about fifteen men under Kootenay pioneer Jack Evans started the work in early May. A smaller crew took over in July and continued to push through. By the summer of 1892, the woods were again full of prospectors. Repairs to the trail were finally completed in September 1892.

In late 1891, Martin Fry and his partner, A.D. Coplen, had collected some ore samples from their brief prospecting trip. Fry remained in the Slocan over the winter, while Coplen took the ore samples to Spokane, where he would have them assayed. The results showed more than 100 ounces of silver to the ton and 78 percent lead. When he received the news, Fry sprang into action. He set out up Carpenter Creek, telling his camp comrades that he was going trapping for marten. He did set a couple of traps, but then cached his gear and made his way to the slide near where he and Coplen had found the float. He climbed up the slide and placed his stakes in the snow, then climbed back down and returned to the creek mouth where he was camped.

Coplen arrived back in the Slocan in March. He and Fry reached the north side of the creek they had located before and found a fallen tree that they could use as a bridge to the south side. Coplen went across first, followed closely behind by Fry. When Coplen jumped down on the other side, the tree trunk rolled. Fry was thrown off his feet and landed hard on the spine of the tree. He was lucky not to have fallen in the creek, but he broke several ribs. He couldn't go on, so the two men set up camp by the creek. For four days Coplen nursed his partner back to health.

Coplen and Fry were just about to start again when veteran prospector Bill Springer wandered into their camp. Springer was pretty sure that Fry and Coplen were on to something, so he persuaded them to let him join their expedition. The three men set out, but only after Springer promised not to stake any claims without Fry and Coplen's approval. They soon came to the slide and the claim above, which Fry had named the Freddie Lee, after his youngest son. Coplen staked the adjoining Cube Load and Budget. An assay on one sample of Freddie Lee ore ran 900 ounces of silver to the ton. Springer earned an interest in the Freddie Lee for his efforts in helping to stake the additional claims.

Other prospectors were in the area too. Eric Conway "E.C." Carpenter, along with partners Jack and Angus McGillivray, staked the Gray Eagle between the Slocan Star and Cody Creek. Carpenter was a twenty-five-year-old British-born real estate agent and former actor, most recently from Victoria by way of Nelson. An early enthusiast for West Kootenay, he had invested heavily in Nelson townsite lots before joining the rush to the Slocan.

Coplen ranged further afield and staked another rich claim high up in the mountains near the divide between the Slocan and Kootenay Lake watersheds. Whitewater Creek is a glacier-fed tributary of Kaslo Creek. The Whitewater basin was thick with prospectors at the time. J.C. Eaton—who had earlier paddled, pushed, and pulled a canoe up the Slocan River—was working his way through the bush near the creek when he came across a patch of mineralized earth atop a small cliff. He swung his pick to pull himself up but instead dislodged a forty-pound piece of solid galena ore. His excitement was tempered when he learned the ground had been staked by Coplen less than two weeks earlier. He tracked Coplen down and persuaded him to sell a two-thirds interest in the Whitewater claim for two hundred dollars.

While much of the prospecting activity in May and June was near the Payne, Noble Five, or Slocan Star discoveries, most of the good ground was quickly staked. So some prospectors, like Coplen, ventured further afield. A few set out to explore Seaton Creek and the ground near Bear Lake. When a snow slide came down from the mountains, exposing a rich outcropping, Jim Shields was first on the scene and (with the help of Charlie Drouin) staked the Lucky Jim just south of Bear and Fish Lakes. Shields, a forty-four-year-old Irishman newly arrived in West Kootenay, grandly claimed the Lucky Jim had a vein of high-grade ore that was twelve feet wide. Others put it at a more modest thirty inches. All agreed, however, on the quality of the ore.

Just under four miles south of Carpenter Creek, another large creek empties into Slocan Lake. In May 1892, Mike Grady and Charlie Laatz hiked into the area just north of Four Mile Creek. They found a trail of rich float and followed it to a large outcropping of solid galena ore. On May 23, Grady staked the Echo, and Laatz the Alpha. In later years it was said that Grady had first been shown the site by members of a local Indigenous community. Whether true or not, the crowds of prospectors combing the mountains would have soon found the spot with or without help. Still at the site of their discovery a couple of days later, the two partners were joined by another man, Len Briggs. After Briggs staked the Standard, an adjoining claim to Grady's and Laatz's Echo and Alpha, the three men made a pact. Each agreed to sell two-thirds of his claim to the others.

There were several other rich claims located in the Four Mile Creek area, including the Vancouver, the Climax, the Lancaster, and the Reed and Robinson. The Reed was likely staked by Major Al Reed. The major, in his fifties, had a troubling history south of the border. A veteran of the First Colorado Cavalry during the American Civil War, Alonzo S. Reed was appointed Indian agent at the Milk River Agency in Montana in 1868. It was by virtue of this appointment serving the Assiniboine Peoples that Reed acquired the honorific of "Major." However, Reed's tenure lasted only four months. He was fired for malfeasance, accused of—among other things—selling liquor, agency blankets, horses, hay, and other resources to the Nakoda Oyadebi (Assiniboine). He was also accused of shooting and killing one.

Several years later, in 1874, Reed and his partner, John Bowles, established a trading post on Montana's Carroll Trail. By all accounts Reed continued his dubious trading practices. However, the post was an important stopping place for many western pioneers. American naturalist George Bird Grinnell stopped by, as well as characters such as "Liver-Eating" Johnson and "Yellowstone" Kelly. Kelly, who was seldom critical of any man, remembered Reed as being "dashing and brave, a gentleman of the old school and a fine frontiersman."[8] In 1892, Reed decided to take out Canadian citizenship—probably a wise decision given the consequences he might have faced if he returned to the US.[9]

Just south of Four Mile Creek, Coeur d'Alene prospector Con Doherty and his partners, likely including Billy Childs and James L. Smith, located the Grover and the Stevenson. The float was so plentiful on the swampy ground that they were soon "digging out ore like farmers digging potatoes."[10] Hence, the claims became known as "The Galena Farm." Billy Childs located the Cleveland nearby. By naming their claims Grover, Cleveland, and Stevenson, these prospectors were showing their preference for the Democratic Party in American politics.

There were still some locations to be made in the heart of the mineralized area, but prospecting was delayed by the lingering snow at higher elevations. One prospector said climbing the mountains was "like going backward in time."[11] While it could be spring or summer down by Slocan Lake, it would still be winter above. Many rich claims were located as prospectors followed the receding snow line. Jimmy Moran, of Seattle, wrote of his experiences in the Slocan to a friend in Victoria:

> During the week following the Fourth of July he had the roughest experience of his life. One day with a party of prospectors he started to go 11 miles, across a range of hills. On the summit they found snow 10 feet deep, and late in the afternoon the same day they found ripe strawberries in the valley below. Before the week ended their

> provisions gave out, and for a time they lived on porcupine without salt. At last they came upon a deserted mining camp and in one of the cabins found a loaf of bread, which all agreed was the best food they ever tasted.[12]

Moran started his prospecting jaunt in the Slocan with a classic case of tenderfoot luck. When he and his group first set up camp in late June, he was separated from his companions and—worried about bears roaming the area—decided to wait in camp for their return. He picked up a small boulder while waiting and, feeling how heavy it was, broke it open to reveal rich galena. He traced a trail of float up the slope to the mineral ledge and staked a claim he called the Queen Bess.

German mining expert Louis von Ruecau arrived in the Slocan on July 4 and set up camp with Charles Brown and Oscar Hill. After firing off a few rifle shots in recognition of American Independence Day, the three men almost immediately came across a claim they named the Ruecau. Von Ruecau offered to buy out the other two. Instead, Brown and Hill sold out for a higher price to Sam Wharton, Johnny Harris, and Fred Kelly. Stories that circulated years later had Harris down to his last dollar when he went in on the deal. But he had a lucky rabbit's foot and liked his chances.

A native of Virginia, Harris arrived in the Slocan earlier in 1892, from Wallace, Idaho. While unlikely, Harris later claimed to have been a barber in Tombstone, Arizona, where he shaved Wyatt Earp on the morning of the gunfight at the O.K. Corral. Harris spent several years in the Coeur d'Alene district before setting out for the Slocan. He was interested in mining, but most of his time and energy went into land speculation, particularly townsite promotion. He evidently took his work seriously. In January 1891, he and a companion put four bullets into a man in a dispute over an acre of land that Harris had fenced off and claimed for his own. The Slocan would give him a fresh start.

Von Ruecau staked subsequent claims by himself. He might have missed some of the luxuries of Brown's camp, though. Brown suffered few of the hardships experienced by other prospectors. According to one account, he had "a sheet iron stove, two tents, canned oysters, mushrooms, cherries, and several other articles strictly unknown to a million prospectors when they are in active service."[13]

Von Ruecau soon left the Slocan. Before the end of the year, he was promoting a diamond field in Idaho. While he didn't stay long in the

Slocan, the Slocan stayed long with von Ruecau. He had explored the Alps, traversed the Himalayas, and crossed the Andes, but nothing he found compared with the Slocan. He later waxed rhapsodic in an interview with the *Spokane Review*:

> I have never yet seen a country that so attracted my admiration and made me realize my own unworthiness and unimportance to God's great universe, as is the wild, rugged grandeur of nature that one finds in the glaciers to the north of the Slocan range in British Columbia. Not only in that especial section, but wherever one may climb in the Slocan or Carpenter creek districts, every yard of ground brings to sight some new and thrilling sight that only some masterly hand could weld into being.[14]

While the original locators of the Ruecau got some quick cash from the sale of their claim, Johnny Harris and his partners, Sam Wharton and Fred Kelly, would reap ongoing benefit from this rich property, which, for convenience, they renamed "Reco."

The Blue Bird (not to be confused with Jap King's Blue Bird) not far from the Noble Five claims, was another rich property staked on July 4. It was located by Jack Thompson and Jack Whittier. Whittier, though born in Nova Scotia, had deep American roots and may have been related to the famous American abolitionist and poet, John Greenleaf Whittier. Whittier and Thompson would become long-standing partners and lifelong friends.

Johnny Harris was nearby when Billy Smith made one of the big discoveries of 1892. Prospecting near Carpenter Creek, within three miles of Slocan Lake, Smith was said to have been fleeing an angry bear when he stumbled across the ore croppings of a claim he named the Mountain Chief (not to be confused with the claim of the same name that adjoined the Payne). After eluding the bruin, Smith traced a ledge for more than three thousand feet, finding rich deposits of silver and lead in three different locations.

There were diminishing returns over the summer as hundreds of prospectors scoured the land. A few prospectors were still at work in August and beyond, including E.A. Bielenberg, who had been prospecting almost continuously since his first, ill-fated excursion with Eli Carpenter. In early August, Bielenberg staked the Jim Fair. John Adam "Jack" Watson—perhaps working with Bielenberg—staked the John W. McKay and the Flood about the same time. Fair, McKay, and Flood were the names of three of the four "bonanza kings" of Nevada's Comstock Lode. Miners could not help but aspire to the success of these silver kings, who were wealthy beyond imagining.

Jack Watson had been in West Kootenay since April 1891. He was a Scotsman of some small means who, like so many others, came to Canada to earn his fortune. Immigrating in 1882, he worked on the CPR through the 1880s. When the railway was completed, he made his way to Victoria, where he befriended two other men who would figure prominently in the early years of the Slocan: David Bremner and Fred Mountain.

Not all the prospectors who climbed the Slocan's slopes were men, and not all were white. Little is known about Caroline Anderson. Claiming to be widowed, she had a young daughter, Lilly, but we don't know if Lilly was with her in the Slocan. Caroline was described in one account as "a little dark complexioned Swedish girl about 26 or 28."[15] She tried her hand at laundry in the growing camp at Carpenter Creek, but decided prospect-

David Bremner and Jack Watson, Nelson, 1891. Photographer unknown, but possibly Fred Mountain. From Fred Mountain's photo album. IMAGE COURTESY OF THE UNIVERSITY OF CALGARY DIGITAL COLLECTIONS

ing held more promise. She staked or purchased at least one claim, the Mazeppa, likely named after Lord Byron's poem of the same name, or the popular nineteenth-century play based on it. One man who saw her in action in 1892 said she used her pick to break rock "like a man."[16] Among the prospectors and miners, she was known as "Fool Hen." Mrs. E.M. Pound was there too that summer of 1892. The wife of a Spokane prospector and packer who was in the Slocan from at least July 1892, she dressed in men's attire and located a rich claim—the Solo.

While most prospectors were of European descent, there were a few Black prospectors too. Alexander Clark was one of the first into the Slocan. In early 1893, he located a claim he named the Noonday (not to be confused with the Noonday near the Noble Five claims) near the mouth of Carpenter Creek. Clark passed through the Slocan with two other Black companions: David Washington and Ralph Jackson. Clark and Washington were from Spokane; Jackson, Virginia. Clark returned the following year to work the Noonday with Tom Duffy, Charles McNichol, and another Black prospector, Jackson Radcliffe. Radcliffe made a home for himself in the Slocan. Joe Butler stayed too. A veteran of mining rushes in California and South Dakota, Butler gave up his itinerant lifestyle when he arrived at the mouth of Carpenter Creek in the early 1890s. R.T. Lowery credited Butler as one of the men who "built" the mining camps of the Slocan.[17]

Most prospectors had a rudimentary knowledge of geology, but often they trusted in luck and good timing more than science. But luck could be good, or it could be bad. On the morning of July 14, 1892, West Kootenay pioneer Joseph William Cockle (sometimes known as "Black Jack") was camped in the valley just below Bruce White's Slocan Star. While either cutting a tent pole or sharpening a claim stake, he discovered a large boulder of almost solid galena ore. Weighing approximately 120 tons, assays indicated that the boulder was 60 percent lead and contained nearly 200 ounces of silver to the ton. Cockle couldn't believe his good luck. He staked the ground surrounding the boulder but was disappointed soon after to discover that the giant rock had rolled down the mountainside from the Slocan Star.

In mid-June 1892, Coeur d'Alene prospectors Billy Tonkin and Sim Tabor set out from their camp early one morning to explore the ground near Martin Fry's Freddie Lee. Not yet done after reaching the Freddie Lee, they hiked to the top of the divide above. In the early afternoon, a sudden storm rolled up. The two men sought shelter under a pair of stunted pines, but

One-hundred-twenty-five-ton galena boulder, c. 1892. Photographer unknown.
IMAGE COURTESY OF SANDRA OSTROM AND THE ROYAL BC MUSEUM AND ARCHIVES

there was to be no shelter from the gods of thunder and lightning. Three times the skies roared with thunder, and three times the rich metallic rocks of the mountain ridge were struck with lightning. Tonkin and Tabor were directly in the path of one of those strikes.

Tonkin was killed instantly by the lightning strike, which carried enough current to melt a piece of ore he was holding. He had a hole in his hat and a burn mark just above his right temple. His beard was scorched and his clothes in tatters. His watch was stopped forever at 1:20 in the afternoon. Tonkin's companion, Tabor, was also struck. He was stunned but, remarkably, escaped serious injury. When he regained his senses, he looked around for Tonkin. At first, he couldn't find him, but crawling through the tangled undergrowth, he soon enough came across his partner's lifeless body.

Tabor managed to make his way down the mountainside. He stumbled into a couple of prospectors, who helped him to a crude shelter. When he spoke his first words, he said, "get someone to go and see for Billy, maybe he isn't quite dead yet."[18] And the man was a sorry sight: "His hair was singed close on both sides of his head, his whiskers were burnt off, and a smell of burnt hair and flesh filled the hut." A prospector helped get Tabor's wet clothes off, revealing shocking wounds. His shoulders and one of his forearms were badly burnt, the fronts of both his thighs were burnt, and there was a scorch on his stomach "as big as a cheese plate." Tabor's clothes were in shreds, and the ends of both boots were ripped asunder.[19]

News of Tonkin's death spread quickly through the throngs of prospectors. It was a sobering reminder of the dangers and uncertainty of life in the mountains. And if Tonkin's death wasn't enough, the decomposing corpse of another unfortunate prospector was discovered the same day. It was believed the remains were those of Charles Randall, a prospector who had vanished late in 1891. Before his disappearance, Randall had purchased more than a hundred dollars' worth of supplies on credit from J. Fred Hume. When he didn't return, Hume took the case to court. The court ordered Randall to appear within thirty days of a notice published in the *Spokane Review*. Sadly, Randall would never read the notice nor show up in court.

COURT CASES PROLIFERATED IN THE early days of the Slocan rush. In October 1891, the *Hot Springs News* noted that there were already "threats of litigation over claims in the Slocan."[20] As the initial rush quietened down, more and more claims ended up in court. Partnership disputes and grubstaking cases were especially common, but there were other cases too. Given the proliferation of roughly hewn stakes littering the mountainsides, it's not surprising that boundary disputes increased as the prospecting season progressed. Sometimes cases would take years to work their way through the courts.

Prospecting partnerships were often a matter of convenience rather than commitment. Half-mumbled pledges made between shots of whisky often took on special significance when a "partner" was lucky enough to make a rich strike. In early November 1891, Charlie Chambers and Ed Becker showed up in Ainsworth with news of the "monstrous" ledge of galena ore they located about a mile southeast of the Noble Five claims. Within days, Becker, Tom Shearer, and Charley Kent filed suit against Chambers. They argued that while only Chambers's name appeared on some of the location notices, they were entitled to an interest in the claims because of an earlier understanding they had with Chambers. When the case reached county court in Nelson the following June, Justice Drake ruled that a partnership was proven. The plaintiffs were each entitled to a quarter interest in the contested claims. The evidence showed that the four men had prospected, camped, and grubbed together and, as a result, had a de facto partnership agreement.

Grubstaking arrangements usually worked to the benefit of both prospector and speculator, but sometimes they turned sour. The Nelson *Miner*, likely inspired by legal action launched a week earlier by Ainsworth saloon keeper Charles Olsen, pointed this out in November 1891. Olsen claimed he had grubstaked Bill Hennessy, Jack McGuigan, and Frank Flint, and wanted the court to award him an interest in each of their Slocan claims. It seems likely that Olsen did have an agreement, but his suit was dismissed.

Captain Hayward and W.A. Hendryx of Pilot Bay had better luck when they began an action against Bill and Jack Hennessy, claiming the two brothers had entered into a prospecting agreement with them in May 1891. Hayward and Hendryx felt they were entitled to a one-fifth interest in the Noble Five claims. Bill Hennessy admitted he had an earlier agreement with the two men but argued that it had expired before the Noble Five discoveries. His case was not helped by testimony that when he reached the Slocan, he "might" have still had "some" of the grubstaking supplies provided by Hayward and Hendryx. The fact that Hennessy and his partners staked a couple of claims in the Slocan under Hayward and Hendryx's names wouldn't have helped either. When the case was finally decided in 1894, the jury found that there was a grubstaking agreement between Hayward, Hendryx, and Bill Hennessy, but no agreement with Jack Hennessy.

While the Nelson *Miner* offered sympathy to grubstakers, the Nelson *Tribune* and *Hot Springs News* came down squarely for the prospector: "It is an absurdity that the locator of a claim should be compelled to 'divy' it with everyone with whom he has had business relations."[21] All parties agreed, though, that any grubstaking agreement should at least be in writing.

The *Miner*'s criticism of prospectors who would turn their backs on those who grubstaked them seems to have been justified. The *Coeur d'Alene Miner* in Wallace, Idaho, heard complaints from returning Slocan prospectors: "It is claimed a number of discoverers of very rich claims violated faith in this matter, locating the grubstakers in poor claims and corralling the good ones by locating in other names than their own."[22] While perhaps not widespread, there were certainly instances of this in the Slocan. It was also clear—and perhaps understandable—that prospectors tended to locate the most promising claims for themselves, reserving lesser claims for their grubstakers.

There were, of course, grubstakers who gained rich claims for very little outlay and without having to resort to the courts. The Dardanelles was a claim staked by John Fitzgerald on June 15, 1892. He had a thirty-two-dollar grubstake from E.E. Coy. Elihu Embree Coy was an important figure in Kaslo's early days. A Union soldier in the Civil War, he arrived in Kaslo in May 1892, after being run out of northern Idaho as the result of a townsite scandal. He hit the ground running in his new home, starting several business initiatives. He built a hotel, operated a pack train, invested in mines, and may have financed the camp's first newspaper. We don't know if John Fitzgerald won any profits from the Dardanelles, but E.E. Coy certainly did.

Another grubstaker who did well in the early days was George W. "G.W." Hughes. Hughes was a contractor based in Spokane when he and another man grubstaked G.W.'s brother Harry and David Porter in February 1892. This earned G.W. a share in the Best, a promising Slocan claim. Soon he would be on his way north to see how good the Best was.

BY THE END OF 1892, the era of easy opportunity was coming to an end. There were still a few rich strikes to be made, but no longer was it common for prospectors to stumble, literally, over the rich galena float scattered generously up and down the mountains. This, of course, frustrated latecomers who were eager to get their piece of the pie any way they could, even if it meant "claim-jumping." Late in 1892, the Nelson *Tribune* reported: "It is no unusual sight to see horsemen dash up . . . on the way to stake ground that has not been represented according to law and on which they have kept their weather eye during the summer and fall. Already a number of relocations have been made."[23] The Nelson *Miner* noted that "it is all right to be down on jumping. The man who is not should be turned out of the country."[24]

One claim-jumping case that reached county court in Nelson involved Billy Smith. In August 1892, a man named Shaw found the stakes for the Mountain Chief, and seeing that the inscription was somewhat defaced, he placed his own stakes and brought a suit to dispossess Smith. In a decision that was greeted with prolonged applause from a large crowd of prospectors, Justice Walkem ruled in favour of Smith. He condemned Shaw's actions as "unneighborly" and told those assembled in the courtroom that the "object of . . . staking a claim was to give notice that the land was occupied, and if the spirit of the law had been complied with, the claim would be upheld."[25] Canadian capitalist and mine owner "Captain" R.C. Adams gave the *Canadian Mining Review* an account of the attempted jumping of the Bon Ton, a claim staked by W.H. Brandon and his partners. One of the jumpers discovered that in transcribing a notice, the mining recorder had written "S. E." instead of "N. E." in the record book. Though clearly a clerical error, it was enough for a legal claim against the Bon Ton. The case was dismissed. "Nothing daunted, the jumpers proceeded to the property and went to work again, running a new tunnel 75 feet and commencing to ship ore when the leader was arrested and sent up for trial."[26]

While the evidence would, in some cases, contradict him, Captain Fitzstubbs, the recent appointee as gold commissioner, reiterated the government's position a few weeks later in Spokane:

> We rarely have quarrels over mining claims in British Columbia. It is our plan not to notice advance claims without there is broad ground for it. We pay no attention to technical differences and consequently we are bothered very little, comparatively, with mining disputes.[27]

In a testament to the diligence and thorough way in which the ground was covered in the Slocan, very few bonanza claims were discovered after 1892. According to the annual report of BC's Minister of Mines, 750 claims were staked in the Slocan during 1892—and this didn't include the dozens of claims on the Kaslo slope. Some were later abandoned, but the majority lived on, their names marked down for posterity in the government records.

3

CAPITAL

BEARDED AND FLANNEL-SHIRTED, Steve Bailey went into the Slocan during the second week of October 1891 with Frank Flint. Following on the heels of the Noble Five, he later told a reporter that he was the "sixth man to enter the camp after its discovery."[1] He was on the ground for three days and made careful inspection of some of the claims. There were eight to ten inches of snow on the mountain summits, but it had not yet crawled down the slopes to the claims. Bailey hadn't packed any tools with him but managed to fashion a crude wooden shovel that he used to scrape away the dirt from the ledges. Everywhere he looked, it seemed, he found rich mineral deposits. He found an uprooted tree blown down in a recent storm. It had not yielded easily. As it went down, it had stripped the soil away from the rock to which it had clung, revealing yet another ore cropping. Bailey told a reporter for the *Spokane Review*: "I have never seen a country which looked so favorable and so full of rich mineral as this." It was, he said, "the biggest thing on the American continent."[2] He was determined to get in on the action.

Capital was quick to follow the prospectors into any new mineral strike. Mining men like Steve Bailey were looking for quick profits and were prepared to suffer some hardships to find them. Big investment would be needed to turn some Slocan prospects into mines, but not all prospectors had the patience to wait for big investment; nor were they eager to work the claims themselves, despite the Slocan's reputation as a poor man's country. Prospectors, as a class, had a well-deserved reputation for selling claims at bargain prices. Often broke between prospecting excursions, they usually relied on grubstakers to finance their explorations. Prospectors always welcomed ready cash, and some were willing to sell undeveloped claims to mining men who were prepared to gamble on what might be under the ground. Some prospectors would settle for just enough money to finance a spree.

For those prospectors who didn't want to sell their claims outright, bonding was an option. Investors would put up bonds guaranteeing future payments based on negotiated terms. This allowed mine operators to retain an ownership interest in their claim until and if the final payment was made but gave them some confidence that money would be available to hire equipment and pay for labour and transportation. Bonds were time limited, and in many cases the terms allowed the bondholders to skim off the cream of profits in the early production of a mine. This was a gamble for both the mine owner and the bondholder, but both stood to reap profits if the mines proved successful. Bonding claims was a common practice for American mining investors but not as common in British territories. E.C. Carpenter explained the practice to a reporter in Victoria: "The bonding of property is a bona fide transaction, and that while English capital will not be invested until everything is demonstrated to an almost dead certainty, the Yankees are disposed to gamble a bit, and invariably reap the biggest share of the initial profits."[3]

Steve Bailey, Scott McDonald, and Jim Wardner were three men early into the Slocan who had the cash to pick up some claims. They bought a few outright and bonded others. Mining men knew where to find investors if claims looked promising. As middlemen, they would pick up good looking claims for relatively little money, then profit from reselling them or from commissions from stakeholders or investors. They looked to attract major investments from deep-pocketed capitalists with an interest in mines. Wardner had backers from New York; Scott McDonald had access to A.W. McCune and other Utah investors; and Steve Bailey looked to attract capital from Washington State.

Steve Bailey got his start in mining as a "bellboy" for a mule train. His first mining rush was BC's Similkameen River in 1859 to 1860. Though born in Kentucky, Bailey was a Spokane man by 1891. He had been a Spokane city councillor and proprietor of the Windsor Hotel during the great fire of 1889 and happened to be in the right place at the right time for the Slocan rush. He was in West Kootenay in September 1891 looking for mining properties to purchase, promote, or invest in. When word of Carpenter and Seaton's great discoveries reached him in Ainsworth, he was quickly on his way to see the ground for himself.

Steve Bailey knew the inherent challenges and risks but was determined in his pursuit of the Noble Five and Payne claims. Over a few weeks in October and November 1891 he negotiated deals—wholly or in part—for the Last Chance, Mountain Chief, Maid of Erin, Two Jacks, and Payne. He negotiated $12,000 for the Last Chance; $10,000 for the four-fifths interest in the Noble Five claims belonging to Seaton, Flint, McGuigan, and the Hennessy boys; and $2,000 for a one-fifth interest owned by grubstakers W.A. Hendryx and Captain Hayward. He got the Mountain Chief for $4,500 from Flint and Bill Hennessy and agreed to the same terms with Jack Hennessy for the Maid of Erin. Bailey paid $3,500 to Jack McGuigan for the Two Jacks, and, in what seems almost literally a steal, he purchased Jack Seaton's half interest in the Payne for $500. He badly wanted Carpenter's half too but was beaten to the punch by Scott McDonald.

Scott McDonald ran a mine in Ainsworth for Utah capitalist A.W. McCune. He was a hardworking and loyal employee who had paid his dues in the Coeur d'Alene district. He was there when the Bunker Hill mine was staked. McDonald staked his own claims too, including the Poorman, but never quite hit the jackpot. He had been involved in lengthy litigation on one Coeur d'Alene claim, something he likely didn't want to repeat in West Kootenay. Like everyone else in Ainsworth, McDonald was infused with Slocan fever after hearing of Carpenter and Seaton's first discoveries.

While overseeing McCune's mine, McDonald kept a careful business eye on the Slocan. He was determined to find a mine and might have had an inside track on the Payne. While the evidence is by no means clear, there was contemporary speculation that Eli Carpenter was grubstaked by either A.W. McCune or G.B. Wright, or perhaps by both. Since McCune was McDonald's employer and Wright the uncle of his wife, either relationship could have given McDonald an "in" with Eli Carpenter. Another account has Carpenter selling his interest in the Payne to John Retallack, but however it played out, somewhere along the way McDonald ended up with Carpenter's half interest in the Payne.

Given the Slocan's proximity to Spokane and that city's connections with many of the prospectors, it's not surprising that a number of the early investors in Slocan claims were from Spokane. John "J.B." Wilson, who had prospected in the Cariboo in 1868, told the *Victoria Colonist* in early 1892 that "everyone" in Spokane was enthusiastic about Slocan mines. In March, a Spokane investment syndicate picked up the Excelsior claim on Carpenter Creek for a reported price of $10,000. Already invested in Coeur d'Alene silver mines, Spokane capitalists saw the Slocan as an extension of the "inland empire" mining frontier they were already familiar with. Men like Patsy

Clark, J.M. Burke, J.A. Finch, Amasa Campbell, Jerome Drumheller, and others picked up some of the most promising Slocan claims.

Despite lacking the Spokane capitalists' familiarity with West Kootenay, investors from Seattle and Tacoma were still quick to see the Slocan's potential. In early 1892, there was a flurry of transactions involving western Washington capitalists. Right from the start there were mining men in the Slocan representing Seattle and Tacoma interests. In late 1891, Mike Gray inspected the Bonanza King and World's Fair claims of Frank Flint and the Noble Five for Seattle interests. Joe Young was also early into the Slocan. Young had an office in Seattle and in February 1892 reported being "in constant receipt of letters from all sections of Montana, Colorado, California, Nevada and New Mexico," asking for particulars about the Slocan.[4]

Judge Hiram Bond of Seattle and Charles Barstow "C.B." Wright of Tacoma were two primary movers from the Washington coast. Bond was a recent arrival in Seattle from New York but soon made a stir with his investments in mining properties like those in Monte Cristo, a booming silver camp east of Everett. Wright was a Philadelphia capitalist with extensive interests in Tacoma. A former president of the Northern Pacific Railroad Company, he is sometimes referred to as the "founder" of Tacoma.

In the first few weeks of 1892, Bond purchased the Seattle claim from "Prospector" Price McDonald for $1,000, and two-thirds of his Eagle. Bond also picked up the Lucetta from E.E. Fletcher for $1,500. Wright took the remaining third of the Eagle and also invested in Lorenzo Alexander's R.E. Lee, which adjoined the Eagle. Not long after, Wright sold his interest in the R.E. Lee to Bond. The interest and investments of Bond and Wright would have raised the Slocan's profile and attracted other like-minded capitalists.

Steve Bailey likely had discussions with Bond, on one of his trips to Seattle. On January 18, 1892, Bailey signed an initial agreement with Bond that authorized Bailey to begin negotiations for the Ajax, Treasure Vault, and Crown Point (all claims owned by the Noble Five partnership), as well as Bailey's Last Chance. Bailey's part of the agreement was to secure deeds or bonds for Judge Bond for an amount not to exceed $300,000. Bailey was to receive a payment of $25,000 and the right to a quarter interest in each of the claims. The remainder of any purchase price was to be paid to Bailey by September. Bond reportedly gave Bailey $7,500 up front and agreed to cover half his travel expenses while he pursued the claims. Bailey set off to see the Hennessy brothers in Minneapolis and consummate the deals.

JUDGE BOND WAS EAGER TO inspect his investments and set out for the Slocan. He was in Ainsworth in April with several other Seattle capitalists who were closing out deals on mining properties, but the snow was still too deep for him to get into his claims. He tried again in June when he had a large outfit set to make the trip in. This time he was stymied by the lack of trails. Winter had wreaked havoc on the rough trails cut in late 1891, and crews had not yet cleared them. However, he managed to get in by picking his way up the Slocan trail and boating up Slocan Lake with his mining expert, Milligan.

After visiting the mineralized area, Bond returned to the log hotel, rough shacks, and scattered tents that were Slocan City. He was frustrated to find there was no pack train available and had to spend a few days in Tom Mulvey's log hotel. Mulvey later recalled that Bond tried fishing in the lake but upset his boat and had to swim to shore. Discouraged and embarrassed, Bond quit the Slocan. One account reported that he "has just returned from a visit to his properties. He couldn't find them, nor apparently does anyone know where they are."[5] It made for a catchy story, but the report that his mining expert didn't approve of the claims, or the district, is closer to the truth. Bailey, Bond, and the Noble Five owners landed in an American courtroom, and Bond came out on top. There was some satisfaction, however, when Bond's abandoned claims, including the Last Chance, yielded silver riches to others.

Litigation involving Slocan claims, particularly the incident involving Bond, gave the Slocan a "black eye" for a time, but the recovery was swift, and soon American capital was flowing into the Slocan in ever-increasing amounts. Steve Bailey and Scott McDonald had done much to bring the Slocan to prominence, but they paled in the shadow of Jim Wardner. Born in Wisconsin in 1846, Jim Wardner was a larger-than-life character who blazed a trail through the mining regions of the west. A Civil War veteran, he spent the latter years of the 1870s running a store, a saloon, and a lunchroom in Deadwood, South Dakota. In the 1880s, he promoted the famous and later infamous Bunker Hill and Sullivan mines in Idaho's Coeur d'Alene district. We know from his autobiography, *Jim Wardner, of Wardner, Idaho*, that he wasn't modest. His book includes the following description written by his newspapering friend, Randall Kemp: "We have long since become convinced that there is only one Jim Wardner. Not only is he a man of excellent judgment, but he is a worldbeater for nerve in all his undertakings. While other men hesitate and wonder, he advances with a smile of perfect confidence, and is indeed a master spirit of energy and enterprise."[6]

While unabashedly full of himself, by all accounts Wardner delivered the goods. He certainly proved himself in the Slocan. Before travelling there in June 1892, Wardner had been following the excitement from south of the border. He was taken with the new district right away, and as soon as he arrived, he was on the hunt for investments. The "Reco" was offered to him for just $1,500, but before he could finalize the deal, it was snapped up by Sam Wharton, Johnny Harris, and Fred Kelly. Wardner didn't despair. He was soon regaling a group of prospectors around a campfire at Bear Lake with tales of the Coeur d'Alene's Bunker Hill mine. Perhaps Toughnut Jack was in the audience. Wardner and Toughnut knew each other in Deadwood. Prospectors would likely have lined up to interest Wardner in their claims, but Toughnut didn't have much to offer. The man who did catch Wardner's attention was Bill Springer.

When Martin Fry and A.D. Coplen were looking to make a deal for their Freddie Lee claim, Springer offered to help find an investor. He went to Jim Wardner, who came out to have a look. He liked what he saw and agreed in principle to Fry and Coplen's asking price of $20,000, with a $1,500 down payment. The deal was consummated in Spokane, and the parties sealed it by getting "liquored up."

SOMETIMES, MEN LIKE BAILEY AND Wardner would start work on their claims themselves. Their goal was to expose some of the mineral riches and thereby make the claims more attractive to outside investors. In April 1892, Bailey took tools and supplies up to his Noble Five claims. He boasted he would be the first to use explosives in the Slocan, but Jim Wardner might have beaten him to the punch. In early July, shortly after his investment in the Freddie Lee, Wardner sent a force of men, the equipment for a blacksmith's shop, and other "necessaries" up the mountain. He was working within a six-month window, and pulled out all the stops to make sure he earned his profit. Martin Fry, Bill Springer, and A.D. Coplen had given him a head start by stockpiling twenty tons of ore, which they had mined with just picks and shovels. Wardner's men worked steadily on the mineral ledge, and Wardner couldn't have been happier. Every swing of the pick increased the stockpile of high-grade ore. He took to boasting he had the greatest mine on earth.

Work in the mines at the start was crude and labour-intensive. The principal tools were pick and shovel. However, once tunnels and shafts were timbered, explosives were critical, and the focus shifted to drilling holes to place the shots. Mike MacGowan, a Gaelic-speaking Irishman, described what his work was like in the silver mines of Montana:

> I knew nothing at all about work of this kind and I didn't know what was in front of me. The first time I went down the shaft, I had to walk a mile and a half from the place where I entered. Two miners were working there all day with a mechanical drill and at the end of the day they would put charges in the holes and detonate them. A heap of stones and clay would be left. I had to get into these holes on a night shift and put the stones and earth onto a little car to be taken out. At the beginning, my heart was up in my mouth with fear.[7]

The work was similar in the Slocan, but in the early days at least, mechanical drills were something of a luxury. Manual drilling was accomplished by either the "single jack" or "double jack" method. In the first, a miner wielded an iron rod and heavy hammer by himself to pound out a hole for the explosives; in the latter, a team of two would carry out the task, with one man holding and turning the rod and the other swinging the hammer. Frank Crampton, who mined in Colorado's Cripple Creek district, described what it was like underground:

> Single jacking was a one man job with no resting, but the double jacking gave some rest with striking and turning being alternated at one or two minute intervals. It was hard working by candlelight that flickered every time one moved, but there was nothing else used for light.[8]

•

BEARS WERE A PARTICULAR DANGER for Slocan prospectors and miners. Marauding bears were so plentiful in some locations that they drove prospectors right out of their camps. Miners were not guaranteed safety even when inside the mines. A story was told of two miners who were partway down a tunnel when one of them heard footsteps close behind him. Thinking it was his companion, he at first paid no attention, but when he called out and got no response, he turned around and realized, to his horror, that he was being stalked by a grizzly. He threw his pick and yelled at the bear, which, surprised, reared up on its hind legs, hitting its head on the low ceiling of the tunnel. With a growl of rage and pain, it retreated back outside.

In another case, a mine owner took a party to visit his mine. He waited at the tunnel mouth while the others ventured inside. About twenty feet in they surprised a large bear, which dashed for the entrance—knocking over everyone in the party. The owner heard the commotion, and when the bear emerged from the tunnel, he killed it with a single pickaxe blow to the head.

There are many other bear tales, but perhaps none so bizarre as the case of the "exploding bear." A miner at Sproule's, between Slocan and Kootenay Lakes, left several sticks of dynamite lying outside the camp. He later noticed they were missing. Hearing a noise in the bush, he caught sight of a bear close to camp. He got his rifle and fired on the bear, which exploded when hit, with bear parts flying in all directions, thus solving the mystery of the missing dynamite.

WITH CAPITAL FLOWING IN AND development work on the mines under way, there was a race to ship ore to market. It was a race Jim Wardner was determined to win. With typical bravado, he vowed he would be shipping ore from the Freddie Lee by the end of July 1892. His success would depend on several factors: First and foremost, he needed ore rich enough to produce a profit over and above steep shipping costs; he needed a passable pack trail or wagon road that would connect with rail or steamboat routes with access to smelters; and he needed the pack animals and packers to transport the ore.

Once Wardner had the ore stockpiled, he needed to pack it out. A few horses of doubtful provenance were available from the Ktunaxa Nation, but there wasn't enough pack train capacity in West Kootenay to satisfy Wardner. He had forty animals shipped in from across the border by way of Nakusp. He had rafts built at the head of Slocan Lake to ferry them to the mouth of Carpenter Creek. There was a decent trail from the mouth of Carpenter Creek to the forks and a passable trail from there to Sandon Creek, but between Sandon Creek and the Freddie Lee, he had to build a trail to get the horses to the mine. He and his men worked tirelessly. By the end of July, they were ready to ship ore. How far they progressed in such a short time can be judged by mining expert Walter Davidson's account of his visit just after Wardner invested in the claim. Davidson noted the twenty tons of ore in stockpile but other than that, reported "very little" work had been done. He was aware of

Wardner's vow to ship ore by the end of July but probably wouldn't have been willing to bet on it: "There was no trail when I was there within five miles of the mine."[9]

Choosing the route to ship the ore wasn't an easy decision. Much would depend on where it was going. There were smelters under construction in Revelstoke and Golden, but neither was proven. The best options were smelters south of the border. One way or another, Wardner had to get the ore to the Columbia or Kootenay Rivers. At this early date, the construction of wagon roads had not yet been started on any of the three major routes into the Slocan, and despite a lot of talk, there were no firm plans in place for any of them. In the end, Wardner decided to ship his ore out over the rough pack trail to Nakusp and then down the Columbia River. It would be an epic journey. On July 22, 1892, Wardner and the Freddie Lee crew loaded a pack train and started down the mountain. The lead animal was a sturdy white mule packing a 300-pound load of ore. At the mouth of Carpenter Creek, the ore was loaded on to rowboats and paddled to the head of the lake. From there it was loaded on to another pack train, this one run by John Patrick "Dad" Allen, a colleague of Wardner's from the Coeur d'Alenes and other western mining districts.

Wardner couldn't have found a more experienced or reliable packer than Dad Allen. Strong and sturdy, though in his sixties, Allen had a reputation for his expert horsemanship. If all Dad's tales can be believed—and his contemporaries found no reason to doubt him—he went to California for gold; was a veteran of the American Civil War; had partnered as an Indian scout with Wild Bill Hickok after the war; had shot a sheriff in Texas who had killed his eldest son, Charlie; and had been the inspiration for a character featured in one of Mark Twain's Silver City tales. (Allen never forgave Twain for stealing something so personal.)

Dad Allen brought Wardner's pack animals into the Slocan from Kellogg, Idaho. He was accompanied on the journey by his teenaged son Bob, who later recalled the trip. Arriving in Nakusp with the forty head of pack animals, the party camped on benchland just above Nakusp before setting out for the head of Slocan Lake. Dad went on to the mining camp at the forks of Carpenter Creek to secure the contract with Wardner. It wasn't long before horses were being loaded with 200- to 300-pound sacks of high-grade ore tied down with diamond hitches. Dad and his men started with three strings of horses—eight horses to a string—each with two men to manage them. Dad's son Bob rode the bell mare.

SS *Lytton*—docked in Nakusp, c. 1893. Photographer unknown. The *Lytton* carried the first ore out of the Slocan. IMAGE COURTESY OF THE ARROW LAKES HISTORICAL SOCIETY

As Wardner knew he would, Dad Allen got the ore to Nakusp. There it was transferred to the *Lytton*, one of the Columbia River steamboats. The *Lytton* puffed its way down to Little Dalles, Washington. The ore was then loaded on to a railway car and taken to Spokane, where it was transferred to the Northern Pacific Railway and finally delivered to Helena, Montana, for smelting. By the end of July, Wardner had shipped out forty tons of ore. The Freddie Lee was the first Slocan mine to ship. Wardner had made good on his vow.

Wardner's ore proved rich and earned him a profit. Mining at the Freddie Lee and other claims was now in full swing. By August, Wardner could report that nearly every pack train carried in an anvil and bellows, and the sound of shots from Bailey's mines sounded like a "small bombardment."[10] Wardner continued to ship ore by way of Nakusp, but he was furious when the provincial government reneged on a promise to build a wagon road from Nakusp to the mines. In November 1892, he switched his business to the growing camp at the mouth of Kaslo Creek. And having

"Pack train laden with baled hay leaving for the Slocan mines," Kaslo, c. 1893. Photographer unknown, but probably Fred Mountain. From Fred Mountain's photo album.
IMAGE COURTESY OF THE UNIVERSITY OF CALGARY DIGITAL COLLECTIONS

just received more than a hundred pack animals, he had to ship hay in as fast as he could ship ore out.

Other mines, besides the Freddie Lee, were soon shipping. They all chose the Kaslo Creek route. In early August, E.E. Coy's pack train carried 960 pounds of ore from the Washington mine. The ore was put aboard the steamer *Galena* and taken to a sampling mill in Spokane. This was likely the first ore shipped by way of Kaslo. In September, J.C. Eaton managed to get a sample shipment of seven tons of Whitewater ore out through Kaslo and Bonner's Ferry. The shipment yielded more than 200 ounces of silver to the ton. The importance of the event was not lost on the residents of Bonner's Ferry, who anticipated the increased business resulting from steady ore shipments.

A visitor arriving at Kaslo on August 28, 1892, aboard the steamer *Nelson* was there at just the right time to see the sacks of Whitewater ore lined up on the wharf ready for shipment. J.C. Eaton was there too, looking over his treasure with obvious pride. "The wharf presented a lively sight as we made fast, there being about 30 people and two express wagons waiting to welcome the new arrivals, but what puzzled the newcomers, was the strange sight of a large number of little sacks made up of strong 'canvas' or 'ducking,' neatly done up. 'These,' said a miner in answer to our question, 'are sacks of ore waiting for transit to Great Falls smelter.'"[11] Eaton netted about $900 in profit on this initial shipment. He later boasted that the Whitewater had paid for itself right from the start: "Practically never a dollar has been put in the mine."[12]

IN ADDITION TO THE MINING "brokers" like Bailey, McDonald, and Wardner, there were plenty of mining "experts," some schooled in geology, eager to visit the Slocan and see the rich galena ores they had heard so much about. While a few could legitimately claim the mantle of "expert," many had questionable qualifications and dubious experience. In 1893, the Nelson *Tribune* welcomed the opening of the School of Mining in Kingston, Ontario, but suggested that students should have a year or two of practical schooling before enrolling. Sharing an opinion widespread in West Kootenay, the *Tribune* thought there were already "too many mining 'experts' in the business."[13]

The Slocan was no different than most other western mining camps. There was an ingrained prejudice against "educated" mining men. Many in the Slocan would have nodded in agreement with a popular witticism: "How are things in Cripple Creek? Oh, they are about the same as usual. The tenderfeet are taking the ore out where they find it, and the mining men are hunting for it where it ought to be."[14] Canadian mining man Hector McRae, who had cut his teeth working at Montana's Drumlummon mine, said he was taught by his devout Presbyterian parents to avoid mining experts like the "pestilence."[15]

While it could be difficult to distinguish one expert from another, R.T. Lowery warned against "the dude expert with the white pants and the scientific expression." He also had advice for those wishing to make the distinction:

> The expert expert is occasionally in sight. His clothes are generally covered with candle grease, powder, soot, and other things a man runs against underground. This kind of an expert is all right. He may look like a tramp, who has been chased by a bulldog, but if he says that a mine is worth so much, you may depend it is, unless he has an interest in it.[16]

Thomas Edward Chandler of London, England, however, was an acknowledged expert. He didn't wear the powder and soot of the underground, but he had other things in his favour. He held memberships in the Institute of Civil Engineers and the Federated Institute of Mining Engineers, and was a fellow of the Geological Society of London. When he visited the Slocan in July 1892, he had never seen anything that looked as favourable: "the highest grade silver-lead ore ever mined."[17]

Other visiting experts included John R. Toole of Butte, Montana, and Walter Davidson. Toole represented the Anaconda Company and Montana capitalist and railroad magnate Marcus Daly. Davidson, after inspecting several Slocan claims, including the Noble Five group, the Slocan Star, and the Freddie Lee, wrote an account of his visit for *The Canadian Mining and Mechanical Review*. You could tell he was an expert from the credentials he listed after his name—"F.G.S., A.R.S.M., etc." Davidson was impressed. So were others. Professor George Adrian of Minneapolis declared the Slocan "genuine."[18] Victoria's Joshua Davies, after meeting with another mining expert, Professor Parks, noted in September 1892 that "the surface showings are away ahead of anything ever found anywhere else." He predicted: "If the quantity is there . . . the district will be the greatest and richest on the continent."[19]

Investment in Slocan mines continued throughout 1892 and into 1893. The Slocan mines were advertised widely, and Spokane capitalists led the way north. There were a few investments in early 1892, but things picked up as the year advanced. Billy Lynch worked hard developing and marketing his Washington claim. He was rewarded in April 1892, when Spokane's Tom Jefferson acquired an interest in the claim for $22,000. In June, Samuel "S.K." Green secured another interest for $20,000. Green spent a month in the Slocan, and having made up his mind to try his fortune in BC, he considered moving his headquarters from Spokane to Nelson.

Other Spokane investors joined in. John Muse "J.M." Burke first visited the Slocan in July 1892 with O.D. Garrison. It was reported that their original goal was to look at the Wellington. However, they also toured the Washington with Tom Jefferson and inspected several other mines. Instead of the Wellington, they ended up with an interest in the Blue Bird, along with E.E. Coy and W.H. Taylor.

J.M. Burke was born to wealthy slave owners on a Virginia cotton plantation. He set out for the west after the Civil War, eventually landing in the Coeur d'Alenes. Burke was a businessman, but he also had political ambitions.

In November 1892, he ran for governor of Idaho on the Democratic ticket. He lost, but this allowed him to pay more attention to the Slocan.

Later in the year, H.D. Scribner and Jerome Drumheller bonded the Alamo group of mines for $40,000. J.E. Boss bonded the Queen Bess and put money into the Mountain Lilly, Lucky Move, Roulette, and Rebound on the north fork of Carpenter Creek. Big money was moving. In December, Patsy Clark invested in the Wonderful and Johnny Harris's Reco. He was in partnership with others, including J.A. Finch, Amasa "Mace" Campbell, and J.M. Burke. Clark knew how to get a mine started. He had 6,000 pounds of supplies shipped to the Reco in late December 1892, expecting it to be worked through the winter. Scribner followed suit, shipping 5,000 pounds of supplies to the Alamo early in January 1893.

Charles and W.P. "Wake" Russell, lately of Spokane but originally from Burr Oak, Kansas, arrived in the Slocan in late 1892. They got right down to business. In October, they bonded the Ruby Silver, one of the early Slocan claims, for $25,000. Russell also invested in the Noble Five claims and picked up several others, including the Keno from Quebec-born prospector Joseph Martin. Just before he completed the deal for the Ruby Silver, Russell was in Helena extolling the Slocan's virtues to Montana capitalists. According to one account, the Russell brothers thought themselves "already millionaires."[20] The thought was not far-fetched.

There was American investment from outside Spokane, too, of course. Frank Farrell of Butte, Montana, bonded the Silver Glance and Summit Queen on Bear Lake for $42,000 in late 1892, and a New York syndicate picked up the Aspen near the Idaho in January 1893 for $20,000. Utah's A.W. McCune, who already had investments in Ainsworth, had his eye on the Slocan too. He likely provided financial backing to Scott McDonald and the Payne.

The only mines that attracted British investment in 1892 were the Great Western and the Reed and Robinson group. Both were managed on behalf of a London syndicate by F.M. Chadbourne and his Canadian associate, William Jowett. Some Canadian investment money finally found its way to the Slocan when Edward Watts bonded the Wellington claim for the Kootenay & Columbia Mining Company of Ottawa. Watts was eager to get work started after a trial shipment of ore yielded profitable results. By the close of 1892, ore was being packed out in volume, and more investment money was flowing in. The Idaho, Dardanelles, Washington, Whitewater, and Best had all joined the Freddie Lee as shipping mines. Wardner's reputation alone attracted other mining men. And the richness of the ore he had shipped was beyond dispute.

GIVEN THE NUMBER OF AMERICAN prospectors and miners in Kaslo and the Slocan and the amount of American capital flowing in, it's no wonder that some Slocan residents—Canadian as well as American—thought they might be better off annexed to the United States. The American influence was nowhere more evident than in Kaslo, where one American proclaimed, "We are the people and demand respect."[21] Another American visitor described Kaslo in its early days as "a thorough American town built on Canadian soil" and declared,

> Americans prevail in everything. They have secured control of all the best mines there and the bulk of the business is being done by American supply men. The miners and prospectors are Americans and nearly every article of food and clothes eaten and worn are of American manufacture, sold by tradesmen of this country and paid for with coin that bears the head and emblem of Liberty.[22]

A British visitor a few months later confirmed this state of affairs and noted that the "sober Englishman" had to put up with the feelings of the preponderant Americans. The topic was the subject of debate in late 1892, and much of it played out in the pages of the local newspapers. What was surprising was that a proponent of annexation, E.C. Carpenter, was Canadian, and a principal defender of Canadian sovereignty, E.E. Coy, was American.

E.C. Carpenter expressed his support for annexation on a November 1892 trip to Spokane:

> We need American institutions in our country. We need to grow and we want your push and enterprise and liberal capital to shove us ahead and make something out of the country. I'll tell you candidly that I am a British subject, but as a business proposition, I would give a whole lot of money to see British Columbia annexed to this country. It is the only way we can ever hope to build up the wonderful stock-raising and mining country that should belong to the United States.[23]

Carpenter's support for annexation was surprising given his background. Born in London, not far from King Henry VIII's Hampton Court, he had a privileged upbringing, educated at the prestigious Marlborough College. After immigrating to Canada, he became a fixture on the expat social and sports scene while living in Victoria in 1890 and 1891. He hobnobbed with Chief Justice Matthew Baillie Begbie, Clive Phillipps-Wolley, and other champions of British breeding and culture. He was an active participant on the playing field, adept at rugby, football, and lawn tennis.

What could lead a seemingly dyed-in-the-wool British expatriate like E.C. Carpenter to support the annexation of British territory by the United States? In short: money and self-interest. Like many others with money invested in the Slocan, Carpenter could see the willingness of American capital to promote the district. He could imagine the wealth that might be generated if there were no borders and no duties or trade restrictions. Writing to the Victoria *Daily Colonist* shortly after his trip to Spokane, Carpenter was dismissive of opinions in Victoria: "There will probably be very few who care a farthing for what the miners want."[24]

Carpenter wasn't alone. A couple of weeks later, John Retallack, whose English father had once accompanied the Prince of Wales on an American hunting expedition, was in Spokane. According to the *Spokane Review*, Retallack "expressed a sentiment that every miner feels when he said that he regretted that the Kaslo and Slocan countries were not on American soil."[25] But while there was certainly some local support for annexation, there was just as much opposition. Even men like Retallack and E.C. Carpenter were, to some degree, "playing to the audience" while they were in Spokane. They didn't offer such bold support for annexation back in West Kootenay.

After E.C. Carpenter's pronouncements in favour of annexation, Coy stood on the other side of the fence. E.E. Coy—American citizen and proud Civil War veteran—took a strong stand for Canada when he wrote to the *Spokane Review* after reading what E.C. Carpenter had said in that paper:

> After a six month's residence there I unhesitatingly declare that we are much better off as we are. I can think of but one way we would be benefitted by annexation and that is the removal of duty on lead . . . So much am I in love with the country, the people and the laws, that immediately on my return I am going to swear allegiance to the crown and become a full-fledged Canadian, for the people

> there are at least a grateful people, thankful for kindness shown and assistance rendered, and this is much more than can be said of the people of the United States.[26]

Coy felt the laws in Canada were "ten to one" better than those in the US.

Clive Phillipps-Wolley, an early visitor to the Slocan, looked at the annexation debate in West Kootenay from a particularly British Empire perspective:

> Men talk of annexation, and the conquest of Kootenay by the American miners. Kootenay had been opened up very largely by the miners of America and the enterprise of American capitalists, and there is a certain amount of annexation going on, *but* it is the annexation of American citizens by Canada, seduced from their loyalty to the Great Republic by the attractions of Western Canada, within whose borders they find that they can mine securely and rest confident in the protection of a justice which does not miscarry.[27]

The *London Advertiser* (Ontario), while acknowledging that up to 90 percent of the Kootenay's population was American, believed the infusion of seasoned American prospectors, miners, and investors would be "highly beneficial" to Canada.[28] Roger Pocock was another champion of British culture. He visited West Kootenay just before the Slocan rush and, like Phillipps-Wolley, had respect and admiration for American prospectors and miners. He could be critical of fellow Britons, but he was fiercely British in outlook and would never have supported annexation: "Canada was a bigger, wilder country, where men went safe without a weapon, where aliens had human rights, where judges were not bribed, Legislators not of the criminal classes, and honesty was not become effete."[29] British travellers J.A. Lees and W.J. Clutterbuck had earlier expressed similar views. Often disparaging of the Americans they met in the west, they finally concluded that "their faults are about the same as our own, but with the accents differently placed."[30]

4

BOOM TOWNS

THE FIRST MINING CAMP IN the Slocan was located on Slocan Lake at the mouth of what would soon be named Carpenter Creek. The Nelson Miner noted that the camp, staked in late 1891, might one day surpass Leadville and Butte. On the other hand, it could within a year be populated only by "owls and jack rabbits."[1] The smart money at the time was on the former not the latter.

In the earliest days, the crowded little huddle of tents and log shelters was simply called "Carpenter Creek" or, briefly, "Slocan City." Typical of the unbridled optimism that permeated new mining camps, the name that stuck was "Eldorado City," perhaps suggested by Nelson *Miner* editor John Houston. Surely the untapped wealth in the surrounding mountains would come to rival the Eldorado of legend. The floating population of about twenty at the camp over Christmas 1891 hunkered down to await the arrival of the New Year and the hordes of prospectors and speculators who would soon arrive.

Most arrivals in early 1892 were eager to stake mines, but more than a few were intent on locating townsites. However, the provincial government threw a wrench into the works by freezing all townsite development within ten miles of Slocan Lake. This had an immediate effect on about forty townsite applications already made. Frustrated townsite speculators complained loudly. The government confirmed that the land reserve would apply only to land staked after December 31, 1891, though the land freeze would still apply so long as the land reserve was in place. In March 1892, it was announced that the reserve would be lifted by June. But it was also reported that "government reserves" would be established at Eldorado City, and at the head of Slocan Lake. This left the parties who had staked land there out in the cold, both literally and figuratively.

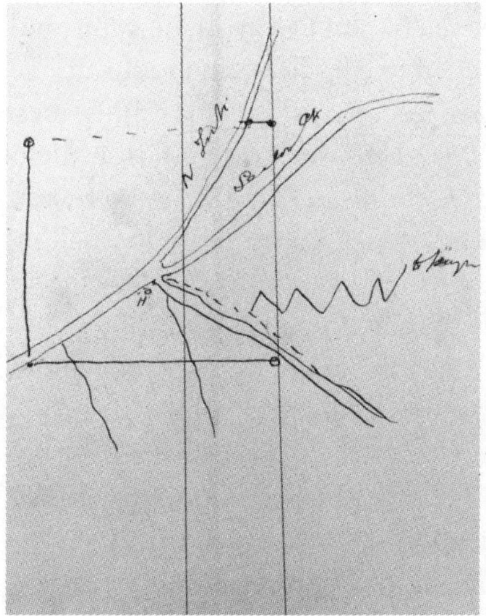

Charles Perry's sketch map of Three Forks, December 1892. Photographer: Author. Note the site of Carpenter and Hugonin's original hotel (H) and the zigzagging trail to the Payne. AUTHOR'S COLLECTION

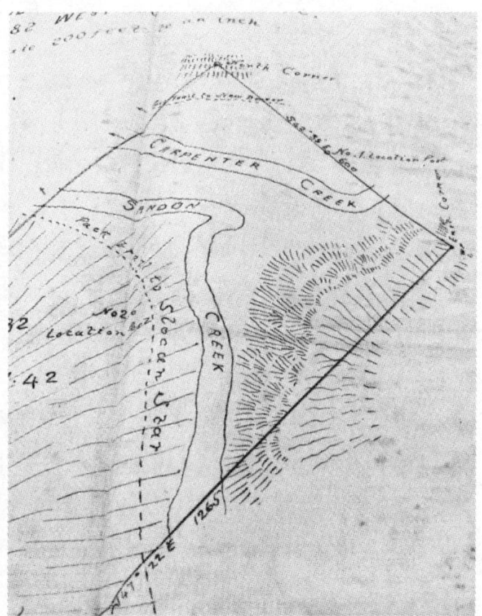

Early survey sketch of the Blue Jay claim, c. 1893. Photographer: Author. The sketch shows the pack trail to the Slocan Star and a trail to New Denver (Eldorado). Things might have been clear on a survey plan, but they were seldom so on the ground. AUTHOR'S COLLECTION

The principal sites, besides the reserves at Carpenter Creek and at the head of Slocan Lake, included land at the south end of Slocan Lake and along Slocan River, and at the mouth of Four Mile Creek. They also included a few inland sites such as the claim staked by Charlie Chambers, Bruce McCulloch, and Tom McGovern at the mouth of "Carbonate Gulch" on Seaton Creek; the site owned by Chambers and John Sandon where Sandon Creek joined Carpenter Creek; as well as the Cody camp, which was up a small creek that fed into Carpenter Creek above Sandon Creek.

Many of the prospectors who staked townsites in 1891 had lost interest by the time the land reserve was lifted, but those who persevered were joined by a host of others. Townsites sprang up like spring weeds. Joining Eldorado City were Three Forks, Four Mile City, Watson, Bear Lake City, Wilson Creek, Cody, and, of course, Slocan City. These were the principal mining camps of the early Slocan.

Boom towns depended on businesses to survive and thrive. Most incomers were eager to climb the mountains to seek their fortunes, but as in all mining rushes, there were some who were content to stay in the camp and "mine the miners." Fortune seekers needed to eat, sleep, and outfit. In the early days, the services provided by hotels, restaurants, packing outfits, merchants, and assayers were essential. By May 1892, Hunter and McKinnon had their store open at Carpenter Creek, Gething and Henderson were welcoming guests to their log hotel, Spokane's W.G. Merryweather was selling general merchandise, and a resourceful baker was offering sandwiches to the hungry crowds waiting for the snow to melt.

Enterprising entrepreneurs set up "half-way" houses on all three routes into the Slocan. Offering cheap meals and rough beds to the men and women crowding the trails, the keepers of these houses were practically guaranteed to make money. Gorman West, who served hot meals to the trailblazers clearing the Slocan River trail, had announced early on his intention to open a stopping place for pilgrims coming in from Nelson. However, he was beaten to the punch by Charles "Chipmunk" Brown and his partner Rufus Evans. They were soon doing a roaring business catering to the multitude heading to the new Eldorado.

> This "hotel" was a long, single storey log building, situated on a bank of land overlooking a bend of the river. The main building contained, under one narrow, low pitched roof of split cedar shakes, the bedrooms and stables. Various "lean tos" which looked as though they might have been thrown at the main building, posed as dining room, kitchen, woodshed, and bar, of which the last named was the largest and most frequented.[2]

One of the men who stopped at Brown and Evans's half-way house was Victoria resident and big-game hunter Clive Phillipps-Wolley. English-born and upper class, he was an old-school Anglophile, but for his trip to the Slocan, he donned a flannel shirt and lived with the prospectors and miners. Interviewed a year later, he explained, "I got into miner's clothes and tramped all through the country 'with the boys,' living in their camps and carrying my pack with the rest." By doing so, he felt he was "more likely to get at the real truth over a pipe at night, or on the trail."[3]

Armed with a Winchester rifle and accompanied by a mining "expert," Phillipps-Wolley was more interested in bears than silver. Still, Phillipps-Wolley couldn't avoid the hordes of prospectors—hundreds had preceded him. He described the clutter of men following float trails as "behaving generally like a lot of demented and erratic rabbits."[4] On reaching the Slocan,

Phillipps-Wolley erected a crude hut to shelter in while he hunted bear. The hut would also serve as a temporary infirmary for Sim Tabor after he was struck by lightning.

John Proctor, better known as "Death on the Trail," was just ahead of Phillipps-Wolley on the trail to Eldorado. Proctor was a signature character on the western mining frontier and had been at Kootenay Lake in the late 1880s and early 1890s when the country was just opening up. At six feet, six inches from tip to toe, and with his wide-brimmed sombrero hat, beaded buckskin shirt, and long hair and goatee, he must have seemed, to the more timid denizens of BC, like a relic from an age when giants walked the earth. Proctor—who had scouted for Custer in the Indian wars—rarely talked about his alias, but one of his contemporaries explained that in the 1880s, Proctor had gone with a party of prospectors to explore the upper Kootenay country. A mixed group of Indigenous and white people attacked them, killing everyone but Proctor, who escaped. The attackers were all later found dead, the only clue to their demise: the words "death on the trail" carved into a piece of bark.[5]

Two other early visitors to Chipmunk Brown's half-way house were E.C. (Easy Come) Carpenter and E. Percy Whalley—both strays from Victoria. Jim Bolander and a few Coeur d'Alene companions stayed at the half-way house too, but because it was full, they camped outside. Bolander later recalled, after a hearty meal of bacon, bannock, and beans, the pleasures of sitting around a roaring fire "spinning yarns" until they were ready to turn in.[6]

Brown and Evans, to simplify their accounts, charged a dollar for pretty much everything. A bed was a dollar; a meal—whether a breakfast of beans, bacon, and bread, or a supper of bread, bacon, and beans—was also a dollar. Drinks were a quarter each, but one was expected never to order less than four drinks at a time. Whalley later described the accommodations:

> The bedroom consisted of a long alley-way, with a double tier of bunks on either side. As Easy and I were the last arrivals that evening all the sleeping accommodations was bespoke; but through the kindness of a packer on the mule train, who was too far gone in drink to know or care where he slept, I secured possession of a lower bunk. Easy Come was not so fortunate, having to content himself with a plank bed on the floor of the dining room.[7]

By June, the McDonald brothers, who also ran a pack outfit, had a half-way house ten miles from Kootenay Lake on the trail from Kaslo to the Slocan. They

"10 Mile House." June 5, 1893. Photographer: Henry Woodside. The "Blue Ridge House" on the Kaslo-Slocan wagon road. LIBRARY AND ARCHIVES CANADA

called it the Blue Ridge House, but most people referred to it as "Ten Mile," or the "Half-Way House," though not to be confused with the half-way house on the Slocan trail. The Nakusp route was slower to develop than either of the Slocan River or Kaslo Creek routes, but packer Jack Walsh operated the small "Summit House" by a pretty little lake. Risdale and McKay took over management of the hotel in 1893 and renamed it "Half-Way House."

Though not strictly speaking in the Slocan, the camp that thrived most conspicuously in the first few months of the rush was Kaslo. Buoyed by hopes for a railway, it was some distance from the mines but proved a popular and populous gateway. It was also beyond the reach of the government's land reserve. Fortune seekers—most from south of the border—took one of the steamboats from Bonner's Ferry, Idaho, down the Kootenay River and up Kootenay Lake to assay the mecca of their dreams. The population grew from one in 1890 to between four to five hundred by July 1892. And the crowds kept coming—seven to eight hundred by November, and two thousand by May 1893.

The owner of the Kaslo townsite, George Kane, proved a capable promoter. He had staked the townsite before the Slocan rush, but the rush

Kaslo, c. 1893. Photographer unknown. IMAGE COURTESY OF THE UNIVERSITY OF BRITISH COLUMBIA LIBRARY DIGITIZATION CENTRE AND ITS GENEROUS DONORS

accelerated his development plans. He attracted high-rolling investors from BC's coast and, by early 1892, had established the Kaslo Kootenay Land Company with railway schemers John Hendry, Alex Ewen, Daniel "D.J." Munn, and Robert Irving. The company hired Victoria's John Keen as engineer and Tom Norquay as the principal real estate agent. Building lots sold briskly. As an added incentive, the company put up a hotel to house prospective investors. In March, Norquay and another Victoria recruit, William Haywood, were in Winnipeg, in Norquay's home province, drumming up business. In the afternoons and evenings, they held court in the Manitoba Hotel. Norquay's name alone was likely to have attracted interest. Tom's father, John, of mixed Cree and Scottish descent, was premier of Manitoba from 1878 to 1887.

Advertising was critical to success, and local West Kootenay newspapers were full of promotional information on the competing townsites, each boasting of its particular advantages. Advertisements for Kaslo lots were carried in newspapers as far away as Vancouver Island. Speculation in town lots was rampant, and by early 1893, Kaslo could legitimately be described as a "boom town."

The rapid growth of Kaslo was bad news for Ainsworth. Many residents left for the growing camp up the lake. Ontario-born assayer Maurice Andrews "M.A." Bucke was among them. Bucke's father was Richard Maurice "R.M." Bucke, a renowned psychiatrist, or "alienist," in charge of the London, Ontario, Asylum for the Insane. A man of many talents, the elder Bucke was a close friend of American poet Walt Whitman and was celebrated in his own right for his novel theories on hysteria, insanity, and cosmic consciousness. As a youth, R.M. Bucke travelled west, pioneering on the famous Comstock silver lode.

On the other side of the Slocan, on the shores of Upper Arrow Lake, Nakusp would become another staging ground for travellers. Land for a townsite at the mouth of Nakusp Creek was first staked in October 1891, and soon attracted the interest of the CPR. The CPR could see that the only viable way of accessing the mineral-rich Slocan would be down the Columbia River and Upper Arrow Lake from Revelstoke. In early 1892, the government allocated money for a trail from Nakusp Creek to the Slocan mines. By May, the CPR had forty men clearing a townsite. The site was slow to grow. It was not as attractive a destination as Kaslo, as most of the Slocan incomers were arriving from the south. One visitor to Nakusp in late June 1893 referred to the camp dismissively as consisting "essentially of 3 hotels on a desolate field of stumps enclosed by forest."[8]

The future townsite of Eldorado was first staked by Angus McGillivray in late 1891. However, the land was caught up in the land freeze, and then the bulk of McGillivray's townsite claim was reserved by the government. In the meantime, residents laid out makeshift streets and built wherever it suited them. In early May 1892, the government dispatched surveyor C.E. Perry to Carpenter Creek to untangle the mess. Perry and his team finished their survey by June and sent the plans off to the government. Perry described the site at the mouth of Carpenter Creek "as pretty a situation for a townsite as he ever saw."[9]

In preparation for the auctioning of town lots, Gold Commissioner Fitzstubbs was there in late May, posting notices that warned people not to build or make any other improvements on the government-owned land. The warnings came a little late for those who had already put up log cabins and makeshift shacks. Buildings that landed in the middle of streets after the survey was completed had to come down. This included the first cabin at Carpenter Creek, the humble residence put up by Neil Gething, George Henderson, and Billy Will in late 1891. Will made a show by burning down the historic building.

With the streets and lots of Eldorado City now laid out, a debate arose over the name of the new metropolis. Some argued that "Eldorado" was not appropriate because it intimated a land of gold, not the silver that it was hoped the Slocan would become famous for. Some thought the name "hackneyed, fanciful and extravagant."[10] It was agreed that a name change was in order. What to name the new town? Several options were bandied about. According to one account, Thomas Lowthian, a well-known mining expert from Denver, Colorado, who was in the Slocan at the time, suggested "New Denver." The name stuck, and the new "Eldorado" became New Denver. Eldorado lived on as the name of the street fronting Slocan Lake on the new townsite plan.

With Perry's plans in hand and the new name, the government was ready to put townsite lots up for auction. Auctioneers Jowett and Haig of Revelstoke and Nelson were given the task. The sale was set for eleven o'clock in the morning, July 20. The *Miner* described the momentous day in detail. The weather was miserable, but though rain soaked the assembled crowd, "it did not dampen their enthusiasm for New Denver real estate."[11] Somewhere in that crowd was R.T. Lowery, newly arrived from Ontario.

Visiting Victoria after the auction, William Jowett told a *Daily Colonist* reporter, "I suppose you know that I have lately held a very satisfactory sale at New Denver, at the mouth of Carpenter Creek, Slocan lake. Since the sale, many tenders have been made at advanced figures for some of the lots."[12] One of the purchasers might have been a woman—Nelson's Annie Eagan—an unusual occurrence for a male-dominated mining camp. The successful auction behind them, residents of New Denver looked to the future. The auction marked the end of Eldorado and its rough-hewn collection of log shacks and itinerant prospectors, and the birth of New Denver, full of hopes and dreams. Newly marked-out streets still sprouted stumps and boulders; the bridge over Carpenter Creek was a large cedar tree, but no one there that day doubted the future prosperity of the new "town."

The confidence was not misplaced. It soon became apparent that the government reserve was not large enough to accommodate all the incomers to New Denver. This was good news for Angus McGillivray, George Bigelow, and Mike Malloy. McGillivray learned that the government reserve didn't take up his entire original claim, so the leftover land became "McGillivray's Addition." But even this was not enough to satisfy demand. George Bigelow and Mike Malloy had staked land in late 1891, and once the land reserve came off, their land became "Bigelow's Addition." Just to the north of the government townsite and McGillivray's Addition, it boasted access to a small bay on the lake.

New Denver was a popular destination for incomers, particularly in the early months of 1892. It quickly expanded from twenty-one buildings in mid-March.

By early April, there were nearly a hundred buildings completed or under way. The population fluctuated wildly. There were as many as three hundred men and perhaps a few women camped at Carpenter Creek, but this number would shrink significantly once the ground was open to prospecting.

Attention to the Slocan silver strikes came from all over North America. This was at no time more evident than when W.D. "Walter" Middaugh arrived in the Slocan in the fall of 1892. Middaugh was manager of the mining department for the American Development Company, an investment syndicate based in Duluth, Minnesota. Middaugh and his wife were on vacation in Banff when news reached them of the Slocan strikes. Middaugh decided to investigate and invested widely. According to the Nelson *Miner*'s account of Middaugh's Slocan visit: "He thought he would like to see it. He came and saw it. He has bought it—at any rate 2,500 acres of it."[13] During his short visit, Middaugh committed $65,000 to purchase fifty silver claims. It was clear that he made an impression on his Minnesota colleagues. Not long after, the Duluth syndicate arranged to buy all of Bigelow and Malloy's lots in their New Denver townsite addition.

The townsite that attracted the most attention in the early days, closer to the mines, was the land at the confluence of the principal creeks flowing through the Slocan. There wasn't much level ground, but the site was right at the crossroads of the main routes in from Slocan and Kootenay Lakes. Billy Lynch reportedly staked a townsite there in late 1891, and for a time the spot was known as "Lynch's." Jack Watson, who was running a pack train out of Ainsworth with his partner David Bremner at the start of the Slocan rush, staked a site in the area too, but his claim was later ruled invalid as he apparently posted a defective notice. Eli Carpenter also hoped to get a piece of the action. In early January 1892, he hired a Spokane man to stake the land at the forks, but the claim was disallowed because of the government's land reserve.

The site was finally successfully claimed by E.C. Carpenter. During his first few weeks in the Slocan, Carpenter had prospected with Angus McGillivray. The land reserve had only just been withdrawn on most Slocan lands, but McGillivray's townsite claim at the mouth of Carpenter Creek was still in the clutches of the government. One can imagine McGillivray and Carpenter discussing townsites. In June 1892, Carpenter applied for pre-emption of the site that Lynch, Watson, and Eli Carpenter had earlier tried to claim. E.C. Carpenter's partner in his townsite scheme was Charles Hugonin, a friend, rugby teammate from Victoria, and schoolmate

Three Forks, c. 1893. Photographer: Edwards Brothers. From Harry Abbott's photo album. An early photo of Three Forks, notable for showing how thickly forested it was in the beginning. IMAGE COURTESY OF THE CITY OF VANCOUVER ARCHIVES

of Rudyard Kipling. Sometimes referred to as Carpenter's Camp, Carpenter's Forks, or simply The Forks, they named the new site Three Forks—descriptive, if not particularly imaginative.

Three Forks was bustling in 1892, but so were other camps. Jack Watson, who had tried to stake the site of Three Forks, had better luck with the Central City claim between Bear and Fish Lakes. At first, the camp was called by the name of the claim, "Central City," but by mid-summer it was generally known as "Watsonville," which likely suited Watson. He had the townsite of "Watson" surveyed by J.A. Kirk in October 1892. Lots were put up for sale, and Watson opened a store, to ensure that settlers would have supplies. The *Vancouver Daily World*, perhaps numbed by the steady flow of new townsites, greeted the new arrival with a certain weary cynicism: "And still another townsite has sprung into existence. The town of Watson, 'the natural centre and distributing depot of the Kaslo-Slocan camp' has bobbed up serenely near Bear lake."[14] Watson engaged his friend, John Retallack, to act as estate agent. By the end of November, all available lots in Watson had been sold. Writing back to Scotland, Watson was upbeat:

"Watson." The view across Bear (now Fish) Lake to Watson in June 1893. Photographer: Henry Woodside. LIBRARY AND ARCHIVES CANADA

> Should the supply of silver emanating from the mines keep coming out in the way it has been doing, nothing can keep us back and my town of "Watson" is right in the heart of the mining country. Everything comes to him who waits, surely some faint rumours of the richness and wealth of this Slocan country must have crossed the ocean, if anyone mentions that name to you, you can inform them that I am fairly in it![15]

Not far from Watson, G.M. Sproat established the rival townsite of Bear Lake City, on land first claimed by Fred Jarvis, and named by him Summit City. By the end of November 1892, Ben Lee, general agent for the townsite, could report that over a hundred lots had been sold in that "coming great."[16] G.M. Sproat's son Hector had one of the lots. Sproat's other son, Alex, appointed mining recorder for the Slocan in June, settled in New Denver. In December, the elder Sproat was busy organizing a Christmas carnival to promote his townsite. He promised it would be a first-class affair, with surrounding ranchers providing fresh turkeys, geese, butter, and eggs. The Nelson *Miner* was legitimately skeptical but suggested a "teeny tiny drop of whiskey" might compensate for any shortcomings in the selection or stock of food.[17] We don't know how the celebration turned out, but we do know that immediately afterwards, G.M. Sproat headed to Victoria and Hector set out for England. G.M. Sproat travelled from Victoria to Seattle, where he was interviewed by a reporter for the *Seattle Post-Intelligencer*. While he confessed that he was generally a skeptic about mines, the Americans in the Slocan had convinced him that it was destined to be one of the "best districts in the country."[18] He presciently noted that the ore was of such a high grade that it could be worked at a profit even if there was a fall in the price of silver.

THREE OR FOUR MILES SOUTH of New Denver, a large creek flowed into Slocan Lake. In 1892, rich silver strikes were made up the prosaically named "Four Mile Creek." But even before the mineral strikes, the mouth of the creek was recognized as an attractive site for a mining camp. In late 1891, merchant William Hunter staked a townsite for himself and his financial backer, Nelson's J. Fred Hume. Capitalist John Cook staked an adjoining site. However, they couldn't do much with the land until the government land reserve was lifted later in 1892. Even then, the townsite was slow to develop. Jack Kelly and Harry Waugh stopped there in early 1892. They found a fine grove of birch trees and a lovely pond, but there wasn't much else. Hume remained in Nelson, where the headquarters of his West Kootenay mercantile business was located. William Hunter, the only one of the townsite owners who resided in the Slocan, was busy in New Denver with his general store and his plans to build a steamboat. Cook invested in the steamboat and several mining claims, but he didn't seem too interested in the townsite.

In the summer of 1892, William Hunter arranged to have C.E. Perry survey part of the townsite. The mines up the creek looked promising, and the natural shipping point for ore would be on the shores of the lake at the mouth of Four Mile Creek. The camp was briefly known as Leadville, but by the time lots went on sale in February 1893, it had become "Four Mile City." Sales were reportedly brisk, with inside lots going for $75 and corner lots for $100.

Hunter and Hume were offering deals on a half cash down basis with the balance to be paid within four and eight months. Before the end of February, 185 lots had sold. Hunter and Hume were trying to attract businesses. They offered

$50,000 to anyone willing to set up a concentrator. They knew they were not likely to get rail connections, but a concentrator would make shipping ore by steamboat almost as attractive an option. By mid-March, it was reported that more than 250 Four Mile City lots had sold. If true, these were better numbers than any other Slocan townsite on the market at the time. One newspaper noted "not a single lot was sold to 'suckers' from the outside. The purchasers all live in this section."[19] We can get an idea of how good business was by an advertisement that Hunter and Hume had printed in April 1893. Effective May 1, 1893, they were raising the prices to $150 for inside lots and $200 for corner lots.

The value of Four Mile City lots skyrocketed with the arrival of Middaugh's Duluth syndicate. Just as it had purchased all the lots in George Bigelow and Mike Malloy's New Denver addition, the syndicate arranged to buy all the unsold lots in Hunter and Hume's townsite. As part of the deal, the syndicate agreed to manage the time payments on lots. But because the syndicate would be paying double the price that most early purchasers had paid—based on the increased prices that Hunter and Hume had announced—many owners likely looked to resell at a profit. Lots were increasing in value, but in July 1893, the "city" still sported a few rough edges:

> As is the case of a number of places designated as cities, there were about five buildings in course of construction, ten or fifteen tents, and five log huts. The timber has been cleared from two streets, and with careful driving I should think a team could be piloted between the stumps.[20]

AT FIRST GLANCE, THE LAND at the southern outlet of Slocan Lake looked like an ideal spot for a mining camp. The ground was level and could perhaps sustain some agricultural development. Passage to Nelson would be relatively easy following the valley of the Slocan River. Arthur Dick and Harry Ward staked a promising site there. In January 1892, despite a scattering of snow, Dick, Ben Lee, and Alfred Bunker were clearing "streets" in anticipation of cashing in on town lots. The site was quickly surveyed, and by early May 1892, even though the land reserve was not yet lifted, Nelson's Harry Selous was advertising lots at "Slocan City" on a first-come, first-served basis. Inside lots were selling for $50, and corner lots were going for $75. While Slocan City was a fair distance from the mines, it was well placed to capitalize on traffic going in and out and could at least boast—though the claim was not entirely accurate—of being "the only property on Slocan lake with a clear title."[21]

The first hotel at Four Mile City, c. 1893. Photographer unknown. The owner, Jim Bowes, stands just to the left of the doorway—the tall man with his hands in his pockets.
IMAGE COURTESY OF THE SLOCAN VALLEY HISTORICAL SOCIETY

Despite its natural advantages, Slocan City was slow to develop. Early in 1892, Tom Mulvey and Billy Clements built a log hotel they called the Lakeview, but no buildings followed. The Lakeview was described as having a "frontier appearance,"[22] but the bunks were said to be comfortable. For most travellers, Slocan City was but a stopping place on their way to the mines. They might pitch tents for a few nights, or perhaps take a bunk at the Lakeview, but their goal was the mouth of Carpenter Creek and the rich mineral district inland. During the summer of 1892, the population of Slocan City fluctuated daily from about ten to fifty as prospectors and capitalists passed through on their way in or out. Few stayed, and Dick and Ward did not make the "killing" in real estate they had anticipated.

About three miles north of Carpenter Creek, another large creek flowed into Slocan Lake. In late 1891, A.M. Wilson staked the land encompassing the mouth of the creek that would afterwards bear his name. The site was good, but it was too far from the mineralized area to elicit much interest in the early days. Wilson spent most of 1892 further north in the Lardeau district, where he thought the prospects were better.

Several other townsites waited their turn in the spotlight. Steep-sloped McGuigan, and "Reco," the site up Carpenter Creek where it was joined by Sandon Creek, would have their day once the mines started shipping ore. Another site that attracted early attention was Seaton. The mountain slopes, where Jack Seaton, Eli Carpenter, and the Noble Five made their rich strikes, seemed unlikely ground for a townsite, but Jack Seaton thought otherwise: "I took up 160 acres of land, the prettiest little valley you ever saw, just halfway between the two camps, and intend to make a townsite of it. We will have a number there next year, you can bet on that."[23]

Some of his partners decided to follow through on Seaton's townsite dreams. In July 1892, Arthur Farwell surveyed the townsite. Construction couldn't have been easy: Jack Hennessy put up the first building, a log storehouse, and said, "We had to shovel away eleven feet of snow to build our house."[24] The volume of snow that stayed on the ground late into the spring would not help their marketing strategy.

Seaton's townsite was close to McGuigan Lake, a popular stopping place for prospectors. Somewhat surprisingly, given its apparent disadvantages, a visitor from Sacramento described the camp as "lively," and a Victoria traveller who passed through in May 1893 noted that townsite lots were selling well. Louis von Ruecau had earlier reported "quite a city of tents" there.[25] Unfortunately, Jack Seaton would not live to see a mining camp develop in his pretty little valley. He died in July 1893.

To have any hope of permanence, mining camps had to reach a critical mass of services and amenities. They had to have at least a store, a hotel, a restaurant, and a saloon to have any chance of success. A newspaper would be a boon, and stables, a necessity. New Denver came fully equipped, and Three Forks, though at first lacking a newspaper, had the basics. Watson and Bear Lake City were more works in progress. Transportation links were also crucial. Wagon roads and railways would be critical.

THE MINING CAMPS OF WEST Kootenay were like magnets for itinerant newspapers. It would be difficult, if not impossible, to recount the district's history without them. The survival of so many titles is largely due to the efforts of R. Edward "R.E." Gosnell, BC's first provincial archivist. Gosnell visited West Kootenay in 1892. Early on he recognized the importance of local newspapers in telling the history of the province.

As mining camp historian Duane A. Smith has noted: "Newspapers were critical for a community: They promoted, defended, attacked, reformed, motivated, aggravated, reported, and dissected events and activities. Every camp and town wanted one; without a newspaper to promote local highlights, miners were isolated and adrift in an uncaring world, lacking the ability to capture public notice, attract capital, or intrigue investors."[26]

It usually took several hands to run a frontier newspaper. At a minimum, there had to be a financier or publisher, an editor, a compositor (typesetter), someone to run the press, and a printer's devil—a junior position responsible for many of the basic jobs that supported everything else. A reporter was needed to follow and describe local events, and correspondents in outlying camps or mines provided crucial local gossip. Multitasking was common, and it was an asset to have a knowledge of how the whole operation worked. If budgets allowed, more staff could be hired.

At the time of the initial Slocan strikes, there were two newspapers in the silver districts of West Kootenay, both run by John Houston. Notoriously peripatetic in his early career, Ontario-born Houston had worked on newspapers from Chicago to California before settling down in Nelson in 1890 to start the *Miner*. After a stint at the *Calgary Herald*, he started his own paper, *The Truth*, in Donald, BC. He later moved the paper to New Westminster—his last stop before Nelson. The other West Kootenay newspaper he ran at the time, the *Hot Springs News*, served the mining camp at Ainsworth. Houston had editorial assistance from David Blyth Bogle, recently arrived from Scotland, and capable production work from Charles Ink.

Houston did not have the field to himself for long. Newspaper publishers, correspondents, editors, and typesetters flocked to West Kootenay after the Slocan discoveries, hot on the heels of the prospectors and miners. By 1900, as many as seventeen newspapers had come off the presses in the Slocan district and in the gateway communities of Nakusp and Kaslo.

In May 1892, Houston decided to cash in on the Slocan boom. He sold the *Miner* to David Bogle and E. Percy Whalley and took up the life of a prospector and real estate developer. Whalley had come to Nelson from Victoria along with his friend E.C. Carpenter. Whalley and Carpenter visited the Slocan early on. While Carpenter decided to stay, Whalley went back to Nelson and partnered with Bogle to provide notary services. Their short-lived partnership as notaries likely came to an end when they embarked on their newspapering career, though Bogle, at least, continued to advertise his notary services.

Whalley later recalled that as a youth in England, he had once had a "Do Your Printing at Home" kit, "so there was nothing, naturally, about running a paper" that he didn't know.[27] However, running two newspapers proved a challenge, and the last issue of the *Hot Springs News* came off the press in October 1892.

For his part, Houston took out a miner's licence and did a bit of prospecting, but he wasn't as successful as perhaps he had hoped. He missed the newspaper business and the forum it provided for his strongly held political opinions. At first, he thought he might start a newspaper in New Denver, but then he began negotiations with Whalley and Bogle in a bid to buy back his old paper, the *Miner*. But the deal fell through, so in November 1892, Houston started a rival newspaper in Nelson, the *Tribune*. Whalley was incensed, accusing Houston of being "petty and self-seeking in every line he wrote" and of prostituting himself to "further his own ends."[28] Houston probably didn't care what Whalley thought. Not only could Houston fully express his political views, the paper also served as a vehicle for his real estate dealings. Subsequent issues were full of advertisements for the sale of lots in the Slocan's Four Mile City townsite, listing Houston as the sales agent. The Victoria *Daily Times* described the first issue of the *Tribune* as "crammed full of news and racy comments."[29] Whalley would probably have agreed with at least the latter part of the assessment.

Newspaper competition in West Kootenay in the early 1890s was fierce. No quarter was given. By the time Houston got back into the game with the *Tribune*, others were looking to get started. With buildings going up right and left, and people swarming in, Kaslo was an attractive location for aspiring newspaper promoters. In the summer of 1892, it was rumoured that a Spokane man, G.M. Walters, would be starting a weekly newspaper to be called the *Kaslo Nugget*. A prospectus was issued—but nothing else. Residents would have to wait a few more months for their first weekly newspaper. On October 22, an American, Mark W. Musgrove, with the help of printer R.E. Seysler of Missouri, and perhaps financing from E.E. Coy, published the first issue of the *Kaslo-Slocan Examiner*. Musgrove, a lawyer by trade, had since 1882 run the *Kootenai Courier* out of Rathdrum, Idaho. Before that, he had started the *Yankee Fort Herald* in Bonanza City, Idaho. Clearly, he had paid his dues. Looking for new opportunities, he saw the potential in Kaslo and decided to pack up his printing press and haul it through Idaho and up Kootenay Lake to the new camp.[30] In May 1893, R.T. Lowery launched his first BC newspaper, the *Kaslo Claim*, in competition with Musgrove's *Examiner*.

New Denver got its first newspaper in June 1893, when W.D. "Bill" Pratt, an experienced newspaperman who owned a newspaper in Oregon, started the *Slocan Prospector*. Pratt, a man large in both girth and family (he reputedly had eleven children), had considered the prospects in Nakusp but decided New Denver was the better bet. Even before the press arrived, Pratt hired Los Angeles typographical union member and former editor of the *Tres Pinos Tribune*, Thomas B. "Tommy" Tobin, to help get the paper out. "Well printed" and published every Tuesday, the new paper was available by subscription for three dollars per year. The Nelson *Miner* was generous in its opinion: "In its first issue it strikes a rich vein of news in a body of commonsense that may show good assays for the editor if he opens up well."[31]

It didn't take long for Pratt to take a shot at his contemporary, the *Kaslo-Slocan Examiner*, addressing an irritant widely held in New Denver: "We object to the term 'Kaslo-Slocan.' Kaslo has stolen lustre from Slocan long enough. Slocan stands upon its own merits and desires that Kaslo do the same. The term 'Kaslo-Slocan' was invented in Kaslo. It was meant to deceive; to make the world believe that Kaslo had the grip on the Slocan country. Who here in the Slocan would think of calling this the 'Slocan-Kaslo?'"[32] We don't know how committed Pratt was to his new enterprise. By September, while south of the border touting the Slocan, he was offering to sell the *Prospector* for $700.

THE MINES WERE THE FOUNDATION underlying everything else in the mining camps. Whether it be newspapers, hotels, or general stores, as long as the mines produced riches, and investment money flowed in, the camps thrived. If the mines closed down, most mining camps did as well. As we know today, the western slopes of North America are dotted with abandoned "ghost" towns that once rang with gunshots and noisy revelry.

New Denver, Nakusp, and Kaslo, buoyed by their scenic settings, are still with us today, but Three Forks, Watson, and Bear Lake City have slipped into the forgotten pages of history. And who has ever heard of Murphyborough or Daly'sville? For every successful Slocan camp, there were probably three, four, or more that would never amount to much. Nashville and Mahoneyville on Kaslo Creek, at the junctions of the south fork and Rabbit Creek respectively, were launched with high expectations that would never be realized. A man named Fielding surveyed Nashville in July 1892, and in October William Jowett held an auction of 250 lots. It's likely that many went unsold. Other camps fell by the wayside too. By the summer of 1894, the Nelson *Tribune* described Seaton as "the city of snow in fall, winter, and spring, and chipmunks in the summer."[33]

5

BY WAGON ROAD AND STEAMBOAT

DAD ALLEN, BECAUSE HE SHIPPED the first ore, was perhaps the most renowned of the early packers into the Slocan, but he didn't suffer from lack of competition. Pack trains were a critical tool for all stakeholders to get supplies into the mining camps and the mineral claims, and, of course, were essential in getting ore out. Rates were high, and packers could make money with every load they carried. Before the trails were built, Indigenous packers accompanied some of the first prospectors into the Slocan, but they couldn't handle the rush that followed.

Within weeks of the first discoveries, there were packing outfits on all three of the main routes into the Slocan. Jack Walsh, who had two hundred pack animals by July 1892, pretty much had the Nakusp route all to himself in the early days. Competition was keen on the other two routes. The McDonald brothers operated a pack train on the Kaslo trail, but so did Jack Watson and David Bremner. E.E. Coy also had a packing outfit. For a while, E.C. Carpenter ran a pack train from New Denver to the mines, charging two to three cents a pound for the short haul. After injuring his foot in July, however, he quit the business and would focus his energies on the townsite of Three Forks and the hotel he ran with Charles Hugonin.

Angus McIntyre was likely the first packer on the Slocan River route, packing in supplies for Hunter & McKinnon's store, but he soon had competition from Blake Wilson and Billy Perdue, and the Madden brothers. Perdue, an "old cowboy" described as "a wonder on a horse," was familiar with the dry lands of the Okanagan and the foothills of Alberta but would be a mainstay in the Slocan.[1] He and Wilson were charging six and a half cents a pound from Slocan Crossing to Slocan Lake and had an arrangement with Mickey Monaghan to ship goods up the lake. Seven cents a pound was the going rate on the Kaslo trail. Once ore started moving in earnest after Jim Wardner's first ore shipment from the Freddie Lee, multiple packing outfits sprang up to serve the mines. Rates would go down as the year progressed and the traffic and competition increased. By the end of the year, Kaslo's G.O. Buchanan, who ran the camp's first sawmill, reported that packers had contracted to haul out about a million dollars' worth of ore over the winter.

It's likely that Lane Gilliam had a big piece of the business. Gilliam had been caught up in the Coeur d'Alene troubles and looked to the Slocan to build his future. He crossed the border in late 1892. Before his Coeur d'Alene adventures, Gilliam briefly served in Spokane as both a sheriff and marshal. He was eager to find a mine to work, but he loved horses and made good money running a pack train.

In the days before railway connections and reliable wagon roads, the pack trains served as lifelines for the mining camps. New Denver and Three Forks, in particular, were often at the mercy of inclement weather, and it was not unusual in winter for them to run out of one thing or another. This was rued by a man who returned to Kaslo from New Denver in the spring of 1893: "I am glad to get back to Kaslo again . . . in Denver it is difficult to get even pork and beans. The town is out of almost everything and the trails are very bad, and packing rates five cents a pound, from Slocan crossing and Nakusp. Even at these high prices, the packers do not seem to be able to get enough goods in."[2]

Contemporary accounts attest to the hard life endured by pack animals:

> We stopped at Slocan crossing, the nearest approach from Nelson to the Slocan mining district. Here there were some small wooden shacks and a large corral, full of pack horses whose raw backs were most distressing; we deposited such an amount of miner's supplies including a gigantic smelting bellows, to be transported thirty-three miles to the town of New Denver on Slocan Lake, which has 250 inhabitants, it made my heart ache.[3]

Prospectors and miners could put up with running out of most things, but not whisky. Almost everyone dreaded a "whisky famine." In March 1893, David Bremner and T.J. Proctor of Watson made the first boat trip of the season from Kaslo to Nelson. They rowed when there was open water and hauled their boat over the ice when there wasn't. They were warmly welcomed when they returned to Watson with six hundred pounds of whisky. "Their heroic efforts will be told around many a campfire in years to come."[4] Sid Norman arrived in Kaslo a few weeks later aboard the pioneer steamer *Galena*. Partway up its slow trip on Kootenay Lake, the *Galena* nosed its way into the icebound narrows north of Nelson. Norman wondered what was going on. The *Galena* was picking up a sleigh load of whisky destined for Kaslo.

The ever-increasing crowds of merchants, miners, and boomers filling the Slocan were acutely aware of the transportation challenges. Whether it was whisky, potatoes, or building supplies, residents paid a premium to cover the cost of bringing goods in by pack train. Only the richest of mines would be able to profitably ship ore out by pack train. Railway connections to the outside world would be the ideal solution, but in the interim, there was a clamour for wagon roads, improved trails, and a steamboat for Slocan Lake. The flat-bottomed bateaux operated by Palma Angrignon and Mickey Monaghan did yeoman service, but they would be unable to handle the anticipated increase in trade.

When the first trails into the Slocan were being built, champions for the Kaslo route said the Slocan River route would be useless without a steamship service on Slocan Lake. Nelson interests took notice. They realized that a steamboat service in conjunction with the Slocan River trail would be an integral component of a transportation network linking Nelson to the Slocan by way of the Columbia & Kootenay Railway at the mouth of the Slocan River. As early as November 1891, the citizens of Nelson were urged to put up $1,000 to whoever could get a steamboat on Slocan Lake first. American capitalist W.A. Hendryx considered buying a boat in Idaho to bring up Kootenay Lake. However, his plans didn't pan out. Instead, John Cook rose to the challenge.

Cook first travelled to Victoria to enquire about machinery. He knew lumber would be readily available, but he wasn't so sure about shipping a boiler and steam engine in. He must have been encouraged by his inquiries because a few weeks later he was on his way to the Slocan to firm up his plans. He spent Christmas at the mouth of Carpenter Creek, where he found several like-minded individuals, including—and especially—William Hunter.

A week or two before Cook's arrival at Eldorado, Hunter had announced that the firm of Hunter & McKinnon would get out the hull for a steamboat using local lumber. They were just waiting for plans and a model to arrive from Portland, Oregon. As the principal merchants on the lake, and given the steep freight rates they were paying, they would benefit greatly from a steamboat service. But others would benefit too. In January 1892, Hunter was instrumental in organizing the Nelson-Slocan Steam Navigation Company. Cook and some other businessmen were quick to come aboard. The company raised $25,000 in authorized capital and engaged Portland, Oregon, boat builder David Stephenson to construct the vessel. At the same time, a boiler and machinery were ordered from the John Doty Company in Toronto. Frank Doty travelled to Spokane in early February 1892 to negotiate terms and equipment. Hunter was optimistic the boat could be operating by April.

In early January 1892, John Cook advised that arrangements for the steamboat were completed. The model and plans were expected any day. The machinery was on order and expected to arrive with the first steamboat runs up the Columbia River in the spring. According to the initial plans, the new boat would be forty-five feet long and fourteen feet wide in the beam. Cook admitted, however, that it would not be large enough to handle all the anticipated traffic. To resolve this, he announced the navigation company's intention to put on a barge service until another boat could be built.

Slocan sawmills had not yet started operations, so Cook and his partners decided to have the boards they would need whipsawed on the spot. The trees and thick undergrowth that stretched out behind New Denver would still have been in winter's grip in March, when a group of three or four men gathered at the mouth of Carpenter Creek. Pioneer woodsman Jack Evans, who had started a whipsaw mill, was in charge. Choosing several straight trees to work, he and his crew dug a pit in front of Gething and Henderson's hotel. One man on top would guide the large whipsaw through the green timber on the downstroke, while a man below would help with the return stroke. Alex Sproat later recalled that the Bowerman brothers, George and Jack, manned the saw. Soon they had enough lumber for their needs. But things didn't move as quickly as either Hunter or Cook hoped, even though the lumber was ready by the end of March.

David Stephenson arrived at Carpenter Creek shortly after the lumber was sawn. Though living in Portland, Stephenson was a native of Saint John, New Brunswick, where he had learned the shipbuilding trade. He came to the Pacific coast in 1883 and continued to turn out a steady stream of expertly built vessels, including the *Mikado*; the sternwheelers *No Wonder*, *Altona*, and *Messenger*; and the propeller-driven boats *Iowa* and *Baranoff*. Stephenson was recognized up and down the coast as a master of his trade. He had been to West Kootenay before to supervise the construction of the

Nelson, one of the Columbia & Kootenay Steam Navigation (C&KSN) company's steamboats.

The boat for Slocan Lake was a more modest affair, but before starting construction, with the support of Cook and others, Stephenson changed the plans to give the boat more carrying capacity. This delayed the project a bit, though he still thought he could be finished by mid-May. Plans revised, work finally began. One of the key contributors was John Gosson. Born in Halifax, Nova Scotia, Gosson was a "ship carpenter of repute."[5] He had decided to make his home on Slocan Lake and was in the right place at the right time to show off his boat building skills. In early April, Henry Cody—just in from a trip to the Slocan—gave a glowing report to Nelson's *Miner*, expecting the new boat to be "one of the tidiest craft" to ever sail on inland waterways.[6] However, May came and went. It was not until early summer that the sixty-foot superstructure for the twin propeller-driven craft was complete. Unfortunately, those who had been patiently waiting for the boat to be finished would have to wait a bit longer—it could go nowhere without a boiler. In the meantime, Jap King set to work building rowboats.

The delay was a boon to King, and allowed the bateaux operated by Angrignon and Monaghan to continue service. Another vessel appeared too. This was likely built by Bob McTaggart and Conrad Bill. The *Irish Man-of-War* was described as a "pretentious" craft that, for want of nails, was cobbled together from roughly hewn logs "fastened together with wooden pins."[7] It was said to have been twenty-seven feet in length with a capacity of three tons. We don't know how this glorified raft was powered, but for a short time in 1892, it plied the waters of Slocan Lake delivering much-needed freight to the new camps.

In late August, the shareholders of what was now known as the Slocan Trading and Navigation Company held a general meeting in Nelson. Their first order of business was to deal with the delays, cost overruns, and the most pressing crisis, the failure of the John Doty Company. Doty, who had been long established on the Toronto waterfront, suffered significant financial reverses in 1892. Late in the year, he had no choice but to sell out to his major creditors. In retrospect, perhaps Hunter, Cook, and the other investors should have looked south of the border for equipment. While they would likely have had to pay duty, shipping costs would have been much reduced, and the American companies were more experienced and reliable.

Some West Kootenay mines had purchased equipment from the John Doty Company previously. One operator noted that the steam equipment "while undoubtedly strong, does not possess that finish and elegance which American mining engineers have become accustomed to."[8] The equipment delays were costing shareholders in added expenses and lost business. The company was determined to get the boat on the lake as quickly as it could, but it was weeks before the machinery orders could be sorted out.

The engine and boiler finally arrived in October, packed from Nakusp to the head of Slocan Lake by mule, then ferried to New Denver on one of Angrignon's bateaux. Fortunately, the timing was right for Hiram Sweet to install the equipment. Sweet was a West Kootenay pioneer and expert steamboat engineer. Born in Charleston, South Carolina, he arrived in West Kootenay in the fall of 1888. He installed the boiler and engine on the *Galena*, the first commercial steamboat on Kootenay Lake, and afterwards worked for C&KSN with their small fleet of steamboats on Kootenay Lake and the Columbia and Kootenay Rivers. Sweet knew his business. He quickly had the boiler installed. By November the boat was ready for its maiden voyage. It just needed a captain and crew.

The Slocan Trading and Navigation Company had been lucky to have Sweet available to install the engine and boiler. They were luckier still to find a captain of the quality of George Ludlow "G.L." Estabrooks ("Captain Lud" to his family and friends). Estabrooks was born in Swan Creek, New Brunswick, in 1846. By the age of fifteen, he was working on the steamboat *Gazelle*, operating between Fredericton and Woodstock. He soon advanced, captaining a succession of steamboats, including the *Rothesay*, a steamer built for day trips on the Saint John River between Saint John and Fredericton. By the early 1890s, however, the steamboat business in New Brunswick was suffering from railway competition. Estabrooks—like Stephenson before him—decided to try his fortunes in the west. He was on his way to Vancouver when his passenger coach stopped in Revelstoke. A C&KSN man came on board and asked if anyone had a mate's ticket. Admitting he had a master's ticket, Estabrooks soon found himself working for the C&KSN. A few months later he took the position with the Slocan Trading and Navigation Company. He never made it to Vancouver. His son, Otto Estabrooks, later recalled that his father took the Slocan Lake job because he thought it would be "soft."[9]

The new steamboat was christened the SS *W. Hunter* in tribute to the man who had worked so hard to see it built. The construction delays had been frustrating, but there was a great sense of accomplishment and pride once the boat was on the water. The *Hunter* initially operated on an "as required" basis, transporting people and goods as demand warranted. Otto Estabrooks recalled that if prospectors along the lakeshore lit fires, the *Hunter* would take that as a signal that someone needed a ride. A red flag would do the trick too. It was said that the boat's machinery had to stop so she could blow her whistle, and the boat would tip to port or starboard every time the captain switched his chewing tobacco! The Nelson *Tribune* welcomed the new service:

> The captain and engineer of the steamer *W. Hunter* are the most accommodating steamboatmen in British Columbia. They will fire up and run that boat to either the head or lower end of the lake at any time to suit the convenience of travelers.[10]

The *Hunter*'s shallow draught allowed it to nose into almost any landing. Boarding could be accomplished easily enough with a wide plank. However, the steamboat soon adopted a regular schedule with runs up and down the lake, including a daily five o'clock afternoon departure from the head of the lake, carrying passengers and freight coming in from Nakusp. Jack Kelly was hired on as purser and Archie Lee as engineer. After running the boat for a few weeks, Hunter and his partners decided to make a few improvements. By June 1893, a second deck had been added, increasing its carrying capacity. It could only carry about twelve people on deck but could push barges carrying dozens.

Unfortunately, Jack Evans, who had the lumber whipsawed to build the boat, would not live to see it launched. Renowned for his strength and endurance, Evans seemed indestructible to his comrades. But in October 1892, Ike Lougheed was prospecting on the western shore of Slocan Lake with Evans, Jack Buchanan, and Albert Irwin when Evans was taken ill with what was most likely appendicitis. His companions got him into a boat and rowed him to the mouth of Carpenter Creek. According to one account, they got him up to his cabin, but nothing could be done for him. He reportedly got up off his bed one last time, had a drink of water, and looked to the setting sun. "It's getting dark," said Evans, and then he was gone.[11] His comrades were in tears.

The next day, Ike Lougheed and Al Irwin dug his grave. The sudden death of Evans served as a cold reminder to all Slocan prospectors of the transitory nature of life. Shortly after his death, the Nelson *Miner* reported that "some of the boys think it would be only a graceful tribute to the memory of Jack Evans to erect a suitable monument to his memory on his lonely

"First voyage of the SS *W. Hunter* on Slocan Lake," c. 1893. Photographer unknown. While the photograph is identified as the first voyage of the *Hunter*, the picture would have been taken some time after the early voyages as the second deck addition has already been built. Clearly, however, the photograph captures an important event/ time, with many Slocan stalwarts crowding into the picture. The Slocan Star's Bruce White can be seen standing tall just to the right of the main deck entrance, but who is the young woman at the back of the boat on the upper deck? IMAGE COURTESY OF THE ROYAL BC MUSEUM AND ARCHIVES

grave."[12] Twenty-five dollars was raised to mark Evans's grave, but the creek that tumbles down to Slocan Lake near where he was first taken ill and the pristine lake at its source, both now named after him, are far more fitting and lasting tributes to this Slocan pioneer.

THE SS *W. HUNTER* WAS welcomed by the mining camps on Slocan Lake, but it wouldn't do much for the mines up in the mountains. The trails into the Slocan, crudely built in 1891 and repaired in 1892, served their immediate purpose by bringing prospectors, investors, and goods in and by sending ore out on the backs of pack horses and mules. But they could not keep up with the traffic. No sooner were the trails completed and repaired than there was a clamour for wagon roads.

For a time, it looked like there could be two or possibly three wagon roads into the Slocan in 1892. When the Nakusp trail was being built in the summer of 1892, many residents called for the government to upgrade it to a wagon road. In June, the *Kootenay Star* complained the trail "should have been made a wagon road at once, as the route has proved to be so well adapted for it."[13] The government gave assurances in September that a wagon road would be started before the winter. There were calls for a wagon or sleigh road on the Slocan River route too.

To the great disappointment of Slocan boosters, especially Jim Wardner, the government reneged on its promise to build the Nakusp wagon road, and little work was done on the Slocan trail. While the proponents of the Nakusp road were left licking their wounds, an initiative to build a wagon road from Kaslo into the heart of the Slocan moved forward. As with the Nakusp route, those who supported the road turned first to the government for funding. However, they were determined to push a wagon road through with or without government funding. The townsite owners, mine owners, and others in Kaslo and Ainsworth committed to financing the wagon road. In total, about $10,000 was raised by public subscription. The townsite company promised to contribute "about an equal amount."[14] A wagon road committee was formed to oversee construction.

Tenders were opened on September 15, 1892. Eleven bids were received, including one from veteran road builder G.B. Wright. However, the winning bid was from John Lane, of the Spokane contracting firm Lane & Marks. The bid was for $33,300. This worked out to about $1,100 per mile for the estimated twenty-eight-to-thirty-mile road. The road was to be completed to Bear Lake within sixty days and to Cody Creek by August 1, 1893.The contract was short on technical requirements but did include racist provisions typical of the time, prohibiting Lane from hiring any Chinese or Italian workers.

Chinese workers had provided the labour to build the CPR through the Rocky Mountains and were by the 1890s ubiquitous throughout most of BC, but they were not tolerated in the Slocan and suffered abuse elsewhere in West Kootenay. R.T. Lowery was virulently anti-Chinese and lost no opportunity to showcase his bias. His newspapers regularly ran articles denigrating Chinese "heathens." In July 1892, when a trip from Revelstoke to visit the new camp at Nakusp was organized, just before the *Lytton* would carry the first ore out of the Slocan, six Chinese excursionists—all "good Christians" with fares paid—were denied service on the steamer. Lowery would have approved.

Prejudice against Italians was also widespread. Speaking a "foreign" tongue and not quite "white" enough to fit in with many of the other workers in the west, they were dismissively referred to as "dagoes," and shunned by their contemporaries. However, a few early arrivals, like New Denver's

Nick Palorcia, earned the trust of their communities and, against the odds, won a measure of acceptance that would not have been accorded to individuals of Chinese background.

PROGRESS ON THE WAGON ROAD was slow despite the best efforts of the road builders. The project was beset from the start with problems and delays. Building a road through such a heavily forested landscape proved much more difficult and expensive than Lane had anticipated, and he found that payments from Kaslo's road committee were erratic at best. The road was also plagued with small forest fires. A group of travellers in the fall of 1892 complained of having to lead their horses "around burning stumps and fallen trees."[15]

Lane and his crew pushed ahead through October and November, but they expected to be paid for their work. Because of the difficulty of keeping men on the job and the uncertainty of the contract payments, Lane instituted a time-stamp system for paying his workers' wages. Instead of receiving money at the end of their shifts, workers were given a "chit" stamped with the date on which wages would be paid to them. The system was unpopular with the road workers, but it seems to have served Lane's purposes.

As work proceeded, the problems between Lane and the wagon road committee escalated. Soon it appeared the whole project and contract might have to be cancelled. On October 15, 1892, the committee wrote to Lane to advise him they were hiring an independent engineer, W.D. McKay, to oversee and inspect the works. A month later, McKay wrote to Lane & Marks to advise that he was hiring his own crew, but that all costs would be charged to the contract. Lane was incensed.

On December 6, the road committee chair, G.O. Buchanan, wrote to Lane announcing that the committee had decided to terminate the contract. Two days later, Lane wrote to Buchanan advising that "we will have the wagon road completed from Kaslo to Bear Lake on the 15th inst [in this month] ready for your acceptance and we desire that you act in the matter at once as we wish to break up our camps as soon as the work is done to that point for removal."[16] Perhaps the letters crossed in the mail.

The road committee refused to budge. Once Lane, his partners, and the work crew realized they were not going to be paid, they went on the warpath, threatening to fence off the road so that no one could use it until they were paid. If they were not paid, they threatened to go to Victoria to seek an injunction. In all, Lane & Marks had completed just seventeen miles of the road. The committee acknowledged the contractor's bad luck with the "phenomenally bad weather with which they have contended," but still refused to pay Lane more than the contracted price.[17] As a result, Lane could not pay his outstanding bills. The road workers were caught in the middle. To its credit, the committee did pay the workers' outstanding wages.

The Nelson *Miner* was scathing in its criticism. An editorial hit close to the mark when it noted that the committee seemed to think it could get work worth $1,600 a mile for $1,100 per mile. The *Miner* felt that the committee had "itself only to blame" for the problems. In particular, the committee was faulted for not hiring an engineer—something the *Miner* had earlier advised—to go over the wagon road route before awarding a contract.[18] The committee was chastened but determined to carry on. They scrambled to come up with a contingency plan. Belatedly heeding the *Miner*'s advice, they hired C.E. Perry to go over the route and make whatever engineering improvements were necessary.

A contemporary account from the Nelson *Miner* was uncharacteristically circumspect and a bit more charitable than its earlier editorial: "Nothing very definite has been stated to the public, and the slight veil of mystery which hangs over the proceedings is not altogether a good thing, though no doubt necessary. In the meantime, the solid fact remains that the road has been completed."[19] Well, completed almost to Watson, which was no doubt fine with Jack Watson and the promoters of his townsite. They could now boast in large newspaper advertisements: "Watson . . . Terminus of the Kaslo-Slocan Wagon Road."[20]

Late in 1892, Jim Wardner sold his packing outfit to G.W. Hughes. With his purchase, Hughes, who had mining interests too, pretty much had a monopoly on packing contracts to move Slocan ore out through Kaslo. In addition to the Freddie Lee, he also had contracts with the Blue Bird and Idaho mines. He struggled to keep his mules and horses fed but was able to purchase twenty-five tons of feed in late December. Hughes and his pack trains were a godsend for the Kaslo wagon road committee. Having just extricated themselves from their contract with Lane & Marks, they were scrambling to get a makeshift crew to push the road through to Bear Lake. Hughes's business depended on a reliable road. When the road committee's construction crews ran into trouble, he took over. He vowed to push the road through by the end of December 1892. This was an ambitious target considering that Hughes had only arrived in the Slocan in October. His infrastructure was impressive. His camp boasted an office, cookhouse, bunkhouse, ore sheds, blacksmith shop, and stables, all of log construction. With hard work and perseverance, he and his men were able to deliver a reasonably reliable sleigh road.

While G.W. Hughes was getting most of the ore business from the mines, he generally left passenger transport and deliveries to specific mines to others. Sharp-minded entrepreneurs could see business opportunities.

Billy Lynch—with his profits from the sale of the Washington—and William J. Cleary were first on the road. Lynch provided the money and Cleary the business acumen. On December 3, 1892, even before the wagon road reached Watson, the Kaslo Transportation Company began advertising sleigh service from Kaslo to Bell's camp, just short of Watson and Bear Lake. Although they would start with open wagons, Cleary and Lynch promised to soon offer a quality service. In January 1893, Cleary set out to acquire two stylish Concord coaches. Entrepreneurs south of the border were eager for transportation links too. One of them, Rufus L. Cheney, formerly a magistrate in Bonner's Ferry, visited Kaslo in December 1892. He managed to get more than $600 in subscriptions for a winter sleigh road linking the outlet of Kootenay River into Kootenay Lake with Bonner's Ferry. Cheney was likely in cahoots with another ex-magistrate, "Judge" Bill Chambers, Charlie Chambers's brother, who had established "Chambers City" at the foot of Kootenay Lake.

With the $500 already subscribed from Bonner's Ferry businessmen, Cheney—described approvingly in the *Kootenai Herald* as a "rustler"[21]—was confident he could have the road built within a week. He wasn't far off. By early January the road was complete. Travel was not for the faint of heart, though. It took Cheney's stages ten hours through bitterly cold weather to transport passengers from Bonner's Ferry to Kootenay Lake. The stage itself consisted of an old stagecoach box mounted on runners. It had room for nine passengers within the box and another two or three outside with the driver.

By January 1893, G.W. Hughes was running to capacity carrying Slocan ore to Kaslo. The sleigh road was proving its worth for passenger travel too. Cleary and Lynch were soon running daily stages between Kaslo and Watson. Mine manager F.M. Chadbourne made the trip in January:

> I left Nelson on the fourth of January for Kaslo with the intention of paying a visit to the Great Western mine. On the fifth two stages, with sixteen passengers left Kaslo for Bear Lake . . . The road from Kaslo to Bear Lake City makes a first class sleigh road. G.W. Hughes is entitled to all the credit . . . He is a man who does not say much, but he has

> done a whole lot . . . When he started in the wagon road was about three miles below Bear Lake, and there was no probability of its being put through; he cut out the timber along the line of the road and ran his sleigh road through on the snow. On Monday, the 9th of January the first four-horse team went through. I happened to be standing with Mr. Hughes at the time, and he pointed it out to me as the first. Mr. Hughes has now got everything down to a fine point, corrals, stables, stores and relays all arranged to expedite transit.[22]

The work that G.W. Hughes had put into the sleigh road was welcomed, but the wagon road committee knew that Hughes alone couldn't complete the road. He would have had no incentive to extend it to Three Forks. The committee had no idea how they would finance further work. All their funds were exhausted. They were sinking further into debt, owing more than $9,000. With few options available, the committee resolved to seek help from the government. They reasoned $10,000 would do the trick. In February 1893, G.O. Buchanan and Bob Green left Kaslo for Victoria to lobby the government for funding. Jim Wardner and Steve Bailey showed up early on to offer their support.

Buchanan and Green returned to Kaslo in mid-March. While they weren't exactly the bearers of bad news, their trip had not yielded the results they had hoped for a month earlier. They had a vague, largely implicit commitment that some money for the wagon road would be included in the forthcoming supplementary estimates. They were told point-blank, however, that there would be no money to compensate what had already been subscribed and spent. The government also made it clear that if and when money was forthcoming, it would not be put in the charge of any "committee" but would be managed by the government. Residents of Kaslo and the Slocan kept their spirits up in hopes of receiving good news in the upcoming budget. After Buchanan and Green returned from Victoria, the wagon road committee managed to scrape up some funds but estimated they would need an additional $1,500 to keep the road open while they waited for a decision on government funding. However, G.W. Hughes was given assurances that he would not lose any money if he continued working on the road.

Late in March, the provincial government tabled its estimates for the 1893/94 fiscal year. There was $10,000 included for the Kaslo wagon road. The Nelson *Miner* accurately expressed the prevailing mood in West Kootenay: "No one knows just how this appropriation is to be provided for, but no one cares."[23]

6

SIN CITY

IN DECEMBER 1892, A "RUGGED old prospector" named Abbey registered at the Grand Hotel in San Francisco.[1] Under "place of residence" in the hotel register, he entered "Kaslo." Within two hours he had twenty-three letters in his letter box, and there were a hundred people in the lobby. They were all looking for information about Canada's newest eldorado. It was the same all over the west. When Jimmy Moran of the Queen Bess arrived in Spokane in February, he was met by three hundred men who wanted all the latest news from the Slocan.

Kaslo was booming. More than a hundred buildings dotted the delta of Kaslo Creek in early 1893, and new buildings appeared every day. Jim Wardner reported that lots that could be purchased for $50 in the summer of 1892 were now selling for $1,500. The boats from Bonner's Ferry brought in more fortune seekers on every trip. The rich silver deposits were cut off by deep snow, and it would be months before they were accessible. But this didn't stop the incomers. Idle men with nothing much to do crowded the streets. There were plenty of diversions. Not everyone was seeking their fortune in the mountains. Prostitutes, gamblers, and bunco artists would seize any opportunity they could to fleece the gullible. American dollars ruled, but liquor was the common currency and fuelled some wild times.

Several refugees from the labour troubles in the Coeur d'Alenes landed in Kaslo in 1892, including Jack Lucy, a Canadian who had run the Senate Hotel in Wallace, before taking on a job at the Noble Five. No doubt there were troublemakers and bullies among them: "flannel mouths" and "Molly McGuires," as described by Coeur d'Alene mine owner A.M. Esler.[2] Web Leasure, who had been a deputy sheriff in the Coeur d'Alenes, was in the

Slocan in early 1892. A few weeks later he was in custody in the Coeur d'Alenes, accused of murdering a non-union miner.

It should come as no surprise that bad behaviour flourished in the rough and rowdy mining camps. Many blamed this on the rougher element among the Americans who followed the silver strikes north. Even so, it seemed generally accepted by both Canadians and Americans that the mining camps on the Canadian side were more law-abiding than those below the line. This, despite the claim made by American badman "Long Shorty" that he "did not give a damn for the law on this side."[3] Certainly, there were stricter controls over handguns. Canada did not have the same constitutional right to bear arms that existed in the United States, and Canadian law enforcement officers, then as now, did not hesitate to seize guns when necessary.

Canadians prided themselves on their lack of a gun culture. It set them apart from their American neighbours and, for many, was taken as an implicit indicator of cultural superiority. In his novel *Black Rock*, author Ralph Connor has his American miner, "Idaho," whose gun was taken away, express his "amazed disgust at the state of society that would permit such an outrage on personal liberty." Whether in fact or fiction, few opportunities were lost in drawing distinctions between the rough-and-tumble justice of the American West and the "peaceable kingdom" to the north. In fact, the distinctions were never so great as imagined. However, the trope proved popular with a population self-conscious in the shadow of their bigger, brasher neighbour.

BC's justice system in the late nineteenth century combined Britain's county court system, which administered both civil and criminal law, and a magistrate's system in which minor offences were prosecuted. Outside of Victoria and the lower mainland, there were few people with formal legal training. Instead, there were justices of the peace (JPs) appointed by BC's Attorney General. They were responsible for meting out justice for most civil disputes and petty crimes. They were not required to have legal training, but they did need common sense and respect within their communities. More serious crimes were tried by Supreme Court justices, who sat in assize courts scheduled across the province during the year.

While some American visitors might have been impressed with the orderliness they found, the rapid growth of Kaslo and other camps seriously taxed the administrative capacity of BC's government. In the early 1890s, the province's civil administration was thin on the ground outside of Victoria and the lower mainland. One estimate puts the province's entire civil service in 1891 at just over a hundred employees. The regional administrative infrastructure was largely a legacy of the Fraser River and Cariboo gold rushes. This explains why the chief government administrator for the silver-rich West Kootenay district was the gold commissioner, "Captain" Napoleon Fitzstubbs.

Fitzstubbs had local responsibility for policing West Kootenay, but overall responsibility rested with Police Superintendent Fred Hussey in Victoria. Headquartered in Nelson, Fitzstubbs and his constables were expected to cover almost the entire West Kootenay. Often on the road for weeks at a time, they made regular appearances in "hot spots" such as Kaslo. They were also on call for incidents requiring police attention in outlying camps.

When Constable Joseph Dee "J.D." Graham was assigned to Kaslo in October 1892, he spent his first few weeks patrolling the construction camps of the Kaslo wagon road. The camps were filled with itinerant workers eager for a paycheque. With so many men from different backgrounds and classes jostling for meals and money, tempers often flared. Bad language, petty thefts, and fights were common. Sometimes fines were issued. The *Kootenay Star* thought that having to pay fines would have a "wholesome effect" on Americans who had "little or no experience of the law on this side of the border."[4]

As Kaslo grew, the law enforcement challenges increased. The wide open nature of the camp was described by a visitor from Spokane in December 1892: "Gambling houses, maisons de joie and saloons never close their doors, and at 2 o'clock in the morning there are as many people to be seen on the streets as in the day time."[5] A correspondent for *The Commercial* could see through the prospectors and miners on best behaviour: "Of course there are rough characters among them, gamblers and heaven knows what some of them may not have been, but there is no place where the criminal and vagabond class disguise their former selves so completely as in a mining camp."[6]

The cancellation of the Kaslo wagon road contract had an immediate impact on Kaslo. Dozens of suddenly unemployed men streamed into the camp. Some had been paid, some not. Those with money were eager to spend it. Those who had not been paid were intent on raising havoc in any way they could. There were several assaults and street fights. Constable Graham noted the prolific use of obscene language. There were disturbances in the brothels too. In one instance, the piano player at Blanche's complained of being beaten on the head with a revolver at about two thirty in the morning. The suspect was Jim Startsman, one of the owners of the Noble Five Hotel.

Startsman's partner in the Noble Five Hotel was Emery Giles. Giles was an unsavoury young man who was himself no stranger to the wrong side of the law. Expelled from school for rude behaviour as a teenager in 1888, Giles was charged in Vancouver with burglary before moving to Kaslo with his parents. Upon arriving in Kaslo, he befriended Jim Startsman and took an interest in the Noble Five Hotel's brothel. He was soon served a summons for keeping a "disorderly house."

Startsman and his partners had staked a few promising claims, including the US claim on the Kaslo slope. In late 1892, the claim was bonded for $20,000. We don't know how much up front money there was, but certainly Startsman would have received a good chunk of cash. He couldn't seem to profit from his mining claims or his stake in Kaslo's Noble Five Hotel, or if he did, he couldn't hold on to the money (perhaps he spent it at Blanche's). In the summer of 1893, no doubt suffering from the harsh economic times, he took to forging Bank of Montreal cheques. He would cash them in small amounts in businesses in Kaslo and Nelson. He sold his Dolly Varden claim, which he had worked for a while with Giles, and headed for the border. He was caught—and given a five-year prison sentence by Judge Spinks. This was the lightest sentence afforded by the law. It was Startsman's first conviction for this type of offence, and Spinks let him know that if it had been a repeat offence, he would have made the punishment a life sentence. Still, Startsman, more accustomed to the "flexibility" of American justice, reportedly "took his medicine with an effort."[7]

Money flowed more freely in Kaslo and the Slocan with the opening of J.M. Burke's bank on January 1, 1893. The Nelson *Miner* noted at its opening that the first bank in Kaslo had "an imposing display of filthy lucre, guarded by a prominent businessman and a revolver."[8] Burke hired J.J. Barclay to do his books and John Piggott as cashier. Piggott had previously partnered with Lane Gilliam in the packing and mining business, before taking a position as engineer with the Kaslo wagon road. The cashier's position must have seemed more secure than those earlier assignments. Burke was a formidable presence in Kaslo. When Robert Neill wrote home to a friend in Wallace, Idaho, in early April, he reported the many Coeur d'Aleners in Kaslo and noted that John M. Burke was "the boss of them all."[9]

Gambling was ubiquitous. Kaslo's Mike Mahoney was throwing dice and being hustled at his Palace Hotel, and he wasn't alone. Constable Graham had to warn a Black gambler named Jackson to stop using "false dice."[10] The Nelson *Tribune* felt that nearly every man in Kaslo was "a born gambler."[11] Card sharps like Jim Smith ruled the green cloth in 1892 and

1893. Poker was played openly, but other games such as faro and dice were played more surreptitiously.[12] Constable Graham issued a few warnings, but he couldn't be everywhere.

By the close of spring 1893, every steamboat arriving from Bonner's Ferry was packed with pilgrims from south of the border. One of them, a Boston newspaper correspondent named Herbert Heywood, was struck with the familiarity of the scene he encountered:

> We land on British Columbia soil and look for foreign faces, but they nearly all have the American stamp. Surely these are the same prospectors and miners that we have seen on the streets of Butte, Mont., and Leadville and Crede, Colo. It is the restless shifting element of the mining regions of the United States that has thronged over the border and discovered the mines in this new region. No country on earth has such an army of prospectors, ever ready to march on a new district. Here are the veterans of '49 of California, of the '60s of Colorado, of the '70s of Montana, with recruits of the later excitement of Idaho and Washington.[13]

It was certainly true that most of the boomers, dreamers, schemers, and followers filling up Kaslo and spilling over into the Slocan in the early months of 1893 were Americans—principally Coeur d'Aleners. They had been thick on the ground from the start, and their numbers continued to grow during the ongoing labour troubles south of the border. By June 1893, no less than two thousand Coeur d'Aleners were estimated to be in the Slocan.

The correspondent from Boston viewed the crowds of Americans in Kaslo as the "vanguards of civilization." The Nelson newspapers weren't so sure. In February, the Nelson *Tribune* anticipated that a considerable number of the Americans arriving in Kaslo would be of the "undesirable hobo element."[14] By late March, the *Tribune* claimed that Kaslo was "overrun with toughs" and felt it was high time they were sent packing.[15] The Nelson *Miner* went further, fearing a crime wave in Kaslo. It worried that the camp "might form a disgraceful exception to the good order prevalent in British Columbia." "Disorder," the paper proclaimed, "must not be allowed to make headway."[16]

West Virginian Ira Jenkins, who had done a bit of prospecting in 1892, noted that in early 1893 Kaslo had "no less than twelve gambling houses," all oblivious to the rules of "good order."[17] Brothels and saloons were operating around the clock. Fraud and bunco artists had begun to make their appearance too. On the borderline were the real estate agents selling Kaslo lots on speculation. The sales pitches were intense, and many buyers ended up with small lots for big prices, often on the margins of the camp. E.P. Whalley was caught up in the fever. He bought a lot in a townsite up the lake from Kaslo. The seller told him it was a "big lot for its size."[18] Worse than the real estate agents were the fraud artists selling mining claims they didn't own. The *Spokane Review* cited the case of a man who was selling out a claim in eighths. He forgot to stop when he sold the last eighth and sold an extra three.

Thick with Americans, West Kootenay was an ethnic and racial hodgepodge at the time, and disputes could flare up at the drop of an insult. At the close of March, Graham noted the "town overrun with drunks."[19] Free-flowing liquor fuelled egos and tempers. Graham found himself intervening in disputes involving Black American "toughs," "drunken Swedes," and a few French Canadians cited for their overuse of obscene language.

In truth, rowdy behaviour was typical of a booming western mining camp. But Kaslo went beyond "typical." By March 1893, the camp was being referred to by its Nelson rival as the "wickedest city on Kootenay Lake."[20] Confined to the mountains or mines for long stretches by weather and work, men were desperate to seek out entertaining diversions whenever they could. One Vancouverite who visited Kaslo at the time gives a good idea of what things were like. Back in Vancouver in early May 1893, he told the *Owl* that he had a new name for Kaslo: "'What is it?' enquired his interlocutor. 'Kash-low, by Jove. I went there flush, a month ago, had a good time with the boys, bucked the Bengal; shook dice for the drinks, went the whole quadruped generally; got busted wide open and had to beat my way back.'"[21]

A visitor from eastern Canada, perhaps after hearing all the tales of drunkenness and debauchery, was surprised to find Kaslo relatively "orderly," but noted "far too many saloons."[22] Ironically, as wild and woolly as Kaslo seemed to residents of Victoria and Vancouver, and to visitors from eastern Canada, it wasn't wild enough for some of the Americans who passed through. George Datch of Montana—perhaps one of the "toughs" the *Tribune* was concerned about—visited Kaslo in June 1893. He described the camp as a "puritanical town." Constable Graham had likely cleaned things up a bit.

> The saloons are not open Sundays, although there is not a great deal of trouble getting drinks there. No saloons are permitted except in connection with hotels. A man must run a lodging house, restaurant and stable in order to run a saloon . . . The police are very strict. No one can carry a weapon, and for fighting the penalty is 60 days in jail.[23]

Regardless of nationality, incomers to Kaslo were all looking to win their fortune—one way or another. Despite George Datch's opinion, the Nelson newspaper accounts were not entirely inaccurate. Prostitutes and con men flocked into Kaslo. A writer for Spokane's *Northwest Mining Review* had seen it all before: "The country will be fairly overrun by men who will make no attempt to prospect or get work, but who will go in, spend the few dollars they have or beat a board bill, come out and damn the country. Such is a mining boom."[24]

Constable Graham had his work cut out for him. In the summer of 1893, he reported wheeling drunks about in a wheelbarrow. The prostitutes of Kaslo did perhaps the best business of all in the early weeks of 1893, but they were a constant source of police interest too. There was no shortage of choice. There was Maggie's House, Emma Dale's, and perhaps the most notorious of all, Emma Starr's Noble Five brothel.

As in other West Kootenay mining camps, warnings and cautions seemed the order of the day. On receiving a complaint that "the girls" were using obscene language in the streets in the early hours of the morning, Graham simply advised them to be more careful. He also had to warn them several times to tone things down late at night and to refrain from firing off guns early in the morning. There were other issues as well. In January 1893, he warned them about "wearing male attire."[25]

Almost all the prostitutes who flooded into West Kootenay in the early 1890s were from the mining camps of Idaho and Montana or the urban demi-monde of Spokane. Many were Black and thus something of a novelty in BC. A few Japanese women also made early appearances. One of those women might have been a teenaged Koto Kennedy (née Shimuzu). Her backstory was more fantastic than most. According to some stories, she was shipwrecked off the BC coast in a fishing boat along with her father. She was an early arrival in Kaslo and lived out the rest of her life there. In many respects, Koto and the other prostitutes in West Kootenay were no different from the miners, capitalists, and other entrepreneurs who flocked to the mining districts. They aimed to get in early and seize as much market share as possible as quickly as they could.

Constable Graham was respected for his even-handedness by even the toughest Coeur d'Alene "toughs." But he lost his temper on at least one occasion. While subduing a "big Swede" on a Kaslo street, someone in the crowd of onlookers—likely Jack Lucy—threw a stone that hit the constable in a particularly vulnerable spot "amidships." In obvious pain, Graham straightened up and vowed prison time for the guilty culprit. The crowd murmured its disapproval, but no one admitted guilt.

Graham's policing seems to have been both effective and pragmatic. Effective, perhaps, because it was pragmatic. In some cases, he would allow events to unfold without interference if it appeared the results would in some way align with his sense of natural justice. Graham's approach to law enforcement earned high praise for the "excellent judgment" he always showed. In December 1892, he came across a disturbance at the Noble Five brothel where Jack Buchanan was hurling expletives at a man named Skinner. Skinner gave Buchanan "a good thrashing."[26] Graham decided to give Skinner until the next day to get away. There was some practical reasoning for this approach. One of Graham's challenges was the lack of a decent lock-up. He complained about this several times in his diary, and his concerns were shared by the justices. The Nelson *Tribune* joined the chorus calling for a jail in Kaslo, noting that "if an officer has to handcuff his prisoner's arms around a telephone pole, he can not very well enforce the law, or even make people respect it."[27]

Lacking a jail, Constable Graham had to keep a close eye on his prisoners. Often, this meant organizing work parties. In April 1893, Kaslo's cemetery was moved to a site along the wagon road leading to the Slocan. On April 15, 1893, a group of citizens moved the remains of veteran prospector Jim Brennand and E.E. Coy's infant daughter—the first two recorded deaths in Kaslo—from the old cemetery to the new one. However, a few days earlier, Graham had two of his prisoners dig what was likely the first grave in the new cemetery. The burial was for an itinerant Black man who had died in Kaslo's Montana Hotel. "Major" Pointer's departure from this world was anything but dignified. Graham and his charges had to slide the coffin sideways over the snow before slipping it into the ground.

Graham's business increased when Kaslo's Theatre Comique opened in May 1893. Spokane businessman Samuel Jacob Holland saw a great opportunity in Kaslo. Along with his brother John, Sam Holland ran the Theatre Comique in Spokane. The Spokane Comique was a variety theatre that offered plenty of low-brow entertainment but made most of its money from beer and whisky pushed aggressively by seductively dressed women known as "box rustlers." The Holland brothers set up the Kaslo Comique in a three-storey frame building on Front Street. John Holland was the manager; Sam Holland, proprietor; and J.J. Belladeau, stage manager. Since the California gold rush, "comique" type theatres, like Al Swearengen's infamous "Gem" in Deadwood, had become staples of mining camps across the western mining frontier. But Kaslo's Comique was the first of its kind in Canada, and the authorities were wary.

Constable Graham noted the arrival of the Comique troupe aboard the steamer *Nelson* on April 27. It must have been quite a scene. Several hundred Kaslo residents greeted the steamboat. On board, there were as many as thirty girls, dressed to the hilt to impress the civilization-starved citizens of Kaslo with their burlesque finery. Most of the Comique girls travelled a circuit that had them moving between Spokane and Kaslo.

The first performance at the Kaslo Comique took place on May 1, 1893. The correspondent for the Victoria *Daily Colonist* wasn't impressed. Noting that the troupe came from Spokane, he felt the residents of Kaslo would have been better off if the troupe had stayed there. Nevertheless, the house was jam-packed. Every seat was taken, and every inch of standing space was occupied. Profits from opening night amounted to more than $1,300. Even the *Colonist* correspondent was impressed with the acrobatic performances, but overall, he found the programme of "no account" and the performance of the "nature seen only in low concert houses."[28]

But even if some local critics were dismissive, the crowds of prospectors and miners kept coming back. A Montana man there on opening night, no doubt more familiar with mining camp entertainment, thought the entertainers put on "a great show."[29] Coeur d'Alener Charles Harris found the show "quite as good" as those in Spokane or other western camps.[30] Over and above the entertainment, the Comique had two things the miners and prospectors couldn't resist: cheap drinks on the floor, and for those with a bit more money to spend, female companionship.

One of the prospectors who likely attended Kaslo's Comique was Jim Shields. In the spring of 1892, he and Charlie Drouin were prospecting near Seaton Creek when a snow slide came down and exposed a rich ledge of ore. Shields was first on the spot and staked the Lucky Jim. He reportedly exclaimed, "I'm lucky and I'm rich!"[31] But perhaps he wasn't so lucky after all. In a bizarre turn of events, "Lucky" Jim Shields was attending a show at the Comique theatre in Spokane when an acrobat landed on him, leaving him with a life-long disability.

The Comique Theatre, c. 1893. Photographer: A.T. Garland. ORIGINAL IMAGE COURTESY OF THE KOOTENAY LAKE ARCHIVES, KASLO, BC

On entering the Kaslo Comique on the ground floor, patrons would find seating, a well-stocked bar, and a stage at the front. Upstairs, there were rows of boxes on either side. Each box was accessed through a door that could be locked. Inside, there was a table, chairs, a call button for ordering drinks, and a view of the theatre. Male customers who ventured upstairs were greeted by women who would invite them to sit down and order drinks. The drinks were more expensive than on the floor but were no doubt worth the cost to men starved for female company. Box rustlers would stay and flirt so long as the money and liquor flowed. Inevitably, there were incidents fuelled by excessive drink and unrestrained libido. The *Spokane Review* reported on an incident in that city's Comique that involved a newly recruited box rustler named May Wrenly, a man named Patrick Murane, and a beer mug. According to Murane, Wrenly came into his box, sat on his lap, and made suggestive promises. When he tried to collect, she crowned him with the beer mug and called for assistance to throw him down the stairs and out the door. Accusing her of assault with a beer mug, Murane bore the scars as evidence when he appeared in court. In her defence, Wrenly, herself sporting a black eye, testified that she was only protecting herself from Murane's improper advances. "Is it not a fact," asked the prosecutor, "that women down there in the Comique go into boxes with men, sit on their laps and embrace them?" The witness reluctantly confirmed that this was the case. The judge concluded that the Comique was a standing invitation to "drunken and jealous brawls" and fined the unfortunate May Wrenly fifty dollars.[32]

Constable Graham recorded a similar incident at Kaslo's Comique. A man named Russell—quite likely "Colonel" Wake Russell, once a sheriff in Arizona—complained that he had been dragged into the Comique, where a diamond ring was stolen from him. Graham interviewed Russell but found no grounds for the complaint. Graham explained to the justice that Russell "was in the Comique at 3:10 AM and did not appear particularly desirous of leaving the place . . . The ring was held in safekeeping for him by the Comique staff and returned to him once he sobered up.[33] The case was dismissed.

It didn't take long for the Comique girls to get up to mischief in their off-hours. On May 11, Graham warned them, as he had done earlier with Kaslo's prostitutes, "not to be running around the streets drunk."[34] Some of the women, it seems, also found they could earn extra money working in the local brothels. Graham cautioned Emma Dale, one of the madams, for encouraging them. She denied it, but Graham had witnessed two Comique girls entering her house.

One of the key attractions at the Comique was the Kittie Goodwin Burlesque Company. Kittie was quite a character. She makes several appearances in Constable Graham's diary. On one occasion, he was called out of bed at quarter past two in the morning to deal with a complaint from a man named Reno, who complained that she had assaulted him by boxing his ears in. Kittie received a caution. Kittie could take care of herself. Before coming to Kaslo she had worked at the Casino, a variety theatre in Spokane run by the notorious Big Bertha. Kittie made headlines in January 1893, when she and two other box rustlers were arrested for assaulting Josie Wilson, one of their co-workers. Josie was "a free-lance in the business, and delights in nothing more than taking the other girls' friends away from them and making them buy beer."[35] This didn't sit well with Kittie.

The incident in Spokane likely led to a change of venue for Kittie. By June, she was working at John Considine's Standard in Seattle. Considine was grooming a younger Lillie Masterson to become his star attraction over Kittie. The two women got into a knock-down, drag-out fight. Considine managed to break it up, but not before Lillie slashed Kittie's arm with a penknife. Sewn up with thirteen stiches, Kittie was soon off to Kaslo with her own burlesque company.

As evidenced by the very visible presence of prostitutes and brothels, there was sex on the western mining frontier. But what really went on behind closed doors? Historians cannot ignore the obvious, but they should look behind the closed doors too. The challenge is in finding sources. There are a few cases of sexual assault in the court records, but then, as now, we can assume that cases that went to trial were only the tip of a very large iceberg.

While there were rumours of lesbian relationships among the mining camp prostitutes, it stands to reason that in such a male-dominated society, there would have been homosexual liaisons too. There were, but one wouldn't know it from the evidence. It generally wasn't talked about, or written about, and certainly rarely admitted to. In addition to public approbation, men who engaged in homosexual acts or activities could suffer the full force of the law if they were caught. Charges on the books in the 1890s included "attempted buggery," which could net a perpetrator ten years in prison; "assault with intent to commit buggery," which included the ten years plus a whipping; and "gross indecency"—also ten years and a whipping.

At least one relevant case has come down to us through the court process. Frank Hughes was out on the street in Kaslo in 1893 when he ran into a prominent Nelson lawyer. The two shared a few drinks and some casual conversation. The lawyer was looking for a room and Hughes suggested the Leland Hotel. Hughes was invited up to the room, and the two men had a couple of glasses of claret. Then, according to Hughes, the lawyer asked him if he knew of places where "men had intercourse with one another." Hughes didn't know and asked, "You would not do it, would you?" The lawyer nodded his head and said, "Yes."[36]

The two men differed on what happened next. According to Hughes, he tried to leave the room, but the lawyer came at him and pleaded for his secret to be kept. According to the lawyer, it was he who tried to leave the room, but he was pulled back by Hughes, who said, "I know all about you, I'll ruin you." Many behaviours were tolerated on the western mining frontier, but homosexuality was not one of them. Hughes asked for and received a cheque for fifty dollars. Blackmail would be a lucrative sideline for Hughes until about a year later when the lawyer had had enough and pressed charges.

The incident between Frank Hughes and the lawyer was not widely reported at the time, but other events likely had tongues wagging. The mysterious death and contested will of John Sandon was at first front and centre. Sandon operated a ranch on Kootenay Lake just south of Kaslo. He often commuted from there by rowboat. On February 11, 1893, his boat was found overturned on the lake. Sandon and his companion, Kenneth McLeod, were both missing. Things looked bad, but people were at first reluctant to accept his death. Sandon was an experienced boatman. He had confounded everyone once before when he was prematurely declared drowned. In that instance, his empty boat, oars, and hat were found floating on the lake after a storm. At first presumed dead, he was found safe and sound on his ranch. This time, however, no trace was ever found of him or McLeod. Suspicions were raised later in 1893 when Sandon's purported will surfaced. In it, he left his entire estate to his hired hand, John Hetherington. Sandon was known locally as something of a "scholar." Certainly, he knew how to read and write. However, the will was signed with a "mark." Sandon's family was convinced he died as the result of foul play, but nothing could be proved.

Another near tragedy took place in Kaslo on May 23. Dick Hughes, a mining camp cook prone to liquor and spousal abuse, suspected that his wife, Catherine, was unfaithful. Hughes had married Catherine—a widow with five young children—in 1890. In a fit of jealousy, Hughes decided to kill himself, his wife, and their youngest son, Richard. He got hold of a stick of dynamite. When he went to bed that night, he put the dynamite under the pillows, lit the fuse, and waited for his trip to eternity. Fortunately, Catherine was awakened by the sound of the sizzling fuse. She got out of bed before the dynamite went off, which it did, with a terrific explosion. Both wife and child escaped serious injury, but Hughes was badly concussed. When Constable Graham arrived, he found a four-foot section of the floor blown out, a fire burning, and feathers everywhere. Hughes recovered, but his actions earned him a trip to the Provincial Asylum for the Insane in New Westminster.

The mystery surrounding John Sandon's death and the violence attempted by Dick Hughes paled in comparison to the sensational trial of E.E. Coy for the alleged sexual assault of a married woman, Hannah Ewin. Coy was a prominent figure in Kaslo, and his trial both captivated and scandalized residents.

In June 1893, BC Supreme Court Justice George Walkem held his first session in Kaslo. The principal case to be tried was the charge against Coy. At the opening of the proceedings, in which other cases besides Coy's would be heard, Justice Walkem said he was "surprised" by the energy shown by the people of Kaslo in building up their town. He was impressed with the orderliness and general respect for law and order. He also paid special—if condescending—attention to the large numbers of Americans in the audience: "The judge complimented the Americans and told how it was his experience that citizens of the United States lay their bowie knives and pistols aside after coming to Canada and seeing how well the laws are enforced."[37]

Ironically, the first case that Walkem heard involved a knife fight. Jack Beaudoin was charged with assault after a fight with Gus Carney. Beaudoin was an unsavoury character, prone to violence and gunplay. During the fracas, the night watchman who tried to separate the two men was stabbed in the leg. Carney swore that Beaudoin had pulled a knife, but the night watchman hadn't seen it and couldn't swear as to who might have stabbed him. Regardless, the case seemed straightforward to Justice Walkem. He lectured the jury on the need, in a new mining camp, to make an example of the perpetrator of the crime. He seemed surprised when the jury actually wanted to retire to consider the case and their verdict. He was positively incensed when they returned a verdict of "not guilty": "Fire flashed from the judge's spectacles; trembled his wig; quavered his voice; the jurymen shivered in their seats. After rebuking them severely for their disregard of the law . . . his lordship concluded with the remark, that he had his opinion of a Kaslo Jury."[38]

The stage was set for Coy's trial. While it was well attended, the trial was afforded minimal coverage in the local papers. The *Tribune* reasoned that "the facts in this case are generally well known to the people in the lake country and the morals of those on the outside would not be improved by reading the evidence given at trial."[39] Reading Justice Walkem's bench book for the trial, it's hard not to sympathize with the *Tribune*'s stance.

According to Mrs. Ewin's testimony, a few weeks before the alleged assault, Coy had come to her house wanting to discuss some properties. She let him in, and they made small talk. Mrs. Ewin asked after Mrs. Coy, who was away visiting family in the United States. Then the conversation took a left turn. Coy told her he had an offer of $50,000 on his interest in the Dardanelles mine. If Coy got it, he told Hannah that if she would "skip" away with him, he would give her half the money. She thought he was joking, but he said, "You think I'm joking but I'm not."[40] Then he sprang up and put his hand on her shoulder and told her that he loved her, had always loved her, and "better than he had ever loved his wife." She slapped him across the face and asked him to leave. He did, but he was back a few days later knocking on her door. She opened the door thinking it was one of her lady friends. He either talked or pushed his way in and was soon making advances.

Hannah tried to push him away, but despite her struggles, Coy lifted her, carried her to the bedroom, and threw her down on the bed. She continued to struggle and cried for help but could not hold off Coy's advances. He spread her legs, straddled her, undid his pants, and put his left hand on her "private parts." She wriggled about "to hinder him from obtaining his purpose" but it looked like she would succumb to his advances. Just then her husband came through the front door. Both Hannah and Coy sprang up from the bed, and Hannah ran to her husband. Robert Ewin produced a revolver that was immediately pointed at Coy. Terrified, Hannah pleaded with her husband not to commit murder: "Oh Robert, don't murder him! Don't let us have a murder on our hands."[41] There was a tense standoff. Coy grabbed the gun but Robert Ewin seized another. However, neither revolver was loaded. Mrs. Ewin testified her husband was looking about for cartridges. While he was doing so, Coy overpowered him, took the other revolver, muttered a few curses, and made his way out the door and down the street.

Coy did not deny the circumstances but vigorously denied it was a case of assault. In his version of events, Mrs. Ewin had invited him into her house. They were pursuing a mutual "assignment." It was hard for Coy's defence to overcome the evidence against him, including the statements of both Robert and Hannah Ewin and the fact he had been "caught in the act." However, the most damaging evidence probably came from Dr. Bruner, recently arrived from the Coeur d'Alenes. Bruner testified before the jury that he had examined Mrs. Ewin after the alleged assault. She was emotionally distraught, but he found no signs of physical assault. Perhaps to comfort her, he then told her that "she was not the first woman he [Coy] had so assaulted."[42]

If the jury had any sympathy for Coy's claim of innocence, Bruner's bombshell might have blown doubts away. How many other women might have been assaulted but told no one other than their doctor? Coy was done. Even if he was truthful and his liaison with Hannah Ewin had been by mutual consent, he would be judged on wider implications. Still, a conviction was not a sure thing. Coy was well respected in Kaslo, and the week preceding the trial, the Kaslo-Slocan *Examiner* had run a story practically eulogizing him under the heading "Kaslo's best friend."[43]

Juries sometimes confound and frustrate public expectations. At about the same time that Coy was on trial in Kaslo, a young woman named Lizzie Borden was before a judge and jury in Bedford, Massachusetts. Accused of brutally murdering her father and stepmother with an axe, the evidence—

though circumstantial—seemed stacked against her. A conviction was expected, but the jury unexpectedly acquitted her.

It seems that Justice Walkem wanted to ensure that the jury in his courtroom had no doubt about the verdict he thought they should reach. His instructions to them after the defence and prosecution had rested went on for almost an hour and a half. His bias was clear. This was noted with astonishment by the newspapers covering the trial. Walkem concluded that there was no attempt at blackmail on the part of Mrs. Ewin or her husband. He rambled on about his experiences with similar cases. He found Hannah Ewin's testimony credible and was particularly critical of Coy's "unmanliness . . . in alleging consent upon the part of the woman."[44]

After deliberating for two and a half hours, the jury approached the justice to advise him they could not reach a verdict. Furious, Walkem gave them fifteen minutes to reach one, or he would have the case retried elsewhere. Coy was called into the jury room to face a "fusillade of abuse" from Walkem.[45] The jury retired briefly and returned with the verdict the justice wanted. They found Coy guilty of indecent assault. While the maximum sentence for the crime was three years in prison, Walkem felt that a year's hard labour in the Kamloops prison would suffice.

Coy was led away to the steamboat to await his transport to Kamloops. The *Kaslo Claim* reported a touching and emotional parting between Coy and his wife, Belle—who had stuck with him throughout the ordeal. She had lost her young daughter only months before and would now have her husband taken away. Sometime after his trial, Coy did sell his interest in the Dardanelles. It was reported that he got $16,000 for it. It was not the $50,000 he had hoped for, but he would not be sharing the returns with Hannah Ewin.

After the trial was finished and the sentence passed, a man who was in the audience for Justice Walkem's charges to the jury approached Attorney General Davie (also premier at the time) and commented: "It seemed to me that your efforts were superfluous and that Justice Walkem conducted the case for the prosecution exceedingly well." "Well," answered Davie, "I myself thought I was kind of a fifth wheel."[46] There were many who thought the conviction unjust and believed that Coy was badly treated. Coy himself thought he would have been acquitted had he been a British subject. A numerously signed petition was sent to Ottawa asking that he be pardoned or his sentence commuted, because he was "a valuable member of society."[47]

E.E. Coy was not well regarded in Bonner's Ferry, Idaho, but even the *Kootenai Herald* came to his defence, questioning Hannah Ewin's morals. The trial and conviction of Coy was a sobering moment for Kaslo and perhaps other West Kootenay camps too. Kaslo was a rough-and-tumble town, and a certain amount of rowdy behaviour was tolerated. However, there were boundaries, and Coy was convicted of crossing them. The Nelson *Tribune* had declined to cover Coy's trial, but, without naming names, it did include a small nugget of moral judgement in its June 8, 1893, edition: "Married men who attempt to wreck the happiness and peace of mind of other married men are not deserving of sympathy. A man should protect his wife's honor and there is no better way to do it than by letting other men's wives severely alone."[48]

One would have thought that the downfall of Coy would have served to discourage others from similar acts. Not so. A few months later, U.S. Thomas, a prominent Nakusp resident—postmaster and proprietor of the Nakusp House Hotel—found himself similarly charged. This time the newspapers were not so reluctant to publish salacious details of the first hearing and subsequent trial, including the account of his alleged victim, Mrs. Mary Jane Hesketh:

> I was in bed sleeping Thursday morning, the 18th of January. Accused knocked at the door of my residence but I took no notice of it. The second time he knocked I asked who was there? Accused answered "Mr. Thomas." I got up, put on some clothes and opened the door. He stated that he wished to inform me that Mr. Hesketh was at Three Forks living with another woman. I said "Mr. Thomas, you are no gentleman to come and tell me this even if it were so." I asked him to leave the house but he refused . . . He caught hold of me and thrust a $10 bill into my hand and saying that I should have to go to bed with him because I could not help myself. He then attempted to lift me into my bed, but I caught him by the neck and he lost his grasp and I escaped . . . When accused attempted to raise me on the bed, I noticed his trousers were all undone and he appeared very determined. It was between the hours of 2 and 4 o'clock in the morning.[49]

The Hesketh, both born in Britain, were recent arrivals from Australia. Thomas denied the charges entirely and instead accused Mrs. Hesketh and her husband, Ellis, a blacksmith, of trying to blackmail him for $160. Ellis Hesketh admitted confronting Thomas. He said to him "damn your dirty heart" for the disgrace he had brought to his family.[50] Ellis Hesketh demanded that Thomas publish an apology in the local newspaper, but he denied asking for any money.

When the case came to trial, it was again prosecuted by Attorney General and Premier Theodore Davie. But in this instance, Thomas had a capable defence lawyer, the recently arrived Robert Bird "R.B." Kerr, who would soon become a thorn in Davie's side, both in and out of the courtroom. Kerr was able to produce witnesses who testified they were with Thomas on the night in question. At the time that the offence was alleged to have taken place, according to testimony provided by George Hardy, Thomas was passed out "paralyzed drunk" in his barroom. The trial came to an unexpected end. According to a newspaper account, Attorney General Davie proved that the accused committed the assault, but Kerr proved a perfect and clear alibi for Thomas on the night in question. In the circumstances, Thomas was advised to plead guilty to common assault, which he did. He was then dismissed with a few cautionary words from Justice Crease, who congratulated Kerr "for the able manner in which he handled the defence."[51]

The *Tribune* perhaps felt that justice was served with the conviction of E.E. Coy. However, the acquittal of Beaudoin on the charge of knifing Carney and a few light sentences handed out in similar cases led the newspaper to a crisis of confidence in the much-vaunted British system of justice.

In May 1893, a churchman from Spokane arrived in Kaslo. He wanted to see if the camp was as wicked as Spokane. He would not be disappointed. Kaslo had twenty-nine outlets for the sale of liquor, and more expected. The population exceeded 2,500. But there was only one church.

Presbyterian Church, Kaslo, c. 1893. Photographer unknown. IMAGE COURTESY OF THE KOOTENAY LAKE ARCHIVES, KASLO, BC

7

CHURCH AND COMIQUE

AT ABOUT 11 PM ON the night of Saturday, July 8, 1893, Fred Laing arrived in New Denver. No doubt tired from his long day's journey from Sanderson's Hot Springs, north of Nakusp, he took a room at Gething and Henderson's Slocan Hotel. Arising on Sunday morning, he made his way downstairs for breakfast. Passing through the barroom, he was asked: "Have an eye-opener?"[1] Back at the hotel after breakfast and a walk, he found the Methodist Reverend James Turner. The two knew each other, and Laing sat down to have a chat. The chips on the poker table lay undisturbed from the previous night.

Turner seemed unperturbed by his surroundings and was probably glad to get a little breakfast. Before dinner, he and Laing visited the site of the little church then under construction. There was a church in Kaslo, but this one would be the first in the Slocan. In the evening, Turner preached a sermon in the general store. There were about fifty people present, including four women and one child. Afterwards, the chairs were cleared away and the store resumed business.

Turner's church would be built, but religion would be a hard sell in those early days. It didn't matter whether it was Methodist, Presbyterian, Catholic, or the Church of England; to most American prospectors and miners, the Church was part of the conservative, largely British establishment they shunned. They had come to the Slocan to strike it rich and weren't particularly interested in having their souls saved. This disinterest in organized religion was welcomed by R.C. Adams. Adams was president of the Secular Union of Canada. When he first visited West Kootenay from Montreal in 1892, he found the country much to his liking:

> I traveled several hundred miles and never saw or heard a church or a parson until one day I saw a large log building abandoned when about half built. "What is that?" I asked of the driver. "Oh!" said he, "a minister came along one day and coaxed some of us into building a church for him. We started it, but we got discontented about it and left it off. I worked two days on the damned thing!" The tone in which this was uttered expressed, more fully than a written volume could have done, the indifference and contempt that is generally felt toward religion by the workingmen of the west.[2]

The men who ministered in the mining camps faced a formidable task. They usually had large, intractable areas to cover; were often received with indifference or disdain; and unless or until churches were built, had to give their services in hotels, stores, or saloons. Some fared better than others. To achieve any measure of success, they had to adapt to circumstances. When R.E. Gosnell visited West Kootenay in late spring 1892, he had some advice for the churches then setting up shop. He thought they should tone down their clericalism and do what they could to fit in with the prospectors and miners. It was good advice that wasn't always followed. Some preachers were just not suited to the mining frontier. A Presbyterian missionary writing in 1892 about his experiences in West Kootenay provides some context:

> My territory is eighty miles long. I pass by rail over thirty of it, the other fifty must be traveled by boat. This is a great difficulty. I cannot walk on water, and the steamer makes no regular trips to the camps which ought to be visited by the preacher. I want a light skiff or canoe in which I can take a life preserver and my bible and some hymn books. The whole Christian status of this region may be described in very few words. The appalling destruction of the bodies, intellects and souls of our brothers and sisters here, by giving free rein to every passion, cannot be written.[3]

The missionary further described a trip up into the mountains—possibly from Kaslo—where he met an old miner who told him: "I've been in every camp between here and Mexico and there's more drunkenness here than any other camp in America." The magnitude of the challenge can perhaps be gauged by the reaction of the Nelson *Miner* on learning that a Church of England curate from St. Luke's Parish in Toronto would be assigned to West Kootenay. "God help us," pleaded the *Miner*.[4]

In May 1892, though in poor health, Acton Sillitoe, the Church of England Bishop of the Diocese of New Westminster—which stretched to the Rocky Mountains in the east—travelled to Nelson to introduce the Reverend A.J. Reid to his new flock. Reid, formerly of Toronto, gave the first Church of England service in Kaslo on May 30. Reid's parish included the Slocan, and he was determined to give services wherever he could. He made a trip through the mining camps in October 1892. He should be given credit for making the journey, because it couldn't have been an easy one. E.C. Carpenter reported on a stop Reid made, probably in Three Forks. According to Carpenter, Reid insisted on holding a service, though the facilities were far from ideal: "In the improvised church a screen of blankets separated the gin palace from the sleeping compartment, and in the latter, the service was held."[5] Circumstances were certainly no better in Watson:

> The Rev. A.J. Reid has been on a pastoral tour through the Slocan country, and on his way to New Denver held a service at the town of Watson. There were 40 or 50 of "the boys" present and as some of them had been selling claims lately, they were having a high old time. The service, held in a saloon, went all right until the part of the prayer was reached where the Prince of Wales was commended to the mercies of Divine Providence. Here mr. Reid was very solemnly interrupted by a prospector: "Stop right there partner. You can pray for the Queen—that's all right—she's a woman; but praying for that——— don't go." He then went to the bar counter, and scratched the Prince of Wales' name out of the prayer book with a pencil, saying: "There! I've knocked him out."[6]

Reid must have missed Gosnell's advice. Violet Sillitoe, who usually accompanied her husband on his travels, knew Reid and later retold the story of the young parson's encounter with Slocan prospectors, noting that his "regular prayer book service" was unwise in the circumstances.[7] The prospector who had it in for the Prince of Wales was likely Thomas "Scotty" McDougall. The story of Scotty and the Prince was soon firmly embedded in the annals of Slocan folklore and spread far beyond the bounds of West Kootenay.

It is difficult now to separate truth from apocrypha in the tales of Reid. In one account, Reid was asked what he was going to do with the ten dollars collected during the service. He supposed he would use it to get to the next mining camp, and he didn't know how to respond to the curious prospector's reply: "I'll play you a game of draw poker—ten-dollar freeze out—double or quits."[8]

Another story had Reid giving a service in a billiard hall. The hat was passed around at the end, but when the man holding the hat approached the door, Reid reportedly yelled: "If that man goes out the door with that hat, he will be damned." A voice was heard from the back: "I'll be damned if he ain't gone."[9] Reid lasted less than a year in West Kootenay. In April 1893, he announced he was resigning his commission to return to Toronto. He would be succeeded by H.S. Akehurst, formerly vicar of St. Peter's Pro-Cathedral in Qu'Appelle. According to Jim Wardner, Reid simply "tired out." Reid's farewell service was in May. Wardner's account of Reid's speech was colourful and perhaps included some small bits of truth:

> Brothers and sisters, I come to say good-bye. I don't believe God loves this church, because none of you ever die. I don't think you love each other, because I never marry any of you. I don't think you love me, because you have not paid me my salary. Your donations are mouldy fruit and wormy apples, and "by their fruits ye shall know them." Brothers, I am going to a better place. I have been called to be chaplain of a penitentiary, "Where I go, ye cannot now come. I go to prepare a place for you," and "may the Lord have mercy on your souls."[10]

The groundwork for the Methodist mission in West Kootenay was largely laid through the efforts of the Reverend Turner. Described in earlier years as a "ranting radical," he had likely mellowed by the time he got to West Kootenay.[11] During his long-serving career, he became known as the "Minister of the Interior" or the "Saddlebags Parson," due to the large territories for which he was responsible and his fondness for travel. Transferred from Revelstoke in 1891, Turner arrived in Nelson about the same time as a Presbyterian minister, the Reverend Thomas H. Rogers. The two men joined forces to operate a "Union" church where both Methodists and Presbyterians could attend services on alternating weekends.

Turner set about organizing a Methodist congregation to serve Kaslo and the Slocan. But it wasn't without challenges. During the first year, just $250 was raised for Turner's salary, although he also had a mission grant of $149. The average salary for an unmarried Methodist minister at the time was less than $500 per year. Presbyterian clergy were somewhat better paid, but it seems clear that Turner, Reid, and other clergymen who served in

West Kootenay were not in it for the money. On receiving a grant from the Methodist Board in 1893, Turner wrote to Ebenezer Robson, president of the Methodist Conference in British Columbia and brother of Premier John Robson: "I am so glad you secured a grant for my work and though not covering half my indebtedness it will be of considerable help. I hope they will send it on soon as I do not want to pay interest any longer than I possibly can."[12]

Despite his indebtedness, Turner was patient, willing to work hard, and abundantly optimistic. The future of the mission looked promising. At the time of the Slocan rush, Turner wrote enthusiastically to Robson, confident that he could secure for the Methodists their position as "leaders" in the Slocan. Despite cooperation between the Methodist and Presbyterian ministries in Nelson, there was competition between the various Christian denominations elsewhere. Turner aggressively pushed Methodist interests and was eager to get into Kaslo and the Slocan early. In late 1891, he approached John Hendry and Alex Ewen, of the Kaslo Kootenay Land Company. He secured a promise for townsite lots to build a Methodist church. However, he was much chagrined when shortly afterwards, Hendry and Ewen offered the Presbyterian Church first choice of lots and "also large contributions besides."[13]

Turner was determined not to give further ground to the competition, so he focused his energies on New Denver. Thanks to his efforts, the Methodists did indeed secure the lead in the Slocan. Turner, often accompanied on his trips by David Birks, a divinity student sent to assist him in 1893, cheerfully tramped into even the most remote camps. A resident of Kaslo recalled seeing him coming down from the mountains on foot "wet to the knees" with his overshoes "loaded with the mud of the lower part of the trail."[14]

Turner was prepared to hold services in any available venue. It's likely the first service in New Denver was in Gething and Henderson's roughly hewn Slocan Hotel. New Denver pioneer Jack Cory passed the hat around. When it reached Turner, it contained an impressive sixteen dollars. The money would help fund Turner's purpose-built church on lots donated by Angus McGillivray. Like the townsite owners in Kaslo, however, McGillivray also donated two lots to the Presbyterian church.

A travelling Presbyterian missionary, G.A. Wilson, held one of the first services in Nakusp. The "church" was an empty store, and boards on empty beer barrels served as furniture. All the improvised seats were filled, and latecomers sprawled on the floor. A borrowed organ accompanied the ad hoc choir singing old, familiar hymns such as "What a friend we have in Jesus."[15] Satan had not been idle in the camp, but Wilson concluded that he had never addressed a more appreciative and attentive audience.

The Reverend D. Martin was the first clergyman to permanently locate in Kaslo, arriving in the spring of 1892. The Presbyterian missionary found a small flock there and room for growth. A church on the lot donated by Hendry and Ewen was soon started. It must have been frustrating to Turner to see the Presbyterian church going up while he was delivering Methodist services in the schoolhouse. Other Christian denominations were served by travelling ministers operating on circuits. The Church of England's Reverend Reid, and then Akehurst, passed through Kaslo occasionally. Reverend Bédard served the district's Catholics, although the Reverend Guertin from Kamloops also occasionally visited.

Reverend Martin performed his first service on May 22, in a temporary church on B Avenue. He was beaten to the punch, however, by the Reverend Rogers of Nelson, who had preached a sermon a week or two earlier. Martin was grateful for the support of a group of god-fearing Christian women who were not intimidated by the rough-and-tumble prospectors who made up the largest portion of the population. It was the ladies who took the initiative in raising funds for a permanent church. In the summer of 1892, one of them walked into the Green brothers' store. Without hesitation, she walked up to a prospector at the counter and explained her mission to raise money for a church organ, handing him the book of subscriptions. Before the prospector could take it all in, his partner stepped into the fray: "What've you got there, pard?" Without skipping a beat, the church lady explained her purpose. She got a quick response: "I'll tell you what I'll do, Bob," said the man to his partner. "I'll flip the dice with you to see who gives the girl five dollars."[16]

And that's what they did. The lady walked away with five dollars towards a church organ. The man who witnessed this, perhaps a visitor from eastern Canada, was startled: "No one seemed to look on the event as in any way humorous or unusual, although it could not help but strike a stranger as extremely so." The visitor concluded that while most prospectors were "not religious in the ordinary acceptance of the word," they were quite willing to contribute to good works, provided that they were left alone and not preached to by the "sky pilots."

Like Turner, Martin was approachable and always ready to pitch in where he could. He took to collecting newspapers, magazines, and books to send up to the mines, a service the miners likely preferred over prayers. When Martin was asked to contribute to the Kaslo-Slocan wagon road, he replied: "I have no money but I have two hands." The next day he was out with the construction crew wielding a pick and shovel. The Nelson *Miner* noted that Reverend Martin, Reverend Turner, and the Roman Catholic priest were known and respected throughout West Kootenay "even by those who refuse to listen to them." They had "worked hard, lived hard, and taken the knocks with the remainder, and yet work on. More valuable factors in the building of a new country could not be found."[17]

In the early years of the Slocan rush, the Reverends Martin of Kaslo and Rogers of Nelson were the only Presbyterian ministers between the Okanagan Valley and Lethbridge to the west and east, and Revelstoke and the American border to the north and south. The difficulty in attracting missionaries to serve in the west was common to most Canadian denominations with roots in the eastern provinces. "When the young students of the east are offered a field in the wild west, they generally seek some time to consult with the Lord, and invariably they report that he advises them to wait for a call nearer to home."[18] On learning that he would be posted to Nelson, T.H. Rogers was at first disconsolate. He had heard of the "wickedness" and "depravity" of the West Kootenay camps. However, after a pep talk from the Reverend Doctor James Robertson, the superintendent of western missions for the Presbyterian Church, Rogers accepted his posting.

Like Rogers, the Reverend Martin was from eastern Canada and presumably of a conservative, god-fearing nature. However, this did not prevent him from getting caught up in the Slocan mining fever. Not long after his arrival, he took up mining speculation. Together with C.D. McKenzie, assayer Henry Horrocks, and Horrocks's partner, E.E. Rice, he recorded the Snowbird claim in Whitewater basin. The claim was unusual for the Slocan as it apparently assayed high in gold—between 608 and 907 ounces of gold to the ton. Or so Martin thought. The assay was likely conducted by Rice and was highly suspect. Soon after staking the claim, Rice took off from Kaslo for Bear Lake with all his assaying equipment. Rice sold his interest in the claim and then set out for Vancouver, where he likely flipped the bird again before hightailing it to Arizona. All Martin and his partners were left with was a bad taste and some worthless paperwork.

Martin must have been disappointed with his mining experiences, but he still had his church and congregation. To compensate for how thin their clergy were on the ground, Methodists and Presbyterians in Kaslo, as in

Nelson, occasionally held joint services, with both Martin and Turner presiding. Martin's church was also open to Church of England adherents, but it doesn't seem that any took up the offer.

Martin was a sick man. He had to vacate his post from time to time for treatment on the coast or back east. G.O. Buchanan proved a capable lay preacher, or Turner would sometimes fill in. Nelson's Reverend Rogers was also willing to cover. On one visit in early summer 1893, Rogers proved a match for the adversities that missionaries faced in the west. He set out walking from Kaslo to give a service in New Denver but had to bed down on the trail for the night "with a pocket handkerchief as his sole blanket."[19]

There was undoubtedly underlying competition between Christian denominations, as made clear in Turner's letters to Ebenezer Robson. But despite, or perhaps because of, the challenges they faced, there was also a degree of mutual respect that sometimes seemed absent in more settled regions. The Nelson *Miner* noted with approval: "The Rev. Messrs. Turner, Rogers, Reid and Father Bernard [*sic*] carry the doctrine of their various denominations into the surrounding country and we imagine from the goodwill they show towards each other at home that they lay more stress on the points on which they are agreed than on those on which they differ."[20]

Turner had for months been urging Ebenezer Robson to visit West Kootenay. Early in 1893, Robson was preoccupied with establishing a theological college in Vancouver, then took up the minister's pulpit at the James Bay Methodist Church in Victoria that June. But in September, he took time out from an eastern trip to finally tour West Kootenay. Turner met him in Nakusp on September 14. After a meal at the Leland House, Robson held prayers with several families, led a Sunday school class, and, in the evening, gave a lecture on pioneer days in BC in "a building erected same day, with blanket for window and sail for door."[21] He remarked in his diary that the lecture "amid present surroundings suggested coals to Newcastle."[22] The next day, Robson and Turner set out for the head of Slocan Lake, sharing one grey mule between them. They took the steamer *W. Hunter* to New Denver and put up at a "nice" hotel. This was likely the new frame-built Slocan Hotel put up to replace the humble log structure that had hosted F.W. Laing just weeks before. In the evening, Robson gave his "Pioneer Days" lecture to an attentive audience in Turner's new church.

The next morning, they started for Kaslo at five o'clock and made Three Forks before breakfast. They took a stage from there, arriving in Kaslo that evening after a very rough ride. Robson's account of his trip was not particularly flattering to the government crews who had only recently extended and "repaired" the road:

> After breakfast we took stage (freight-wagon style) to halfway house where we waited an hour till noon. Then dined & took another stage—rockaway—worse than lumber wagon tho' more pretentious—in which we made about 2 miles when we came to a 4 foot tree lying across the road. Having no means whatever of cutting it we walked on to send relief. Met lots of teams & concluded the log would give way to their treatment. So we went to the next "house" where we waited a long time for our stage. Mounted & rode on to *Kaslo*. The road was rough & many deep holes in it—especially near Kaslo. One passenger thrown from driver's seat to the ground.[23]

Robson paid a visit to the Presbyterian church before retiring to the Hotel Slocan. The next morning, he preached to a good congregation "considering the coldness of the buildings," and led another Sunday school class. He was expected to preach again at the Presbyterian church, but the service was instead led by the Reverend Martin, who unfortunately fell sick midway through his sermon. Before departing for Nelson the next day, however, Robson did manage to give his "Pioneer Days" lecture to another well-attended house.

In the summer and fall of 1893, one thing that all the religious denominations in Kaslo and the Slocan agreed on was the corrupting and immoral influence of Kaslo's Theatre Comique. The moral crusade to get rid of the Comique started early. In May 1893, just after it opened, it was added to a blacklist that also included all the brothels in town. A petition was circulated for the benefit of a grand jury scheduled to hold court in Nelson on May 30:

> WHEREAS a grave danger seems to threaten us in the establishment of places of resort ostensibly known as theatres, but in reality are places for the sale of liquor by the disgraceful method of "box rustling," locally so called, one such place having already obtained a foothold in your district.[24]

The Nelson *Tribune* felt that a theatre in Kaslo was not the business of Nelson, but the grand jury did note the irony that the building in question had previously been used for court services. It recommended discontinuance of the practice.

The Reverend Martin mounted a scathing attack on the Comique, calling it a "menace to the moral welfare of the young men, and a lasting disgrace to the people of Kaslo."[25] He was in the middle of a sermon dealing with the story of Paul, the silversmith Demetrius, and the dispute over the temple of Artemis in Ephesus when he launched his tirade. No quarter was given in the struggle between Church and Comique. Comique show cards were prominently displayed near the Church—some affixed to the walls of the building itself.

Sam Holland did not seem worried by Martin's attack. Demetrius was a silver worker, and Holland would likely have backed him in any dispute with an apostle. Holland was buoyed by the crowds filling the Comique every night and by the money he was raking in. Advertising manager Bert Colville travelled to Spokane looking for talent to fill out the orchestra and stage. Holland would later cast a wider net and looked to Butte, Montana, for female beer slingers with a sense of adventure.

BY JUNE 1893 THE POPULATION of the Slocan was still largely American, and visiting Boston correspondent Herbert Heywood could describe a wishful vision of "an American Eagle, bird of prophecy, up from the south spying out his future land."[26] However, talk of annexation had faded into the background. On the ground, Canadian and British businessmen found they could do just fine riding the coattails of the Americans. And American entrepreneurs like Sam Holland found they could thrive on the Canadian side of the border. There was no need to upset the status quo. Americans seemed content exchanging Uncle Sam for "Aunt Peggy." Indeed, the two communities learned much from each other.

New Denver residents can thank Sam Wharton for what was probably the first barbecue in the Slocan. R.T. Lowery later recalled that because New Denver did not have celebrations for the Queen's birthday in 1893, a committee was struck to find something to celebrate.[27] Sam Wharton was elected chair. He suggested a barbecue to celebrate July 4, which—in the early days at least—was celebrated with more gusto than Dominion Day. Someone asked him to explain what a "barbecue" was: "'Yes sah,' replied the chairman. 'In the state of Georgia, whar I come from, we have them every year. You take a whole ox and roast him at an open fire, sah. Then with bread and butter and other eatables, all jine in and eat.'"[28]

The barbecue was a great success. However, some Americans—like Spokane's F.Z. Alexander—couldn't help but tease their Canadian hosts.

> The Slocan is populated by Americans anyway. One wouldn't realize he was out of the United States if he didn't catch sight of the bob-tailed dogs that accompany the English "Chawley's." I was at Watson on the Fourth of July and we celebrated in true American fashion. We fired a salute of thirty-one guns with giant powder, and then poked fun at the Britishers, who had only managed to fire eight guns on Dominion day July 1.[29]

English "chawleys," or "chollys" were at the time a great source of amusement to many Americans. But nationality took a back seat to prosperity. The mines had proven themselves; mining men were confident; capital was flowing in; and wagon roads were completed or under way. Leo Kaufman, a merchant, wrote in June from Kaslo to a friend in Spokane. While things were quiet in the camp, he said, this was only because fortune seekers were abandoning the saloons and brothels for the Slocan's silver-heavy hills. The slopes were peppered with prospectors, but there were few strikes. Nevertheless, the mood was optimistic.

Sam Holland returned to Spokane after the successful opening of the Comique. He reported of Kaslo: "The people all speak in the highest terms of the mineral wealth of the country. There is not a croaker in the camp."[30] Slocan mine owners all believed they would soon be millionaires if they weren't already; miners aspired to be mine owners; property owners prided themselves on getting into the market early; merchants dreamed of newer, bigger stores and more of them; and saloon keepers had visions of endless streams of beer and whisky.

Kaslo's *Examiner* predicted great things for the future: "Nothing (not even an earthquake) . . . can prevent the rush of immigrants to the Kaslo-Slocan country."[31] The future looked bright. With its rapidly growing population, residents began thinking about Kaslo's incorporation as a city.

8

THE GREAT PANIC

FINE SUMMER WEATHER BLANKETED KASLO late in June 1893. The streets were dirty and dusty from the traffic of packers and freighters driving their animals between the wagon road leading to the Slocan mines and the wharves clinging to the shores of Kootenay Lake. The loud hustle and bustle was suddenly pierced by a shriek that cut through the mutterings of horses and mules and quieted the chatter on the streets. A young woman was in a panic: "My gawd; and all the money I have in the world—$300—in it."[1]

Kaslo and the Slocan mining camps were booming in late spring 1893. Town lots were selling like hotcakes. Merchants, rustlers, tinhorns, and sporting ladies were landing in Kaslo by the boatload. Though he had heard the glowing reports, a visitor found the camp exceeded all his expectations: "It is a city of about 2,500 people, with fine hotels and stores of all kinds and classes."[2] Another visitor noted that "building is very lively, and about the only music is that from the saw and hammer."[3] Nobody was expecting the bubble to burst.

But it did. In June, telephone lines carried worrisome news from Spokane. Word of mouth from the crowds of travellers arriving daily confirmed the bad news. Bank failures were widely reported. Both the Nelson *Tribune* and the Nelson *Miner* tried to gloss things over. The *Miner* reported: "The trouble in Spokane is practically over. G.B. Wright received a telegram on Wednesday afternoon stating that there had been no more failures, and it was believed that the crisis was then over."[4] It wasn't.

The word on the street in Kaslo was grim. The *Kaslo Claim* on June 8 reported "all sorts of rumors of the breaking of banks in Spokane."[5] Six employees of the Comique and many others in Kaslo had money tied up in Spokane banks. There were stories of frightened depositors bursting the doors of closed institutions in desperate, futile efforts to retrieve their money. Then, most alarmingly, the price of silver dropped ten cents an ounce in just over a week, hovering at about $0.73 an ounce before falling to $0.69 an ounce by the end of June. The *Tribune*, at least, could no longer ignore the new reality: "The fates seem to be in league against us."[6] Things hit home on June 29, when the private bank operated by J.M. Burke closed its doors, leading to the young woman's shrieks.

Still, the *Miner* tried to calm the waters: "There is not much uneasiness evinced by the local merchants."[7] But if merchants were not "uneasy," their customers certainly were. A few days before the closure, there had been a run on Burke's bank by nervous depositors. Withdrawals totalled $30,000. Burke left for Spokane, ostensibly to secure additional funding. People waited anxiously, but Burke didn't return. The new safe he had ordered for the bank sat abandoned on the Kaslo wharf along with a placard that read CLOSED FOR WANT OF FUNDS.[8]

The mining camps of West Kootenay were now fully caught up in what came to be known as the "Great Panic" of 1893. Railway magnate D.C. Corbin described it as "like a thunderclap out of a clear sky."[9] Earlier in the year, money markets along the eastern American seaboard had begun to collapse. Several large American railway companies failed, including the Union Pacific, and the Atchison, Topeka & Santa Fe. As financial instability grew, the depression moved inexorably westward. Dozens of banks collapsed in Washington State. While banks did not collapse wholesale in BC, some smaller private banks with American connections, like Burke's, went under. Silver mining regions on both sides of the border were hard hit. This was widely attributed to monetary policy in the United States and India, the two biggest purchasers of silver in the early 1890s.

The Sherman Silver Purchase Act, enacted in the United States in 1890, required the American government to purchase silver using notes backed by either silver or gold. The act was largely a response to an overproduction of silver from western American silver mines. While the American economy had relied on the gold standard since 1873, western silver mining regions were strong proponents of bimetallism, a system that would see a dual standard using both silver and gold. The Sherman Silver Purchase Act was a compromise offering some stability for silver while not fully embracing bimetallism.

In early 1893, the government of India announced that it was closing its mints to silver and would establish a gold standard. This hit world silver markets hard. The price of the white metal dropped 15 percent overnight.

American investors began trading in their silver notes for gold, thus depleting gold reserves and putting the American government in the embarrassing position of having to borrow from tycoon J.P. Morgan to shore up the gold reserves. The newly elected Democratic president, Grover Cleveland, a strong supporter of the gold standard, began marshalling the political resources he would need to repeal the Sherman Silver Purchase Act. The price of silver went into freefall. Dozens of low-grade silver mines closed in the western United States, never to open again. The Slocan mines were rich in high-grade ore, but even that couldn't save them all.

In retrospect, there were plenty of warning signs about the deteriorating financial situation. Like troubling grey clouds, they popped up here and there, briefly casting their shadows on those below. In April, an executive committee for San Francisco's unemployed issued a circular: "The city of San Francisco is crowded with idle men. There are thousands of us tramping the streets, hungry, hopeless and destitute. For God's sake keep away from this city."[10] Circumstances were similar in Washington State. The bloom was off the rose in the Slocan too. An "old prospector" hired by Montana capitalists to scout the Slocan reported back in May: "Dear Sirs: The gamblers are playing solitaire and the girls are doing their own washing. Yours, D.C."[11] The message was clear enough.

Perhaps Mark Musgrove was attuned to the warning signs. In late May 1893, he sold his interest in the *Kaslo-Slocan Examiner* to "Colonel" Coy, the adult son of E.E. Coy. The younger Coy had been a minority partner with Musgrove but vowed to improve the paper with his ascendency to owner. Coy had a staff of six to help him run the paper. Unusual for the time, his employees included two young women, Margaret O'Rourke and Mary van Buren. Coy also employed Benjamin "B.R." Atkins, R.E. Seysler, R.F. Wells, and the printer's devil, "Little Frank." His father, E.E. Coy, assumed the role of "society editor."

For weeks leading up to the crisis, Spokane newspapers carried stories about bankruptcies and bank failures back east and the occasional unexplained suicide of one or another businessman. On May 19, 1893, Charles S. Rogers, president of the Northwestern Cordage Company of Saint Paul, Minnesota, killed himself by diving headfirst off a bridge into the Mississippi River. Rogers gave two letters to a boy passing by and asked him to take care of his horse and buggy. He then climbed over the railing and, exclaiming that he could fly like an angel, made his fatal leap. For two hours preceding his jump, he had been in conference with his bankers.

Most Slocan residents too often glossed over these gloomy and depressing reports without realizing their significance. They were more interested in exotic news from faraway places, lurid gossip from the courts of Europe, or political intrigue in Cuba, Hawaii, or South Africa. In early 1893, the story that captured the most interest and excitement was the great fair that was to take place in Chicago. There was poetic irony in the coincidence of the Great Panic and the great fair.

The World's Columbian Exhibition of 1893, a year late, was meant to celebrate the four hundredth anniversary of Columbus's "discovery" of America, but it was also intended to showcase a thriving and prosperous Chicago, which had recently overtaken Philadelphia as the second largest city in the United States. More than showcasing Chicago, the fair would advertise the United States to the world. While it wouldn't open until May 1893, planning had been under way since 1890. The great Paris Exposition of 1889, which dazzled with Eiffel's tower, was fresh in everyone's mind. The Chicago organizers knew they had to pull out all the stops to match or exceed the Paris exhibition. They largely succeeded.

The crowds eventually flocked to a fair that dazzled with architectural splendour in the famed "White City," and bristled with exciting new technology. Innovations in electricity loomed large, including the first large-scale implementation of Westinghouse's new alternating current system and the first fully electric kitchen. Six different electric cars were on display—a promising invention that seemed a clear sign of things to come. "Typewriters," female stenographers who operated gleaming black Remington typing machines, were stationed strategically throughout the fairgrounds, ready to display their skills. Products now familiar to us that were first introduced at the fair ranged from Cracker Jack and Juicy Fruit gum to Shredded Wheat and Quaker Oats. While the fair focused on technology, there were other delights for the broad-minded. "Little Egypt" dancing the hootchie coochie delivered shock and awe in equal measure. Her belly dancing would inspire performers and scandalize puritans for years to come.

Many Slocan residents had been diligently following preparations for the fair, and some became directly involved. The BC government planned to participate. In July 1892, Charles F. Law of Golden was appointed to collect minerals from throughout the province to display in a metallurgical exhibit. Law had volunteers like Charles Hugonin and Police Constable J.D. Graham gather ore samples. Law was in Kaslo in December 1892 to collect samples from more than forty Kaslo and Slocan claims. By the end of January 1893, he had more than four hundred BC ore samples to choose from.

Once the fair opened, Slocan residents were eager to hear how their local ores fared. They didn't have long to wait. Noble Five pioneer Bill Hennessy visited in early June and returned to Kaslo later that month. He spent a full seven days at the fair and was mightily impressed. Newspaper accounts could give "but the faintest idea of the actual reality." He thought the most complete mineral exhibit was that of Australia's New South Wales. He was also impressed with Ontario's exhibit and California's, "with fruit of almost every imaginable variety." Hennessy was at the fair early, and many of the exhibits were not yet complete. He was too early to witness the unveiling of Montana's solid silver statue of *Justice*, and he missed the opportunity to ride the giant passenger-carrying wheel designed by a Pittsburgh engineer named Ferris and constructed by Andrew Onderdonk of CPR fame, but he had seen much:

> The richest and finest silver ores to be seen in Chicago are those of the Slocan, and I say it without fear or favor. The exhibit was not fully prepared while I was there but it is a collection of absorbing interest to all connected with mines and mining who visit the fair. Mining men from Colorado, Montana, Idaho, New Mexico and Arizona who have seen the exhibit are unanimous in declaring the Slocan ores the richest in silver and lead that they have ever seen. Our ore simply "lay over them all."[12]

Residents of Kaslo and the Slocan were filled with pride at having the district's ores in the world's eye.

The Chicago World's Fair succeeded in entertaining and astonishing people through 1893. It drew more than twenty-five million visitors and closed with a profit, but when it closed, the reality of the depression would sink in. Bill Hennessy returned to Kaslo just before the failure of Burke's bank. Back in Chicago, several banks failed shortly after he left. At the fair itself, several suicides, including the sad demise of a woman who leapt from a fifth-floor window, dashing her brains out when she landed on a hotel skylight, were graphic reminders of the hard times.

On October 28, 1893—two days before the fair closed—Mayor Carter Harrison was assassinated by a disgruntled office-seeker. By December 1893, after the fair closed, it was estimated there were nearly 117,000 unemployed in Chicago, including thousands of homeless men and women who sought shelter in city hall and other public buildings. In January 1894, the famed White City fairground caught fire and was quickly reduced to a pile of blackened rubble. Martha Black, a Canadian icon who was raised in Chicago, later recalled "a winter of misery, especially for women and children."[13]

The effects of the depression were keenly felt in the Slocan. In Canada there would be no marches on Ottawa—at least not in the late nineteenth century—but there was hardship and suffering enough in the western silver camps. There seemed no immediate prospect of silver prices recovering. The lingering depression and the brutal winter chilled the hearts and hopes of those who remained in the half-deserted camps. A flock of wild geese had circled Kaslo in September 1893, and members of the local Ktunaxa Nation, familiar with the seasons and portents, predicted a hard winter. The prediction proved true.

As early as July 1893, mines started closing like rows of falling dominoes. Marginal prospects were abandoned, and low-grade mines shut down. Some mine owners and operators looked to get out of the business entirely—while they could. Investors started pulling out and new investment virtually dried up over the summer. One of the first mines to go down the spout was the London Mercantile's Reed and Robinson. London investors could be finicky about silver at the best of times, and these were not the best of times.

Most Slocan residents had never heard of the Sherman Silver Purchase Act or participated in debates about bimetallism before the collapse of silver prices. Afterwards, however, "the silver question" was talked about everywhere in West Kootenay. One couldn't pick up a newspaper that didn't have an expert report or editorial on the benefits of a dual standard. Bimetallic clubs sprang up in western mining regions. Public forums for discussing the issue were common. From saloons to campfire gatherings, the topic could not be avoided.

Jack Watson, the founder of the mining camp of Watson, writing back to Scotland in October 1893, gives a good indication of the passion with which bimetallism was discussed:

> This silver question has knocked the supreme stuffing out of silver for the present, and this camp being practically composed of the white metal has in common with others over the line suffered from the drop in value of said metal. Were it only as last summer I could have cleaned up a fairly good sum this summer. However, there is one comfort and that is this: the ore in this camp being generally of so high a grade enables mine-owners even at the present low price of silver to ship their ore at a profit. Were silver only once established internationally

> upon a standard basis, the same as gold, as will without a shadow of a doubt, eventually be done, all silver camps both here and all over the world would be eminently prosperous.[14]

Watson apologized for imposing his opinions, explaining that "to me, it means everything."

There are some who see in L. Frank Baum's *The Wonderful Wizard of Oz*, which he wrote in 1900, a commentary on the depression of 1893 and the political struggle between the supporters of the gold standard and those who favoured bimetallism. The yellow brick road represented the gold standard. The Emerald City was Washington, and Dorothy's silver slippers (changed to ruby for the celebrated 1939 movie) symbolized the free silver movement. Baum was living in Chicago in 1893 and would have visited the fair and its White City, but he would also have seen the terrible effect the depression had on the city and country.

In September 1893, newspaperman and land promoter David Bogle gave a lecture in Nelson on the financial crisis, including the silver issue. The Nelson *Miner* suggested several other lecture themes that would bring out an attentive audience: "Collections made easy"; "How to get money out of people who have none"; "Where are we going to eat, or how to select winter quarters"; and, "Will it make it another winter, or our old overcoat."[15]

There was a very real human cost from the market collapse and depressed times. Drunkenness was rampant, and suicides were common. A Kaslo pioneer, Henry Kern—better known as "Old Jerry"—was jailed for three months for public drunkenness and for threatening to cut his own throat, which seems a harsh penalty for actions likely driven by alcohol and/or depression. George Whitten, a well-known and widely respected Slocan prospector, came into Kaslo from the Slocan in mid-September 1893 and drank heavily for about ten days before waking on September 21 in the Montana Hotel when—whether depressed by the downturn in silver prospects, perhaps "tired of life," as the Nelson *Miner* suggested, or in a state of temporary insanity as determined by the coroner's jury—he decided to kill himself by cutting his throat. His death was discovered only when a pool of blood was found on the floor of the barroom below his room. He was about forty years old. His funeral the next day, high up in the hills above Kaslo, was a sombre affair attended by many of his prospecting companions. It wasn't just depressed prospectors either. In June 1893, one of mining man and freighter G.W. Hughes's horses walked into Slocan Lake and drowned itself. It was a bad omen.

AND WHAT BECAME OF J.M. BURKE? Many Kaslo and Slocan residents wondered this as the warm summer months of 1893 faded away and the first signs of yellowing tamaracks heralded the coming fall and winter. For the first few weeks, he was in Spokane, confident he could secure funds to repay his depositors. The Slocan, he claimed, was "looking better than ever."[16] Interviewed in July, he said, "all would come right shortly as he was then engaged in securing the necessary funds."[17] Nelson's George Bigelow met Burke in Spokane about this time and reported that he seemed to be leading a lavish lifestyle, showing no effects of the depression that had enveloped the Slocan.

The weeks passed. By August, it was clear that Burke wasn't returning to Kaslo. John Retallack was appointed receiver to seize and dispose of Burke's Slocan and Kaslo assets. Burke managed to stay afloat south of the border. An "inveterate faro player," he frequented the saloons and gambling tables of Spokane.[18]

There is one story of a disgruntled Kaslo resident tracking Burke down. Joe Davis was a long, lean Missourian who had come to Kaslo from the Coeur d'Alenes. He borrowed the money to get to Spokane, and when he found Burke having drinks at Natatorium Park, he walked up to him and demanded the $700 he had lost in the bank failure. Burke insisted he was broke. Davis didn't want to hear about it. He reached into his pocket, pulled out a pistol and laid it on the table. "This yer shootin' iron don't sit well in my pocket," he casually remarked. Reappraising his financial situation vis-à-vis his will-to-live situation, Burke agreed to pay the funds in full the next morning. Luckily, it was a good night at the faro table. Burke was able to settle his debt to Davis and live to play another hand.

Many Slocan prospectors with claims bonded to outside capitalists for rich prices had spent what money they had with wild abandon. They hadn't anticipated the precipitous fall in silver prices. Johnny Harris and Fred Kelly, two of the owners of the Reco, who had bonded their claim to American investor Patsy Clark, spent Clark's $4,000 down payment freely, using it to visit their homes in the United States. They were counting on future payments. Both were practically broke when they returned to the Slocan in May, just before the great "thunderclap." Then, when it came time for Patsy Clark and his partners to make the second payment on their bond, they decided to let it lapse. This sent a clear message to other investors. Bonds were thrown up on other claims too, often leaving the original owners high and dry.

The shine was off silver, but some of the richer mines continued to ship ore while there was still some profit in it. In July, the Idaho mine made one last shipment of 167 sacks of ore to the smelter in Tacoma. While the ore still brought in a profit, it was felt the most prudent course of action was to suspend operations and hope for the price of silver to recover. Other mines followed suit. G.W. Hughes, the owner of the Mountain Chief, bucked against the trend. He explained his philosophy to a reporter for the Nelson *Tribune* in the summer of 1893:

> HUGHES: I suppose I have had as anxious a summer as anyone, but I did not allow myself to get the blues over it. Much of the trouble we have been passing through is caused by people getting the blues and spreading them round.
> INTERVIEWER: What is the outlook for the winter?
> HUGHES: Very good. There is quite a little ore coming out now. I shipped seventy-five tons of Mountain Chief ore this week. I think there will be a greater production and more development this winter than last.
> INTERVIEWER: How much ore do you calculate to ship from the Mountain Chief?
> HUGHES: I am afraid to tell you. I have things pretty well blocked out there and you will see later on.
> INTERVIEWER: Would it not pay you better to ship by way of Nakusp?
> HUGHES: Perhaps when the road is open. But I can't wait till it is. I am one of those men who must be doing something all the time. I would rather make $10,000 now than $20,000 ten years hence. Some men are content to sit down and wait till they can work at the least cost. But I want to go right ahead if I can work at a profit at all.[19]

Wake Russell, with interests in the Noble Five, Ruby Silver, and other mines, was similarly minded: "Even with silver at 65 cents we can make a profit, and should silver rise again, which we firmly believe, we are just that much ahead by having turned out ore and developed the mines."[20] Russell had the Keno, the claim he bought from Joseph Martin, assayed. It yielded 1,200 ounces of silver to the ton. He was not ready to give up on the Slocan. Johnny Harris, likely still reeling from the collapse of the deal with Patsy Clark, was determined to ship ore from the Reco. When he had a carload ready to ship, he told other prospectors in the neighbourhood that he expected to net $8,000. They laughed at him. He had the ore packed down the mountainside, hauled over the Kaslo wagon road, boated down Kootenay Lake to Nelson, and shipped by rail to the Omaha and Grant smelter. He ended up with a net profit of $9,000. No one laughed.

Just as claims were abandoned, so too the camps. Fortune seekers who had flooded into Kaslo and the Slocan just months earlier returned in droves to the towns and cities many had started from. They carried with them tales of hardship and despair resulting from the busted boom. James Holler had been in Kaslo for three months but returned to his home in Columbia City, Montana, in June. He reported the Kaslo boom had "flattened out as flat as a pancake."[21] When Charley Walker returned to Philipsburg, Montana, in August 1893, he described the Slocan as "almost totally depopulated . . . everybody who can get away at all is doing so."[22] A.M. Barnes also returned and confirmed that "the bottom has dropped completely out in that section."[23] One man described Kaslo as "too dead to skin."[24]

James Holler claimed that "every one with the price of a steamer ticket is getting out."[25] Trouble was, not everyone had the price of a steamer ticket. Many prospectors and speculators found themselves stranded and

"Mtn Chief Mine." June 1893. Photographer: Henry Woodside. Dinner at the mine. The cook, in white, is likely Charles Miller, later to marry Caroline Anderson.
LIBRARY AND ARCHIVES CANADA

broke, far from their homes, with no way to return. William Jessen, who arrived in Spokane in late July, vividly described the scenes of desperation he left behind. Men tried to stow away on the steamboats, but they were usually found and driven ashore. However, returning home wasn't an option for more than a few Slocan prospectors who had long ago come untethered from the concept of "home." Up in the mountains above Carpenter, Seaton, and Kaslo Creeks, men with no means of support struggled to survive. Stranded by the collapse of the silver market, some sought to escape while others chose to wait out the hard times in hopes of a quick recovery. Living was cheap, but conditions were primitive. Tents and makeshift cabins were scattered through the forests, occupied by shifting knots of itinerant miners and prospectors.

Some fortune seekers adapted to the changed circumstances and looked for new opportunities. Some tried to get work with the few mines still operating. Sid Norman, who arrived in the Slocan just before the depression, was one of the lucky ones. He got a job with Lane Gilliam's packing outfit, which paid just enough to keep him clothed and fed. Several prospectors headed south through Nelson to the Salmon and Yahk Rivers, following some promising placer showings. A few continued to explore the Slocan and surrounding area. Bill Springer decided to explore the ground down Slocan Lake near its outlet. He and his partners made a rich strike on what was later named Springer Creek, displacing the Sinixt name that had likely been in place for centuries. However, due to the depressed times, the strike didn't elicit much interest.

The 1893 downturn was devastating to townsite speculators. Kaslo was hit especially hard. The value of lots plummeted. When A.L. Howard returned to his home in Montana late in June, he reported that lots purchased for $2,000 in Kaslo just two months earlier could not be sold for $200. Many investors lost almost everything. There was sympathy for family men who had purchased lots in Kaslo in good faith, but little sympathy for the real estate promoters who had done whatever they could to drive up prices before the depression hit.

Other townsites suffered too. Real estate agents and townsite owners scrambled to find incentives that would lure buyers. In New Denver, newspaperman and real estate promoter John Houston was offering lots in the McGillivray Addition at "nominal" prices to prospectors and miners who would agree to put up cottages within a "reasonable time."[26] Nakusp and Three Forks fared somewhat better, but sales were slow, and prices reduced.

"Seven men seated outside a mine building. Ore sacks nailed to exterior of building," c. 1893–94. Photographer unknown. ORIGINAL IMAGE COURTESY OF THE KOOTENAY LAKE ARCHIVES, KASLO, BC

Hotel Slocan, Kaslo, c. July 1893. Photographer unknown. While the Hotel Slocan was in receivership, it remained open, hosting dozens of itinerant men looking for work—or at least a means of fleeing Kaslo. IMAGE COURTESY OF THE KOOTENAY LAKE ARCHIVES, KASLO, BC

Businesses that had thrived earlier in the year sank like stones. The last edition of R.T. Lowery's *Kaslo Claim* was published on August 25, 1893. A tombstone featured prominently on the front page. Advertisements within were printed in a variety of configurations. Delinquent accounts had their advertisements printed upside down. Those who had paid in part had ads printed sideways, and those who had paid in full were rewarded by having their ads printed conventionally. One contributor described the *Claim*'s final "spasm" as a "nightmare of topsyturveydom."[27]

The bad times had a serious impact on the good times that had been a hallmark of Kaslo's Comique. By August it was reported "running to empty benches."[28] From listening to the sermons or reading the newspaper accounts, it might have seemed that the Comique was universally in disfavour. However, once it opened it proved very popular and—while there were certainly disorderly incidents, according to the Nelson *Tribune* at least, it was "one of the most orderly resorts" in Kaslo.[29] The Comique "girls," though, could not in good conscience be described as "orderly," but their mischief was generally carried out on the streets of Kaslo late at night, or in one of the brothels, not in the Comique. The Comique was not without its defenders, however. Several men wrote letters to the *Kaslo-Slocan Examiner*. One writer, who admitted being a frequenter of the Comique, plainly stated his case against closing it:

> Any man can go there free of charge and enjoy a sociable entertainment, and make no more a fool of himself, than he does in any saloon. The only difficulty is, there are actresses at the Theatre who are very sociable and entertaining and will take a drink with a man if he feels inclined to do so, but he doesn't have to . . . Where are the workingmen, the breadwinners of this community you may call them, going to find enjoyment? Does it not stand to reason, that after toiling month in and month out in the mountains, that they want a little amusement, and goodness knows, this place has a very small percentage of it.[30]

In September 1893, while the Reverends Robson, Martin, and Turner were all in Kaslo, a number of citizens and saloon keepers began organizing measures to get rid of the Comique. Reverend Martin was an early critic, and perhaps the visit by Robson and Turner was an opportunity for him to enlist two influential allies. The Nelson *Miner* noted that "a meeting of the Star Chamber variety was called for Saturday last and the fight may be expected to commence shortly."[31] The *Miner* felt the Comique was doomed, largely because of an unholy alliance between the Church and the saloon keepers of Kaslo. The Church wanted the Comique gone so that it would no longer be a corrupting influence on the camp's citizens. The saloon keepers wanted it gone because they couldn't compete with the Comique's liquor prices. However, the Comique faced a more formidable threat than either saloon keepers or church people could mount. Kaslo was incorporating as a city. Incorporation would give the city local control over permits, bylaws, and fines. A city council might allow the Comique to stay open but would likely look to raise cash from permit sales and fines.

On August 14, 1893, Kaslo became BC's newest city. There was some irony in the fact that incorporation came right in the middle of the depression, but for residents, it was a narrow ray of sunshine that briefly pierced the gloom engulfing them.

There was considerable competition between the principal camps in West Kootenay—Nelson, Kaslo, New Denver, Nakusp, and Three Forks. Incorporation was a coup for Kaslo. Nelson, which saw itself as the "capital" of West Kootenay, was particularly chagrined by the incorporation of Kaslo, years before Nelson would become a city. However, in a district where most of the population was American, it proved difficult finding British subjects to stand for office. By one account, there were only seven eligible men in the whole camp of Kaslo.

Robson, Martin, and Turner were united in their opposition to Kaslo's Comique, and eventually they would achieve their desired result. But the other challenges they and the new city authorities faced were formidable. Drunkenness, cursing, prostitution, and other "sins" were rampant. The adult male population was largely irreligious. Martin had first-hand experience of duplicity in his mining endeavours. However, as hard as the challenges were for the "sky pilots" that served the Slocan, most were unlikely to give up on their missions. Meetings seemed to be well attended when they were held, and there was an almost endless supply of souls to save.

The smaller camps faced serious setbacks too. Watson would benefit from a new sawmill and Three Forks got a provincial police constable, but one of the only improvements at Bear Lake City was one hotel's new poker table. By September, when the Duluth syndicate's Walter Middaugh arrived back in the Slocan, he confirmed what William Hunter and Fred Hume had already figured out—his company was getting out of real estate at Four

Mile Creek. They would not honour the terms of the agreement they had earlier negotiated with Hunter and Hume to purchase all the unsold lots in the Four Mile City townsite. Their focus would be the mines, and their goal was to maximize profits as quickly as they could. Middaugh gave a graphic account of how badly the depression was affecting business interests south of the border:

> I have just come from the coast, where we have large investments, and you people in the west have no idea of what the crisis has been like in the east. In Duluth and northern Minnesota, we have 12,000 men out of work and on the Duluth exchange 40 percent was being paid for call loans. No one who has not walked the boards during the last month or two can realize what the crisis has been like.[32]

Despite the reversals, Middaugh was confident that, except for the Four Mile Creek townsite—renamed Silverton a few months earlier—all the Duluth syndicate's liabilities would be discharged "to the last cent." Regarding mining operations, Middaugh said, "The ball will roll from now on."[33]

Expatriate Henry Horrocks tried to raise British interest in the Slocan with a letter he wrote to the *Preston Journal* in July 1893: "It is not the fact that the ore bodies are large and in places that give the people of this section so much confidence, but their confidence is due to the fact that they know that they have ore that can be shipped at a profit notwithstanding the depressed state of silver in the market."[34]

It's unlikely that Horrocks's letter raised much interest in Scotland or England, but for prospectors and miners hit hard south of the border, the rich Slocan mines were rife with opportunity. One man who made his way north during the hard times of 1893 was Ben Fennell. The one-time foreman of the Idaho Mining Company in Murray, Idaho, spent much of 1891 and 1892 in Alaska as part of an exploring expedition sponsored by the Smithsonian Institute. Fennell reported that while some money could be made mining the placers, the high cost of living restricted profit. He thought the Yukon River might one day yield its riches, but he noted that "life was entirely too short" to wait for that day.[35] Instead, he cast his lot with the Slocan mines.

Fennell was just one of many American miners and investors who saw the opportunities north of the border. At about the same time that Horrocks wrote to England, the Nelson *Miner* noted of the Slocan that "the District offers some wonderfully good buys to those who have ready money to invest and sufficient courage to stay with silver through the few dark days which seem to have closed around the white metal."[36] The depression was hard on those who had invested heavily at premium prices, but it also opened opportunities for investors looking for bargains who could afford to wait until the markets—and hopefully the price of silver—bounced back.

In August 1893, Noah F. McNaught of Seattle, who had been in the Slocan since May, bonded the Black Bear and Alpha, two claims that formed part of the Grady group, principally owned by Mike Grady, Charlie Laatz, and Len Briggs. The deal called for McNaught to provide a $5,000 down payment, to be followed by additional payments at three-, six-, nine-, and twelve-month intervals. The full price was $70,000—a real fortune, especially in such hard times—but nowhere near the $250,000 the partners had wanted before the depression hit. However, the sale was timely. Mark Twain once said that "a beggar with a silver mine is a pitiable pauper indeed if he cannot sell."[37] Before the sale of the Black Bear and Alpha, the story was out that Grady, Laatz, and Briggs were having "a hard time raising a dollar to buy beans and bacon."[38] With the down payment they received from McNaught, they could do much better than beans and bacon.

Another capitalist who saw the silver lining in the dark clouds of the depression was J.A. Finch. An English immigrant who came to America with ambition and high hopes, Finch was in Spokane by 1887. Along with his business partner, Mace Campbell, he invested heavily in Coeur d'Alene mines. Finch was an early investor in a few Slocan mines through his connections with Patsy Clark and J.M. Burke, but for most of 1892 he was preoccupied with his Coeur d'Alene investments. In particular, as secretary for the Coeur d'Alene Miners' Association, he was deeply involved in the ongoing labour troubles there. By late 1893, however, discouraged with silver prospects in the eastern US, and with most Coeur d'Alene mines closed, he paid closer attention to opportunities in the Slocan. In September 1893, Finch made what was likely his first visit to the Slocan. He was in a party with fellow capitalists Patsy Clark and Tom Jefferson. They visited some of the claims they had earlier invested in but were also on the lookout for new properties at bargain prices. Finch was impressed with what he saw and lost little time picking up mines. Despite his earlier abandonment of the Reco, Patsy Clark was still interested in Slocan mines and together with Finch, he bonded the Reed and Robinson, abandoned earlier by the British syndicate that had operated it.

The investments of McNaught and Finch were welcome bright spots in an otherwise depressing year for mines in the Slocan. The annual report of the Minister of Mines for the year 1893 tried to put a positive spin on things. While acknowledging that there was a "decided decrease" in the number of claims dealt with in the Slocan compared to 1892, the report noted that only six abandonments were recorded (though the number of unrecorded abandonments would have been substantially higher). The report provided a cautious but optimistic summary:

> In the spring of the year there was a rush of prospectors, capitalists, brokers and others to this part of the district, but the general depression so affected their operations that this camp has not quite realized the anticipations formed of its activity and prosperity last fall. Nevertheless, such work as has been done, and there is a great deal of it, has been satisfactory to those bearing its cost, and gives promise of and encourages increased vigor in mining operations for the future.[39]

G.W. Hughes's earlier prediction for the winter proved true. Once ore could be hauled down the mountains and packed out over sleigh roads, shipping costs were considerably reduced. In August 1893, at a stopover at the Rainier Hotel in Seattle, Jimmy Moran conceded that a few Slocan mines had shut down, but he claimed that several were getting ready to ship again: "The only ore that is shipped is ore running 150 ounces and over."[40] By December, a dozen or so mines were shipping ore, but many were operating by the skin of their teeth. Meeting payroll was always a challenge. There were few mine owners with pockets deep enough that they could keep mines running without the returns on ore shipments. If they didn't ship ore, they couldn't pay their bills—or their men. It was as simple as that.

Writing to Ebenezer Robson on November 24, 1893, Reverend James Turner hoped that Robson would "remember us earnestly in prayer for this whole sin cursed district."[41] The depressed mood was pervasive, even falling on the Kaslo Literary Society. The question up for debate one Sunday in December 1893 was "is life worth living?" After the debate concluded, a vote was taken. The "nos" were heavily in the majority.

Silver would not in the 1890s reach the heights it had before the Great Panic, though it did recover slightly. Nor would the dreams of bimetallism be realized. But if silver was in the doldrums, the price of lead (the other main ingredient in the rich galena ore that characterized the Slocan) rose steadily in the latter years of the nineteenth century. This was fuelled in part by the demand for batteries for the electric cars that were then faddish in eastern American cities. Despite the lower price of silver, the Slocan would eventually recover from the Great Panic and flourish in the later 1890s. But there was no denying the setback of 1893. Before the depression, there were predictions that the population of Kaslo would reach ten or twenty thousand before the end of the century. Of course, we know that never happened, but it well illustrates the optimism that reigned supreme in the early months of 1893.

9

HARD TIMES

IN THE DARKEST DAYS FOLLOWING the 1893 depression, people grew hardened to the hard times, and no crime—no matter how despicable—was beyond belief. It was little solace, but things seemed worse south of the border. Many Slocan residents would have read the tragic account reported in the *Spokane Review* of a train wreck in New York State. Before the dead and wounded could be removed, they were stripped of valuables by survivors and witnesses—thieves of convenience. The corpse of one man, known to be carrying $6,000 in cash, disappeared entirely.

Things weren't quite so bad in the Slocan, but with money and work in short supply, robbery became an option for some hard cases with few other opportunities. In the summer of 1893, a man named Harry Tracy was offering shaves and haircuts in Nakusp, but by 1894, he had taken up robbery and was up for trial for breaking into Lane Gilliam's warehouse at Bear Lake City. Tracy spent time in Three Forks in early 1894 while working on a packing contract. Then he got some work at Gilliam's warehouse. On March 2, he stopped in at Gorman West's Bear Lake Hotel. West knew Tracy as "the barber." After a few drinks and card games, Tracy left for Three Forks with two other young men. The allegation was that Tracy—either alone or with his two companions—hit Gilliam's warehouse on the way to Three Forks.

The next morning, when it was discovered that clothing, tools, dynamite, and a sled full of beef were missing, the local constable was called in. When he went to Tracy's cabin with a search warrant, he found clothing, tools, and powder. Tracy claimed it all belonged to a man named Rochon. The constable didn't buy it. Tracy was committed for trial. He was sent to the jail in Nelson, but "the barber" soon escaped and likely crossed the line into the States.

Was this the same Harry Tracy who would later become infamous in the annals of western crime? It seems unlikely, but the notion isn't as far-fetched as it might seem. The Canadian border was an attraction for American fugitives looking for respite from troubles to the south. Harry Longabaugh, better known as the "Sundance Kid," spent time in the early 1890s working at the Bar U Ranch in southern Alberta, just across the provincial border. It has also been suggested that John Jarrette, a Quantrill raider and member of the James gang, could be found in the 1890s in BC's Boundary district—not far from the Slocan—where he had taken up prospecting. One of his prospecting partners might have been the Slocan's Ike Lougheed. In 1895, then a young man and fugitive from the law, notorious outlaw Harry Tracy was laying low in a cabin north of Spokane. Could he also have spent time in Canada?

Curly Robinson was a much celebrated local character in the Slocan's early years. Flitting between Kaslo, New Denver, Nakusp, and Three Forks, Curly told his tall tales from one end of the Slocan to the other. In early 1894, he was in Nakusp, planning a trip to Alaska. Those plans were rudely interrupted when, within a week of his arrival, he was hauled before a JP on a charge of theft. On the night of May 24, two workers were bunked down together in a bed. While they slept, someone stole $10 from one and $7.50 from the other. Curly, the primary suspect, had been in the bed next to them. The trial lasted the better part of a day and involved numerous witnesses giving evidence on the travels of a ten-dollar bill that was alleged to have passed through Curly's hands. Money was tight in the mining camps, and people took notice when ten- or twenty-dollar bills were flashed about. The Imperial Bank of Canada note was marked in blue pencil and was identical, its alleged owner claimed, to the bill he had lost. This wasn't enough evidence for a conviction, however, and the case against Curly was dismissed.

Witnesses who attended Curly's trial might have been familiar with a parallel case that happened up the Columbia River. Professional thief and safe cracker Jack Black, who would later gain fame for his tell-all autobiography, *You Can't Win*, was stopped in Revelstoke on his way to Vancouver. He couldn't resist the temptation of his hotel's safe and was soon on the CPR train to Vancouver with a fat roll of bills in his pocket. When it came time to pay his fare, he peeled off a well-worn twenty-dollar bill and handed it to the conductor. Not long after, the train was stopped by a snow slide. Two constables from Revelstoke caught up with the train, and after a few inquiries, they arrested Black. He was convicted of the burglary on the testimony of an old prospector who had most recently owned the purloined twenty-dollar bill. Black later recalled the circumstances:

> An old prospector, who was wintering at the hotel, testified that he had changed a twenty-dollar bill at the hotel bar the evening before the burglary; that it was the only bill of that denomination he had, that he had carried it with him for six months and had looked at it so many times he remembered the big serial numbers on the back of it. He swore further that he went to the hotel man the next morning and gave him the numbers. The arresting officers now told of following the train, getting the conductor's statement, and arresting me. They produced the fatal twenty-dollar bill the only one in the roll that could have hurt me, the prospector's bill.[1]

Curly was luckier than Jack Black, but his reputation suffered regardless of the trial's outcome.

Gun crimes were relatively rare in the Slocan, but there were a few. In one incident, a miner heading back to Bear Lake City after "getting a jag on" in Kaslo in November 1893 was held up at gunpoint by a mounted, masked rider and ordered to "stand and deliver."[2] There were knife crimes too. Jack Beaudoin, who had been tried and found not guilty of a knife crime against Gus Carney, was just one knife-wielding "tough" in a crowded field. If American prospectors in the Slocan weren't carrying a gun, they most likely had a knife. In January 1894, a man named John Sandholm got into a stabbing affray in Nakusp, slashing the shoulder of J. Hector, the bartender at the Prospect House. At his trial, it was adduced that Sandholm was a professional in the knifing business, having had several previous sharp-edged encounters. Thrown in jail, he tried to escape by chewing at the cell door, leaving a trail of splinters and blood.

Another gun crime came to trial in early 1894, but it didn't involve theft. Rather, it was an early case of "road rage." In January, Jim Delaney was on the Kaslo wagon road driving a sleigh carrying several of the "girls" from the Theatre Comique on an excursion to New Denver. About ten miles out from Kaslo, Delaney came upon an ore sled headed in the opposite direction. He claimed the right-of-way and demanded the ore sled move aside. Due to his heavy load, the driver refused. Then, according to the driver, Delaney pulled out a pistol and threatened him with violence. The driver moved aside but lost part of his load in the process. When news of the incident reached Kaslo, Constable Graham laid charges against Delaney. The case came before G.M. Sproat a week later. In his defence, Delaney claimed it was not a gun but a tobacco box he had pointed at the driver. The prosecution's key witness apparently skipped the country just before the trial, and the case was dismissed. However, this did not stop Sproat from issuing a well-thought-out sermon on the "rules of the road."

Sometimes desperate people resort to desperate measures. Gun crimes might have been uncommon in the Slocan at the time, but arson was not. On a Sunday morning in late February, the Bon Ton restaurant in Kaslo was set ablaze. This was the third time in three weeks that someone had tried to burn it down. In one incident, someone saturated a pile of wood with coal oil and lit it on fire. Fortunately, the fire was discovered and extinguished before it could do any real damage. Unfortunately, the third attempt was successful.

Fuelled by a strong wind, the flames spread rapidly. The Kaslo fire brigade was out in full force, braving the freezing weather, but it was not enough to save Kaslo's business district. The fire swept along Front Street, incinerating everything it encountered. Some residents, worried about the wharf, used 150 pounds of dynamite to blow up Byers Hardware to create a firebreak. The wharf was saved, but windows were shattered throughout the camp. A high wind swept the flames out towards the lake, but before

Kaslo after the fire, c. 1894. Photographer unknown. IMAGE COURTESY OF THE ROYAL BC MUSEUM AND ARCHIVES

the fire could be extinguished, nine hotels, several large stores, and many restaurants and offices were reduced to ashes.

There were some daring rescues—Frank King pulled a mother and child from a burning building—but, fortunately, no deaths and only a few minor injuries. Sam Holland, who was in Spokane at the time of the fire, was relieved to learn that the Comique had survived. The local newspaper—unsubtly referring to Holland's Jewish ethnicity—reported: "The Almighty had, as usual, taken care of his chosen people."[3]

R.T. Lowery was in Kaslo at the time of the fire. He vividly described the scene he witnessed when he was finally roused from his hotel room: "The lurid flames shot upward, seeming anxious to kiss the stars."[4] There was something else Lowery witnessed that deeply troubled him. It shouldn't have been surprising—given the hard times—that there would be widespread looting during the fires. There were several arrests. Peter Smith, for example, a brewery owner, was arrested and sentenced to ninety days at hard labour for stealing two hams from the butcher's shop. It seems his sense of civic responsibility was overcome by his love of bacon. Lowery quite rightly noted: "It is wrong for people to take pork, ham, bacon and other articles the owners save from a fire. When a man saves his bacon, he ought to have it."[5]

Apart from the looting, there was the larger mystery as to who might have set the fire and for what reason. One suspect was Paul Savage, who ran the New York Chop House on Kaslo's Front Street. He was arrested

H. Giegerich store, Kaslo, c. 1894. Photographer unknown. Built in three days following the fire in 1894 as a temporary store. Included in the picture: Charles Kane, Archie Jardine, "Shady" Giegerich, [E.A.?] Bielenberg, Al Palmer (saloon keeper), C.W. Roe (bookkeeper for H. Giegerich), H. Byers, J.L. Pierce. IMAGE COURTESY OF THE KOOTENAY LAKE ARCHIVES, KASLO, BC

in Nelson a couple of weeks after the fire and transported to Kaslo for trial. There was an interesting and unusual twist to the proceedings. Because Kaslo's new city council had decided to send all their legal work to Vancouver, local lawyers refused to act for the city. As a result, Mayor George Kane was tasked with handling the prosecution. There was little evidence against Savage other than the use of some "foolish language," which the court believed was a misguided attempt at humour, and the fact that he and two or three other men were in or about the Bon Ton shortly before the fire started.[6]

Savage was acquitted but couldn't stay out of trouble for long. It seems Mayor Kane and his city council didn't take kindly to the acquittal. A watch that went missing at the time of the fire was found in Savage's Nelson hotel room when he was seized on the arson charge. He soon found himself under arrest again for theft. The Nelson *Miner* thought a conviction unlikely, but Savage was held over for trial nevertheless.

Savage was in dire straits after his acquittal on the arson charges. His reputation had sunk through the floor. He couldn't get a job. He spent most of his time drinking, playing cards, and looking for people he could cadge money from. His wife, Antonia, was with him in Kaslo, but she was tiring of his drunkenness and brutality, and they likely lived apart for at least some of the time.

Savage shared a cheap hotel room with Frank King. On the evening of March 21, Savage and King went to the Comique, where they both got good and drunk. Savage went back to his room, but King stayed out. There was a break-in at Mike Mahoney's Palace Hotel that night. The thief made away with 10 bottles of Hennessy brandy, 4 bottles of Canadian Club whisky, and 150 cigars. Early the next morning, King came into the room he shared with Savage, brandishing bottles of brandy and flashing cigars about. Savage asked King to remove the liquor and cigars. King did so, but the next afternoon—no doubt planning his getaway—he asked Savage to get him some sandwiches and a pair of oars. Savage later claimed that King had a .44 revolver and threatened to "give him the contents" if he gave him up.[7] King made a successful getaway. A hero only weeks before, now a fugitive. All the authorities were left with was Savage.

It seems the break-in at Mahoney's hotel was the last straw for the Kaslo city council. They couldn't get their hands on Frank King but decided they'd had enough of Paul Savage. They instructed the police chief to run him out of town. If Savage can be believed, Chief Adams was reluctant to do so, but his job depended on it. He told Savage, "I would advise you to leave as these people have it in for you and there has been a whole lot of monkey work going on here lately and if you don't get it on one thing you will on another."[8]

Savage was stubbornly defiant and vowed to stand his ground. He had his lawyer write a letter to council threatening action for wrongful prosecution. This was too much for the Kaslo city council. After being run out of Kaslo, Savage was arrested in Nelson on charges of being an accessory to burglary and locked up pending trial. He must have finally realized how the cards were stacked against him, so he flew the coop. Left alone in the Kaslo lock-up while awaiting trial, Savage wrenched one of the bars loose and made his exit. Soon he was across the line in Washington State, where his life continued to spin out of control. Savage was apprehended in August by a pair of detectives in Seattle and scheduled for trial in Kaslo. But he would never appear. His wife, Antonia, was in Spokane, and in early August 1894, she secured a divorce, pleading drunkenness and violence as the grounds. When he heard that he had been divorced, Savage left Seattle for Tacoma. About a week later, he died by suicide. He was just twenty-eight years old. The Kaslo city council was left with nothing but bad memories.

If Paul Savage didn't start the Kaslo fire, who did? Why would someone want to burn Kaslo down? What was the motive? Perhaps the target wasn't the Bon Ton but the building in which it was located. The Bon Ton occupied space in the Noble Five Hotel—a building that also just happened to house the notorious Noble Five brothel. Could the arsonist have been targeting the brothel—or one of its "inmates"? Such a thing was certainly not unheard of. We know that the manager of the brothel, Emery Giles, had enemies, and likely some of the "girls" did as well. Capitalist W.E. Mann had a more mundane but perhaps more plausible theory: "Kaslo is cursed with a few residents who would destroy the world if they saw a prospect of stealing a ham and sack of flour out of the ruins. I think there has been a determined effort to start a fire for the express purpose of pillaging the burnt district."[9] Although Paul Savage had been acquitted, suspicion continued to swirl about him and Frank King. Savage, in particular, an alleged thief, drunkard, wife beater, and fugitive from justice, certainly seemed capable of arson. If Mann's theory was true, however, it was a sad testament on the desperate state of affairs in Kaslo.

Many prospectors and camp followers like Savage struggled through the Great Panic and its aftermath. George Cleveland was in the vanguard of

"Mary van Buren, stage actress." Undated. Photographer: Thors. IMAGE COURTESY OF THE UNIVERSITY OF WASHINGTON LIBRARY SPECIAL COLLECTIONS

men who braved the Slocan's snowy slopes in late 1891. He did not profit by it, suffering numerous reverses in the months and years following. In early 1895 he was aboard the Kootenay Lake steamer *Nelson*, heading down the lake from Kaslo. A couple he had been in conversation with turned away for a moment, and when they looked back, Cleveland had jumped overboard into the frigid waters of the lake.

Like other businesses, newspapers struggled through the hard times. After R.T. Lowery closed down the *Kaslo Claim*, Colonel Coy had the newspapering field in Kaslo all to himself. But he still couldn't make ends meet. In September 1893, he was in court defending his paper, the *Kaslo-Slocan Examiner*, against actions launched by three of his employees seeking back pay. The Nelson *Miner*, sympathetic to Coy, noted: "Running a newspaper is not the easiest kind of puzzle in hard times, especially when those employed expect payment."[10] Coy settled with Margaret O'Rourke and R.E. Seysler, but he balked at paying out B.R. Atkins.

According to the testimony, Coy approached Atkins and told him he could no longer afford to keep him employed. Atkins responded by telling

Coy that if he was paid his back wages, he would quit immediately. Coy didn't have the money, so dismissed Atkins without pay. This didn't suit Atkins. He continued working. Coy told the court that "he was aware that Atkins was hanging around the office but added that he had incidentally mentioned to Atkins that if he did not cease loafing around the office he would get a policeman to assist him in keeping away."[11] Coy never called the policeman and was ordered to pay Atkins's back wages. Another of Coy's employees, Mary van Buren, also left the *Examiner*. She would make return trips to BC, but the attractive young woman moved to Los Angeles, where she would embark on a successful career as an actress. Seysler relocated to Wallace, Idaho, where he took on the management of a union newspaper, the *Idaho State Tribune*. Down Kootenay Lake at Nelson, David Bogle and E. Percy Whalley sold their interest in the Nelson *Miner* to Clive Phillipps-Wolley. Bogle's twin brother, Andrew, arrived from Britain. Together, the two Bogles tried to make a go of Bogleville, a townsite they were promoting at the foot of Trout Lake. The timing was most unfortunate.

By July 1893, the *Vancouver Daily World* reported that Bogleville was "completely deserted." Not quite. A visitor found David Bogle perched on the roof of his hotel with everything surrounding flooded. Not long after, a correspondent for the *Victoria Daily Times* reported that a voracious water rat, the only remaining tenant at the Bogles' hotel, had devoured all furnishings except for the chandeliers. Andrew Bogle was soon back in Britain, while David contemplated his next move.

After abandoning Kaslo, R.T. Lowery moved to up and coming Nakusp, whose star seemed to be waxing just as Kaslo's was waning. Lowery started a stationery store in Nakusp. Then, in October 1893, he started the *Nakusp Ledge* with Ananias Wallbridge and typesetter Ricardo Fraser. In an early edition, likely in reference to the earlier failure of Burke's bank in Kaslo, Lowery waggishly noted that "last spring we had a bank account. To-day we have no account of the bank."[12]

Lowery visited Kaslo shortly after starting the *Ledge*. There was no welcome mat. One correspondent was scathing in his criticism of Lowery's newspaper abilities. The failure of the *Kaslo Claim* had been entirely predictable, he felt, as Lowery was better suited to running a peanut stand than a newspaper. Lowery wasn't the only one to turn away from Kaslo, but unlike most others, his newspaper gave him a platform to rail against his former domicile. He claimed that the citizens of Kaslo wanted to lynch him for "speaking the truth."[13]

Colonel Coy decided in early 1894 that he was ready for a career change. Lowery visited Kaslo again in October 1893, just after E.E. Coy's court appearance. Lowery thought Colonel Coy "looked weary and worn as though his crown was all of thorns, and the farmers had ceased to bring in turnips for subscriptions."[14] Coy put the paper up for sale in February 1894. He had not been able to solve the puzzle of how to make money on a newspaper in the middle of a depression. Circulation had dwindled as the hard times dragged on. At first, it looked like Coy had a deal to sell the *Examiner* to Captain D.C. McMorris, most recently the purser on the steamship *Nelson*. However, Coy received a better offer and reneged on his agreement with McMorris. Instead, he sold the paper to Nelson businessman George Bigelow.

Bigelow admitted he was buying the operation on speculation but vowed to make improvements while he was looking for another buyer. He hired Will Hanks to edit and manage the paper, though Bigelow allies and fellow "oppositionists" Samuel Park "S.P." Tuck and David Bogle also took turns editing. Hanks had previously edited the *Tribune* in Great Falls, Montana. He had also been president of the Merchant's Bank of that city. The bank had failed in the Great Panic, and Hanks's time in BC may at least in part have been to avoid legal troubles south of the border.

The first edition of Bigelow's new paper—now rebranded as the *Kaslo Times*—came out on March 3. It was described by the *Victoria Daily Colonist* as "a clean and bright looking eight-page sheet that does great credit to those who are connected with it."[15] If it was to succeed, it would need to expand its subscription base. At the time of its relaunch, it had only six paid-up subscribers.

With the lingering clouds of the depression still weighing heavily and the collapse of silver prices, it might have seemed like things in the Slocan couldn't get much worse. Many residents were shocked then, in April 1894, when it was announced that the Methodist minister, James Turner, was being reassigned. Turner had worked hard and earned the respect of the prospectors and miners, whether they were believers or not. The *Nakusp Ledge* noted that few missionaries had been more successful than Turner. His departure would "cause many heartaches among the miners and settlers generally."[16] He left a legacy of fond memories.

In early May 1894, it was learned that Martin, the Presbyterian minister in Kaslo, would also be leaving his post to return to eastern Canada. Newly married but in poor health and in debt due to bad investments, he had likely had enough of the Comique and the hard times in West

Kootenay. In a happy instance of serendipity, however, the departures of the Reverends Martin and Turner were concurrent with the demise of the Theatre Comique. Martin, in particular, had fought for months against the Comique, but both men must have been pleased to see the curtain finally come down on the notorious "palace of sin." No doubt they felt they had played an important part in its closure, but others thought it a toss-up whether the end had been hastened by the crusade mounted by virtuous citizens or was simply a result of the hard economic times and Kaslo's incorporation.

There would be a provincial election in the summer of 1894. For the first time, the new Slocan communities would have an opportunity to express themselves at the ballot box. While there were no "party" politics at the time, many politicians had ties or sympathies with the federal Liberal or Conservative Parties. The sitting government of Premier Davie was generally Conservative in outlook, though it also included some members with Liberal leanings. Voting was open to British subjects—as long as they were male—and to Americans and other nationalities naturalized as Canadians, and to Kanakas (Hawaiians). Indigenous members and Chinese Canadians were not allowed to vote.

Given the large number of recent American arrivals in the Slocan, the voting requirements meant that the majority of the local population was ineligible to vote, leaving the electoral future of the district largely in the hands of a few Canadians and British expatriates. In Watson, for example, there were only twelve registered voters. Regardless, there was considerable local interest. When a Nelson *Tribune* correspondent visited New Denver in late January 1894, he was surprised to find the election "one of the principal topics of conversation."[17] This would also have surprised coastal pundits, who viewed the West Kootenay camps as "an exceedingly doubtful quantity in Provincial politics."[18]

In the wake of the Great Panic, there was much speculation on the election's outcome. Premier Davie could legitimately claim that he had little or no control over the worldwide downturn, but incumbent governments often suffered when their electorate was experiencing hard times. There was a redistribution bill on the agenda in the legislature in the weeks leading up to the election. In recognition of the expanding population, the West Kootenay riding would be given two representatives. Prior to the election of 1894, the Slocan was included in the West Kootenay riding, represented by J.M. Kellie. Kellie had been an opposition member when Premier Robson was in power but joined the government side when Premier Davie succeeded Robson.

The redistribution bill passed in February. The West Kootenay electoral district would be split into two ridings—north and south. Nomination conventions were held from February through April. Though the voting pool was small, there was no shortage of prospective parliamentarians willing to throw their hats into that pool. It was expected that Kellie would run for the government in the north riding. D.A. McDougald, the proprietor of the Leland House in Nakusp, offered himself up as an oppositionist candidate. But it was William M. Brown, a Revelstoke hotel keeper, who got the nod.

There was no incumbent in the new southern riding, so the field was wide open to both government and oppositionist candidates. The movers and shakers behind the oppositionist forces in the south riding included newspapermen John Houston, David Bogle, and George Bigelow. It was clear that Bigelow would use his newly acquired *Kaslo Times* (née *Kaslo-Slocan Examiner*) as a mouthpiece for the opposition forces up the lake.

There was plenty of discussion in Kaslo, New Denver, Three Forks, and other Slocan camps about who could best represent them in Victoria. Race and nationality played an important role. Government supporter John Retallack, though of English sentiment, declared himself a "Canadian boy" who should be entitled to the same rights as any Canadian-born British subject. English-born John Keen, on the other hand, insisted the district would be better represented by a "good, live English man" rather than a "North American Chinaman"—a derogatory term that English expatriates sometimes used to insult Canadians.[19]

After the meetings, debates, and backroom wrangling, the candidates for the southern West Kootenay riding were finally announced. Kaslo sawmill operator G.O. Buchanan, who had long had political aspirations and Liberal sympathies, emerged as the government candidate. A number of Kaslo's British expatriates had written to Buchanan urging him to run. His campaign would be managed by G.M. Sproat. David Bogle sought the oppositionist nomination, but it went to J. Fred Hume. The respected Nelson merchant and businessman's campaign would be managed by John Houston.

In mid-May, Hume gave a speech in Kaslo's now-empty Theatre Comique building. The building was full nearly to capacity, but not all attendees were Hume supporters. A large contingent from the Buchanan camp also turned up. The Nelson *Miner*, a government paper, reported that Hume was met with "feeble" applause and said "very little of importance."[20]

Shortly after Hume's appearance, G.O. Buchanan also gave his opening speech in the vacant Comique. For him, the venue was personal. A prominent opponent of the Comique, he expressed his satisfaction with this more "legitimate" use of the building, and he likely played up his role in having the Comique shut down. Buchanan defended the government's record and to the best of his ability, promised to "protect and promote the interests of the district."[21]

Hume barnstormed through the mining camps in July. He was greeted warmly at stops in Watson, Three Forks, and New Denver. He was supported in Three Forks with speeches from R.B. Kerr, David Bogle, and E.C. Carpenter. Buchanan held a meeting in Three Forks too. The *Tribune* noted that Buchanan's campaign could not find a British subject to chair the meeting. Instead, Curly Robinson, an American, was elected to the chair. Unfamiliar with the Canadian political system, Curly introduced Buchanan as a "delegate for congress."[22]

The election was set for mid-July. The debates and rhetoric became more heated and rancorous as the date approached. In the weeks immediately preceding the election, Premier Davie toured West Kootenay, making stops in Nakusp, New Denver, Three Forks, Kaslo, and Nelson. He was shadowed for much of the journey by opposition members Colin Sword and Thomas Kitchen. Davie gave a speech in Nakusp, and Sword spoke on behalf of the opposition. Kitchen, a leader of the oppositionists, declined to join the debate while Davie was there but denounced the premier after he left.

After touring the Slocan Star, Davie headed into Three Forks. He expected a good crowd as the camp was doing relatively well despite the downturn. However, he faced a quandary. It was Sunday morning, and his candidate, G.O. Buchanan, had urged him not to hold a political meeting on a Sunday. Davie sidestepped the issue by calling his Sunday appearance in Three Forks a "reception." We don't know if this was enough to mollify Buchanan, but we can be reasonably sure that the throng of miners and workers who attended the "reception"—most of whom were less devout than Buchanan—didn't much care whether it was Sunday or not; they were just happy for an opportunity to support the government or air their grievances.

The next day, the premier was in Kaslo. After addressing a crowd there, he headed to Nelson for a showdown with the oppositionists. The meeting was organized by opposition supporters, who invited Davie and government candidate Buchanan to say a few words. George Bigelow was in the chair. The speakers, in order of appearance, were Fred Hume, Buchanan, John

Houston, Premier Davie, and, last but certainly not least, R.B. Kerr, who was likely eager to take on Davie outside the courtroom.

The meeting included the usual mix of self-congratulatory speeches and politically motivated attacks, with Kerr, in particular, delivering a fiery blast critical of the government. Davie felt disadvantaged in the time allotted to him. He felt he did not have a full opportunity to rebut some of Kerr's points. According to Houston's Nelson *Tribune*, biased in favour of the oppositionists, Davie insinuated after the meeting that the opposition was afraid to give him more time to respond to Kerr. For his part, Kerr offered to debate the premier anytime, anywhere. Kerr was a gifted debater and by all accounts had the best of Davie.

Davie was in Nelson when the ballots were counted. He was gracious when it was clear that Hume would defeat Buchanan. He joined a crowd at the Phair Hotel celebrating Hume's victory; perhaps Davie even joined in on some of the songs. There were 909 registered voters in the South Kootenay riding and approximately 683 votes cast. Buchanan carried Kaslo and the small communities of Rykert's and Duncan City but lost to Hume everywhere else. Nelson and New Denver were particularly hard on Buchanan. Overall, discounting spoiled ballots, Hume won the contest 401 votes to Buchanan's 258.

The *Nakusp Ledge* speculated—with good cause—that Buchanan (a devout Methodist and confirmed teetotaller) likely lost votes in the rough and ready Slocan district "because he sang hymns in church sometimes and was not an adept at studying astronomy through inverted ale bottles."[23] A commentator for the *Province* later said of Slocan voters that "it is nevertheless a curious fact that many electors here think more of a man's power to drink whiskey than they do of his political creed."[24] Buchanan and Davie at least had some consolation when it was learned that Kellie had won the North Kootenay riding. Pat Gannon of Three Forks had spoken in favour of Fred Hume, but we don't know who he voted for. Whoever it was, Gannon's dog was reportedly so disgusted he crossed the border to join the Republican Party.

THE CAMPAIGN LEADING UP TO the election had provided a brief diversion, but the hard times had not gone away. Drunkenness was prevalent in the Slocan right from the start but was perhaps more common and visible during the depression. John Gibb "J.G." Devlin, a Scot from Glasgow, was better known as "the Gunner from Galway." His nickname came from his habit of singing the song for which he was named. He regularly sang it when he was in his cups, and he was regularly in his cups. Devlin was no stranger to the underside of the law. In 1887, he was arrested in Toronto for blowing a safe. In December 1894, he decided to make his home in Three Forks. He soon ran into problems. Gold Commissioner Fitzstubbs had Devlin arrested after one of the Gunner's drunken bouts and tried to make him pay for his trip to the jail in Nelson. The story that later emerged—whether true or not—was that the Gunner switched places with the rookie policeman placed in charge of him. When they arrived in Nelson, the Gunner was wearing the uniform, and the policeman was in custody.

With the election over, Bigelow and Houston lost interest in the *Kaslo Times* and were only too happy to bequeath the operation to David Bogle. There was likely another reason too: profitability, or the lack thereof. The *Times* had come out strongly in the election in support of Hume over native Kasloite G.O. Buchanan. This would not have sat well with friends and supporters of Buchanan. As historian Duane Smith has noted, in politics, most western newspapers threw their support completely behind one side or another, thereby alienating a large portion of their readership. Advertisements and subscriptions to the paper did not meet expectations. The *Times* threatened to pull up stakes and leave Kaslo if the business community there was not willing to support it.

The support did not materialize, and Bogle decided that New Denver, where most voters had strongly backed Hume, might be a more amenable home. The printing plant was packed up and moved to New Denver, and the paper was rechristened the *Slocan Times*. The first issue appeared September 1, 1894. Will Hanks continued as business manager, and Bogle took on the role of editor. Ricardo Fraser, who had once set type for R.T. Lowery, also worked for the paper. Lowery, who himself was interested in the New Denver market, was scathing in his opinion of the paper, run by that "intellectual giant, D.B. Bogle."[25] Lowery, who perhaps felt betrayed by Fraser's involvement, was convinced the new paper would be a "losing speculation."[26] Lowery stuck by his friend Bill Pratt, who "manfully sticks to the little camp, and prints cheering words to brace up the boys who first made the town."[27] John Houston's Nelson *Tribune* had a much different opinion of Bogle's relocated sheet, describing the *Times* as "newsy, brainy and independent."[28] The *Times* continued its anti-government and anti-establishment sniping.

To R.T. Lowery's chagrin, the *Slocan Times* soon gained the advantage in New Denver. It was all too much for Bill Pratt. He decided to move his *Slocan Prospector* and its cylinder press to Three Forks. Pratt was a staunch Republican in American politics and a strong supporter of BC's Premier Davie and his government. Perhaps he felt that local New Denver readers would be more inclined to subscribe to the *Times*. Or he may have just felt that the grass was greener in Three Forks. Like some other business owners, he had been struggling in New Denver.

The *Kootenay Mail*—like Lowery's *Nakusp Ledge*—lamented Pratt's departure from New Denver, though it would not earn any kudos for calling New Denver a "village":

> The *Prospector*, owned and edited by W.D. Pratt, has up anchor and sailed away to Three Forks, "driven from home" by the advent of adverse *Times*. The *Prospector* was born in the village at a time when the site was dotted with the blackened stumps created by the camp fires of the first settlers, and stayed with it through hard times and prosperity, never forgetting that its mission was to make known to the outside world that there was no ore so rich as Slocan ore nor a town so well placed as New Denver.

R.T. Lowery's *Ledge* office, New Denver, c. 1898. R.T. Lowery, Charles Smitheringale, Harry Walker. Photographer unknown. IMAGE COURTESY OF JANICE WILKIN

But times have changed since then, old pal;
Hard times has come to stay.
New faces and new men, old pal.
Have driven us away.[29]

Pratt would thrive for a time in Three Forks, but John Houston wasn't impressed with the first Three Forks issue, speculating that "the *Prospector* is now edited by the mule on whose back the press was packed from New Denver."[30] Pratt called Houston's criticisms "churlish" and accused him of being envious of the *Prospector*'s success in Three Forks.[31] In early 1895, Pratt delighted in announcing that two of Houston's most valued employees, including veteran newspaperman Randall Kemp, had deserted the *Tribune* for the *Prospector*. Kemp was a skilled newspaperman and contributed to several Slocan newspapers in addition to the *Prospector*.

It also seems that R.T. Lowery got some satisfaction in his rivalry with Bogle and the *Slocan Times*. Lowery first contemplated starting a newspaper in Rossland. He visited in 1893, and in 1894 issued a prospectus for the *Rossland Paystreak*; but never followed through. Instead, Lowery—along with Charles E. "C.E." Smitheringale—relocated the *Nakusp Ledge* to New Denver in late 1894. The *Slocan Times* didn't roll out the welcome mat. Bogle thought that Lowery had surely established his reputation as a "humorist" for introducing a paper "into a field where there is but scanty browsing."[32] Indeed, and Lowery had the last laugh.

The paper Pratt had dubbed the "Bogle Bugle" ceased publication shortly afterwards.[33] Lowery later claimed some of the credit, but Bogle acknowledged the difficulties of running a newspaper in a country where ready money had disappeared. However, there was life after death for the *Times*. In January 1895, Bogle got a telegram from John Houston urging him to move the paper from New Denver to Rossland, the fast-growing camp tucked away on the margins of the Monashee Mountains to the south. So, the pioneering printing press that had perhaps been shipped down Kootenay River and up Kootenay Lake to Kaslo by Mark Musgrove, and then hauled over the mountains to New Denver, now made the return trip over the mountains and down the lake on its journey to Rossland, where it would be reborn as the *Rossland Miner*. Houston's rivals at the Nelson *Miner* summed up the travails of the *Times*: "After having failed to charm the people of Kaslo and being driven from New Denver by the energetic and bright little *Ledge*, the defunct *Slocan Times* is transporting its dyspeptic plant to Rossland."[34]

By the end of July 1895, Bogle could claim sole ownership of the *Rossland Miner*, but he sold out soon afterwards. Unfortunately, after some initial success, Lowery's friend Pratt could not sustain his operations in Three Forks. He briefly moved the paper to Kaslo, where R.W. Northey, late of the *Kootenay Mail*, joined as "all-round" man, before following Bogle in a final, unsuccessful move to Rossland.[35] Lowery lamented the passing of the *Prospector*'s Three Forks iteration: "It climbed the golden stairs a few days ago and was deposited in the journalistic boneyard."[36]

Despite the failing newspapers, the economy was picking up, and with the newly created newspaper vacuum in Kaslo, Lowery decided to revisit the site of his first BC newspaper. As early as January 1894, he felt he had been forgiven by the citizens of Kaslo, who had seen "the error of their ways."[37] Just before launching his new paper, the *Kaslo Claim Relocated*, Lowery travelled to Vancouver to solicit advertisers. At about the same time, he got some help with the *Ledge* when W.P. Evans, formerly of the *Edmonton Bulletin* and short-lived *Edmonton Times*, landed in New Denver. Evans appeared to be in it for the long haul. In September 1895, his wife and son joined him from New Westminster. By September of the following year, he had a new house nearly built. Another newspaperman on his way to the Slocan in late July 1895 was Charles Davis of Oregon's *St. Helens Mist*, but we don't know if he was looking for work in New Denver. If he was, he would be disappointed. He fared better in Rossland, where he got a job at the LeRoi mine.

The first edition of the *Kaslo Claim Relocated* appeared in August 1895. Iowa-born Dave King, ex–railway camp cook and former editor of the *Tekoa Globe* and *Spokane Daily Times*, oversaw printing operations until December, when he abandoned the press for work at the Dardanelles mine. John Langstaff came to Lowery's rescue. Langstaff had apprenticed as a printer in Vancouver, but he was a victim of the 1893 depression. He relocated to New Denver in 1895 and took up prospecting. But then he heard from Lowery. Langstaff donned a backpack and hiked thirty miles through the snow to help Lowery get the *Claim* out.

THE GREAT PANIC OF 1893 was a major setback for the Slocan and caught everyone off guard. Recovery would be difficult, but those still left in the Slocan were determined to restore their camps to prosperity and productivity. However, the path to prosperity would not be easy. The hard times would last for another couple of years.

Many of the American "croakers" and idlers who had filled the streets of Kaslo before the Great Panic returned to their homes south of the border. Those who remained were invested in the Slocan and Canada. J.J. Barclay, who had managed the books for Burke's bank, stayed in the Slocan after the bank's failure and turned to mining investments. Interviewed on a visit to Portland in late 1893, he acknowledged the early tensions between Americans and Canadians but felt that "the hatchet has now been buried. The Canadians join with the Americans to celebrate the Fourth of July, and the latter always are ready for a good time on the Queen's birthday."[38]

If things seemed to be settling down in the Slocan, circumstances were much worse south of the border. From California to Ohio, thousands of unemployed men were organizing in "armies" to march on Washington. Among the marchers was a young man from San Francisco named Jack London. He got as far as Niagara Falls, New York, but after spending thirty days in jail on vagrancy charges, he decided to head back to the west coast by way of Canada. Living a hobo's life—like many others on both sides of the border—he rode the rails from Ottawa to Vancouver.

London passed through the northern margin of West Kootenay in the fall of 1894. It has been rumoured that he spent some time working in West Kootenay, and certainly he knew the area. But on that trip in 1894, he wasn't looking for work. Nearly dead with cold and desperately hungry, he crawled out of a boxcar just east of Kicking Horse Pass and scrounged a few scraps of lunch leftovers and a splash of coffee from some sympathetic railway workers. A freight train got him over Kicking Horse Pass but stranded him just short of Rogers Pass. After two days without food, he started walking out towards Revelstoke. Though he would later experience the excitement and exhilaration of the last great mining rush of the nineteenth century, the poverty and hardship he witnessed on his trip across North America would stay with him for a lifetime and form a solid base for his socialist leanings.

10

NATURE'S WRATH

THE SPRING OF 1894 IN West Kootenay and most of BC was generally wet and cold. However, in late May and early June, the weather turned very hot and quickly dried out the forests and melted the snowpack, leading to widespread flooding. The Fraser River experienced the worst flooding ever recorded both before and since. West Kootenay was hit hard too. Rivers and creeks were swollen with snowmelt, and Kootenay, Arrow, and Slocan Lakes rose to record levels. CPR tracks were washed away on low-lying lands. Hundreds of travellers were stranded in Vancouver, and hundreds more in isolated mountain stations all along the line.

CPR surveyor Henry Cambie witnessed some of the human tragedy: "Never did I behold such pitiful scenes and such helpless people . . . the ranchers are homeless and without food and in many cases the end will come soon if they are not rescued."[1] Workmen on the Fraser River near Ruby Creek came across a small raft with the dead bodies of an entire family. All five members had been lashed securely to the raft.

The waters of Slocan Lake and its incoming creeks had been rising for weeks. Late in May, Carpenter Creek was described as "an angry stream."[2] Bridges were washed out up and down the creek. By early June the lake was rising a foot a day. Logs, lumber, and anything else on the shoreline that could float was carried into the lake. Then, at about five o'clock in the afternoon on Sunday, June 3, a storm struck New Denver from the north with an intensity no one there had before experienced. Sweeping through town, it left a swath of destruction in its wake. The government wharf was broken in two and thrown out in the lake, to crash later on the shore near Wilson Creek. A canoe pulled up on the lakeshore was picked up by the wind and blown over the Slocan Hotel, coming to rest at the shoemaker's shop uptown.

Some buildings were twisted into misshapen caricatures of the carpenter's craft. Others were destroyed entirely. The local madam rushed out into the street to confess her sins after her building was shifted several feet by the storm. The winds knocked down hundreds of trees. A logjam on Carpenter Creek added to the havoc. Residents along the Carpenter Creek flats were forced to move to higher ground.

Other communities on the lake suffered too. The new camp at Wilson Creek was reported "down among the fishes."[3] At Silverton, the Alpha ore house was submerged, and a store owned by Walter Middaugh was destroyed. Two men in a boat travelling from New Denver to Four Mile Creek had a narrow escape when the storm hit. Their boat was tossed onto the shore and turned into "kindling," but they both escaped serious injury.

Three Forks was hit hard too. While residents didn't have to contend with a rising lake, they had other worries. The storm cleared the timber at the lower end of town "as effectively as a Missouri wood chopper."[4] Brush clearing fires in the upper part of town were fanned into a fury by the winds. Buildings were quickly set ablaze. Police Constable Sandilands organized a bucket brigade, which saved some of the buildings. However, six houses along the junction of Seaton Creek and the north fork of Carpenter Creek were not so lucky. All were consumed by the flames. The whole town might have been lost, but a timely downpour saved the day.

As bad as it was in New Denver and Three Forks, it was worse in Kaslo, which would soon be known as the "city of calamities."[5] Kootenay Lake and Kaslo Creek rose to record levels. Within days, most buildings east of Third Street were flooded and could only be reached by boat. The "lavishly furnished" two-storey building on A Avenue occupied by madam Ida Williams and her inmates sank, along with a piano and other luxuries.[6] As many as a dozen houses belonging to prostitutes—"disreputable women" as described by G.O. Buchanan[7]—were washed away.

Then came the great storm of June 3. The day was oppressively hot. Late in the afternoon, successive waves of hot wind blew through town. Mrs. Mackay was on the verandah of the Leland Hotel having tea with a neighbour when she noticed unusual cloud patterns in the sky and a peculiar stillness in the air. A dark cloud appeared. Within minutes, the stillness was succeeded by hot winds and then a terrific gust. The full brunt of the storm followed and raged unchecked for almost an hour. Fires burning along the wagon road raged out of control. Huge waves on Kootenay Lake struck the town with unbridled ferocity. The winds picked up almost everything in their path and hurled the debris across town and out onto the lake. Before Mrs. Mackay and her neighbour could get inside, the wind swept away their tablecloth and dishes. Foreign objects were flying about in all directions.

Dogs and cats were picked up by the winds or swallowed by the waters. The storm carried away more than fifty buildings. The Galena Trading Company's store and the new jail were both washed out into Kootenay Lake. The Great Northern Hotel went too. But the day the storm hit had started clear and fine. Many residents were enjoying a relaxing Sunday. Some even took their boats out on the lake, which early on was as calm and placid as a millpond. People were curious to see the flooded and floating buildings. Mr. A. McGregor, a contractor, decided to take his wife for an outing on the lake. He drifted a bit too far and, seeing the oncoming storm, frantically tried to reach shore. Almost there, the boat was overturned. Mrs. McGregor disappeared under the storm-driven waves.

Based on the contemporary descriptions, the June 3 storm that ravaged West Kootenay was likely a tornado that touched down in both New Denver and Kaslo. The *Kaslo Times* was one of the few newspapers to describe it as such. The Nelson *Tribune* called it a cyclone. While rare, tornadoes are not unknown in the interior of BC. Altogether, the tornado, floods, and storms that swept through BC in 1894 caused millions of dollars of damage, leaving a trail of destruction from Vancouver Island to the province's farthest reaches.

"Kaslo during the flood," June 1894. Photographer unknown. IMAGE COURTESY OF THE ROYAL BC MUSEUM AND ARCHIVES

Kaslo had little time to recover from the storm when, within a week, it was struck by another disaster. Kaslo Creek was flooded with runoff from the snowmelt and jammed with logs and debris. In the middle of the night, the creek suddenly changed its course and cut a new path through Kaslo and out to the lake. Several cabins were directly in the way of the creek's new path. People who had gone to bed thankful they had survived the great storm were now in a panic to escape the raging creek. A small boy who had lived in a cabin nearby, when asked how his family had fared, answered: "Oh, the house is alright but the lot has gone."[8] Fortunately, no lives were lost. However, more buildings were carried out to the lake, to join those already bobbing incongruously on the waves. A visiting newspaper correspondent was shocked:

> The hospital, back broken and canted in different ways, stands half buried in shingle in the middle of the stream. Over against it and around, the houses are tilted about and pushed out of their places, knocked endways and sideways and upside down. Some have a side or a front torn off. Some have opened out until the roof lies flat on the floors, and now and again, one sails calmly out into the lake like a ship going to sea.[9]

One day, the steamboat *Nelson* found the hardware store floating peacefully in the middle of the lake. The *Nelson* hooked a rope on to it and towed it back home.

The floods and great storm caused havoc with the transportation routes in and out of the Slocan. The Kaslo wagon road was littered with hundreds of fallen trees, and whole sections were washed out. In some places, the road would have to be rerouted and rebuilt. No one used the wagon road as much as G.W. Hughes, and people thought it a sure thing he would be helping with repairs. He almost didn't get the chance. He was walking along the road into Three Forks just before the worst of the flooding when the section he was on suddenly slipped into the creek, taking him with it. Fortunately, he was carrying his coat with him, and his companions were able to pull him out using the coat as a life rope.

After the terrible storms and floods of June, Slocan residents had a brief respite. At the end of July, though, disaster struck again. This time it was fire, always a danger in mining camps, built as they were with wooden buildings cheek by jowl. As dry as parchment in the summer, they were stoked with roaring stoves and fireplaces through the winter.

Fire was a constant threat. The *Kaslo-Slocan Examiner* noted that there was hardly a day in Kaslo in the summer of 1892 when a fire didn't break out in one or another of the tents littering the camp. Fire brigades were critical. These locally organized fire brigades were reasonably effective for small fires—a hearth fire caught early for example—but they were no match at all for the destructive power of a forest fire.

Several small forest fires leftover from the storms burned intermittently throughout the late spring and early summer of 1894. One, started by lightning, was reported "burning merrily" in mid-June in the forest beside the Kaslo wagon road near Watson. Another was blazing along the trail between New Denver and Three Forks. In mid-July, two men travelling the trail had their faces badly blistered trying to force their way through. Less than two weeks later, on July 31, the fire rushed towards Three Forks. Leaping the north fork of Carpenter Creek, it reduced eight cabins to ashes before moving on in the direction of Bear Lake and Watson. The flames quieted down overnight, but the next morning the fire crossed Seaton Creek.

Some thought the camp would be spared, as it had been in June when Constable Sandilands and the rain saved the day. However, it was not to be spared this time. Reminiscent of the earlier storms, rising winds stirred the flames into a rage: "About 1:30 PM a terrific cyclone joined forces with the red demon and together, they made another rush at Three Forks."[10] One eyewitness described the fire bursting out like an "explosion." This time the flames swept through the "pronged city," burning buildings indiscriminately. The terrified inhabitants sought whatever refuge they could find. Just outside Three Forks, Arthur Farwell, who was surveying a claim, only had time to place his surveying equipment in a tunnel before running to safety. Many residents escaped to the ore house of the Slocan Star just below the town. Others fled into the mines, where they ran the risk of asphyxiation. With nowhere else to go, a few were forced into the waters of Carpenter and Seaton Creeks. Burning cinders were falling like fiery golden leaves in a nightmarish vision of autumn in hell. The clothes of Mrs. Bowen's children caught fire as the young ones desperately tried to escape the flames. A guest at the Bowen House fainted and had to be carried to safety. Mr. and Mrs. Weaver, who ran a bathhouse, fled to the creek, where they spent two hours up to their necks in water before they were rescued.

After consuming Three Forks, the winds carried the flames to Bear Lake and Watson. Many Bear Lake residents saved themselves only by paddling logs out on to the lake. The log hotel owned by Fred Jarvis was destroyed, as was everything else in the camp, including Gorman West's hotel and Lane Gilliam's feedstock. At Watson, twenty buildings were consumed. Thirteen women and children found safety in Ed Atherton's fireproof root cellar. Atherton, covered with a wet blanket, stood at the front door throwing water at the building while terrified women and children huddled inside. The roof caught fire and a pony tethered twenty feet away burned to death. Assorted domestic animals were "roasted," including several pigs, a cow, and five horses. Fortunately, the women and children survived.

For the residents of Watson, Atherton's root cellar offered a convenient refuge. Others had to travel further afield. The course of the flames was unpredictable, and those seeking safety gambled on escape routes. Wildlife, too, sought shelter or escape. One observer noted that rabbits, whistlers, and other ground squirrels were so thick on the patches of ground untouched by the fires that they could hardly be kicked aside by their two-legged kin. It must have been a chaotic scene, with men, women, children, and animals running this way and that, desperately trying to outrun, outflank, or outsmart the flames. The *Nakusp Ledge* described it as "a wild rush for life" and, with the election just over, wryly noted that no one stopped to "talk politics."[11] Kaslo was at some risk too. W.D Pinkston, a mining machinery man from Butte, Montana, reported Kaslo residents "trusting to luck and nothing else."[12] Fortunately, luck was with the "city of calamities" this time, and Kaslo escaped the deadly fires.

A Three Forks businessman, Jack Lowes, has left us a stirring first-hand account of his adventures during the fires. Once he realized the fire was coming directly at Three Forks and there was no hope of stopping it, he rushed into Lemon's store to save as much as he could. He managed to get the counter scales, two cases of canned goods, two stoves, and his bedding out to the middle of the street when he had to drop everything and run for his life. In the end, he saved only the clothes he was wearing—but he was thankful to get out alive. John Winter, who was running the hotel's dining room, had better luck and escaped the flames after retrieving most of his clothes. Herb Pitts and Bert Crane were each left with only a pair of pants, a shirt, and a hat. With Three Forks a smouldering ruin, Lowes decided to make his way to Bear Lake and then out to Kaslo. He left his partner, Crane, sitting on the only remaining goods left from the hotel—a barrel of whisky saved by rolling it into the creek.

Lowes got about a half mile out of Three Forks when he came across five head of beef. He tried to drive them back to Three Forks, but the way was blocked by fallen trees. Giving up on the cattle, he started for Bear Lake again. He made it about a mile and a half, but the fire had jumped ahead of him, and he had to turn back. He retreated to a tunnel that Gorman West had driven the previous winter. While waiting there, he was joined by about thirty more refugees from Three Forks. Lowes and three others tried again to make for Bear Lake, but they were again forced back. Lowes then decided on a different tactic. With E.C. Carpenter, he tried to return to Three Forks. It's not exactly clear what they hoped to accomplish by returning to Three Forks, since it would have been particularly hard for Carpenter to see the town he founded in complete ruin. In any event, they were unable to complete the journey when they were cut off by more flames. Instead, they had to make for the relative safety of Seaton Creek.

At Seaton Creek, they found packer Brown with his animals and Bill English with his four-horse wagon, huddled together in a patch of undergrowth. English had his wagon backed into Seaton Creek. Leaving Brown and English, Lowes and Carpenter worked their way along the creek until they returned to Gorman West's tunnel at about four in the afternoon, where G.W. Hughes had since arrived. Not one to give up easily, Lowes again set out for Bear Lake, this time with Hughes. They hiked about a mile before they were forced by the flames to detour up the mountainside. They had a lucky break when the winds died down and they were able to get to the road and reach Hughes's main camp just outside Bear Lake City. They had hoped to get food there but found nothing but ashes and the scorched iron remains of Hughes's premium wagons.

Proceeding to Bear Lake City, Lowes and Hughes found Gorman West and another man surveying the ruins. West had managed to save two bottles of whisky and a bottle of wine that he was keeping cool in the lake. The bottles were retrieved, and the four men passed them around while sharing experiences. Lowes learned that the men at Hughes's camp had seen the fire coming and had hitched up two four-horse teams. Taking along six other animals, they reached Bear Lake City ahead of the fire. They unhitched the teams and saved themselves and their animals by taking to the lake. Lane Gilliam, who had a camp at Bear Lake City, managed to get to his pack animals in time to saddle them up and run them down the road to safety. Gilliam rode his own animal up the trail to the Solo mine to warn the men there. It was believed that packer Hugh Mann was not so lucky, and it was feared that his four-horse team was lost.

As the flames died down, several deaths were rumoured. There had been some worry that Callahan, the telegraph operator, and another man,

Frank Price, had perished, but both men turned up alive—though Callahan was badly burned. Some accounts of bodies being found in Carpenter Creek and along the trails included the report of a charred corpse on the route between Three Forks and Sandon Creek. There was relief when none of the rumours proved true. Nobody was asphyxiated in the tunnels, and nobody drowned in the creeks. Still, given the large number of prospectors up in the mountains, some feared that "perhaps a pile of charred bones may some day be met with to tell the sad fate of some unknown who perished in that awful avalanche of flame and smoke."[13]

Relief turned to dismay when Three Forks resident Joe Forbes succumbed to injuries he suffered during the fire. He had been carrying water in a futile effort to fight the flames when a tree fell on him. His back broken, he lingered for two days in great agony before dying. The Nelson *Tribune* paid Forbes a well-deserved tribute: "He met his death, after a life of hardship unknown and poor, in the attempt to save other people's property. Such is the life and similar too often is the death of the prospector."[14] Forbes's death cast a pall over the homeless survivors of Three Forks. One prominent businessman—who had lost everything in the fire—put things into perspective: "This accident is worse than the loss of the town."[15]

On the ground, the Slocan Star ore house at Three Forks was saved thanks to precautions taken by Byron White. Atherton's root cellar was saved in Watson, and the slaughterhouse operated by Billy Perdue survived. Almost every other building in Three Forks, Watson, and Bear Lake City was destroyed. The loss of the Three Forks Hotel was especially hard felt. The newspaper headlines summed it up well: "The Red Demon cremates Three Forks, Bear Lake and Watson." The July fire completely devastated the three camps. More than a hundred buildings were destroyed in the inferno, including the sawmill at Bear Lake. Of Three Forks, it was reported that "practically nothing was saved, as there was no secure place to store goods. The fireproof cellars in connection with two of the stores caved in and the valuables contained therein destroyed."[16]

Twelve hundred pounds of dynamite and detonators in Lemon's cellar survived the fire. "The powder was removed the next day while the boxes were still hot."[17] Little else in the cellar survived. Rummaging through the ruins, Herb Pitts managed to salvage his charred account books. Some of Lemon's books, badly burnt, were also saved. Remarkably, some bacon and hams stored in Wilson and Burns's cellar made it through the flames, along with a few hundred dollars' worth of case goods.

At Watson, four hotels and three stables were destroyed in addition to Atherton's store. Another ten buildings were destroyed at the small camp at Sandon Creek. Many residents lost everything but the clothes they were wearing. Some losses were due to the fire—others to looting. While no specific accusations were made, there were plenty of suspicious circumstances. Six hundred dollars was missing from a trunk in Lemon's cellar. Five hundred dollars was missing from another cellar, and a woman reported losing the $150 that had been tucked into a pocket in her skirt.

The losses for Jack Watson were devastating. Kaslo pioneer G.O. Buchanan later recalled "the rising town of Watson went up from earth in a chariot of fire."[18] In late August Watson wrote to his sweetheart in Scotland and provided more details of the fire:

> "Watson" was completely gutted and of course besides losing three good building[s] the standing of the place has been considerably hurt, thereby materially affecting the condition of my pocket book . . . The fire left me nothing except the clothes I stood up in—books, papers and everything I had was licked up by the flames, the only single thing I saved being my grandfather's watch which I had in a safe in Kaslo.[19]

In the aftermath of the fire, the little camp at Sproule's on Kaslo Creek turned into a refugee camp as it filled up with the crowds of exhausted men, women, and children who had escaped the fires. The Kaslo Relief Committee, with government funds leftover from the recent flood, sent wagons with blankets and other provisions to aid the homeless. Other refugees headed out by way of New Denver.

The damages roads and bridges suffered during the storms and floods had not yet been fully repaired when the fires struck. More trees, toppled by the forest fires, fell on the Kaslo wagon road and other trails. Many bridges and much of the wooden cribbing and corduroy work on the wagon road were burned beyond repair. Telegraph lines were hit hard. Some that survived the heavy winds succumbed to the fires. The mines suffered too. Cabins and other buildings were destroyed at the Alamo, Queen Bess, Young Dominion, Payne, and Noble Five. Steve Bailey narrowly escaped with his life. Twenty-five Noble Five miners saved themselves by taking refuge in the mine's tunnel. One of them, John Ward, graphically described the scene when he reached Three Forks: "You have had a fire here but I tell you there were oceans of fire round us up yonder."[20]

Just at the time the fires were raging through the Slocan, Mrs. E.W. Ferguson of Chicago, the wife of one of the owners of the Surprise mine, was in Kaslo preparing to cross the Noble Five divide and see the mines for herself. Donning a pair of bloomers, she set out with her husband and his party. She gave the following account:

> The day after our party reached Kaslo Mountain forest fires started up and swept great tracts. The flames were so fierce that they jumped hundreds of feet. The trees are covered with a hanging maze that in fire is like tinder. High up in the mountains, where the fire did not reach, our travelers were afterward told that the men thought it was a volcanic eruption, the sight was one so grand and awe-inspiring. Droves of mules used as pack animals and men who had escaped the fire only half clad fled down the mountains into Kaslo.[21]

The West Kootenay forest fires of 1894 were cataclysmic. Their effects would be felt for decades to come. Most Slocan residents were too close to the action to see the bigger picture, but William Drewry wasn't. In the summer of 1894, the provincial government surveyor was camped south of Kootenay Lake, 7,200 feet above sea level, looking out over an apocalyptic vision: "From the neighbouring peaks it was observed that apparently most of the surrounding country was on fire, great volumes of smoke rising from Slocan district, both sides of Kootenay Lake, Sixteen-Mile Creek, Salmon River and Slocan River. During the greater part of three weeks, the smoke was so dense as to be painful to the eyes, even at our height above the sea."[22] Drewry lamented the loss of old growth timber: "The damage done cannot now be measured in money, for it will be felt most years to come . . . I do not think I am going too far in saying that at least one-fourth of these forests have been destroyed, much of it beyond redemption."[23]

THE REVERENDS TURNER AND MARTIN were not there for the worst of the fires. Their absence and lack of comfort was keenly felt. However, a replacement for Turner was announced not long after the floods and just before the fires struck. The new minister was Albert John Gaebel. He arrived in Nakusp in mid-July but likely didn't get to New Denver until after the worst of the fires. In his mid-twenties, A.J. Gaebel was born and raised in Ontario. It didn't take long for him to make an impression, but perhaps not of the kind he was intending. It rained in the Slocan in late August, giving residents a welcome respite from the lingering forest fires. In one of his early sermons, Gaebel announced that he had prayed for rain and the raindrops began falling. He prayed harder, and the rain came down in torrents, thus proving the efficacy of prayer. The *Inland Sentinel* of Kamloops carried a largely verbatim account of his sermon:

> A few days ago, New Denver town was threatened by fire and storm. The heavens were black with smoke and everybody was looking up and saying "I wish we could get a good shower," "I hope it will rain," etc., but no one seemed to express any faith in getting the blessing by prayer. My heart was pouring forth pleadings for the needed rain and the few drops that came seemed to me as the "sound and abundance of rain." At midnight I was awakened by the pattering of a few drops on the shingles, and I lifted my soul in thankfulness to the Lord, because he was still mindful of his people. I had scarcely despatched the first message of thanksgiving, when the rains descended in torrents till the waters ran in streams about the house. The answer of prayer was so clear to me, that I could not mistake the fulfillment of our Master's promise and the thought came to my mind that showers of spiritual blessings were lingering over us ready to be poured out.[24]

Gaebel went on to tell those in attendance that though "the sky is black with clouds of disappointment, losses and discouragement and we can hear the thunders of financial bursts, and bankruptcy," salvation was at hand for those who had faith.

Gaebel endured a certain amount of ridicule over his claims, especially from R.T. Lowery, who did not suffer the church or those who represented it with any degree of tolerance, regardless of denomination. However, Lowery was prepared to throw his lot in with Gaebel if by prayer the minister could raise the price of silver. Lowery went further and, rather bizarrely, questioned Gaebel's manliness: "He is a fine specimen of physical strength and it would be more manly on his part to earn a good living hammering a drill than to endeavor to scare people into being saints instead of common sinners that most of us will always remain."[25] Lowery's sarcastic skewering of Gaebel and attack on his manliness didn't have quite the effect that he probably intended. Clearly favouring Gaebel's optimism over Lowery's cynical attacks, the Methodist minister's congregations steadily expanded. Due to the increased demand, Gaebel added Three Forks to Nakusp and New Denver as regular stops. It's unlikely that Lowery's readership increased in like manner.

WHILE THE RESIDENTS OF KASLO and the Slocan suffered through fires and floods during 1894, nature had other trials in store. Winters were always hard. Snow fell early in the mountains and lingered long. The snow was deep and dangerous. High up in the mountains where most of the mines were located, snow slides were a constant threat, and the power they unleashed was almost unimaginable. Thundering down a mountain slope like a herd of overstoked locomotives, snow slides routinely snapped sturdy timbers like spent matchsticks, turned buildings into splinters, and tossed miners aside—or buried them as easily as the winter winds swept away the withered leaves of autumn.

Slocan pioneers had an early taste of winter's wrath. Late in 1892, a few days of warm weather caused some thawing at higher elevations. This significantly increased the risk of snow slides. On one of those days early in 1893, Bill Springer, who was supervising the outside workers at the Freddie Lee mine, issued a warning to his men to expect snow slides and to be careful. Frank Switzer (or Sweitzer), Martin Flaherty, and James Harrison were working outside sacking ore between the mouth of the tunnel and the blacksmith shop. Suddenly a snow slide was bearing down on them. The blacksmith and a miner who was in the blacksmith's shop could see it coming and raced for the tunnel. They shouted for Switzer, Flaherty, and Harrison to come too, but perhaps fearing they would be buried in the tunnel, Switzer and Flaherty stayed where they were. It was the last time anyone saw them for the next few months. The only evidence left of their demise were their hammers and a few spilled sacks of ore.

Harrison survived and wrote to Switzer's widowed mother Mary in California with the sad news of her son's passing. Martin Flaherty's body was found in July. He had been carried 2,800 feet down the mountain, sandwiched between twenty and twelve feet of snow, top and bottom. In its rather macabre coverage, the Nelson *Tribune* reminded everyone that it was originally thought that Switzer's and Flaherty's bodies had been ground to a pulp by the snow slide. Instead, "the corpse, when taken from its icy tomb, was natural as the instant when the unfortunate young man lost his life but exposure to the air soon made a change that necessitated burial at once."[26]

It took longer to find Frank Switzer. His brother Charles finally recovered Frank's body in August. Thankfully, this time the newspapers did not report the condition of the remains. The loss of Switzer and Flaherty hit Jim Wardner, who was managing the mine, hard. Switzer had worked for Wardner for years as an ore porter and sacking man in the Coeur d'Alene mines. Flaherty, too, was most recently from the Coeur d'Alene district and had only just arrived at the Freddie Lee. Wardner was aware, as were all who worked on the mining frontier, that the work was dangerous.

Miners from the Coeur d'Alenes would be especially familiar with the risks posed by snow slides. On one day alone in the winter of 1889 to 1890, ten men died in Coeur d'Alene slides. Despite the tragic loss of life in both the Coeur d'Alenes and the Slocan, work on the mines would continue. Snow slides would be a common threat in the Slocan over the years. Despite the lessons learned in the slide that killed Switzer and Flaherty, and precautions taken in ensuing years, dozens of men and horses were swept away over the decade. By the end of the 1890s, the bleached bones of horses and mules littered the Slocan's mountainsides.

A visitor to the Slocan late in 1896, describing the hardships the country had faced—the floods, fires, storms, heavy snows, and snow slides—concluded that nature demanded a heavy price for its treasures. But even amid all the hardships, desperate times, and rogue weather, there were still prospectors in the Slocan convinced they could beat the odds and come out ahead. One of them was Chipmunk Brown. In December 1893, Brown—Slocan pioneer and proprietor of the half-way house on Slocan River—set out with a companion, John Dolan, late of Winnipeg, to inspect a claim for A.J. Marks of Nelson. The claim was located in the mountains not far from the Kaslo wagon road. Nothing was heard from them afterwards, and a worried Marks offered a reward for their recovery—dead or alive. Six months later, in June 1894, their corpses were found lying as if asleep, blanket-covered, in their snow-filled tent.

Some in the Slocan were discouraged, but others held tightly to their dreams of silver. The mines still attracted investors, and there were good deals to be had. In July 1894, E.H. "Bill" Tomlinson bought W.A. Hendryx's interest in the Last Chance for just $1,000. The claim, originally staked by the Noble Five, would reward Tomlinson handsomely. Prospectors still combed the hills, often ranging further afield, hoping to discover riches that others had missed. John Gosson and a French Canadian prospector—perhaps Joseph Martin—worked their way from Four Mile to Ten Mile

E.H. Tomlinson's camp at the Last Chance. June 1897. Photographer unknown.
ORIGINAL IMAGE COURTESY OF THE SILVERY SLOCAN HISTORICAL SOCIETY

Creek in the summer of 1894. Others followed. Tom Mulvey found some promising ore, and Andy Murphy, who made a "flying trip" to Springer Creek—where Bill Springer had made a rich strike in 1893—was "surprised" at how rich the ore was. He was certain the country at the foot of the lake would be "heard from in 1895."[27] Like other Slocan residents, he likely wanted to put the years 1893 and 1894 behind him.

11

RAILWAYS

SOMETIME ON SUNDAY, OCTOBER 28, 1894, tracklayers for the Nakusp & Slocan Railway (N&S), dirty with the grime of the road and weary from the final push, entered the Slocan mining camp of Three Forks. However, they did not have enough fishplates—used to connect the rails—to complete their work. The rail link with Nakusp would not be finished until the following day, but this did not deter the officials on hand to mark the occasion. The first through train from the end of the tracks near Three Forks arrived in Nakusp at midnight. It carried the federal member of Parliament, J.A. Mara; Captain Troup of the C&KSN; and railway contractor Dan McGillivray. There was no celebration that night, but Slocan residents would have been relieved that the dream they had carried for more than three years had finally come true—they had rail connections to the outside world.

The *Nakusp Ledge* summed up popular sentiment: "But now, after battling with difficulties innumerable, delays from various causes not less frequent, and despite the jibes and jeers of zealous opponents, the Nakusp & Slocan Railway is an accomplished fact, redounding in credit to the Government which fostered the scheme to the lucky men who undertook the hazardous task."[1] The *Slocan Times*, which had been critical of the government-sponsored railway, was less magnanimous, describing the foul-up with the fishplates as "typical."[2] However, even the *Times* had to acknowledge the fact that the railway had arrived, confounding skeptics.

On Monday, October 29, a small celebration in Three Forks marked the arrival of the N&S. But while the celebration might have been modest, the accomplishment celebrated was not. The arrival of the N&S was a milestone. It brought life to camps that had been smothered by the depression and hammered by the weather. Three Forks had been substantially rebuilt after the summer fires, and the future now looked bright. Property prices were on the rise and townsite agent C.J. Loewen must have been all smiles.

Bringing railway connections to the Slocan had been a priority right from the beginning. Everyone—miners, merchants, capitalists, and the government—understood that the long-term success of the new mining district would depend on rail connections to the outside world. While the richest Slocan ores could be shipped by pack train or wagon at profit, it was difficult and laborious to do so. A railway would significantly increase profit margins. And everyone was interested in increased profit margins. The N&S was a step in the right direction for mines close to New Denver and Slocan Lake, but it was the wrong direction for mines tributary to Kaslo. The N&S and the SS *W. Hunter* were of little use to mines further up Carpenter and Seaton Creeks or down the slope to Kaslo. Mine owners and operators along this stretch would not be satisfied until they had rail connections to Kaslo.

There had already been some railway development in West Kootenay before the Slocan discoveries. To the north, there was access from the CPR mainline in Revelstoke. Just south of the border, Daniel Corbin had a line—the Spokane Falls & Northern (SF&N)—running from the Northern Pacific mainline in Spokane to the Columbia River at Northport (Little Dalles). From there it connected with steamboats plying the Columbia River into Canada. Corbin was eager to push his line into the rich mineral districts to the north. He began acquiring railway charters and his company, the Columbia & Kootenay Railway and Transportation Company, received a large land grant for a line between Nelson and the site of present-day Castlegar. However, the Canadian government disallowed the charter. Instead, others stepped in.

In May 1891, the Columbia & Kootenay Railway & Navigation Company (CKRN), which included Harry Abbott, John M. Browning, and William F. Salsbury—Vancouver capitalists with ties to the CPR—opened a short line from Nelson to Robson, on the northeast bank of the Columbia River. The Nelson *Miner* uncharitably called the short line—the Columbia & Kootenay—a "jerkwater" railway, but it provided a link between the steamers operating on Kootenay Lake and those on the Columbia River, connecting to the CPR mainline at Revelstoke.[3] This made reasonably regular and reliable travel possible between West Kootenay and the rest of Canada via the CPR. Destinations in the US could be accessed via the SF&N, or through the steamboat connections to Bonner's Ferry.

Corbin would not be denied. In August 1890, Ainsworth's G.B. Wright and Corbin met and set the wheels in motion for Corbin's eventual entry into Canada. In early 1891, British Columbia granted a charter to the Nelson & Fort Sheppard Railway (N&FS). The principals behind it were Cariboo pioneers Wright, Charles Major, and Peter Dunlevy, along with Charles Dupont and Henry Sly Mason, but Corbin was pulling the strings. Corbin was intent on crossing the border, and the N&FS offered him just the opportunity to do so. However, the Canadian government delayed the federal charter approval for a year. Corbin was frustrated. He was eager to lay iron to West Kootenay. He wanted to get moving, but the charter delay once more opened the field to Canadian railway promoters. A year later, in February 1892, Wright, along with Peter Dunlevy, again met with Corbin. Soon after, Dunlevy announced that construction on the N&FS would start as soon as the snow was "off the ground."[4] Corbin visited West Kootenay in early 1892 and was enthusiastic about the new discoveries in the Slocan. He could see the railway potential and was eager to "open up this magnificent mining district."[5] He would soon invest in Slocan mines, and many hoped that he would lay rails to tap the mineral riches.

Slocan boosters knew that a railway into the mineral district was inevitable, but though numerous schemes were floated, by the start of 1893, none had materialized on the ground. The best hope was the Kaslo & Slocan (K&S). In December 1891, the Victoria law firm of Belyea and Gregory announced they would be pushing for a railway at the next sitting of the Legislative Assembly. A petition to incorporate the Kaslo River and Kootenay Lake Railway Company was duly introduced in the legislature by Slocan representative J.M. Kellie on February 2, 1892. On February 15, Kellie introduced a bill to incorporate the Kaslo and Slocan Railway Company. There were a few minor changes to the Bill after its second reading, but by March 30, all the loose ends were tied up and the bill was given third reading and royal assent.

The K&S was just one of a mixed bag of railway proposals that surfaced between 1891 and 1895—many intended to capitalize on the Slocan's mineral discoveries. A successful railway charter could bring windfall profits from the generous terms offered by the federal and provincial governments, both eager to promote development through land grants and financial incentives. "Charter mongering" was common in BC in the late 1880s and early 1890s, particularly among capitalists in Vancouver, Victoria, and New Westminster.

Between 1890 and 1900, eighty-seven railway companies were incorporated in BC. Another early proposal for a link to the Slocan was promoted by the CKRN's Abbott, Browning, and Salsbury. They were seeking an amendment to their railway's incorporation act to allow it to run a line—the Columbia & Slocan—into the Slocan. Their petition failed. For a while at least, it looked like the K&S would be the only game going.

The men behind the K&S were Alex Ewen, Daniel "D.J." Munn, John Hendry, and Robert Irving. Munn and Irving both joined Hendry and Ewen in the Kaslo Kootenay Land Company—inextricably linked to the railway. The K&S principals started ambitiously enough once the railway's enabling legislation was passed and the charter granted. In May 1892, the *Victoria Daily Colonist* was optimistic that residents of Kaslo and the Slocan would, before many months, "hear the shrill whistle of the locomotive at their very doorsteps."[6] But while the business end of the railway company seemed to be moving ahead, progress on the ground was slow to materialize. Munn visited Kaslo in October but was tight-lipped on when construction would start.

The initial excitement in Kaslo gradually turned to frustration as the months dragged on with no sign of progress. 1892 turned into 1893, and there was still no sign of construction. By early 1893, Slocan residents were wearying of rumours and promises and wary of each new one. There was good reason that Hendry and his partners did not begin construction—they couldn't afford to. Suffering from a lack of cash, they courted J.J. Hill of the Great Northern Railway (GNR). Meeting with Hill in Seattle in January 1893, Hendry and Munn were pleased to learn that Hill was indeed interested in building feeder lines into Canada from his American transcontinental railroad. However, things were slow to advance.

While progress on the K&S was slow, there was another development. On April 12, 1893, the BC Legislative Assembly passed an act to incorporate a railway running into the Slocan from Nakusp. It was good news for Slocan boosters. In early February, Charles Major (also a principal in the N&FS scheme), Johann "John" Wulffsohn of Vancouver, and Arthur Jones of Victoria petitioned for the incorporation of the Nakusp and Slocan Railway Company. The idea was to run a line from Nakusp to Three Forks. Enthusiasm in the Slocan was unreserved, and support quickly grew. New Denver residents, who were unlikely to benefit from the K&S, wanted to petition the government to proceed. They didn't need to. The government strongly supported the proposed line. There was good reason—it was politically expedient to do so. While the K&S, if built, would funnel valuable silver ore south of the border and facilitate the transport of American goods into West Kootenay, the N&S would at least ensure that some of that trade stayed in Canada.

Tenders for the N&S were opened June 7, 1893. Four bids were received, but three were rejected as they did not comply with the form of the tender. The one bid remaining belonged to Dan McGillivray. McGillivray was an experienced railway man who had worked with Andrew Onderdonk on the CPR. McGillivray set up the Inland Construction and Development Company to build the line and hired a host of subcontractors who were assigned specific portions of the line.

Men flocked to Nakusp looking for work. Describing the N&S railway workers who she encountered when she first came to Nakusp from Ontario in August 1893, Blanche Jordan later exclaimed, "My knees began to shake, for I never in my life had seen such a melee of faces, all races and conditions, as belonged to these workers and followers of the railway camps in the west."[7]

Railway workers came from a variety of backgrounds. Premier Davie estimated—when interviewed in August 1893 by the *Colonist*—that of the approximately 700 men at work on the line, there were about 250 Swedes, 100 Italians, and the remainder "our own people." While it seems Italians could now get labouring jobs in West Kootenay, the premier was quick to point out that "there are no Chinamen."[8] Early in 1894, Nakusp's Fred Fauquier took it upon himself to enumerate the camp on the shores of the Lower Arrow Lake. He counted 419 residents, of whom 48 were Italians, likely railway workers. The four Chinese residents he counted definitely wouldn't have been working on the railway. The other group he singled out were nine Black people.[9]

In an environment where steady work was often hard to come by, the railway camps offered itinerant workers a place to sleep, decent meals, and, occasionally, a paycheque. Other than the offer of regular meals, however, conditions in the camps were spartan. As railway man Dan Alton remembered from his days on the Columbia & Kootenay, men slept in their clothes as often as not. An amusing incident was reported in a N&S camp involving a man in a white nightshirt. Nightshirts reeked of civilization. When a man wearing one got up in the middle of the night at a camp at Wilson Creek, he was taken for a ghost and pelted with boots by a wakeful railroader!

Wages in the railway camps averaged about $1.75 to $2.00 a day. Right-of-way men usually earned slightly more than graders or tracklayers, as their

"A roadway slashed at Nakusp" and "Going back to camp, Nakusp," c. 1893. Photographer unknown. "It is when the axemen have cleared the right of way that the first view of the railroad in embryo is obtainable. And very queer it looks. It is a wide avenue through the forest, to be sure, yet it is little like any forest drive that we are accustomed to in the realms of civilization."[10] IMAGES COURTESY OF THE ROYAL BC MUSEUM AND ARCHIVES

work was judged more difficult. They followed the surveyors and trail cutters and were responsible for cutting a swath through the forest for the railway bed. A good right-of-way man had to be handy with a broad axe, particularly in the Slocan, with its thick, heavy timber. Graders took over after the right-of-way men, and they, in turn, were followed by tracklayers. Railway construction offered relatively steady work, but it was a challenge in the Slocan to keep workers from succumbing to the temptation of rich silver strikes.

Shortly after construction got under way, in September 1893, the steamer *Columbia* carried Archduke Franz Ferdinand of Austria from Revelstoke to Nakusp on its way to Northport, Washington. The archduke didn't particularly enjoy his trip. The steamer was crowded with prospectors, and he noted their torn clothes and complained of them lying about on the sofas and deck chairs "spitting everywhere."[11] When they stopped in Nakusp, the boat was met by crowds of workers from the N&S railway eagerly awaiting the payroll the *Columbia* was carrying.

Three Forks, September 28, 1894. Photographer: Neelands Brothers. AUTHOR'S COLLECTION

Anticipating its new distinction as the terminus of the N&S, Three Forks grew by leaps and bounds. Many Kaslo residents, including Thomas Norquay and his wife Hilpa, relocated to Three Forks. The destruction of the camp by fire in the summer of 1894 was a serious setback, but almost immediately, tents began to spring up on the charred landscape. J.B. Wilson opened a store in a tent in early August 1894, and other tent businesses soon followed. With its log buildings turned into firewood, there was an immediate demand for milled lumber. The destruction of the local sawmill hampered reconstruction, but it wasn't long before George and Sam Lovatt set up a new mill. People seized the opportunity to build back better.

The N&S would prove to be a lifeline. A few weeks after the camp was reduced to ashes, Bessie Maxwell, a travelling correspondent for the *Dundee Courier*, was in Nakusp. She didn't go into the Slocan herself, or even get off the steamboat, but watched with condescending interest the transfer of goods to the N&S train preparing to carry supplies: "We had brought up all sorts of things with us for those poor neglected miners—meats, fruits, vegetables (canned of course), biscuits, stoves, rails, nails, and countless other things. What a good time they would have when they got them."[12]

Soon Three Forks would become a thriving camp of frame buildings and constant hustle. It was true that its citizens would welcome the supplies, but like Franz Ferdinand, Bessie Maxwell was content to judge the prospectors, miners, and railroad workers she saw from the boat by their appearance rather than on any interaction with them. She disapprovingly described them "sprawling over barrels" in "tattered felt hats."[13]

Many thought that when the N&S was announced in April it would spur the K&S into action. Indeed, this at first appeared to be the case. Slocan residents anticipated a "lively race" between the N&S and the K&S, to see who would reach Three Forks first. There were calls for the N&S to extend its tracks to Kaslo, but also opposing speculation that the K&S would extend its rails to the shores of Slocan Lake. In early May 1893, the K&S called for bids to clear the right-of-way and cut ties on the first section of land out of Kaslo. William Baillie, public relations point man for both the railway and the townsite company, stated: "Our plan is to follow up the clearing as closely as possible with grading and get the iron on thereafter as speedily as may be desirable."[14] A party of surveyors was soon on the ground, along with their camp followers. It looked like the race was on. When contracts were tendered in early May, the *Kaslo-Slocan Examiner*, perhaps not quite convinced that the K&S was serious, reported the developments under a banner headline exclaiming "Glorious (?) News!"[15] Things at first looked promising. As it turned out, the work didn't amount to much. Those who speculated that it was all a public relations gambit were probably close to the truth.

Behind the scenes, Hendry and the other K&S principals had hit a bump in the road with J.J. Hill. Munn had telegraphed the GNR president on March 8, seeking a response to earlier letters. He hadn't received a reply by mid-April and, clearly impatient, sent both a telegram and a letter to Hill on April 12, 1893. Munn again stressed the importance of starting work on the line as soon as possible. A distinct advantage of doing so, he argued, would be the labour pool created by the crowds of incomers.

Munn felt that the risk of not going forward with construction was that "we may expect discouraging reports sent broadcast and as a consequence outside public interest in that Section will subside and retard travel very much."[16] In addition to the railway workers flocking to Nakusp, hundreds of prospectors and miners, as well as "tramps, adventurers and destitute men," were crowding the stump-strewn streets of Kaslo, as they had done in early 1892.[17] The labour conditions touted by Munn were corroborated by G.B. Wright, who reported Kaslo at the time "literally alive with strong, able-bodied men, anxious to get something to do."[18]

Munn's letter to Hill was en route when Hill finally replied to the earlier correspondence. It was a discouraging response. Hill felt the time was not right to approach his financial backers in New York. However, he promised to go to them later in the month, when he would put the matter "in shape for favorable consideration." He finished by reassuring Munn and the others: "While delay in starting your work may be inconvenient, as I said before, it would be much better to have your arrangements thoroughly complete before commencing work."[19] Munn and his partners were disappointed, and in this context, one can understand the dilemma they faced. They had to keep the people of Kaslo and the Slocan on-side while they waited for Hill to come up with financing. Delaying construction on the K&S brought its backers head-on into the Great Panic.

WITH THE ONSET OF THE depression, D.J. Munn finally came to understand J.J. Hill's hesitancy in financial matters. Munn wrote to Hill: "By watching the financial reports from New York we to some extent understand the situation."[20] Hill was an astute businessman. Under his leadership, the GNR was one of the few American railroads to come through the depression relatively unscathed. He was not ready, however, in the uncertain economic climate, to commit completely to the K&S, but neither was he ready to abandon it. Instead, his strategy seems to have been to do just enough to keep Munn on-side. In June, Munn and Hendry met with Hill in Saint Paul, Minnesota. Hill agreed to provide $20,000 in stopgap funding. This was the money that allowed the K&S to do some clearing and grading over the summer.

Their shaky alliance somewhat steadied, both Munn and Hill took measures to reassure themselves of the K&S's viability. Munn hired Professor Parks, the mining expert, to prepare a confidential report on the outlook for the Slocan mines. The success of the railway depended entirely on the output of the mines. J.J. Hill had his trusted locating engineer, John Frank Stevens, to go to the Slocan to look over the proposed line. Professor Parks's glowing report was well received by Munn, who forwarded a copy to Hill. According to Parks, "from fourteen years experience in visiting and reporting on the various mining districts of the North American continent I am safe in stating that the Kaslo-Slocan District as a silver-lead section is much higher grade than any other camp of the same size known to exist on the continent."[21] He estimated that by the time a railway could be constructed, mines would be ready to ship a minimum of fifty to sixty tons of ore a day, with that figure steadily rising as the camp developed.

Stevens's report was equally encouraging. The locating engineer, who was generally credited with discovering the Marias Pass in Montana and Stevens Pass in Washington State (both crucial to the GNR's advance to the Pacific), found the K&S's route into the mines eminently suitable for grade construction. He was impressed with the mines too: "As to the permanency & richness of the mines, the grade of ore is high, remarkably so. I saw large quantities of ore coming down by wagons & pack trains."[22]

Construction work on the N&S was one bright spot during the dark days of late 1893. However, there was tension between the government, the railway company, and McGillivray's Inland Construction and Development Company. This tension, coupled with the onset of winter, effectively brought construction to a halt. In early November, about $40,000 was paid out to the railway workers. Most packed their belongings and left. Slocan residents were stunned by the stoppage. The future of the railway, which had sustained their hopes and dreams through the hard times, was now uncertain. Things would get worse before they got better.

As part of the original agreement with the railway company, the government had guaranteed interest on investment bonds in an amount of "up to" $25,000 per mile. This was very much a "guestimate." To determine a more accurate per mile estimate, the government contacted the CPR. Based on what was learned, Premier Davie recommended that the per-mile guarantee on principal and interest for the N&S construction be fixed at an average of $17,500 per mile. The new figures were incorporated in An Act Respecting the Nakusp and Slocan Railway, introduced in the Legislative Assembly on February 26, 1894.

Opposition members raised a great hue and cry when the proposed legislation was introduced. Opposition leader Robert Beaven said he thought the only way the government would have given such a favourable deal to the railway company was if one of the members of the government had an interest in the company. Beaven went so far as to suggest that the premier had purchased shares in the railway company—which would have been a clear conflict of interest. Matters came to a head when one of the members for Nanaimo denounced the government for corruption and incompetence and accused Premier Davie of working for the railway company and not for the province.

The citizens of Nakusp, New Denver, and Three Forks followed the proceedings with a sense of bewilderment. Because the accusations had been made in the legislature, the response and any investigation could not be handled by the government. Instead, in April 1894 the legislature approved the establishment of a Royal Commission to look into the matter. The commission was to be jointly chaired by Chief Justice Matthew Baillie Begbie and G.W. Burbidge of the Exchequer Court of Canada. The full effects of the hard times fell down on the Slocan as heavily as the thick winter snows.

THERE WAS A GLIMMER OF light in May 1894, when the Royal Commission exonerated the government and railway construction resumed. Dan McGillivray announced that work on the N&S would commence shortly and "would not cease until such time as the whole road was completed."[23] But he didn't anticipate the terrible weather that plagued BC in 1894. The construction crews were almost immediately tormented by violent storms. Leona Leon, who had served as a volunteer nurse for the Confederate army during the American Civil War, was hired on by the N&S to assist Dr. Brouse, the doctor assigned to the railway camps. She later wrote of enduring "all kinds of wheatherhardships [*sic*]."[24]

There was good news for Slocan residents in June, however, when Captain Nathaniel Moore of the Duluth syndicate announced that he was going to build a concentrator on Howson Creek, just below Three Forks and conveniently located alongside the proposed tracks of the N&S. This was a welcome development. The whole purpose of a concentrator was to separate the rich ore from the dross, thereby "concentrating" the ore content and making it easier to ship at profit. The few buildings that would rise around the concentrator would be known as New Duluth.

In early July 1894, tracklayers and surfacing men, who were making $1.75 a day, went on strike, demanding $2.00 a day. The strike was short lived. Within a week it collapsed, and the striking workers returned to work. The *Nakusp Ledge* reported that "all spikers, men on iron cars and good able men" were being paid $2.00 a day, but it appeared that most everyone else continued to earn $1.75 per day.[25] While there were other intermittent labour disruptions, construction delays due to supply shortages were more common and more serious. Even before the storms and fires wreaked havoc on the supply chain, track-laying came to a standstill for a week in early

June when the crews ran out of spikes. Work was halted again in August when the supply of bolts ran out, then they ran out of spikes again.

Not all the delays could be blamed on labour troubles, the vagaries of Mother Nature, or gaps in the supply chain. In September, there were outbreaks of "mountain fever" in the railway camps, and a steady stream of sick workers washed into Nakusp for treatment. The symptoms seemed similar to sunstroke and included fever and delirium. Mountain fever was a catch-all for any number of unspecified flu-like ailments, and sometimes included early stages of typhoid. The influenza strain that swept through West Kootenay in 1894 was debilitating but does not appear to have been deadly. Still, it was widespread and certainly slowed down the construction and operation of the N&S. Of more serious concern, in late October, it was learned that Charles O. Parsons, a mining expert who had visited the Slocan six weeks earlier, had died of typhoid in a Spokane hospital. Sure enough, there was at least one case of typhoid reported at the time in the Slocan—J.C. Whyte, the superintendent of the N&S.

As the construction season moved into late August and early September 1894, it was becoming clear that Dan McGillivray's Inland Construction Company, despite its enthusiastic resumption of work earlier in the year, was in serious financial difficulty. McGillivray was operating very much on the margin. Cash flow was increasingly problematic. One of the casualties of cost-cutting was the railway camp hospital and physician. However, the company continued to deduct one dollar a month from workers' paycheques. Paydays were becoming so infrequent by late 1894 that the dollar deduction might have escaped the notice of workers impatient to get money—any money—from the company. There was a payday at the end of August—the first since the strike. However, there was only enough money to pay about a quarter of the workers. Paymaster Sampson had somehow lost a roll of twenty-dollar bills—where and how, he knew not. The *Slocan Times* was not impressed nor surprised, believing that "a worse engineered, worse financed, worse managed road" had never before been constructed.[26]

Not everyone felt as strongly as the *Times*, but frustration with the slow pace of construction was widespread. Despite the delays, however, by early July the railway had passed the half-way house at Summit Lake and was in operation for a seventeen-mile stretch out of Nakusp. A big mogul locomotive was hauling supplies to the railway camps. By late August, the tracks were within six miles of Three Forks and the railway was expected to reach Three Forks by September 15.

Upon completion, the N&S was almost immediately congested with traffic as merchants tried to bring goods in and mines tried to ship ore out. On the day after the railway arrived in Three Forks, three carloads came in carrying the equipment for Moore's concentrator. The railway's station agent told the *Kootenay Mail* that on average during November, he was taking in $300 per day in receipts for ore shipments. The heavy traffic exacted a toll on the newly constructed grade. As might be expected, McGillivray's makeshift crew encountered wrinkles they had to smooth over or adjust to. They found, for example, that the steep grades on part of the line were very hard on brakes, wearing them out sooner than expected. This was perhaps the cause of a fully loaded ore car jumping the tracks in early November outside Three Forks. In December, another five cars went off the tracks between New Denver and Three Forks. On the last day of the year, a flatcar came untethered at Three Forks and ran at high speed all the way down the line to Wilson Creek, where it came to a safe and self-satisfied stop. In a more serious incident that occurred in the Nakusp rail yard, Frank McGowan, a fireman, misjudged the distance to the end of the runway and was thrown from the cab when the engine braked. He struck his head on the boiler during his flight and narrowly missed being thrown under the locomotive's big iron wheels.

The N&S was backed by the CPR, who negotiated a deal to manage the railway once construction was complete. As a result of the derailments and other mishaps, there were concerns in some quarters that the quality of workmanship on the railway might not be up to CPR standards. This could scuttle the planned transfer. This was not the case, however. Despite the concerns of the *Slocan Times* (the railway's principal detractor), when government engineer Ed Mohun and a party of CPR and N&S officials inspected the line in November, the CPR officials proclaimed they had "never seen a mountain road constructed better."[27] The CPR's Richard Marpole paid particular attention to the bridges, roadbed, and trestle work and found them all satisfactory. The CPR was satisfied with the quality of construction but wanted the N&S company to put up enough money to repair the line in the spring of 1895, expecting damages over the winter. Given the washouts, fires, and other devastations earlier in 1894, the request was prudent.

Mohun's official report confirmed his earlier opinions. The CPR officials, with the benefit of their own inspections, agreed with Mohun's assessment, and a date was set for the official transfer. The N&S would become a branch line of the CPR on January 1, 1895. The opinions of

Mohun and the CPR, and the confirmation of the transfer date, were welcome news to Dan McGillivray, who was struggling to keep his company afloat as he tried to finish up the railway in time for the handover. This proved a challenge due to his financial difficulties and—unlike the circumstances when construction began—a general labour shortage. In mid-November McGillivray was still trying to finish ballasting the railway but could only get a crew of fifty or sixty men instead of the two hundred he needed. It's likely that word of his company's dire financial straits had spread, and some men stayed away as they could not be sure of receiving a paycheque. Other railway workers took up work in the mines, and a few packed up for California where there were rumours of track-laying work. While McGillivray worked feverishly to tie up loose ends, the CPR started putting its own crews on the line.

The N&S railway was formally handed over to the CPR, as scheduled, on January 1, 1895. There was no great fanfare to mark the occasion, but residents were confident the railway would be well managed under the new regime. There was even some sympathy and forgiveness for Dan McGillivray and his company, the *Ledge* noting: "That the road is well built its acceptance proves, and however lax the Inland Construction Company may have appeared in the eyes of some, none can assert that they shirked their contract in that respect."[28] Dan McGillivray could have used more than sympathy and forgiveness. Even with an additional government subsidy, constructing the railway under the terms of the contract on which he had underbid basically bankrupted his Inland Construction and Development Company.

The company did its best to make ends meet and ensure that all workers and suppliers were paid, but this was often a hit-or-miss prospect due to the intermittent payroll, a poor reputation with suppliers, and a propensity to wait for accounts to be settled by lawsuit. One of the first to resolve his overdue account through litigation was Ned Thomas. Thomas delivered a load of hay to the company just before the fire that wiped out Three Forks. The hay was consumed in the fire, and the company wasn't eager to pay for hay that it had never been able to use. The court sided with Thomas and ordered the company to pay him $522.60 for the hay. The company's Three Forks office and its contents were seized by the sheriff to ensure payment.

The CPR introduced operating and safety procedures, but there were still mishaps as the new crew familiarized themselves with the equipment and the route. Weather and terrain were the biggest impediments, particularly through the winter. Heavy snowfalls and snow slides often blocked the tracks. It was a huge amount of work when the train or tracks had to be dug out or cleared of snow. The icy conditions also presented safety hazards for the train crew.

Fireman Frank McGowan, still recovering from his near-death experience when he fell off the locomotive in Nakusp, again came close to meeting his maker in January 1895. He was back on the job after time spent at one of the hot springs on Arrow Lake. On the way from Nakusp to Three Forks, he climbed to the top of the tender to throw down some firewood. Slipping on a cake of ice, he tumbled to the ground and then bounced back on to the tracks. He grabbed one of the train's truss rods and pulled himself clear just before the wheels would have run over him. He hung on for about a thousand feet while the ridge in the centre of the track tore at his clothes and flesh. Noticing a trail of blood along the tracks, the caboose crew got the train to stop, and McGowan was rescued. He was quickly taken to Three Forks for medical care. Bruised and battered but with no broken bones, he was sewn back together to mend. It was his third narrow escape since joining the N&S.

The line itself took some getting used to—both for passengers and crew. One early passenger was no less a railway man than Donald "Dan" Mann himself. After supplying the CPR crews through the Kicking Horse canyon in 1884, Mann and partner William McKenzie laid tracks all over North and South America. In February 1895, Dan Mann took a trip on the N&S to Three Forks to visit his brother, Slocan packer Hugh Mann. Dan had ridden trains all over North America. He reported feeling "sea sick" after riding the N&S.[29]

While there were some growing pains, Slocan residents were confident the N&S would open up new opportunities. The railway's arrival and the imminent start-up of the Slocan's first concentrator were exciting developments for long-suffering residents. Despite the low price of silver, the *Nakusp Ledge* predicted that the output of the mines for the winter of 1894 to 1895 would be five times any previous year. Regular shipments of ore out to smelters boosted local confidence. When the annual report of the Minister of Mines for 1894 was published, Gold Commissioner Fitzstubbs noted that silver mining was "being pushed forward satisfactorily, notwithstanding the depressed prices of that metal and lead."[30] As a government appointee, he couldn't help but toot his employer's horn: "Much of the progress and of the confidence entertained by investors is due to the improvements in communication and notably to the construction of an important and necessary work—the Nakusp and Slocan Railway."[31]

THE ARRIVAL OF THE N&S in Three Forks raised spirits throughout the Slocan. Captain Troup used his time in Three Forks to visit some of the principal mines. With the new railway link, he expected mines to start shipping ore in volume: "You see, the beauty about Slocan ore at the lowest prices touched yet for either lead or silver, there is a handsome margin of profit left."[32]

Troup was right. Undoubtedly, the most significant railway development to date in the Slocan occurred in September—even before the line reached Three Forks—when the first Slocan ore shipped out by rail. The mines close to Slocan Lake were in the best position to take advantage of the new rail connections, and the Alpha, near Silverton, had the distinction of being the first mine to ship ore to Nakusp by rail. Fifteen tons were shipped on September 11 and another sixty tons the following day. Over the next two weeks, more than five hundred tons of ore were shipped from the Alpha. The ore was transferred to steamboats in Nakusp and shipped to Revelstoke. By November 20, the Slocan Star had shipped 850 tons of ore. Other mines began to ship by rail too. E.H. Tomlinson's Last Chance, famously abandoned by Seattle's Judge Bond, was proving a wonder. The more Tomlinson's men dug, the richer the ore became. Work started only in August, but by December, 125 tons of ore had been sledded to Three Forks and then loaded into railcars for the trip to a smelter in Great Falls, Montana.

While Three Forks was the centre of attention in the Slocan in late 1894, other camps thrived too as a direct result of the railway. The townsite at Wilson Creek, originally staked by A.M. Wilson and located on a sheltered bay on Slocan Lake, owed its development almost entirely to the N&S. By April 1894, just before the floods, the townsite had been surveyed and christened "Rosebery" after Archibald Primrose, the fifth Lord Rosebery, who succeeded Gladstone as prime minister of the United Kingdom in March 1894. Rosebery had visited some of the silver districts of western America but never made it to his namesake camp. The railway company built a wharf, freight shed, and station house there, and Wilson was employed to operate a box- and railcar repair business. Contractor J.T. Nault also saw the site's advantages. He got a contract to clear the townsite and picked out a choice lot on which to build a hotel.

Rosebery was soon the connecting point for the steamer *W. Hunter* and destinations south on the lake. The steamer came up the lake in the morning and left Wilson Creek for New Denver every day at 4 PM, except Sunday. By May 1894, J.T. "Tref" Nault had completed his Rosebery Hotel. It was filled immediately with railway workers. Nault hired Dad Allen's son, Bob, as a dishwasher. However, it didn't take Bob long to realize he preferred packing to dishwashing. He had never seen so many dishes. He worked from four in the morning to nine o'clock at night, all for fifty cents a day plus board. He soon returned to packing. The Rosebery Hotel continued to thrive, however, even after the line was complete and the construction workers were gone.

In addition to Nault's hotel, Milton Martin, the bookkeeper for the Slocan Star, ran a store. A few other buildings were randomly scattered across the townsite. A correspondent for the *Kootenay Mail* took the train from Nakusp down to Rosebery in early December 1894. He described "the tasteful nucleus of a coming town."[33] Another visitor, who was at Rosebery in early September, when the warm glow of summer still fell on Slocan Lake, was equally impressed. He lauded the fishing in Wilson Creek, the bathing in the lake, the airy rooms in the two-storey Rosebery Hotel, and the fine meals set out, courtesy of Nault's chef, Joe Libby. The influx of traffic through Rosebery from the railway reportedly kept Nault and his staff so busy he had to hire two bartenders to keep the drinks flowing for thirsty travellers.

View of the Nakusp & Slocan's Three Forks station from the north, c. 1896. Photographer: R.H. Trueman. IMAGE COURTESY OF THE UNIVERSITY OF CALGARY DIGITAL COLLECTIONS

12

SETTLING IN

BY LATE 1894, THE SLOCAN was settling into a period of relative stability. The effects of the Great Panic lingered, and times were still tough, but the weather had calmed down, the election was over, and the coming of the railway offered hope for the future. Mines could ship ore more economically, and the N&S brought in families. The presence of women and children had a profound effect on mining camp social life. Bachelor newspaper editor R.T. Lowery, attracted to the rough-and-tumble early days of the mining rush, when women were as scarce as blue roses and children were a rarity, must have looked on with some trepidation at the changing social fabric. He could see that "civilization" was trickling in one family at a time.

While prostitutes were among the first women into the mining camps, a few other pioneering women made early appearances and did much to shape the development and social structure of those camps. Among the women who arrived early were Sarah Thorburn, Annie and Amy Eagan, Maud Donahue, and Mary Layton. Prospecting women like Caroline "Fool Hen" Anderson and Mrs. Pound arrived early too, but they didn't stay long and didn't have much impact on community development.

Sarah M. Wilds and Grant Thorburn, though both born in Canada, were married in Olympia, Washington, in 1891. However, they likely met in Vancouver. Grant was a veteran of Louis Riel's Manitoba rebellion and later ran Vancouver's first livery stable. Sarah was young, attractive, and ambitious. By September 1892, she was helping Grant run the Leland Hotel in Nakusp. Sensing new opportunities in the Slocan, Sarah and Grant packed their bags in 1893 and moved to Four Mile City, soon to become Silverton. Grant opened the Thorburn House, but before it was finished, he and Sarah

"Pack train leaving Slocan Hotel, New Denver, [for] the Thompson Group on Fennell Creek, September 27, 1894." Photographer: Neelands Brothers, Nelson. IMAGE COURTESY OF THE SILVERY SLOCAN HISTORICAL SOCIETY

were hired to run the dining room at Gething and Henderson's Slocan Hotel in New Denver, which, with Sarah's arrival, could boast "one of the prettiest waiter girls in the country."[1] In May 1894, Sarah Thorburn was hired to run the dining room of the Rosebery Hotel, where business was heavy with N&S workers. No doubt she was also helping Grant with the Thorburn House, which opened in the summer of 1894.

Annie and Amy Eagan, mother and daughter, likely arrived in New Denver in 1893 or 1894. Prior to that, Irish-born Annie was running a laundry in Nelson. In 1892, Annie was the owner of a lot in New Denver, which would have originally been bought in the government auction at Eldorado in July 1892. By 1894, she had fixed up a house in New Denver to operate as a laundry and bathhouse, but then she moved to Three Forks. She described herself as a widow and had two children with her. Her daughter, Amy, helped her at the laundry, and her son, William Thompson, presumably worked in the mining industry. In 1894, Annie was managing the dining room at Hart's Silverton Hotel, which would have put her in direct competition with Sarah Thorburn at the Thorburn House.

Maud Donahue was born in 1871, perhaps in Memphis. She was given up for adoption at an early age. Taken in by a wealthy family in small town Illinois, Maud Morris enjoyed a privileged childhood. However, when she turned eighteen, she learned of her adoption and discovered her birth mother was still alive and living in Wardner, Idaho.

Maud made her way there. She was young, beautiful, cultured, and strong-willed—certain to be a centre of attraction on the mining frontier. Clarence Donahue was shift boss at the Coeur d'Alene's Bunker Hill and Sullivan mines. He was a big, strong, handsome man. He drank and gambled a bit, but Maud was attracted despite or because of these traits. They were married in January 1891, and within a year had a son. Then, one drunken night, Clarence won more than $1,500 at the card table.

Clarence quit his job and went into the saloon business. Soon he was drinking and gambling every night and every day—it didn't take long for him to lose the saloon. He drifted to Spokane and took a bartending job. Then he headed north and got a job at the Slocan's Surprise mine. Maud and her birth mother crossed the border too, likely arriving at New Denver in the late summer of 1893. Clarence and Maud separated, and in early 1894, Maud filed divorce papers in Spokane.

By this time, Maud was running a private school in New Denver and likely served as a midwife in the days when no doctors were available. Her contributions were appreciated, and she was readily accepted into New Denver society. She was still trying to obtain her divorce when fate intervened. On July 22, 1894, Clarence was working by himself in a cut on the Surprise mine when one of the earthen banks, saturated from heavy rains, collapsed on him. He didn't have a chance. He was dead in an instant, smothered in a damp slurry of rocks and dirt. His friends, worried when they didn't hear from him, found him completely buried with only a stiff, dead hand protruding above the ground to mark his makeshift grave.

While Maud could not have anticipated Clarence's death, and no doubt she felt some twinges of sadness, the death of her husband separated her from him more effectively and permanently than she could ever have expected from a divorce. She was free to pursue her heartstrings. On October 24, 1894, at the Methodist parsonage in Revelstoke, she married Alex Sproat, New Denver's mining recorder. Sproat's friend, J.D. Graham—formerly constable in Kaslo and by 1894 Revelstoke's government agent—was best man. Twenty-nine-year-old Sproat gladly traded in his bachelorhood for the pretty twenty-three-year-old widow. In the bargain, he gained a stepson, two-year-old George Morris Donahue. For her part, Maud gained a reliable husband with a steady income, and solid connections through his father, G.M. Sproat.

Mary Layton, once of Butte and the Montana mining camp of Granite, was an early arrival in Kaslo, having come in by way of Burke, Idaho. Mary first picked up work in a restaurant on Kaslo's Front Street. In the winter of 1894, she was working as a cook at the Noble Five mine. Then she landed at the McDonald brothers' Blue Ridge House on the Kaslo wagon road, though she expected to continue at the Noble Five when the snows returned later in 1895. These women and others like them were catalysts for social interaction.

Marriageable young women were still uncommon in the Slocan in the mid-1890s. There were prostitutes of course, but they usually weren't considered marriage material. J.G. Devlin, "the Gunner from Galway"—a bachelor himself—believed he had a solution. On a trip back east, he told reporters that if fifteen hundred "nice girls" were sent out to West Kootenay, each one could be assured of a "good husband." His idea was picked up by several newspapers, including the *New York Times*, which reported there were women "talking up the matter seriously" and "the first lot of would-be wives will be arranged for next spring."[2] A Nelson newspaper complained of a flood of letters arriving every day from "would-be captors of husbands and homes."[3]

While the mining camps in the earliest days were overwhelmingly male, this was largely dictated by context and not by preference. There were male prospectors and miners who treasured their bachelorhood, but for many, the dream of wedded bliss was second only to the quest for material wealth. The western mining camps were generally more tolerant than settled communities in the east in matters of religion and social mores, and many men had only tenuous ties to organized religion. However, the sanctity of marriage was something few prospectors or miners were prepared to abandon. For many in the mining camps, the rising tide of weddings marked the transition from camp to "town."

The first marriage in New Denver possibly took place on August 18, 1893, when prospector John Gill married Maggie B. England. There was another early wedding in New Denver on December 26, 1893, when the Reverend James Turner joined together—in a union destined to have a tragic ending—Charles Miller, a German-born cook at the Idaho mine, and Caroline "Fool Hen" Anderson. The next day, on December 27, 1894,

Ed Terrill and Kate Dryden, both of the Pacific Hotel, celebrated the first wedding in Three Forks since the town had been rebuilt: "Of course, the first wedding in the town provoked a chivari—strangers stopping in town were frightened and will remember it for years. Whether it was the noise, the whisky or the Tom and Jerry, it is certain the crowd got hilarious and a bloody scrapping match occurred before morning."[4]

With all the weddings and the increasing influx of couples and families, there was soon a baby boom. The first children born in a mining camp were sources of great celebration and pride. No matter what happened to the camp in the future, it meant that for as long as they lived, there was someone who could say "I was born in New Denver," or Three Forks, or Silverton.

By mining camp tradition, the first baby born in a camp was usually given a town lot. This was the case with Denver Teetzel Shannon, the first baby in New Denver. Denver was born September 16, 1893. Maud Donahue likely attended Denver and his mother, Janet. Denver's proud father was Slocan pioneer Ed Shannon—the town's baker and owner of Shannon's Hall. More than a year passed before the camp's first baby girl appeared. Mary Clever arrived in January 1895. Mary joined an older brother, Bill. Their parents were Herman and Rosamunde Clever. German immigrants, they came to Canada in 1893, after spending time in the American mining camp of Neihart, Montana.

The first baby in Kaslo might have been Christina Eliza Kane, born December 10, 1892, to George Kane and Dick and Justine Fry's daughter, Julia. Christina may have been descended from a Sinixt First Nation Chief through her grandmother, Justine Fry, a.k.a. Irie; Sust-eel; daughter of Soqu'stik'en.

Kaslo's first male child was probably "Dickie" Hughes, born January 2, 1893. The first baby in Silverton was John Edward Brownrigg, born October 11, 1893. He didn't stay long, leaving with his family for Pilot Bay in 1895. The first birth in Nakusp was a son for Constable Fauquier and his wife. The first baby in Three Forks—a son for George Thomas and his wife—was born August 5, 1895. The first girl was Mr. and Mrs. McGregor's daughter, who arrived in October 1895. On May 11, 1895, Mrs. Kellett, whose husband was a section foreman on the N&S, gave birth to the first baby in the small community that was springing up in the shadow of New Duluth's concentrator—an eight-pound baby boy named Ernest. As there were no lots available, the *Ledge* suggested that the newborn be given a mining claim.

Other children soon followed these "firsts." Alex and Maud Sproat's baby girl, Katherine Ivey, was born in New Denver in July 1895. Over in Kaslo, Hannah Ewin gave birth to a daughter in November 1895—the first child for her and husband Robert.

Many of the women who arrived in Kaslo and the Slocan in the 1890s were dedicated to the Christian churches they belonged to. The church served as a safe refuge within the predominantly male mining camps, and it was one place where women outnumbered men. In April 1895, several "church ladies" in New Denver organized a Ladies' Aid Society. By the end of April, inspired by their counterparts in New Denver, the women of Three Forks, led by Hilpa Norquay, had formed their own society. Kaslo, too, had a Ladies' Aid Society. These women were instrumental in organizing social and cultural events that offered opportunities for interaction between men and women who perhaps would not have been comfortable quaffing down beer and whisky in the company of the men who frequented the camps' saloons and hotel bars. The churches were also reasonably tolerant of race and ethnicity. Arvell Perkins, a Black woman living in Kaslo, was welcomed into the Methodist Church and joined the Ladies' Aid Society.

Ladies' Aid Society, Kaslo, c. 1895. Photographer unknown. Arvell Perkins sits somewhat uncomfortably at the back of the photo to the right of the window frame.
ORIGINAL IMAGE COURTESY OF MABEL COLLINS

Social interaction in the mining camps, which were often isolated and far distant from large cities, was of paramount importance. Whether in the saloons, brothels, or clubs, or at dances and other events—some sponsored by the churches—people valued their opportunities to get together and confirm their shared community bonds. With a limited cast of characters, gossip flowed freely.

In 1895, the New Denver Ladies' Aid Society sponsored a "pink supper." The programme consisted of a "choice and varied" dinner, followed by musical entertainment and recitations.[5] The decorations and waiter girls' costumes were all in pink. Highlights of the musical entertainment included a cornet solo, a violin solo, and a duet performed on clarinet and cornet. According to the *Ledge*: "The programme was far and above the average and the participants came in for a liberal allowance of applause."[6] The pink supper was financially successful. The Ladies' Aid Society concluded the evening with a profit of more than twenty dollars. Newspaper editor and noted boozer R.T. Lowery later wondered if a pink nose would get him admission to a pink supper.

In addition to the Ladies' Aid Societies, churches sponsored various clubs intended to promote social discourse among their followers. Methodists had their Epworth Club, but other Christian denominations had their own versions. Epworth League clubs got their start in Canada in 1889, reaching a peak in 1896 with more than 82,000 members and almost 2,000 clubs across the country. Primarily aimed at young adults, they were intended to provide a "moral" forum for social activities. They were especially important to women, who normally outnumbered men by a margin of two to one in most clubs.

The opportunities for women in the Slocan who wanted to work outside the home were limited and usually consistent with social stereotypes. Several women in the Slocan ran hotels or lodging houses, and others operated hotel dining rooms and restaurants. Women travelled from camp to camp following opportunities and advertisements. Judging by the advertisements that ran in Slocan newspapers, one needed an impressive résumé for the job. One advertisement called for a woman with twenty years' experience in the hotel business. Another asked that only "respectable" women apply.[7]

Sarah Thorburn, Annie Eagan, and Mary Layton weren't the only dining room divas in the Slocan. Having a kitchen or dining room run by a woman was good for business. Bremner and Watson proudly advertised that the dining facilities at their hotel in Watson were "in charge of female help of experience."[8] Mrs. McConnell and Miss Purcell—"two ladies well known in Montana and California"—later took over the dining room at Silverton's Victoria Hotel.[9] Miss Purcell had previously run the dining room at the Paragon House in Butte, Montana.

Miss Josie Foley arrived in Kaslo from Spokane in early 1893 to run the Dardanelles' dining room. In Nakusp, Mrs. Crawford managed the Hotel Nakusp with the help of Mrs. Whyte, who ran the dining room. Sarah Manuel, formerly of the Barnard Castle in Vancouver, took the reins at Nakusp's Madden House along with her daughter, Sadie. Late in 1894, Mrs. Whyte travelled to Three Forks to investigate the possibility of opening a hotel there.

As well as running dining rooms, women were also employed in them. "Pretty waiter girls" were popular in the mining camps. Historian Mary Lee Spence has noted: "Prospectors or miners would flock into any restaurant or establishment where a winsome woman worked."[10] In his mining camp novel, *The Lost Cabin Mine*, Frederick Niven tried to explain the reverence that such waiter girls were accorded on the western frontier:

> A woman in such a place, I should imagine, must constantly find it advisable to remind herself that there are very few of the gentler sex in the land and a vast number of men, and tell herself that it is not her captivating ways alone that are responsible for the extreme of respect that is lavished upon her.[11]

In addition to Sarah Thorburn at the Slocan Hotel in 1893, other hotels and restaurants were quick to hire their own "pretty waiter girls." The *Kootenay Star* referred to Jack Madden's wife—who helped out at his Bonanza City Hotel—as his "agreeable, good looking partner." Before Sarah Manuel took over, the Madden House Hotel in Nakusp had the "popular" Agnes Horton serving hungry patrons. The Hotel Slocan in Kaslo jumped on the trend, hiring a "young woman waiter" in January 1895. Maud Sproat too, who once described herself as a "waitress," may have worked in New Denver as a "waiter girl."[12]

ANOTHER TYPICAL ROLE FOR MINING camp women was teaching. Most of the teachers in the Slocan during the 1890s were women, many from eastern Canada. There was no requirement in BC for teachers to have any specific training or experience. All that was needed was a high school equivalency test. Even then, a mark as low as 30 percent was good enough for a certificate. In an era when women faced gender bias in many professions, teaching was an attractive proposition for young women who had advanced in their schooling. Indeed, they may have had an advantage over men, in being allowed to take the teacher's examination at the age of sixteen rather than eighteen.

Miss McLennan was teaching in Kaslo as early as 1892. Eleanor Caldwell, a native of Ontario, was teaching in Nakusp by 1893. New Denver had to do with Sunday schools and the private school run by Maud Donahue in 1894, but in 1895 Martha McDowell and her brother were hired to teach there and in Three Forks respectively. Martha didn't last long and was succeeded by Eliza Livingstone.

A few women in the Slocan found work in less traditional fields. The first newspaper to specifically serve the Slocan, the *Kaslo-Slocan Examiner*, employed Margaret O'Rourke and Mary van Buren. Other women with talent or passion for writing sought opportunities as correspondents. Perhaps O'Rourke and van Buren were inspired by Vancouver's Sara Anne McLagan. In 1884, Sara Anne married John McLagan. Together, the two founded the *Vancouver Daily World*. Born Sara Anne Maclure, her younger brother was Samuel Maclure, a noted Victoria architect. A champion of women's suffrage, Sara was very socially active. When she visited the Slocan, she was just as impressed with the district as most other visitors.

While women played an important role in the mining camps of the Slocan, and families were a sign of stability, there were other indicators of growth. As the camps developed, social institutions common to larger population centres were eagerly sought. The brass band was a symbol of status in up-and-coming mining camps and an institution familiar to British expatriates. The camp that could organize a brass band was demonstrating that it had a future. It didn't much matter how qualified the members might be as musicians; residents felt a sense of pride whenever the uniformed bands marched up and down the streets or greeted visiting dignitaries. As New Denver's *Ledge* noted: "Nothing enlivens a town so much as a band."[13] When Canada's Governor General, Lord Aberdeen, visited Kaslo in 1895, Lady Aberdeen noted that they were greeted "in grand style with dynamite salutes and prolonged discordant strains of 'God Save the Queen' by the band."[14]

The idea for a brass band in New Denver was first floated in November 1894 and quickly gathered momentum. A subscription was started and almost seventy dollars pledged right away. By the end of the month, a tidy sum had been collected for instruments. Fundraising continued through December, culminating in a Christmas Eve ball at Shannon's Hall. The band was yet to be formed, but several residents with musical talent contributed to the entertainment. The highlight of the evening was the house band consisting of Tom Trenery, Jack Delaney, and Wilson Hill. It was a far cry from Brahms or Strauss, but some thought they produced "the best dance music ever heard in the Slocan."[15] According to the *Ledge*, Trenery and his bandmates were "away up" the whole evening.[16] Given the number of Irish and Scottish immigrants, the music likely included lots of jigs and reels. At one point, one of the dancers gave a lively step-dancing demonstration.

There was already a cornet or two among the prospective band players, but additional instruments were ordered in January 1895 from Claxton & Company in Toronto. In late February 1895 the instruments finally arrived. There were two shiny new cornets, a snare drum, and a bass drum. For days following, New Denver was treated to the wayward sounds of band members becoming acquainted with their new devices.

The band's first official appearance was at Shannon's Hall on March 22. Attendance exceeded all expectations as New Denver residents crowded into the hall to hear their band boys raise the rafters. By all accounts the band put on a creditable performance considering they only had three weeks to practice. After a lively evening of music and refreshments, the band ended the concert with a raucous performance of the "The Maple Leaf Forever"—Canada's de facto national anthem at the time. New Denver residents left well satisfied and proud of their new band. Two weeks later, the band made their first foray out on to the streets of New Denver and, though somewhat shaky, acquitted themselves with honour.

WHILE THE FORMATION OF A brass band was symbolic, the mining camps had other, more critical requirements. Health care might have been at the top of the list. Certainly, women had an important role to play. Dozens of unnamed women bandaged miners, fed hungry prospectors, and looked after ailing members of the community, old and young, both before and after doctors and nurses arrived. In fast-growing camps, where men were prone to injury and the general population was always at risk from typhoid, tuberculosis, or pneumonia, a doctor was a necessity. The N&S had Dr. Brouse and his nurse, Leola Leon, but they couldn't serve all the scattered camps. For those desperate enough, there were a few "quacks" offering their services. Kaslo's "Doc" Aikens, for example, believed to be a former veterinarian, was known to have a store of drugs he was likely willing to trade for whisky.

By the spring of 1893, Kaslo had three real doctors. First in were Doctors Bruner and Rogers. Bruner, a Coeur d'Alener, followed his countrymen north to the Slocan. He was in Kaslo by at least April 1893 and appeared as a witness at the trial of E.E. Coy. At the beginning of April, though, he was still advertising in Wallace, Idaho. Dr. Rogers, a graduate of Trinity University in Toronto, was enticed west by his brother, the Presbyterian minister in Nelson. Both Bruner and Rogers were registered to practice in BC on May 4, 1893, along with Dr. Mary MacNeill, BC's first female doctor. Bruner and Rogers were soon joined by Dr. Samuel A. Metherell. Metherell had practiced medicine in Ontario before coming west but didn't stay long in Kaslo, opting to join Dr. H.F. Titus on a contract to serve the men building the N&FS railway south of Nelson.

By April 1895, in addition to Dr. Rogers in Kaslo, there were two doctors in the Slocan. Dr. Bruner moved his practice to Three Forks in late 1894. He was followed to the Slocan by Dr. Brouse, who moved to New Denver in April 1895 following his work for the N&S. In September, Bruner was joined in Three Forks by Dr. William Gomm, a native of Savannah, Georgia, and a graduate of Bellevue College in New York.

In August 1895, Dr. Brouse—with community support—opened the Slocan Hospital in the two-storey Dingman building on Sixth Avenue in New Denver. The hospital had twenty-five beds and was fitted with all the latest equipment. From his experience as a railway camp doctor, Dr. Brouse instituted an early health insurance scheme where, for twelve dollars a year, residents could be sure of receiving care when they needed it. Mining companies were encouraged to adopt payroll deduction schemes similar to a system that had been in place for the N&S. Most Slocan mines signed up. Dr. Brouse received many confirmation letters. J.J. Rafferty, a mining man recently arrived from the Black Hills of South Dakota, wrote from the Reed and Tenderfoot: "You can count on five men at present for your hospital list . . . I shall deduct $1.00 from all those who have agreed to sign."[17] Individuals signed up too, including R.T. Lowery.

Dr. Brouse couldn't run the hospital himself and was fortunate to have able assistance, particularly from Julius Wolff, the hospital's nurse. Born in Prussia in 1855, Wolff, a veteran of the Franco Prussian War, emigrated from Germany to the United States in 1882. In the 1890s, after a stint working as a nurse for the CPR, he decided to try his luck in West Kootenay. Before taking on the job in New Denver, he had been in charge of the baths at the Halcyon Hot Springs on Upper Arrow Lake.

The Slocan Hospital was soon taking in patients. "Mountain fever" was endemic. M.A. Bucke, with a case initially described as mountain fever, was the first guest, admitted in late August, 1895. He was followed by a number of patients suffering from typhoid, most of them coming in from Sandon. Bucke had a private nurse, forgoing the attentions of Julius Wolff. This was just as well for Wolff, who would have been preoccupied romancing his co-worker, Annie Thompson, who had arrived at the hospital in September, having previously resided in Vancouver. Bucke was likely oblivious to the romantic pursuits going on outside his room. He was focused on recovery—his mountain fever later diagnosed as typhoid. Conditions at the hospital were generally good. The cooking was much better than he expected and was a welcome respite from hospital routine. He wrote to his father regularly and sent records detailing his daily care and frequent enemas.

Whatever the treatment, it must have worked. Bucke was discharged in late October and returned to his work at the Slocan Star. It seems he had not signed up for Dr. Brouse's insurance scheme. He expected his expenses to be burdensome, but through some arrangement with the Slocan Star, Byron and Bruce White agreed to pay most costs.

The Reverend Gaebel was admitted to the hospital in early November with a severe case of typhoid. He was soon joined by the Slocan Star's Will Bennett, a twenty-seven-year-old miner from Wisconsin. Bennett was suffering from both mountain fever and pneumonia. It was expected that a few days of convalescence would have him back on his feet, but he took a turn for the worse. By early December he had developed "unfavorable symptoms."[18] Bennett required continuous care, but there was hope that he would be well enough to celebrate Christmas. Gaebel was discharged shortly before Christmas, along with several others. This left only Will Bennett in the hospital over Christmas and New Year.

The *Ledge* took to giving weekly updates on the comings and goings at the hospital. In December 1895, it provided a summary of cases handled since the hospital's opening. The forty-nine admissions included one case of mountain fever; two, bilious fever; four, pneumonia; one, erysipelas; one, lead colic; and four, acute bronchitis. There were also twenty-one surgical cases, three cases of alcoholism, two cases of paralysis, and ten cases of typhoid. Remarkably, there had been no deaths. Sadly, this changed in late December when Peter Larson, struck by an ore car at the Slocan Star, died shortly after being admitted to the hospital.

Will Bennett, who had come close to death himself, made a full recovery in early January. He was discharged, but the hospital had new arrivals, including pioneer prospector Charlie Drouin, who later died. There were deaths outside of the hospital too, of course, including the victims of snow slides and Otto Austin's death in Three Forks from tuberculosis, another mining camp scourge.

Like the story of Maud Donahue and Alex Sproat, the romance of Julius Wolff and Annie Thompson caught the attention of many in New Denver. At first blush, they didn't seem to have much in common. Wolff, forty years old, was the only surviving son of the late Jacob Wolff and his wife Charlotte. The elder Wolff had been chief justice of the court of assizes for Rhenish Prussia and a knight of the Order of the Red Eagle. Julius Wolff's love interest, Annie, was a London-born thirty-six-year-old spinster, the fourth daughter of the late Charles Thompson and his wife, Lydia. Julius and Annie were married at the hospital on November 23, 1895, in a Catholic ceremony. Fittingly, Dr. Brouse was one of the witnesses.

ANOTHER ESSENTIAL COMPONENT OF LIFE in the western mining camps was mail service. It's hard to overemphasize how important the mail was to those living in the isolated mining camps. Most inhabitants were far removed from their families and loved ones and depended on the mail to keep in touch. There were dozens of prospectors and miners with sweethearts, mothers, brothers, sisters, and others that they wrote to. They waited eagerly for news from the outside and were disappointed with every mail trip that yielded no letters. Similarly, those at the other end were beset with worry when there was no reassuring letter from their loved one far away.

The postmaster, one of the most important people in the early mining camps, acted as the go-between for communications linking the isolated camps with the outside world. They experienced the joy when a lonely prospector received a letter from a far-off sweetheart, but also shared the sadness when men came in week after week only to meet with disappointment when there was no mail.

In the summer of 1892, J.B. Wilson was appointed the first postmaster at Kaslo. The Kootenay Lake camp was flooded with pilgrims on their way to the Slocan, and bundles of letters followed them. Soon after, there were postmasters in New Denver, Three Forks, Watson, and Nakusp. Assistant post office inspector Dorman was in Nakusp in October 1893, having just been in Three Forks to appoint Herb Pitts as postmaster there. Dorman was interviewed by the *Nakusp Ledge* and, responding to complaints about U.S. Thomas's duties as a postmaster, provided a brief but accurate description of a postmaster's lot on the mining frontier:

> I hear quite a number of complaints here about the Nakusp postmaster. But I hear similar complaints everywhere. I have to protect the postmaster as well as the people. Unless specific charges in writing are made against a postmaster, nothing can be done as general charges verbally made do not amount to anything. The salary of the Nakusp office is very small, considering the amount of business done at this point, and the position of postmaster is not an envious one.[19]

The salary might have been small, but designation as a postmaster, with the guarantee of regular traffic, could provide a significant boost for those postmasters who also ran general stores or other businesses.

Poor mail service would be an ongoing irritant in West Kootenay. In December 1892, a correspondent for the *Victoria Daily Times* complained loudly. With the lack of steamboat service in the winter, he regaled readers with the hardships of the mail carriers who had to ford rivers on waterlogged rafts, stagger over slippery roads, and tramp through three or four feet of snow to get mail into the camps. In May 1893, an American in Kaslo had this to say: "There is practically no mail service here. Occasionally a bag will stray into camp. It takes a letter about three times as long to get here from Spokane as it does ordinary freight."[20]

By 1894, residents' anger was boiling over. Most of it was directed at E.H. Fletcher, the post office inspector headquartered in Victoria. In the summer of 1893, when the mining camp of Watson was still a going concern, someone asked Fletcher about mail service between that camp and New Denver—ten miles to the west. He replied: "Send the letters by way of Kaslo." This meant that a letter from Watson to New Denver would first travel to Kaslo, then down the lake to Nelson, then by steamer up to Nakusp and by pack animal to New Denver—a round trip of about two hundred miles. Dr. E.C. Arthur complained that a letter sent from Kaslo to Nelson took nine days to get there—by way of Victoria. The Nelson *Tribune* was merciless in its criticism: "It is useless to advise Mr. Fletcher for he is as densely stupid as he is servile."[21]

Fletcher visited the Slocan in April 1894, and no doubt got an earful from disgruntled residents. He promised improvements, but they fell far short of expectations. In September, the *Slocan Times* described the mode of delivery for mail from Nakusp to New Denver: "The mail comes into New Denver on a pack horse. The pack horse hops along the ties on the railroad grade and when the train comes along it moves aside and lets the train pass."[22] The *Kootenay Mail* called Fletcher a "relic of a bygone era," and suggested that he should be placed in the Victoria Museum and labelled "An Antediluvian Mossback."[23]

Curiously, several weeks later the *Kootenay Mail* came to Fletcher's defence. In December 1894, it was reported that the chief post office inspector was expected in Victoria from Ottawa. Several employees had quit their jobs to protest working conditions and low pay. The chief inspector had promised to address their grievances, but it was also understood he would review the operation of the Victoria office under Fletcher. The *Kootenay Mail* expected he would find a "big bundle of complaints" from West Kootenay, painting Fletcher as the "arch offender" in the failure of the postal system. However, on sober reflection, the *Mail* came to believe that Fletcher "is doing as well as he can in a new, scattered and unsettled community."[24] Fletcher survived the review. In January 1895, he introduced improvements to the mail system in the Slocan that even some of his harshest critics welcomed. However, it was not enough to satisfy everyone. In April, the *Ledge* described mail service in the Slocan as "the great annoyance."[25] The complaints would continue.

Mail delivery using pack horses and wagons seemed decidedly old-fashioned in the last decade of the nineteenth century. Even telegraphy was beginning to seem outdated. Many camps were embracing instead the revolutionary new technology of telephony. As early as 1891, the news of Carpenter and Seaton's discovery of the Payne had been communicated from Ainsworth to Nelson by telephone. As the Slocan camps grew, so too did the demand for telephone connections. A number of mines started to run their own telephone lines into the various camps. Telephone connections greatly improved communications within the Slocan, but the mail remained the backbone of communications with the outside world. During 1895, mail connections improved somewhat when pack horses were finally replaced by trains, but this would not completely resolve the great annoyance.

13

TRACKS TO SANDON

IN THE WINTER OF 1893 TO 1894, Sandon, the small camp located in the heart of the mining district, consisted of a few tents and log shacks huddled around Bob Cunning's roughly hewn hotel. When Patsy Clark threw up his bond on the Reco, Johnny Harris camped at Sandon Creek on his Loudoun mineral claim. He could see the potential. He worked the Reco to raise cash and planned his townsite. In early February 1894, E.L. Wilson described Sandon as "one of the coming towns" of West Kootenay.[1] The fires in the summer of 1894 swept through but did not diminish the camp's potential. After the devastation of Three Forks, Bear Lake City, and Watson, many burned-out residents from those camps relocated to Sandon.

When Three Forks was being rebuilt after the fires, the townsite agent, C.J. Loewen, with buildings going up all around him, mocked Harris's forlorn dream of a townsite and railway stop up Carpenter Creek. However, Sandon continued to grow, and pilgrims came in from further afield. Three of the earliest arrivals were brothers Mike, Al, and Ed Bartlett. Experienced Colorado packers, they had freighted for the Homestake and other mines in that state. Charlie Lundberg and William Levi, respectively, put up what were likely the second and third hotels in the camp. Before opening the Star Hotel, Lundberg had operated the Palace Hotel in Kaslo. Boosters like Lundberg and the Bartlett brothers believed that Sandon's location, close to the Slocan Star and on the road leading to other nearby mines, would prove the new camp once ore started shipping by rail.

After many delays, the K&S, with the financial backing of J.J. Hill, finally took off in March 1895. The latest plans for the railway—now a narrow-gauge proposition—had it going from Kaslo to a terminus at the mouth of Sandon Creek, with a spur line to Cody, just up Carpenter Creek from Sandon. This would put it right in the heart of the mineralized area with easy access to big producing mines including the Noble Five, Last Chance, Reco, and Slocan Star. Much to the chagrin of the Three Forks townsite agent, the line would bypass his camp. When asked if the railway's terminus would be at Three Forks, the principal contractor replied: "No, at Sandon. We pass near Three Forks, but that town is on a level so much lower than the roadbed that we couldn't get down to it. The terminus chosen for the line will be just as easy of access from all the mines in that vicinity, and just as satisfactory."[2] The fate of Three Forks was sealed.

A representative of the CPR was in Three Forks when the latest news on the K&S came through. In conversation with a New Denver resident, he vowed that the CPR would never let a foreign railway cut them out of their own territory. The understanding at CPR headquarters was that as soon as dirt began to fly on the K&S, the CPR would immediately extend the N&S to Sandon in direct competition. It looked like the railway race anticipated in 1893 was finally on.

Just as Three Forks boomed when it was announced as the terminus of the N&S, Sandon boomed once it was known that both the K&S and

Sandon, June 1895. Photographer: R.H. Trueman. Nakusp & Slocan Railway surveyors at Sandon. IMAGE COURTESY OF STAN SHERSTOBITOFF

the N&S would be building there. The small huddle of log buildings that sprang up in 1893 and 1894 was quickly transformed into a bustling, chaotic knot of buildings crowding along the banks of Carpenter and Sandon Creeks. E.R. Atherton, who had relocated from burnt-out Watson, had a large store that dominated Reco Avenue. Sandon pioneer Bob Cunning was putting up a two-storey hotel to replace his log hotel; Archie Grant was building a barn to house stage teams; and the Hammond brothers were building a store. When Mr. Cockburn, a Vancouver mercantile agent, visited Sandon in July 1895, he described it as West Kootenay's "great centre of attraction" due to the railway speculation.[3]

With the beginning of construction on the K&S, the Slocan experienced a boom not seen since the heady days of early 1893. Tents sprang up all along the line. K&S engine no. 1 arrived in Kaslo on July 31 aboard a barge from Bonner's Ferry. The locomotive was quickly put to work carrying supplies from the wharf in Kaslo to the workers along the line. Kaslo was booming again. According to D.J. Munn: "There is not a house empty in the place, and new buildings are going up every week."[4] No longer the "wicked city," or the "city of calamities," Kaslo began promoting itself as the "city of energy."

Construction on the N&S extension began in August, shortly after the dirt began to fly on the K&S. The narrow valley leading into Sandon was soon thick with railway workers. Construction was just the tonic for a mining district still recovering from the depression and the floods, fires, and snow slides. The mountains were alive as miners worked with new purpose to bring out ore and prepare it for shipping. While winter was the preferred season for shipping ore, when pack animals would haul tons of ore wrapped in the "rawhides" of beef cattle down the snow-packed trails, a few mines would take advantage of the railway connections to ship ore over the summer.

One of the early passengers riding on the N&S out of Three Forks was Bishop Dart of the Church of England. Dart had succeeded Bishop Sillitoe and was making his first foray into the Slocan. The line was not yet to Sandon, so he had to walk part of the way. Just out of New Denver, the train stopped. Dart got off and walked through the trees and stumps to a cemetery, where he presided over an impromptu service for a recently deceased miner.

With the railways headed his way, Johnny Harris decided the time was right to cash in on his Loudoun mineral claim, the site on which most of the growing camp of Sandon was located. With partners Sam Wharton and

Arrival of Locomotive No. 1, July 31, 1895. Photographer unknown but possibly a draughtsman named Wilse. ORIGINAL IMAGE COURTESY OF KOOTENAY LAKE ARCHIVES, KASLO, BC

Fred Kelly, Harris had a stake in the fabulously rich Reco mine. But his primary focus was Sandon. He partnered with G.M. Sproat, who was experienced in townsite development, to seek a Crown grant for the Loudoun. They jointly registered their improvements in August 1895, and in October applied for the Crown grant. The application was approved and recorded on November 18, 1895.

There was a Canadian federal election in 1896. J.A. Mara had represented the Slocan since the first discoveries of Seaton and Carpenter in 1891. A Conservative with a chequered past, he was opposed by the Liberal, Hewitt Bostock, a relatively recent arrival from Britain. The federal election didn't attract as much interest in the Slocan as the provincial election had. Fewer than a hundred votes were cast in the district, with Bostock coming out on top—51 to 42. The election marked the ascendency of a Canadian Liberal Government headed by Wilfrid Laurier. M.A. Bucke, now living in Sandon, reluctantly voted for Bostock because he favoured the Liberal Party. However, he had doubts about Bostock: "He is an englishman of the english and the province is already so loaded to the neck with english office holders that a Canadian has no show in his own country."[5]

Regardless of political preferences or indifference, Sandon was clearly on the path to prosperity. R.T. Lowery seized the opportunity and financed the *Paystreak*, Sandon's first newspaper. He had earlier sold the *Kaslo Claim Relocated* to Dave King, who rebranded it the *Kootenaian*. The *Paystreak* started up in September 1896. Langstaff left the *Kootenaian* to edit the *Paystreak*. The premiere edition noted that "the liveliest and busiest town in the Slocan country is every day assuming a more urban-like appearance than is usually met with in a mining centre."[6] This couldn't be told from the *Paystreak*'s office and equipment. The Gordon press was propped up on shingles, and Langstaff slept on a cot at the back of the building. Sleep was hard to come by with the noise from the gambling emporiums on either side of the office.

Langstaff wasn't Lowery's first choice for editor. That honour belonged to Seneca G. Ketchum. Of Empire Loyalist stock, Ketchum grew up in Ontario but came into his own as a tramp printer in Washington State. He briefly edited *The Idea* in Vancouver but landed in the Slocan in the summer of 1896. If they weren't already acquainted, Ketchum and Lowery would have known each other by reputation. Both were fond of the bottle and likely hit it off when they met. Lowery agreed to finance the Sandon newspaper. Ketchum would raise advertising revenue and serve as editor. However, when given an advance by Lowery, Ketchum spent it on booze and failed miserably to raise revenue. According to Lowery, when he first "assayed" Ketchum, he found that the newspaperman was worth only 60 cents in silver and was 90 percent beer.[7] Tall and gaunt, with a protruding upper lip tucked behind a bushy red mustache, Ketchum must have been quite a sight in the saloons of Sandon. Lowery could see that it wouldn't work out. Ketchum headed instead for Nelson, where he briefly held the position of chief constable after the camp became a city in 1897. Langstaff didn't last long in Sandon either. In 1897, he left the *Paystreak* to run the *Trout Lake Topic*. He was succeeded at the *Paystreak* by Spokane's E.C. Bissell.

Much of Sandon's growth came at the expense of Three Forks, which suffered as it bled businesses to the upstart camp upstream. Colin Bowen sold his hotel to the Sloan brothers and "went fishing," leaving a long line of creditors behind him. It must have been particularly galling to Three Forks residents in July, when George Lovatt decided to move the Lovatt brothers' sawmill from Three Forks to Sandon. However, it was a sound business decision given Sandon's explosive growth and growing demand for lumber. More particularly, the K&S would need a steady local supply of lumber and had been making overtures to Lovatt, encouraging the move to Sandon.

Ignored by the K&S and jilted by the N&S, Three Forks struggled through the early months of 1896. Nelson's *Tribune* attributed the decline of Three Forks not so much to the railways or any particular attraction in Sandon but more to the greed of the Three Forks townsite owners: "If the owners of the Three Forks townsite would be a little more liberal with the men who have made the town what it is, there would be less talk of moving the town further up the creek. Eight hundred dollars a lot is a pretty stiff price to pay for a small-sized lot in a small sized town."[8] A writer for the *Province* could see the future as soon as the railway race to Sandon began. He noted that once Sandon was reached, the "pronged city" would likely "fade away."[9] Still, as the terminus of the Kaslo wagon road and N&S—at least until rails reached Sandon—Three Forks still attracted a few visitors. It also retained a government office and police constable, and along with New Duluth, continued as the base for local staff of the N&S. In January 1896, E.M. Sandilands resigned as constable. Like others in Three Forks, he decided there were better opportunities in Sandon. He planned to go into private banking. His replacement was to be Fred Mountain. Mountain was a Slocan pioneer from 1892, but by the time he arrived back in the Slocan, his old friend Jack Watson and the town he had founded were long gone.

One of Mountain's first tasks was to conduct an inventory of the police office. He did a thorough job. The library was limited to legal texts such as

Constable Fred Mountain and another man in front of Three Forks lock-up, c. 1896. Photographer unknown. IMAGE COURTESY OF THE UNIVERSITY OF BRITISH COLUMBIA LIBRARY DIGITIZATION CENTRE AND ITS GENEROUS DONORS

the criminal code of 1892, British Columbia statutes for 1896, and the 1876 Indian Act as amended up until 1886. There was no literature—nothing that might divert a lonely constable on a cold winter's night in front of a roaring fire of dried fir drawn from the two cords of wood on hand—no Brett Hart, no Mark Twain, no Sherlock Holmes.

In January 1895, Sandon had at least three hotels running, with a fourth, Archie Grant's, nearing completion, as well as four stores, a barbershop, a laundry, and a cigar shop. A Vancouver man named Freshman was building a men's clothing store, and a bakery was imminent. A couple of weeks later another new hotel, the Ivanhoe, opened under the management of Moore and Fred B. Wrong. The Ivanhoe boasted "an appearance seldom seen" with a barroom lined throughout with "antique cedar bark" and a back wall covered in ferns.[10] Competition in the booming camp was stiff, and businesses would go to great lengths to give themselves an advantage. For the Ivanhoe, it was cedar bark and ferns; for the Star Hotel under the new management of Black and McLennan, it was a "fine store of wet groceries."[11] The wet groceries likely proved a better drawing card, particularly when Moore and Wrong's application for a liquor licence was denied. They didn't know it at the time, but the application was rejected because of a complaint from G.M. Sproat. Sproat and Harris had not at that time received their Crown grant for the Loudoun, so it was suspected that Sproat used his political influence to have the liquor licence denied. A frustrated Fred Wrong sold his share of the business to Ira Black.

A correspondent for the *Kootenay Mail* noted of Sandon's rapid growth: "You might as well try to stop water from running down a hill as stop the growth of Sandon."[12] Another resident observed: "This burg looks lively. Wagons laden with goods constantly arriving and pack trains departing for the hills make our one street look animated as a fair day in Ireland."[13] Typical of most western boom towns and much like Kaslo in 1892 and 1893, Sandon was decidedly wild and woolly during its early days. Unlike New Denver or even Three Forks, its proximity to the mines made it more accessible to work-weary miners thirsty for liquor and hungry for good times. Saloon keepers were happy to accommodate them. Most Sandon residents wouldn't have known why the Ivanhoe's liquor licence was denied, and they might not have cared. There were other bars well stocked with liquor. The denial of one liquor licence seemed a very small setback, but residents would soon feel the reach of Sproat and Harris.

Reco Avenue, Sandon, c. 1895–96. Photographer unknown. Sandon in the winter of 1895 to 1896. The newly built Clifton House to the right of the Ivanhoe. IMAGE FROM *BC OUTDOORS*, VOL. 24, NO. 6 (DECEMBER 1968)

By the close of 1895, Sandon's early log hotels, like the Ivanhoe, were eclipsed by a new arrival. The Clifton House, run by John Buckley, first opened its doors on Christmas Day in 1895. By early 1896, it was running at full steam with Grant and Sarah Thorburn in charge of day-to-day operations. The *Ledge* gave the establishment a glowing review: "The Clifton is just what Sandon has been in sore need of, and it fills a position that has been a long want. The rooms are spacious, and so constructed that every comfort that she could well desire is at hand."[14] Soon the Clifton was the most popular hotel in Sandon.[15]

Incorporated as a city in 1893, in the thick of the depression, Kaslo welcomed the railway activity brought on by K&S construction. But with a shrinking population, the city council was desperate for money to finance administrative services. The licensing fees paid by the Comique in 1893 had been a significant source of revenue for a city council struggling to make ends meet. In December 1894, the city wrote to the Holland brothers offering them a business licence for $900. Sam Holland knew he had the advantage. He refused the $900 and instead offered to pay $600. The cash-short city council accepted the deal and the Holland brothers started planning for their return engagement. The churches were upset, but miners applauded the move. A newspaper correspondent likely represented public sentiment when he wrote, "If people are so moral they can not live in a community with a comique in operation they had better return to the pumpkin fields of a more straight-laced community and not try to abide in a mining camp."[16]

When she visited Kaslo in 1895, Lady Aberdeen found the city to be "very much of the American type." She took note of the hardships it had faced but had her criticisms: "It has about 900 inhabitants and a Mayor and Corporation which appears to be a doubtful blessing as they have licensed an American variety theatre of the lowest type, the only one of its kind in Canada, to amuse the miners. But the disgrace of it is felt, and some of the ladies spoke very strongly to me about it."[17] Lady Aberdeen commiserated with the ladies but there wasn't much she could do.

While Kaslo was shrinking, Sandon continued to grow. The rapid growth was unplanned, though it should have been anticipated. Due to the early uncertainty of ownership, the first arrivals built wherever it was convenient, with little or no regard for property rights. Before Harris and Sproat obtained their Crown grant, squatters could go on in ignorant bliss of what was coming. In many other fledgling mining camps, it was customary for the owners of townsites, once they were in a position to develop the properties and sell lots, to give preference to the pioneers who first set up camp. This was not the way things unfolded in Sandon. When Sproat and Harris received their Crown grant in November 1895, everything changed.

The two partners were determined to aggressively exert their property rights. In early December, residents were alarmed to learn there were no assurances they would be able to purchase the land on which they had built. In the meantime, they would have to pay rent to Sproat and Harris. The new landlords were resolute in their efforts to turn their interest in Sandon into a profit centre. They kept a tight lid on building lots, but those that did make it to the market were selling for about $500 in early 1896. As Sandon boomed, Harris held on to most town lots, convinced that they would only rise in value. According to one correspondent, Harris had "an unshaken faith in the city's future."[18] His preference was to rent lots, which had its own challenges.

Many Sandon residents, particularly the pioneers who had been there before there was any hint of a railway, were upset and angry. Some weren't shy about letting Sproat and Harris know how they felt. One resident publicly denounced Sproat with a few choice words. He was fined twenty dollars on the spot. Mike Kerlin, one of the first settlers at Sandon Creek, was particularly irate and launched legal action. Protests, legal challenges, and even a petition to the Legislative Assembly played out over the next few years, but, at least in the short term, none of this slowed Sandon's growth. Despite the complaints, the future of Sandon looked bright.

The K&S was soon past Three Forks on its way to Sandon, where it arrived in late October. On the way, in an impressive display of engineering, the tracks clung to the sheer rock walls of the Payne Bluff, high above Three Forks and the valley leading into Sandon. On October 29, George Keefer inspected the K&S for the province. He noted "everything from road-bed to rolling stock is of the most workmanlike and substantial nature and the company is to be congratulated on a very satisfactory piece of construction."[19] J.J. Hill must have been pleased. On November 1, K&S president D.J. Munn rode the line in triumph. In early November, the first carload of ore was shipped out to Kaslo from the Ruth. There had been small shipments from other mines—such as the Texas and Mountain Goat—as the railway line advanced, but the Ruth, which had made shipments over the N&S, was in the heart of the mineral district. Soon other mines would be shipping, and some, like the Last Chance, switched from the N&S to the K&S.

All along the line, mines set up infrastructure to take advantage of the shipping opportunities. Twenty-five miles out of Kaslo, at "Bailey's Station," Steve Bailey built a large ore shed to store Payne ore destined for Kaslo. The Washington mine started building a tramway to connect to the rail line. The K&S was accommodating and laid out a townsite in anticipation. The K&S would prove a boon to small, grassroots operators close to Sandon and those on the Kaslo slope. The owner of the Wonderful Bird, located just below the Wonderful, used just a pick, shovel, and grub hoe to scrape the ore from the surface of his claim. He shipped just a ton of ore a week during the summer of 1897, but this would not have been possible without the K&S.

THE WEATHER IN SANDON WAS mild when the N&S arrived in November, shortly after the K&S. The two railways had been sniping at one another for months. Things came to a head in December. There was very little room to maneuver in the narrow valley of Carpenter Creek. On entering Sandon, the N&S began staking land claimed by their rival. On December 9, 1895, the CPR's Harry Abbott wrote to Premier Turner advising him of the N&S's intentions. The railway had applied to the Privy Council in Ottawa for approval to take control of "certain lands owned or occupied by the Kaslo and Slocan Railway."[20] The K&S would not stand for this. With a large force of men, they proceeded to pull up all the N&S stakes. The battle was on. It would be fought vigorously both on the ground and in the courts over the next few months.

The legal ground was complex. The K&S operated only in BC and was subject to the laws of the province. The CPR operated under the jurisdiction of the government of Canada. The K&S fired the first shot, applying for and receiving an injunction from Justice Crease to restrain the N&S from trespassing. On appeal, however, the N&S was able to get Justice Drake to dissolve the injunction. CPR workers re-staked the ground, laid track, and built a station house on the disputed land. The K&S fumed and filed for another injunction. They didn't wait for the court to hear their case. On the evening of December 16, about sixty K&S men gathered at the railway station in Kaslo, supposedly preparing to go out and repair a bridge. Instead, they rode a train all the way into Sandon. Arriving sometime after midnight, they poured off the train wielding axes, hammers, and crowbars. It was rumoured that some had been supplied with revolvers. First, they uncoupled a boxcar, then let loose a bunk car. CPR building contractor Clements and telegraph operator Hamilton were in the bunk car. Clements jumped from the moving car, injuring his ribs when he landed on a pile of loose lumber. Hamilton was pinned against a wall by the stove but did not suffer serious injuries.

The K&S men continued their onslaught by tearing down the N&S freight shed. They ripped up the platform, tore down a trestle, pulled up rail irons and ties, and cut telegraph lines. There was an uneasy truce when the K&S troops returned to Kaslo for breakfast. The only building remaining on the disputed land was the N&S station house. The CPR's roadmaster, John Lawrence, arrived in Sandon later in the morning, and with a small crew, tried to replace the ties and re-lay the tracks. He was thwarted at every turn. Back from Kaslo, the K&S men ripped up the ties and tracks as soon as they were laid. Lawrence quit, and things quietened for the rest of the day. CPR officials were burning up the telegraph wires trying to come up with a strategy to deal with the K&S assault.

At about noon the next day, a K&S train pulled into Sandon and a gang of men immediately set about attacking the N&S station house with axes. The destruction did not go as quickly as planned, so they hooked up a hawser line, running it through the dormer windows of the station house and around the back. They attached the line to the locomotive and let the steam engine do its work. Soon there was nothing left of the station but a jumble of broken, splintered boards. Things eventually settled down on the ground, if not in the courts.

The battling railways stirred the emotions and loyalties of Slocan residents. While many with British or eastern Canadian backgrounds favoured the N&S, with its ties to the CPR, Americans, and most residents of Sandon, regardless of nationality, were loyal to the K&S. During the dispute, the N&S had tried to get a warrant for the arrest of Superintendent McGraw, who had led the K&S men, but G.M. Sproat refused to issue the warrant, believing that the K&S people were in the right.

One visible difference in the way the two railways were run was in dress. The CPR insisted its crews wear regulation uniforms. The K&S allowed their crews to wear whatever suited them. One British observer in 1896 described his first impression of the crew operating the K&S as it pulled out of Sandon: "I thought some Comic Opera Company had stormed the train or pirates had seized it."[21] However, an American passenger was dazzled by the train's conductor, "Gus," resplendent in blue and gold.

While Sandon was in the spotlight in 1896, New Denver continued to tout itself as the administrative and social centre of the Slocan. With more women and families, public discourse was perhaps more varied than in other camps. In January 1896, the New Denver Epworth Club held a debate on the subject "Should women be allowed to vote?" Leading the speakers in the affirmative was schoolteacher Eliza Livingstone. Assayer Howard West argued for the negative. Eliza Livingstone's team won the day. Dora Kerr was at that meeting, perhaps the first in the Slocan to discuss the issue of women's suffrage. Dora Kerr and her husband, R.B. Kerr, were committed Fabian socialists and were catalysts in bringing debate on social issues to the Slocan. In a remarkable letter to the *Woman's Signal*, a British feminist magazine, Dora Kerr described a women's suffrage meeting she attended in New Denver—likely the Epworth Club meeting. She applauded the Methodist minister's support for women's citizenship but was more impressed with her husband's impromptu comments:

> The miners among the audience evidently appreciated the fact pointed out to them that a woman works for longer hours and much less pay than a man; that the wife toils from morning till night getting only a bare subsistence, while the husband spends every cent of extra money on his own pleasures. The speech pleased most of the audience greatly, and I think all the women present were delighted.[22]

Dora Kerr was a beacon of enlightenment among the women of the Slocan. Not all social gatherings discussed such weighty topics. A week after the Epworth Club weighed the pros and cons of women's suffrage, they held a pronunciation competition.

The railways stimulated commerce in all the Slocan mining camps. They were integral to the emerging infrastructure needed to fuel boom town economies. When the rails were approaching Three Forks, Slocan businessmen looked to lure a bank to the district. Not just any bank—there was still a bad taste from Burke's failed bank in Kaslo—but an established, chartered Canadian bank. New Denver's Byron White started the ball rolling in 1894. He organized and circulated a petition. Signed by prominent businessmen, it was forwarded to representatives of the Bank of Montreal. The Bank of Montreal would be offered the field first, but if they declined, the Bank of British Columbia would be approached. While both banks were courted, the likelihood of the latter institution opening a branch in the Slocan looked dim after general manager W.C. Ward and Nelson branch manager Grange V. Holt visited in September 1894.

Things started well enough. The two men arrived in New Denver on Monday afternoon, September 10. Ward was impressed: "This is an ideal mining camp. It is the smartest looking place I have seen in the country."[23] A short trip to Silverton impressed as well. The bankers were particularly interested in the Alpha mine. Ward remarked that it gave him a great deal of confidence to see such a pile of ore on the beach awaiting shipment. The trip took a turn for the worse, however, when they left New Denver for Three Forks. Ward's opinions of the country quickly changed:

> It rained most of the time, and then the trail was blocked with trees and he had to walk a longer distance than he cared about. But what worried him most was piloting his horse from New Denver to Three Forks. He particularly objected to those places on the trail where the cayuse has to balance himself on his forelegs and the tip of his nose to crawl down to bedrock.[24]

Ward concluded that "at present there is not business enough in the country to justify us."

At first it looked more promising with the Bank of Montreal. Campbell Sweeny came to the Slocan in late September 1894, accompanied by A.H. Buchanan, the manager of the bank's Nelson branch. Hopes were dashed, however, when Sweeny decided the bank would not open a Slocan branch any time soon—citing a lack of sufficient business to make it profitable.

Slocan boosters were not inclined to take no for an answer. In October 1894, R.T. Lowery's Nakusp *Ledge* pleaded with the established banks in Nelson to open a branch in the Slocan: "Don't hesitate, respected bank folks, but, for Mammon's sake! Give us a bank before all the mineral is dug out and the community bankrupted paying freight on money parcels."[25]

Slocan boosters persuaded the Bank of British Columbia's Holt to come again to Three Forks. Holt almost got there but turned back due to a rail stoppage on the N&S caused by a track washout. The N&S had not reached Three Forks yet, and he described the trail between New Denver and Three Forks as a holy terror.

The prospects for a bank in New Denver seemed to be looking up in 1895. According to the *Vancouver Weekly World*, "influential parties" had approached five Canadian chartered banks inviting them to locate in New Denver. The Bank of British Columbia was "hesitant," the Imperial Bank was "hopeful," the Bank of Montreal was considering a recent proposition made to them, and the Bank of British North America was urged to go forward by "one of the strongest companies operating in the Slocan." In early April, a representative for Molsons Bank also arrived in New Denver to gather information.

Encouraged by the increased activity, Bank of Montreal men Campbell Sweeny and A.H. Buchanan returned to New Denver in 1895 and, like Holt and Ward the previous year, visited the Alpha. However, they were "close as clams" with any talk about banks.[26] Disappointingly, nothing came of the initiatives. Sweeny was back in West Kootenay in 1896, and while he noted "mining in Slocan Country going strong," still there would be no bank.[27]

Lowery and other New Denver businessmen and boosters never stopped pushing, though frustrated at almost every turn. They had mixed feelings then, when in the space of two weeks in November 1896, two chartered banks set up shop in Sandon. The Bank of British Columbia was first, then the Bank of British North America. Both were modest affairs. One visitor judged the Bank of British North America building as being not more than fifteen to twenty feet long with a "camping outfit" occupying the rear.[28] Regardless, Sandon residents were "jubilant." J.C. Eaton drew the first cheque from the Bank of British Columbia. Sandon had the satisfaction of beating not only New Denver to the bank but also its Kootenay Lake rival, Kaslo.

New Denver would have to wait until early 1897 before a branch of the Bank of Montreal opened. R.T. Lowery lauded the move: "It is a great relief for us to know that New Denver will have a bank. For some time we have been worried about the money we have had buried in the ink keg, and now when the bank lifts the wicket, we will be ready with $10 to help them along."[29]

By the close of 1896—much to the chagrin of New Denver and Three Forks—Sandon had clearly become the commercial, business, and good-time centre of the Slocan. With two continentally connected railways at its doorstep, Sandon surged ahead of neighbouring camps. A visitor in the early days of 1896 estimated there were already about 150 buildings and noted that things were "rapidly advancing."[30] But it wasn't just the railways that made Sandon. When the banks arrived, the Sandon correspondent for the *Rossland Miner* was quick to point out: "With two banks Sandon becomes the acknowledged centre of the Slocan silver-lead district."[31]

The mines above Sandon continued producing high-grade ore, but the silver discoveries at the foot of Slocan Lake opened new fields for investment. Interest in the Slocan was at last gaining ground in Vancouver. C.T. Dunbar had sparked that interest earlier in the year with a number of investments. In the summer, several well-known Vancouver entrepreneurs went so far as to relocate to the Slocan. One of the new arrivals was Charles D. "C.D." Rand. Rand was a major real estate speculator and senior partner in Rand Brothers, one of Vancouver's pioneer real estate and brokerage companies. He had been a prime mover in the development of Vancouver in the 1880s, described by one historian as the "maestro to Vancouver's symphony of growth."[32]

Other Vancouver capitalists quickly joined suit. R.C. Campbell-Johnston first visited the Slocan in 1895 and returned in July 1896, presumably to scout locations for Vancouver investors. Certainly, there was lots of talk about the Slocan among Vancouver businessmen like Campbell-Johnston, Archibald "A.M." Beattie, and others. In August, Dunbar—who had already bonded a three-quarter interest in the Two Friends—increased his investment in the claim with his partners, Ernest E. Evans, F.C. Innes, and Osborne Plunkett. Dunbar and his partners incorporated their interest in the Two Friends with $750,000 in capital.

All this action was likely the catalyst that led coast newspapers to finally give West Kootenay its due. The *Vancouver Daily World* had long touted the mining districts, but other papers now climbed aboard the bandwagon.

In September 1896, Francis Carter-Cotton's *Daily News-Advertiser* of Vancouver noted that "after a long period of neglect, the whole district has begun to resound with preparation, and every hill is covered with its knot of prospectors, anxious to be early in the race."[33]

Regardless of whether money came from Vancouver or elsewhere, the significant and steady investment dollars coming in fuelled development work. Business was good for packers like Dad Allen, who had a contract for packing out twenty tons of ore from the Howard Fraction. With new bunk-houses and three tunnels snaking steadily ahead underground, J.A. Finch's Enterprise was another promising property at the lower end of the lake. Finch was in Seattle in June 1896. The *Seattle Post-Intelligencer* praised him as a man making $1,000 a day from his various mines. Finch was modest about his income but suggested that investors from Seattle travel to Sandon to see what the Slocan excitement was all about. He couldn't "imagine a pleasanter trip that might be taken in the way of obtaining information."[34]

The improved transportation links and population growth in the Slocan opened new business opportunities for wholesalers and merchants in Spokane, on the coast, in Alberta, and from points further east. Pat Burns was a cattleman from Calgary. He was a big player in the beef industry and had established a regional presence in Nelson. He started setting up butcher shops in many of the outlying mining camps, often in partnership with local butchers, packers, or general merchants. He opened a butcher shop in Sandon in late 1895. He shipped about fifty head of cattle a month into West Kootenay in 1894. By 1896, the numbers were up to six hundred head a month. He expected to ship a thousand a month during 1897—offering to buy "all the cattle available in southern Alberta."[35]

The Slocan was a lucrative market. Pat Burns had the meat supply locked up, and prairie farmers shipped in boxcars of grain. John Casorso, an Okanagan pioneer, was instrumental in organizing a farmer's co-operative to exploit the Sandon market. Late in 1895, he and four other members of the co-op travelled to Sandon to push for their place in the sun. They found there wasn't much sun there. The dispute between the CPR and the K&S was in full swing, and one of the warehouses they first looked to lease was destroyed in the railway battle. However, they managed to secure a site in a ravine. It wasn't ideal, but they squeezed in a warehouse, and soon had it filled with grain, fruit, and vegetables.

By 1896, Sandon was large enough to be on the circuit for a variety of travelling shows. The railway connections made it all possible. Early visitors included the McKenzie Trio and the Webling Sisters. Rebecca "Sandy" McKenzie, Bertha O'Reilly, and Mary "Elise" Fellows were young, classically trained American musicians. Elise, a musical prodigy from Maine, had studied violin in Europe, where she met Brahms and other musical notables. The trio toured the west from 1895 to 1897, playing in frontier towns and out-of-the-way mining camps. They played two nights in Sandon to sellout crowds and a rapturous reception. Elise noted that more than 150 people turned out for their first performance. Typical of a mining camp, the audience was overwhelmingly male, with just ten or twelve women in attendance. When the trio walked from their hotel to the concert hall dressed in their finery, crowds of men four and five deep lined the street to watch them pass by. They played in Nelson a few days later, and a smitten correspondent for the *Miner* gives some idea of what the fuss was all about:

> Elise Fellows' playing of Raff's Cavatina for instance took us away out of the great mountains and deep pine forests to half forgotten lands across the seas, and awoke in us sleeping memories of other days. Her execution is delightful and if perhaps she lacks a little power that will come later. She is very young and so pretty that even if she could not play it would be worth paying fifty cents to see her smile.[36]

Elise thoroughly enjoyed her two days in Sandon. She described them as "days crowded to the brim and running over into the small hours with good times."[37] It was a visit that would change her life forever. On her second day in Sandon, she was taken on a trip to see the Slocan Star. Her guide and constant companion was Bruce White. White couldn't keep his eyes off her. Returning from the trip to the Star and after a second concert, Elise and her party went to a reception at the Sandon Club organized in their honour: "There we met about 40 of the good people of Sandon and Three Forks, from which a special train had been run. There was champagne and after a while, a little dancing in one room, and all the while plenty of fun-making laughing and talking."[38]

Bruce White was there. After the reception, he walked Elise back to her hotel. He didn't kiss her good night, but he did put his arm around her, and it was clear to her that he was interested. She had to leave to continue the concert tour, but when she reached Revelstoke, there was a letter waiting there from Bruce. He tried to convince her to come back to Sandon. It was the beginning of a long-distance courtship that would eventually lead to marriage.

Peggy Webling arrived in Sandon a few weeks after the McKenzie Trio. Peggy was one of the "Webling Sisters," an English variety act popular at the time. But like Elise Fellows, Peggy Webling was struck by the gender imbalance in the Slocan. Women were scarce: "We did not see a single woman at door or window. Throngs of men stopped in their business, or leisure, to watch us pass by, staring blankly."[39] Only eight women turned up for the performance. But what was noteworthy to the two visitors was simply a fact of life to the bachelors who made up the larger portion of the population. However, appearances can be deceiving. An attendee at one of the Sandon Club's social events later in 1896 noted that "only one gentleman was obliged to dance with a handkerchief around his arm."[40] The handkerchief indicated that another man was taking the lead. While it is certainly true that men predominated, few "respectable" women would have ventured on to Sandon's streets at night.

The Sandon Club was the domain of Johnny Harris and other prominent citizens of Sandon. Harris must have been happy with the camp's growth. Every train brought in entertainers, entrepreneurs, and new renters. One of those trains brought in Johnny's father from Virginia. He must have been proud of his son's success. But Johnny did have challenges. Some people simply squatted on vacant lots with no intention of paying rent to Johnny or G.M. Sproat, while any rent on offer was difficult to collect. G.M. Sproat's son Alex was in the unenviable position of acting as rent-collector for his father. It's clear from his reports back to Sproat senior that he didn't like the assignment. Tenants came up with all sorts of excuses to avoid payment and were often hard to track down. Collecting rent below the "dead line," where most of the prostitutes operated, proved especially challenging. He sympathized with tenants like the Balmoral Hotel's McDonald brothers, who were hard pressed to make their payments.

In May 1896, Johnny Harris and Fred Kelly took a trip to San Francisco "in search of a little city excitement."[41] They put up at San Francisco's luxurious Palace Hotel. Harris gave an interview to the *San Francisco Call*. He seems to have been something of a novelty to the newspaper, coming as he did from some unknown mining district far to the north. The headline for the interview and article read: "Millionaire of Slocan: John M. Harris and his Queer Silver Mine in the Wilds."[42] Throughout the article, Sandon was referred to as "Salmon." Non-plussed, Harris sang the praises of Sandon, the Slocan, and his Reco mine:

"Preparing for a horse race, Christmas Day, 1896." Photographer: R.H. Trueman. Reco Avenue, showing the Bank of British Columbia and Bartlett brothers' offices. A nattily dressed Bruce White, a horse racing enthusiast, can be seen in the lower left of the photograph standing third from the right of the telephone pole. LIBRARY AND ARCHIVES CANADA

> To my mind, this part of the Slocan country is the richest in America in silver and lead. Were it not that the property there is so rich we would be in the same condition as the miners of Idaho, Montana, and elsewhere; we couldn't work the mines at all. But as it is, the ore running so heavy, we get along first rate and work to a profit.[43]

For some, the social events at the Sandon Club and the arrival of entertainers like the McKenzie Trio and the Webling Sisters marked the emergence of Sandon from its mining camp roots. An attendee at one of the Sandon Club's dances noted of the occasion: "It may now be safely averred that this camp has reached the dignity of a town."[44]

14

BATTER UP!

On a rough clearing, rudely hacked from the forest and scrub that still covered much of the New Denver townsite, two teams of hastily assembled baseball players prepared to go nine innings against one another. It was Friday, May 25, 1895. The citizens of New Denver wanted to celebrate Queen Victoria's birthday in a big way. There were lots of other events to entertain the crowds coming in from the surrounding camps, but the baseball game was definitely the main attraction. By mid-afternoon, a large crowd had gathered under warm, cloudy skies to watch the pride of New Denver take on a "scraped together" team from Three Forks.[1] Nakusp, originally scheduled to play, cancelled at the last minute. The Three Forks boys gallantly offered to take their place. The female contingent of New Denver and the surrounding camps—though limited in overall numbers—turned out in force for the baseball game.

The game was tightly contested. The favoured New Denver team went in confident of victory, but it was not to be. Three Forks pulled off a nail-biting 7–6 win. The New Denver players were devastated. Two weeks after the loss, a clutch of baseball enthusiasts filled the office of the Slocan Hotel to organize a baseball club. Mining recorder Alex Sproat was elected chair, and Jimmy Moran of the Queen Bess mine was elected team captain. The newly organized club wasted little time, immediately ordering new equipment from Vancouver. With the assistance of the town's teamsters, they spent a week enlarging, grading, and clearing the baseball grounds until they had a field surpassing "anything in the district."[2] The new equipment arrived by June 13, and the emboldened team issued a challenge to all comers.

Nothing seems to have caught people's interest and imagination in the Slocan in the summers of 1895 and 1896 as much as baseball. Given the large numbers of Americans, it's not surprising the sport was popular. Perhaps more surprising were the numbers of Canadians and British expatriates that caught the bug. Baseball and other team sports were among the ties that bound the pioneer camps of West Kootenay together. They offered an escape from everyday routine, generated community pride, and allowed for the interaction of populations from physically isolated camps. But the rivalries were intense. One government official noted that West Kootenay camps were "as jealous and malicious as rival beauties."[3] A Nelson restaurant visitor in 1894 saw a sign on the wall that read "Eat, drink and be merry for to-morrow you may be in Kaslo."[4] Author Constance Skinner later parodied these camp rivalries in her story "The Spoofing of Hi-unk." In it, she described the infighting between the fictional camps of Flannel Shirt, Salvation City, and Dried Fish Creek.[5]

Outsiders could make fun of mining camp rivalries, but residents took them seriously. Especially, it seems, when it came to baseball. The game was the principal topic of idle conversation throughout the spring, summer, and fall of 1895. The game had been played in West Kootenay earlier. Indeed, a game played in Kaslo on the Queen's birthday in 1892, between Nelson and Bonner's Ferry, Idaho, may have been the first international game played in West Kootenay. But the arrival of the N&S in 1894, and the K&S in 1895, made it possible for teams from Nakusp, New Denver, Three Forks, Sandon, and Kaslo to travel back and forth with relative ease. Teams were fielded, challenges thrown out, fortunes won and lost, and no doubt more than a few friendships and romances kindled or doused. After fires, floods, and hard times, baseball was a welcome escape for long-suffering Kaslo and Slocan residents.

While the 1895 Victoria Day baseball game was likely the first for New Denver, baseball was reported "all the rage" in Nakusp as early as April 1894.[6] There was a team in Nelson at the time too, and a baseball club, but despite the ad hoc game in Kaslo in 1892, baseball was a hard sell in Nelson with its sizeable population of British expatriates. However, the Nelson ball team did play in Kaslo at the celebration for Queen Victoria's birthday in 1894, taking advantage of the easy steamboat journey up the lake. One of BC's best ball players, Sam Schultz, "the demon of the west," was articling as a lawyer in Nelson in 1893, but by July 1894, it was reported that baseball had "given way to cricket on the athletic grounds at Nelson and instead of the cry 'Batter up!' the cry 'Ovah' is the only one that is heard and understood by the crowd of onlookers."[7] This would change in 1895, when the Nelson baseball club was able to round up enough players to form a team—though they had to import some from Spokane.

New Denver finally got to play the Nakusp baseball team in July 1895. The team travelled to Nakusp for the game and on arrival discovered that Nakusp had obtained the services of an ex-professional curveball pitcher plus three or four other top calibre players. The New Denver boys looked handsome in their new uniforms, but they lost the game 15–8. They admitted afterwards that they had not taken their opponents seriously. A New Denver player interviewed by the *Ledge* explained that while his team had a better knowledge of the game and boasted better fielding, they had not practiced against curveballs. The New Denver team was overcome by "the inability to find the puzzling curves of their opponent's pitcher, one or two costly errors and a slight case of razzle dazzle."[8]

Returning to New Denver, the team was met by a "tin can and whistle brigade" unhappy with the loss to Nakusp. However, the team "took their welcome, as also their defeat, with good grace."[9] They managed to salvage a small measure of pride too, in an impromptu July 4 game against a scratch team who called themselves the "Rubbernecks." New Denver was leading 20–0 in the fourth inning when the game had to be cancelled due to a furious rainstorm. The New Denver players retired to Jimmy Moran's cabin for a "sing song."[10]

Soon recovered from the earlier losses, the New Denver boys still believed they had a better team than Nakusp. With fifty to one hundred dollars to back up their bravado, they challenged Nakusp to a return match in New Denver. Nakusp refused the challenge, arguing that as they were the undefeated team, they would only play on their own field. Instead of Nakusp, then, New Denver issued a challenge to Kaslo. George Henderson of the Slocan Hotel carried the details over the divide. New Denver would put up a purse of seventy-five dollars for the first in a series of games, with the first one to be played in New Denver. Kaslo accepted the challenge. On the last Saturday of July, manager Tom Roadley and a hastily organized Kaslo team arrived in New Denver bent on winning the purse. New Denver prevailed, though it must have been a sloppy game. The final score was 40–33. One of the highlights was a spectacular catch by Alex Sproat. Judging by the score, any catch was likely a highlight.

The Three Forks ball team was in New Denver at the time and challenged the winners to a game. New Denver accepted, and won 36–28, avenging their earlier loss. The Kaslo team returned home, blaming their loss on the hospitality they had received in New Denver: "They were used so well in the Slocan metropolis, they did not have the heart to defeat such kind people."[11] Upon returning to Kaslo, they immediately set about preparing for a rematch. The team was to be reorganized and "thoroughly equipped." The *Kaslo Claim* was confident that "with a little practice, of which the club is badly in need, the 'Kaslo's' will be able to put up a good game of ball."[12]

In preparation for the upcoming game, the Kaslo team and its supporters organized "clearing bees" to get a playing field ready. The field was located at the foot of A Avenue, with a spectacular view out over the lake. Finding enough level ground to mark out a baseball diamond could be challenging in the rugged West Kootenay terrain. Even when level ground was found, players often had to contend with stumps, puddles as big as small ponds, and other hazards. Following the game in Nakusp, one of the New Denver players complained "the ground was a very tough one, the right and left field being full of stumps. The first base was several feet higher than the home plate, and the third base was right up against Abriel's store."[13]

The "Kaslo's" practiced while work proceeded on the playing field. Some local enthusiasts began organizing celebrations to follow the game. There's no doubt they were anticipating a victory party. The team's new equipment and uniforms arrived in time, and come game day the players would proudly don grey pants and blue shirts with "Kaslo" boldly emblazoned across the front.

While Kaslo was reorganizing and preparing a playing field, New Denver played an early August game with Sandon. With a winning streak in hand, they were confident. However, they didn't count on a determined Sandon team with strong pitching and capable management under Bruce White of the Slocan Star. New Denver went down to defeat 31–10. Once again, they were forced to lick their wounds and regroup. They must have realized the challenge ahead for their rematch with Kaslo.

The much-anticipated rematch between New Denver and Kaslo took place in Kaslo on August 21. The preparation and practice put in by Kaslo paid off handsomely. Dashing in their new uniforms, the home team bested New Denver 9–1. Kaslo scored a succession of unanswered runs until the eighth inning, when George Long managed to score for New Denver, thus avoiding the ignominy of a shut-out. Recalling the hospitality they received in New Denver, Kaslo treated their defeated guests generously.

After the loss to Kaslo, the New Denver team travelled down Kootenay Lake for a game against Nelson. Badly hungover and suffering from sleep deprivation, New Denver played what team captain Jimmy Moran thought was their worst game yet. The Nelson *Miner* agreed, noting the match "could hardly be called a good exhibition of the great American game."[14] New Denver fielded the same team that had played in Kaslo, but Moran moved to first base, Richardson to left field, Davis to centre field, and Henderson to right field. Tom Roadley was given the job of umpire:

> Chesley, who was in the box for Nelson, and Halley [*sic*] for the visitors, were wild at times, and the game throughout was principally noted for large scores and costly errors. Up to the 6th inning Nelson had slightly the best of it, but at the end of the 7th the score stood tied, 23 to 23. In the 8th both teams changed pitchers, Brown going in the box for Nelson and Maurin [*sic*] for New Denver. In this inning neither nine scored, but in the 9th the Nelson boys seemed to have donned their batting clothes and hit Maurin for 11 runs, while their opponents could only muster 3.[15]

The final score was 34–26 in Nelson's favour. The New Denver boys were likely happy just to have been able to finish the game. They were in no condition to play. The game had been heavily wagered on, and a significant amount of money changed hands. There was no doubt many unhappy New Denver supporters were out of pocket and out of patience with their team.

Their tails between their legs, the road-weary team returned to New Denver discouraged with their successive losses. The baseball season was drawing to a close and they had hoped for better results. A rematch with Sandon set for September 25 offered an opportunity for redemption, but when the day came, the game had to be cancelled because of rain. They closed out the season with fond memories, regardless of whether they won or lost. There was always next year. The baseball rivalry of 1895 captivated the citizens of the Slocan. An English player more familiar with cricket than baseball wrote to the *Ledge* in June 1895, giving a vivid account of his first baseball game. At first, he complained about being pulled into the game and described an unfortunate encounter with a stump. But in the end, he decided he enjoyed the game and would play again for New Denver if asked:

> I hit blindly out with the bat and have a distant recollection of having struck something, on the strength of which I immediately commenced to run to the first base, as if life depended on my getting there before the

Baseball in Kaslo, c. 1895–96. Photographer unknown. IMAGE COURTESY OF KOOTENAY LAKE ARCHIVES, KASLO, BC

> ball, cheered on in the meantime by what I took to be the approbation of the crowd, but which I found subsequently to be quite the opposite.[16]

In 1896, Slocan baseball enthusiasts picked up where they had left off in 1895. As in the previous year, most games were aligned with the various holidays celebrated through the spring and summer. New Denver, Nakusp, and Three Forks faded from competitiveness in 1896, but they still had hope. Both Nakusp and New Denver worked hard on their baseball fields in the spring of 1896, each vying to have the best field in West Kootenay. However, there was a new baseball rivalry that dominated all others. Bruce White's Sandon team set its sights on Kaslo. White wrote to his sweetheart, Elise, in April 1896. He tried to convey the excitement of that rivalry to Elise: "Sandon had an excursion to Kaslo yesterday to play Base Ball and the result was 19 to 3 in favor of Sandon. We had *heaps* of fun. I wish you could have seen the miners play. Kaslo has been practicing for two weeks and you know we have no place large enough up here to play catch or say nothing about a game."[17]

While the 1896 season started in April, things really kicked off in Kaslo on Queen Victoria's May 24 birthday celebration. Junior teams from

Nelson and Kaslo got things started, with the Nelson juniors winning 19–6, in what was described as a "very exciting game." In the first big game, played the following day, Sandon scraped by Nelson, 14–13, advancing to the marquee match against Kaslo. The Kaslo players donned their uniforms from 1895, now somewhat worn from a season of games and practices. Playing for the championship, McLean pitched for Kaslo and Sammy Myers for Sandon. The score was tied into the eighth inning, but Kaslo pulled ahead in the ninth to win by four runs, with a final score of 22–18, avenging its earlier loss. West Kootenay Alderman Cole Murchison promised the Kaslo team new uniforms if they beat Sandon. Soon after their victory, the scuffed-up outfits from 1895 were retired and the team tried on their crisp new uniforms.

The next games took place in Sandon on Dominion Day and in New Denver on July 4. The game between Sandon and Kaslo was the highlight of the day's celebration. The home team triumphed, defeating Kaslo 30–13 (or 30–15 if the *Kaslo Kootenaian*'s account is accurate). Just days later, the Sandon team took their game to New Denver. New Denver prided itself on having the best ball ground in the Slocan. It didn't matter. The Sandon team was on a roll. They defeated New Denver 26–10.

Dominion Day was celebrated in Nelson too, where the local baseball club hosted a Spokane team. The $200 purse was easy money for the Spokane nine, who defeated Nelson 17–3. Some West Kootenay pride was salvaged a few weeks later when a Rossland team travelled to Spokane and won their game 14–5. Of course, not all baseball games were restricted to Sundays or holidays. On August 5, a Wednesday, Sandon hosted the Kaslo Giants. Kaslo was determined to avenge their August loss to Sandon. They reached out to baseball teams south of the border to bolster the Giants. Two of their acquisitions were a pitcher and catcher from the Missoulas of Montana. The efforts paid off. Kaslo defeated Sandon.

The challenge for baseball in Sandon was the lack of level ground for a decent ball field. Nakusp and New Denver had challenges too, but nothing to compare to Sandon's. Bruce White had noted the challenge in his letter to Elise Fellows in 1896. A makeshift ball field was established on the ground between Sandon and Cody, but it left much to be desired. One resident described Sandon as a place of many "switchbacks." He may have been exaggerating when he wrote: "Indeed, there was even a switchback between first and second base on the baseball field!"[18] Exaggeration or not, it's no surprise that many of Sandon's matches were "away" games. Despite some disadvantages, however, Sandon fielded a team that dominated and often intimidated teams from the smaller camps. When the Nakusp team travelled to Sandon for a game, a Sandon booster made the mistake of calling the Nakusp team "the boys from the sawdust town."[19] This raised the ire of Nakusp's Tom Abriel. In a speech after the game, he told the story of the perpetrator of a crime so heinous, that even hanging was not fit punishment. Instead, he was sentenced to life in Sandon.

WHILE BASEBALL WAS IMMENSELY POPULAR in the Slocan during the summers of 1895, '96, and '97, the building of a curling rink and an indoor arena in Sandon in late 1896 and early 1897 ushered in a new era of winter sports.

Early in December 1896, several prominent Sandon citizens met in Johnny Harris's office to organize a curling club. The elected president was Martin Grimmett, a native of Manitoba who was vice president of the lacrosse club too. The newly established club, perhaps influenced by Grimmett's roots, affiliated itself with the Manitoba Northwest Curling Association, a branch of the Royal Caledonian Curling Club. Though long played in eastern Canada, curling was a new sport to BC. Golden and Kaslo had the first two organized clubs, Golden operating from at least December 1894, and Kaslo from December 1895. Horace W. Bucke, who was a champion for the sport in Kaslo, had the distinction of winning the first game played in Golden.

The first game of curling in Sandon took place on January 27, 1897. It attracted quite a crowd, many of whom had never seen the game played. The two teams included the following players, most of whom—with the notable exception of Johnny Harris—had Canadian or British backgrounds: J.M. Harris, A.E. Hall, B. Wilson, M.L. Grimmett, G.H. Winter, R. McDonald, W.W. Fallows, and H. Mann.

The game was won 14–8 by Harris, Hall, Wilson, and Grimmett. Although it sounds like their team might have been a law firm, Grimmett, in fact, was the only lawyer.

Hockey was the other sport that gained momentum in early 1897. Interest grew by leaps and bounds during the 1890s. The sport had been gradually spreading west from its Nova Scotia roots and Ontario heartland, with recent inroads in Alberta. As early as 1893, a few adventurous Nelson residents played a game on Kootenay Lake.

Hockey clubs sprang up in several Kootenay mining camps, including Sandon. The sport took off when the indoor rink was completed early in 1897. An indoor rink in Kaslo soon followed. Local hockey enthusiasts were boosted by incomers from the east, like Kaslo's "Chid" Frost, a star goalkeeper from Orillia, Ontario. One of the early Sandon matches was a novel affair. The two opposing teams were the "fats" and the "leans." The rules were that none of the fats could weigh less than 200 pounds, and none of the leans could exceed 115. A large crowd watched the leans defeat the fats, 2–1. Expecting the worst, spectators were charged a small admission to "defray hospital expenses." Return matches were arranged, all won by the fats. Johnny Harris played forward for the leans, while Fred Kelly was "brilliant" in goal for the fats.[20]

The first game between the fats and leans was followed by other pick-up games. A contest between the "blacks" and the "whites" was a more serious affair, won by the blacks, 6–3. The game featured players who would go on to form Sandon's first representative hockey team. By the end of February, matches were being arranged with other West Kootenay communities. The Sandon team was successful from the start. In their first game, they defeated Kaslo 5–2. This may well have been the first formal intercity hockey game ever played in BC, though one account—perhaps the result of failing memory—has Sandon playing and defeating Nelson in March 1896.

On March 4, 1897, Sandon hosted the Kaslo and Rossland hockey teams, beating Kaslo 10–2 and Rossland 5–2. The Sandon team comprised Bob Hammond in goal; J. Merritt, point; C.D. Blackwood and J. McVichie, cover points; and Andy Grierson, F.A. Walker, and Howard Cameron, forwards. The Rossland team was captained by Chester McBride, and Kaslo by D.J. Young. Sandon won the tournament cup and had a legitimate claim to the championship of BC. However, they had not played Nelson. This was rectified on March 19, when Sandon humbled Nelson, 14–3. Hockey proved popular in Sandon and was certainly an appropriate sport for the wintry camp. Women were on the ice too. Plans for a ladies' club were put on hold when warmer weather arrived in March, but their club finally emerged in December 1897.

Winter comes early to the Slocan, and Sandon's curling and hockey enthusiasts began preparing in October 1897 for their upcoming seasons. The Sandon curling club was confident they would be able to retain possession of the Bostock Cup, a trophy put up by local member of Parliament Hewitt Bostock. Sandon defeated all challengers in early season games. In

Sandon's Curling Team, Calgary, c. 1898. Photographer unknown.
IMAGE COURTESY OF THE UNIVERSITY OF CALGARY DIGITAL COLLECTIONS

January 1898, two Sandon teams hosted a tournament in which they took on two Kaslo teams. Sandon won the afternoon game and tied the evening game, thereby retaining the district medal on aggregate. Later in the month, a Sandon team travelled to Calgary where they defeated the "crack team" of the tournament. In February Sandon's curling team competed at the Rossland Winter Carnival. They defeated Smith's Rossland rink in the final, 11–8. In March the tournament for the Bostock Cup was held in Sandon. There were two curling rinks from Sandon and one each from Kaslo and Nelson. The final was between the two Sandon rinks and resulted in the victory of Wilson's team over Grimmett's.

Curling enjoyed local popularity due in part to its novelty and Sandon's winning ways, but it could not compete with hockey for crowds. In October 1897, the hockey club was reorganized for the upcoming season. Martin Grimmett was again involved and took over as chairman. Other club members included H.H. Martin, G. Henderson, J. McVichie, R. McDonald, and the captain, Andy Grierson. As with the curling club, most of the members were of Canadian or British backgrounds. The club decided the colours for the team would be black and red. Local team members would be responsible for purchasing their own uniforms, but players from the outside would be provided with uniforms. The new season began propitiously with a 6–5 defeat of Nelson, but a 4–0 loss to Rossland followed. Fickle fans were quick to turn on the team. The *Paystreak* noted "one or two of the Rossland players had evidently seen the game played," and lamented that "the Silver City Appolos [sic] wrestled and floundered through till half-time when the flunkeys came forward and led the heroes to their corners to be rubbed down and prepared for the next spasm."[21]

It could have been worse. After defeating Sandon, Rossland moved on to Kaslo. They thumped the local boys 10–2. Things didn't go quite so well in Nelson, where Rossland had to settle for a tie. Sandon's hockey team joined the curling team at the 1898 Rossland Winter Carnival. They had an opportunity to redeem themselves for the earlier defeat. A $100 silver cup and the championship of BC were at stake. Rossland defeated Nelson in the preliminary round 6–1. Nelson fell to Sandon 2–0. The final between Sandon and Rossland proved an embarrassment for the visiting team. Sandon's *Paystreak* of February 19 reported a 3–0 victory by Sandon over Rossland, but the actual score stood 11–1 for Rossland. During the first half of the game, the Rossland goalkeeper was reported to have been frozen to the ice with nothing to do. Regardless, John Dean of Rossland, who watched the game, described it as "splendid," which is surprising, as it seems he bet on the wrong team, losing his hat in the process. Humbled and humiliated, the Sandon players returned home to something less than a hero's welcome. Though they lost that game, the Sandon team would develop into a dominant force over the next few years and go on to win numerous tournaments and championships.

THE APPETITE FOR SPORT IN Sandon did not diminish with the coming of warmer weather. Lacrosse was all the rage in 1897. The game thrived in mining camps with significant populations from eastern Canada, but even Sandon had a team, which was started in May 1897. Clubs sprang up in New Denver, Kaslo, Nelson, and Slocan City too. Two early matches were played at celebrations for Queen Victoria's birthday. Sandon defeated the Slocan City Wildcats in Slocan City, and Nelson, resplendent in their blue jerseys and white trousers, defeated their hosts in Kaslo. New Denver was scrambling in late April trying to secure equipment. However, everything was in order by June, and in July the club issued a challenge to Slocan

City. The challenge was refused, and New Denver may have closed out the season without having played a game.

There were also various attempts to set up football (soccer) clubs in the Slocan, but the results were decidedly mixed. Most Americans preferred baseball, and the majority of Canadians favoured lacrosse or hockey. An attempt to set up a football club in New Denver in 1895 was unsuccessful, but by 1897, there were at least a few teams playing on makeshift fields. A match between Slocan City and New Denver on May 24, 1897, in Slocan City, had to be cancelled five minutes before regulation time due to the ball bursting and there being no spare. New Denver won that first game and a rematch in New Denver on Dominion Day. Later in the year, Slocan City, seeking revenge, challenged New Denver again. New Denver was eager but was having difficulty getting hold of a ball. They had also been challenged to a rugby match by Sandon, so they were on the lookout for a rugby ball too.

By the end of the decade, once a reliable supply of balls was assured, football gained prominence in those camps where Canadians and British expatriates began to predominate. This was particularly true in Silverton, New Denver, and Slocan City, though Sandon had a team too. A serious rivalry between Silverton and Slocan City emerged in the spring and summer of 1899. Slocan City drew first blood in early June, defeating Silverton 2–1. This was followed a couple of weeks later with a hard-fought draw. Then in July, the red-sweatered Silverton team took the Slocan's new steamboat, the *Alert*, down the lake to Slocan City, where they defeated their hosts 1–0. There was rivalry between New Denver and Silverton too. Silverton lost to New Denver in an early match, thanks to the outstanding goalkeeping of "the Prophet," A.J. Cleverley, but Silverton prevailed 1–0 in the return match. Cleverley later revealed that he was paid ten dollars for each of his appearances in goal. In early September, Sandon lost four games straight to Silverton. The season closed with another victory by Silverton over Slocan City.

TEAM SPORTS WEREN'T THE ONLY attractions at holidays. Queen Victoria's birthday, Canada's Dominion Day, and, in most camps, America's Independence Day, were celebrated both formally and informally with ad hoc competitions and novelty races. For those camps with fire brigades, hose reel races were a big draw. The rock drilling contests were particularly popular. The contests consisted of teams of two miners each, "double jacking" to see who could drill the deepest hole into solid rock in a set amount of time.

Horse races were also popular. The stakes could be high and the competition fierce. The streets of Kaslo, Slocan City, and Sandon would occasionally throw up clouds of dust as horses galloped from one end to another. Of all the Slocan camps, Sandon would seem the unlikeliest of venues. The only possible track was up the narrow confines of Reco Avenue—where thundering hooves terrified the unwary. The sport was likely encouraged by Johnny Harris, who had himself owned a racehorse in Wallace, Idaho.

"Greasy Buck," owned by Bob Hammond, was the horse to beat in the summer of 1897. There were serious challengers though. Kate Barger, who had recently taken over Sandon's Waldorf Hotel, created quite a stir when she brought in a horse named Wyanashott. As a two-year-old in 1892, the chestnut mare had won races against long odds in San Francisco and Salem, Oregon. Then she set a track record in Victoria in 1896. How Wyanashott got to Sandon is a bit of a mystery. However, at seven years old, she was past her prime. Still, there were plenty of bettors eager to take a chance. If she raced, the results escaped the notice of the newspapers, and it wasn't long before Kate decided to put her mare up for grabs in a raffle.

Crowds from the Slocan wanting to celebrate Queen Victoria's birthday usually headed to Kaslo, where the celebration had been a tradition since 1892. In 1897, however, most celebrants went to Slocan City. An event there took pride of place as the most notable and talked-about spectacle of the year. The crowds enjoyed the usual attractions and contests. But then they were treated to a sight few expected: Eli Carpenter, "the discoverer of the Slocan," on a tightrope. In years to come, Carpenter's tightrope escapade would take on the cloak of legend. The truth is no less remarkable.

Slocan City's Victoria Day committee had been working behind the scenes to come up with an attraction that could be set apart from the usual fare at such events. Carpenter, who was living in a small cabin close to Slocan City at the time, seemed like just the ticket. Few knew of his circus background. He told the *Slocan City News* that it had been seventeen years since he was last on a tightrope. Eli was in hard times and a guaranteed purse of twenty-five dollars was probably all the incentive he needed to get back on the rope.[22]

An account of the tightrope walk appeared a year later in the *Chicago Chronicle*. While no doubt taking dramatic licence, it at least gives an impression of how things might have played out. Carpenter was in his late fifties and complained he was out of practice, very shaky, and suffering from arthritis. Besides, he had no outfit to perform in. How could he walk the tightrope without tights? Nevertheless, he agreed to take on the challenge. The committee scrambled to make all the arrangements. Unfortunately, they couldn't secure a pair of tights. "Qu' impore!" exclaimed Carpenter, "I say I walk d' rope anyhow."[23] And so he did.

To the amazement of the crowd below, Eli stepped out of a window in Slocan City's Arlington Hotel and proceeded to walk across the street on the tightrope using an iron gas pipe for balance. Then he walked across again, but backward this time. He rested for a bit while the visiting New Denver brass band played a version of "Dixie." Then he got back on the rope and performed on a trapeze suspended from it. Eli's tightrope walk was the highlight of the festivities—a spectacle that none who were there would soon forget. Eli was well satisfied too. In addition to the twenty-five dollar purse, a collection from the crowd yielded another forty-five to fifty dollars.

Holiday celebrations and team sports continued to be popular in the Slocan through the nineteenth century and into the twentieth. There were horse races, hose reel races, rock drilling contests, tug-of-wars, and any number of novelty events. Work in the mines was hard, and people looked forward to the brief respite afforded by holidays and celebrations.

15

GOOD TIMES

JUST AS STEAMBOATS FROM IDAHO had delivered steady streams of boomers to Kaslo in early 1893, passenger cars arriving in Sandon in 1896 and 1897, often packed and "standing room only," were full of fortune seekers with high hopes and grand dreams. Caboose and freight cars were pressed into service to handle the incoming crowds. New arrivals who came in on the K&S knew they were in for adventure once the train reached the Payne Bluff high above Three Forks. One visitor described the railway clinging to the cliff "as if it had claws."[1] Another described the railway as it climbed above and past Three Forks:

> At one point as you look out of the car window it is almost a straight fall of 1,800 feet from the very edge of the track to the bottom of the precipice, and you catch your breath as you think what sliding off the rails would mean at that particular spot. But the road, although a narrow gauge, is substantially built and well looked after.[2]

Once in Sandon, new arrivals would leave the train and enter a dense, self-contained world where the sound of hammers and saws rose above the cacophony of street noises. New businesses appeared daily. About twenty buildings were under construction in September 1896. They were nearly all aligned along Sandon's one main street. Hemmed in by the mountains and with Carpenter Creek running through the centre of camp, there weren't many other options for growth, although a few buildings started going up on the mountainside to the north above the K&S grade. This area became known as "Sunnyside," as it occasionally caught a few rays of sunlight peering over the mountains from the south. But even Sunnyside was in the dark by November. Residents did not expect to see the sun again until late April 1897.

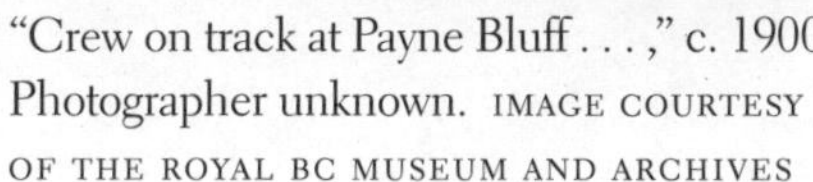

"Crew on track at Payne Bluff . . . ," c. 1900. Photographer unknown. IMAGE COURTESY OF THE ROYAL BC MUSEUM AND ARCHIVES

Payne Bluff near Three Forks, c. 1897. Photographer: R.H. Trueman. IMAGE COURTESY OF THE UNIVERSITY OF CALGARY DIGITAL COLLECTIONS

The flux of incoming humanity made it difficult to accurately estimate Sandon's population. John Moyie visited in early January 1896 and found the camp "very lively. Business places are open night and day. At 4 o'clock in the morning as much goods are sold as at any other time."[3] Moyie estimated that as many as a thousand people had located there. He also noted the transient nature of the "mobile, floating population."[4] When G.H.W. Ashwell visited from Chilliwack in March 1896, he estimated the population at a more modest five hundred; not bad, he thought, "for a town of 12 months."[5] A New Denver resident who visited in February described Sandon, perhaps with a touch of envy, as "grown beyond all recognition since last fall."[6]

Sandon was a magnet that drew in visitors—old and new—from around the world. Vancouver journalist J.T. "Wings" Wilkinson visited early in the fall of 1896 and then again about a month later. He was amazed by the amount of growth in just a few weeks. More than a hundred buildings were under construction, with people arriving every day: "The transformation was something marvelous."[7] Johnny Harris couldn't hide his enthusiasm: "Sandon is rapidly growing. Slocan is now the centre of attraction for British Columbia and British Columbia is the centre of attraction for mining in the world."[8]

For incomers from more staid, eastern Canadian homes, Sandon could be a shock. Harold Platt Christie arrived in early January 1896, shortly after the railways. From Moosamin, in the Northwest Territories, he was more familiar and comfortable with the conservative farming communities of the prairies. Shortly after arriving in Sandon, he wrote to his brother-in-law back in Moosamin:

> Good Lord! I am in a hell of a place. I arrived about an hour ago and feel hopelessly wretched. This is a godforsaken place! It is jammed up in a kind of gully between two mountains, full of folks of apparently the lowest description.[9]

R.T. Lowery had advice for Christie and the flood of incomers to the Slocan:

> If you have little money but plenty of manhood and are composed of the same stuff as the trailblazers of this great country, come along. You will win in the end provided you do not bond yourself to boozereno, cards and the woman in red.[10]

It was good advice, but as Sandon grew, the vices available were powerful attractions for visitors looking for good times. Booze flowed freely, gambling was rampant, and prostitution widespread. Growing pains were inevitable.

Trouble for Sproat and Harris started late in 1896, after their return from California. The hard feelings that had been simmering between Sproat, Harris, and the tenants they shared came to a boil because of a Kaslo speculator named Frank O'Brien. On December 11, 1896, O'Brien staked the townsite of Sandon—already claimed by Sproat and Harris and Crown-granted to them. O'Brien's position was that Sproat and Harris had gained the Crown grant under false pretences. He argued the land was never a legitimate mineral claim, there having been no attempt to find minerals. After staking the townsite, O'Brien went through all the legal requirements necessary, including posting a notice in the December 24, 1896, issue of the *British Columbia Gazette*.

Sproat wrote to Deputy Commissioner of Lands and Works W.S. Gore on February 24, 1897, to complain about O'Brien's staking. He received a response less than a week later confirming that the lands claimed by O'Brien were not open to purchase. That might have been the end of it, but O'Brien was persistent. In early March, he sent Gore a 25 percent deposit on the lands he had staked. Gore immediately wrote back, returning O'Brien's deposit and advising that his application could not be entertained. Undeterred, O'Brien had his lawyer, Robert Cassidy, write to Gore's boss, G.B. Martin, Commissioner of Lands and Works. Not only did Sproat and Harris have to deal with O'Brien, there were rumours that the K&S, or the N&S, or both, were prepared to challenge Sproat and Harris's townsite claim in court.

The residents of Sandon followed developments with great interest. Many of the squatters, who resented paying rents to Harris and Sproat, were hoping for O'Brien's success. Accounts vary, but it appears that a newly appointed justice, Judge Forin, asked an offhand question about how someone with a mineral claim could also claim surface rights. This was just the question that O'Brien and many Sandon residents were asking. Some took Forin's reported question as carte blanche to start staking vacant lots in Sandon. Several women from the lower end of town—home to many of the camp's prostitutes—put up notices in front of their lots claiming them. Alice Crow even threatened to kill any man who dared to build on her lot. Johnny Harris was livid. In Wallace, Idaho, he had brandished a pistol and killed a man when his property rights were challenged. Similarly threatened in Sandon, he armed himself with a sharp axe and went about the townsite destroying all the stakes.

Harris didn't stop there. John R. Cameron of the Kootenay Tailoring and Dry Goods Company had a team of men work day and night to clear the land he had staked. By the time Harris arrived, a building was well under construction. However, Harris had his own team of men. They went up the steep slope behind Cameron's building and started to dig a tunnel into the side of the hill. They showered debris down on to Cameron's building site, quickly putting an end to construction. The men kept digging. No longer could anyone say that Harris hadn't done any mineral exploration. As it turned out, Forin's comments had been misreported and misunderstood. Whether legally correct or not, the report should have included a clause stating "that the owner of a mineral claim had the exclusive right to the use of the surface."[11] Justice Walkem granted an injunction against Cameron and things cooled down.

Forin made his first trip to the Slocan in March, shortly after the trouble in Sandon. He held court on March 24, 1897, in New Denver. The Sandon townsite dispute came up again, and Forin issued a decision—no doubt based on Sproat and Harris's Crown grant—upholding Johnny Harris's right to evict one of his tenants. The resulting mandate induced the holdouts in Sandon who had refused to vacate their lots to do so now. From New Denver, Forin travelled to Sandon. He would have seen squatter's shacks being pulled down, and perhaps he had a look at Johnny Harris's tunnel, which by this time sported a substantially timbered entrance. He likely met with Harris, as he ended up purchasing a town lot for $600, and a thousand shares of Reco stock at a $1.10 a share. Forin was confident that both were sound investments. His purchases also meant that he would be in a clear conflict of interest if he was ever again called on to hear cases involving Sandon property disputes. Perhaps this was part of Johnny Harris's plan.

Harris was by most accounts aggressively assertive in pursuing his interests. He gave no quarter in his mining pursuits or in his stake in Sandon. He was an unpopular landlord and had numerous run-ins with his tenants. He did not hesitate to use litigation and other strong-arm tactics to impose his will on recalcitrant renters.

Take, for example, the case of Nick Palorcia. Italian-born Nicola Palorcia was the pioneer shoemaker of the Slocan. He first opened shop in New Denver but then moved to Sandon when it started booming. Palorcia's shop in Sandon cost him $700, but Harris, with his Crown grant, owned the ground on which the building stood and demanded rent. When it wasn't paid, he would seize Palorcia's property or seek payment through the courts. In March 1897, Harris ejected Palorcia from his building and impounded his tools. Palorcia countersued and charged Harris with "distress of a sewing machine." Palorcia argued that as the sewing machine was a tool of his trade, it should not have been taken. Palorcia lost both cases. A victorious Harris tore down the shoe shop and built the prestigious three-storey Virginia Block, with prime business frontage on Reco Avenue.

While the squatters of Sandon had their supporters, so too did Harris. J.M. Porter, one of his friends from Wallace, Idaho, wrote to Harris in April with words of encouragement: "I am glad to hear you cleaned out the jumpers on your townsite, and that your property is generally doing so well.

'Jumpers' will find out after awhile, that they have the wrong pig by the ear when they try to jump your property."[12] It helped that Harris had the law on his side. He didn't need to win any popularity contests.

While the Slocan attracted incomers from across Canada, the population—of Sandon, in particular—was still largely American. The words of an earlier visitor from Winnipeg rang true: "To an eastern Canadian it is an interesting experience to come out to a western mining camp. Canada is known throughout the world as the Mecca of the respectable and pious. Not so, West Kootenay. A man coming from Ontario or Nova Scotia would think twice about saying 'this is my own, my native land!'"[13]

It was an American who later recalled that, at the time, "every other man you met in the young mining camps up there was from Spokane, and though the country was British territory, the English accent and even the Canadian intonation were the exception to the rule."[14] Most of the big mines were owned by Americans, the main railroad was an extension of the American GNR line, and many residents would call themselves Americans first and foremost regardless of how long they had been in Canada. The most visible reminders that this was Canada and not Idaho were the low incidence of guns and violent crimes, and the presence of a Canadian bureaucracy that managed civil administration, justice, and law enforcement.

Johnny Harris was a proud American and had no desire to become a Canadian citizen. With his power and wealth, he could do pretty much as he pleased. This was an irritant to some Canadians. Dr. Robertson, superintendent of Presbyterian missions in western Canada, had this to say of Harris's Sandon: "The townsite of Sandon is owned by a United States citizen, who is coining a fortune out of ground rents. He is a pleasant, liberal gentleman; but why . . . should not Canadians own the property in their own country."[15]

The church presence in Sandon and the Slocan had changed since the days of the Reverends Turner and Martin. Gaebel had left the field and been replaced by the Reverend Love, who started out in Nakusp but later took over the Methodist church in New Denver. The Reverend Beattie arrived to serve Presbyterians. Love and Beattie both ventured into Sandon, but they were likely uncomfortable in a mining camp where dancing and Sunday openings—sinful behaviours that both men abhorred—were rampant. By 1897, both men had moved on. The residents of Sandon were hoping for replacements more tolerant and attuned to western conditions than Love and Beattie. They largely got their wish.

By most accounts, the Methodists could not have chosen a more suitable representative for Sandon than Albert "A.M." Sanford. He had previously ministered in Truro, Nova Scotia, a long-settled, stable community, but he was enthusiastic about his new assignment. In a letter written to one of his former congregation, he certainly appeared to have the "right stuff": "I am living a very busy and exciting life and have found a most congenial field. This is practically a new field, no real solid work having ever been done here, but I hope soon to see things hustling in good shape. I am pitching in for all I am worth; in fact, I have to do so, for if a man can't hustle he'd better get out at once. This is no country for a slow man, for in every line of business 'hustle' is the word."[16] Sanford went on to describe his modest living conditions. He was sharing a shanty with four other men. There was just one bed, one chair, and some boards nailed together to make a washstand. Even such basic accommodation was costing him three dollars a week.

The Presbyterians assigned the Reverend Menzies to Sandon. The crowded, loud boom town that was Sandon must have seemed foreign to Menzies and Sanford, but they both took to their new assignments enthusiastically. Menzies was ordained at a ceremony in Kaslo on June 2, 1897, where he wittily toasted Sandon as a town that all other Slocan camps looked up to.

Church affairs in Kaslo seem to have been more tangled. The reappearance of the Comique continued to stoke moral outrage. Although the performances were now relatively tame, residents still looked askance at the buckets of beer and the box rustlers' short skirts. This was evident from an incident in early 1896 involving a young Presbyterian missionary. He decided one night to see what the Comique had on offer. We don't know what his motives were, but some church-going "Mrs. Grundys" believed they were suspect.[17]

Church of England adherents in Kaslo were in turmoil too. Reverend Akehurst delivered a Church of England service once a month. In early November 1896, he found the doorway to the Kaslo church—in which he had given services since it was built in 1895—barred with a padlock and a constable standing guard. Evidently, the dispute revolved around a cross that was present on the church's communion table. Former Kaslo mayor John Keen, "the Luther of Kootenay," protesting "high church" ways, had Akehurst locked out of his church.[18] Keen and others in the congregation wanted the cross removed. Akehurst refused. Instead, he broke the padlock and entered the church, whereupon he was arrested by the constable. However, when Akehurst was brought before Mayor Bob Green, the constable was ordered to release him.

Akehurst delivered his service, but when he returned in the evening, he again found his way barred, certain members of the congregation protesting his "papist" ways. While it was true that Akehurst liked his long, flowing robes and certain other "decorative forms of worship," he was not by any means considered an extremist in high-church ways.[19] He was allowed to enter the church to retrieve a few items but was then sent on his way. The church building committee claimed possession of the church and espoused their right to bar anyone, even the pastor, from entering against their wishes. The dispute would not be resolved amicably, and legal proceedings were started.

FOR CANADIAN BUREAUCRATS, SANDON WAS a particular challenge. Sanitary inspector Clive Phillipps-Wolley, who had first visited the Slocan in 1892, summed it up when he complained in one of his official reports that "the inhabitants are very largely Americans, insolently indifferent to our law."[20] It might have seemed to Canadian officials like Phillipps-Wolley that Americans in the Slocan were indifferent to local laws, but most visiting Americans were impressed with how well behaved their compatriots were. A newspaper correspondent who visited in April 1897 commented on the "remarkable order and good government" he found: "One hardly ever hears of a brawl or a saloon fight in any of these towns."[21] The reality lay somewhere between Phillipps-Wolley's insolently indifferent Americans and the news correspondent's picture of peace and harmony.

Phillipps-Wolley made his first visit to Sandon as sanitary inspector in late 1896. He arrived amid a typhoid outbreak. He was not optimistic things could easily be improved on the ground:

> The town is built in a narrow ravine, the sides of which are exceptionally steep. The main street is practically the town. The backs of the buildings on one side of this street abut upon Sandon Creek, which has been used as a natural sewer; on the other side the buildings have their backs against the hill, and in some cases their closets on a level with their second stories. But that the spring freshets scour the town every year it must have been a centre of disease before now.

As it is, unless some serious steps are taken, I have very grave fears for the future.[22]

Regardless of the sanitary inspector's concerns, the good times in Sandon and the Slocan rolled on into 1897. Kaslo, Slocan City, and Sandon were booming. Businesses throughout the Slocan were gaining ground. The price of silver—while not as high as people would have hoped—was at least stable. The railways were going ahead at full steam, and most mines were prospering. Miners, bankers, lawyers, merchants, tailors, hotel keepers, prostitutes, card sharps—all contributed to a dynamic and varied social milieu. While there was still a preponderance of Americans, an increasing number of men—and sometimes families—were coming in from eastern Canada and the prairies, enticed by work in the mines.

In January 1897, the N&S brought in 341 passengers; in February, 468; in March, 695; and by June, 1,040. "Taxed to its capacity" with freight and passenger traffic, it's likely that the numbers were similar for the K&S.[23] The rivalry between the two railways was undiminished. The K&S shipped almost 1,500 tons of ore in a two-week period in January. The railway was popular with Slocan residents, and on a visit to Spokane in February, Munn and Irving boasted that business was "steadily increasing."[24] Some felt that in order to compete, the CPR would need to extend its line down Slocan Lake. This would give it access to the rich silver claims along Springer Creek. The claims at the south end of the lake were in the spotlight in 1895 and 1896. American capitalist J.A. Finch bonded the Enterprise in 1895, and it was soon rivalling the big mines up the lake.

Sandon threw a big party for Queen Victoria's Jubilee in June 1897. J.J. McGrath, formerly an insurance agent in Decatur, Illinois, was there to witness the celebration. He wrote to a friend back home in Decatur: "It is without doubt the wildest place I was ever in. They have horse racing up and down the main business street which is not more than ten feet wide, and the smallest piece of money they use is a quarter. Everything is wide open seven days in the week."[25] Another visitor described a drunken miner galloping his horse up and down the main street, cheered on by the camp's prostitutes. Like others from the east, McGrath was captivated by the wild west atmosphere he found in Sandon. It must have been a bit like stepping into one of the western novels popular at the time, but without the obligatory gunplay. He hinted at this slippage in time and place when he wrote: "Since I crossed the mountain I have not seen a person that I ever saw before in my life."[26]

There was just one major complaint voiced about Sandon's Jubilee Day celebration in 1897. It concerned the lacrosse match. Right from the start, a lacrosse game between Sandon and Slocan City had been planned as one of the day's major events. An invitation had gone out to the Slocan City Wildcats, who arrived in Sandon ready to play. At the last minute, the Sandon committee decided to scrub the lacrosse game in favour of a baseball game. Many spectators expecting to see a lacrosse contest between two local teams instead got to witness a Kaslo baseball team loaded with American professionals wallop the local Sandon team 14–1.

The lacrosse incident highlighted the cultural divide between Americans and Canadians in the Slocan. Sandon was heavily populated with Americans in 1897, and it's understandable that many would prefer to watch baseball rather than lacrosse, a sport unfamiliar to most. On the other hand, there was a core population of Canadians in the Slocan, and more were arriving from eastern Canada every day. It was a Canadian who wrote to complain about the cancellation of the lacrosse game:

> It would appear to me that the lacrosse teams should have been given the precedence, as the game was the first arranged, and the players were amateurs and our own citizens. Further, when we consider the nature of the holiday and that lacrosse is the national game of Canada, the action of the sport committee seems incomprehensible . . . I hope next year when we celebrate it will be borne in mind that we are in Canada and that lacrosse is the national game, and not baseball.[27]

National game or not, baseball remained popular in Sandon over the next few years, but as the ratio of Canadians to Americans increased, so too did interest in lacrosse, curling, and hockey.

When Nelson's Dr. E.C. Arthur visited Sandon in the summer of 1897, he described "a humming hive of humanity."[28] The travelling entertainments that began in 1896, after the arrival of the railways, continued. In the first few months of the year, residents were treated to the Kickapoo Medicine Company, Albini the Magician, and opera singers Madame Renard and Miss McKenzie. Sandon also hosted the Beddard English Comedy Company, which starred Lillian Beddard in a production—appropriate for the Slocan—of the *Silver King*. However, the Columbia Comic Opera Company—later a vehicle for early horror film star Lon Chaney—was judged by the *Paystreak* to be "by far the best company which has ever played here."[29] The entertainments were likely lucrative, but the frontier circuit was not an easy one. Renard and McKenzie's original appearance in Sandon was postponed due to a snow blockade. Then, to make their steamboat connection, they paid twenty dollars to ride on a railway handcart from Sandon to Nakusp.

In March 1897, Sandon was visited by the "Princess of Darkness," a medium for the "past, present and future."[30] She could analyze mineral samples using her psychic powers. She also advertised herself as excellent in providing love and marriage advice and adept at foretelling the particular line of business that people would be most suited for. A seventh daughter of a seventh daughter, she had a room at the Balmoral Hotel—open for business from nine in the morning to nine at night.

If the Princess of Darkness wouldn't do, another option was Dr. Dayohesala, who toured the Slocan in August with his assistant, Professor Sutton. The "doctor" claimed to be a nephew of Oronhyatekha, the first known Oxford scholar of Indigenous descent and Canada's second Indigenous medical doctor. Dayohesala harangued the citizens of Silverton on the ills of the flesh. Fortunately, he had a remedy on hand and managed to sell more than sixty cures for the modest price of one dollar each. Other patent medicine vendors like the Kickapoo company also thrived.

Sandon was literally bursting at the seams from the influx of miners and other fortune seekers, not all of them welcome. As R.T. Lowery put it, "The Slocan is filling up with hobos, tramps, chair warmers, grafters, sure thing gamblers and other members of the human leech family."[31] The railways were the Slocan's gateways to prosperity. They carried ore out and brought capitalists in, but they weren't discriminating about the traffic they carried. By June 1897, Lowery confirmed: "The Slocan is now included in the hobo circuit, and brake-beam tourists are becoming more numerous than welcome."[32]

A correspondent for the *Oregonian* newspaper visited the Slocan in the spring of 1897. He walked the railway tracks from Sandon to New Denver. He and his party travelled part of the distance with a "tramp" who wasn't too impressed with the Slocan:

> He dwelt at length upon the hardships of tramp life here as compared with older-settled communities. He spoke feelingly, just as if it came from the very bottom of his heart, of the total absence of haylofts, potato patches, apple orchards and hen roosts, as well as the incon-

> venience of brakebeam-riding on these poorly equipped roads, not provided with air brakes, and said it was difficult in this wild and woolly west to dispense with steam heat and other modern conveniences.[33]

The sustained growth of Sandon and Slocan City was also an attraction for enterprising newspapermen. In June 1897, another newspaper appeared in Sandon to compete with the *Paystreak*: *The Mining Review*, owned and operated by Charles Cliffe. Cliffe was originally from Ontario, but more recently from Brandon, Manitoba, where he had edited the *Brandon Mail*. The *Mining Review* would provide a counterpoint to Lowery's *Paystreak*. While Lowery liked to think of himself as a champion of the miners, Cliffe's sympathies generally lay with the mine owners. As might be expected, Lowery and Langstaff did not welcome the appearance of the *Mining Review*, which was described as looking like a "starved tramp." A more objective welcome was provided by the *Revelstoke Herald*: "*The Review* is a creditable looking journal and will no doubt fill the bill."[34]

Sanitary inspector Clive Phillipps-Wolley returned to Sandon in 1897 and found things had not improved since his visit in late 1896. He repeated some of the concerns he had voiced then:

> Geographically it is ill-placed for sanitation, in an exceedingly narrow gulley, without room for proper expansion. The sides of this narrow gully are extremely steep; there is no soil to absorb moisture, and the houses are driven from want of space on to the creek which flows through the town. This has been converted into a terribly foul sewer, full of log jambs [*sic*], about which drifting refuse collects, while its discoloured waters are further polluted by the lead from the concentrators of the "Slocan Star" and the "Noble Five" and the sluicings of the "Wonderful."[35]

The *Mining Review* was critical of the sanitary inspector's efforts and poked fun at his double-barrelled name and insistence on being addressed as "Captain." It painted a portrait of a pompous, self-important government official with a "holier than thou" attitude who marched into Sandon "with a flourish of trumpets."[36] However, there were others in Sandon, particularly those like Amy Eagan, who came down with typhoid, who would have welcomed the sanitary inspector's attempts to clean things up.

As bad as Sandon was, it could have been worse. Phillipps-Wolley had to deal with many complaints and unfounded rumours. In 1897, there was "the great cholera scare." Apparently, a homesick Sandon barber wrote to his wife in Tacoma. He claimed that Sandon was under siege from a cholera epidemic. The wife reported this to the newspaper and soon there was an article in the *San Francisco Examiner*: "A short time ago, cholera broke out, gathering its victims at an alarming rate."[37] Other papers picked up the story. In his official report, Phillipps-Wolley took pains to state unequivocally that there was "absolutely no truth in the reported cholera at Sandon."[38]

Residents of Sandon were up in arms over the bogus cholera reports. The first that most heard about it was when some began receiving telegrams from family or friends enquiring about their health. The picture became clearer when copies of the September 3 edition of the *San Francisco Examiner* arrived in the mail. A campaign of indignation was started. Letters were written to the government and to newspapers across North America. All writers decried and denied the cholera claims. In response, some newspapers published fanciful reports that painted a far different picture.

According to the *Spokane Spokesman-Review*, for example, not only was there no cholera in Sandon, life there was so healthy that the town had no need of a coroner or undertaker, and two of the four doctors in town had closed their offices to go fishing. A similar tale was told of Kaslo, where it was said that the undertaker—due to lack of work—gave up his business to take up furniture making. The truth was likely somewhere between the two visions.

If anyone's health was at risk, the most likely target would have been whoever wrote the article for the *Examiner*. Soon after it appeared, M.J. Roche, a newspaperman from Portland, Oregon, toured the Slocan. He found things highly charged over the false cholera report: "The Sandonians were highly incensed at this report and took it so much to heart that they declared that if the writer and manufacturer of the article about cholera symptoms were identified, they would string him up before they could think of a prayer or a hymn. They meant exactly what they said."[39]

It was with some trepidation, then, that Roche took a stroll along Reco Avenue. He grew uneasy when "half a dozen lusty louts" began following him. A rumour was circulating that he had authored the infamous article. Suddenly he heard shouts: "That's the ——! Hang him! Let's lynch him!" Coming from the United States at this time, Roche would have been very familiar with "lynch law." He had every reason to be scared. Fortunately, someone living in Sandon knew him and came to his rescue. There would be no lynching.

WHILE THE RISE OF SANDON was perhaps the biggest story in the Slocan in the years 1895–1897, it was by no means the only one. Transportation initiatives loomed large. Late in 1896, it was learned that the CPR planned to build a large new steamboat for Slocan Lake to connect their rail terminal at Rosebery with Slocan City. However, the CPR's vision for West Kootenay extended much further than a new boat on Slocan Lake. The company entered into negotiations with the C&KSN. If the negotiations proved successful, the CPR would acquire seven steamboats and ten barges as well as the infrastructure to support them. C&KSN principal J.A. Mara (recently defeated in the Canadian general election) and the CPR's Richard Marpole were both in Montreal in December. Things looked decidedly serious when work on the C&KSN steamer under construction in Nakusp came to a halt.

In early December 1896, a private railcar rolled into Sandon. Onboard was the Honourable Andrew George Blair, Dominion Minister of Railways and Canals and former premier of New Brunswick. Sandon residents were thrilled to host so distinguished a guest and rightly saw it as a sign of confidence. Blair was given the usual tour of the Slocan Star and other mines and was guest of honour at a public meeting in Spencer's Hall. Some of Sandon's leading citizens addressed the minister, expressing their loyalty to Canada and the Queen, and lauding the potential of the Slocan. They were also lobbying for more government attention and concessions. In particular, they wanted to know what the status was of the long-talked-about Crow's Nest Pass railway. Blair was gracious in responding and offered his support for the railway but gave nothing away regarding any government commitments. Still, Sandon residents felt that his very presence augured well for the future.

C.E. Perry was not tied to government protocol. He was no politician. He lacked the politician's reticence and inability to commit. Perry had pioneered in the Slocan and knew its people, and a week after Blair's visit, he gave residents the news they wanted to hear. The CPR intended to build a track from Slocan City to Slocan Crossing, at the Kootenay River, which would link up with the proposed Crow's Nest Pass line that the CPR also hoped to construct. The branch line would bypass New Denver and Silverton and would not cross the Slocan bluffs, though such a route might be constructed later.

Instead, railcars would be loaded on to barges and transported by steamboat up and down the lake between Rosebery and Slocan City.

THE ANNOUNCEMENT OF THE RAILWAY link was a catalyst for Slocan City's growth. At the beginning of 1896, there was just one substantial building there—Sam Whittaker's Cumberland Hotel (formerly the Lakeview). As more people arrived, buildings started going up as fast as lumber became available. Like Kaslo in early 1893, the real estate market was booming. People flocked in throughout late 1896 and into 1897. Between them, Slocan City and Sandon were outstripping all other Slocan camps. In early 1897, the population in Sandon was estimated at between 2,000 and 2,500. Slocan City, while not as big, was growing rapidly—one resident, William Brasch, perhaps consumed by boosterism, thought the population would soon be in the "tens of thousands."[40] With "every bed, bunk, house, and cabin" occupied, it was not beyond the realm of possibility.[41] While Sandon attracted a largely American crowd, some of whom were clearly seeking adventure and perhaps a few forbidden thrills, Slocan City seemed to attract a more well-heeled business class—many from eastern Canada, the prairies, and British Columbia's lower mainland. For those coming in by boat from up the lake, the first person they would encounter at the boat landing might have been Dad Allen, who had relocated from New Denver and was running a pack outfit from the boats.

The outlook for Slocan City in 1896 encouraged W.H. Brandon and his brother Dan to set up a rival townsite within spitting distance of Slocan City. At first, it was going to be named Bruce, but Brandon seemed a more appropriate choice and soon stuck. By mid-May 1896, months before the railway announcement, Brandon—where there had been nothing six weeks before—boasted sixteen buildings and a population of more than two hundred.

The rapid growth of Slocan City and Brandon made a fertile field for the churches. The Reverend Beattie, who had been preaching in Slocan City since 1896 as part of his Slocan circuit, was reassigned there in 1897. The Church of England also made appearances, first by Reverend Yates at Schoenberg's Hall, sent to assist Reverend Akehurst in June 1897, and then by Akehurst at the home of Charles S. Mons.

Along with the railway announcement, the big news in Slocan City late in 1896 was the founding of that camp's first newspaper: Daniel "D.R." Young's *Slocan City News*. "Windy" Young, who had newspaper experience from Montana, was described as a man long on promises but short on cash. On arriving in Canada, he was offered a position with the Nelson *Miner*, but chose to hang his hat in Slocan City instead. According to Fred Smyth, who was hired by Young after answering an advertisement in a Spokane newspaper, Young was a man who had never heard the term "inferiority complex." However, Smyth gave Young credit for ingenuity and ambition:

> His printing plant was a washout. He had picked up an old Army press and a few fonts of type that one of the Nelson newspapers had discarded, but not knowing the mechanical end of the business, he had forgotten leads and slugs with which to space out the advertisements. I thought we were up against it, but Young knew better. He sauntered up the street to the Hicks' hotel and was soon back with a bundle of empty cigar boxes under his arm. Then he sat down and took out his knife and whittled out pieces of the wood to the proper lengths while I set the lines of type. The paper came out on time and looked fairly good at that.[42]

Slocan City News office and staff, c. 1897. Photographer unknown. ORIGINAL IMAGE COURTESY OF THE SLOCAN VALLEY HISTORICAL SOCIETY

The *Vancouver Daily World* agreed, describing the first edition of the *News* as "very creditably gotten up."[43] Soon after, W.B. Wilcox of Spokane was hired to run the printing operation. John M. Cole joined the staff in the summer of 1897. And Lester Ackley, as compositor, would add some professionalism to the typesetting. R.T. Lowery was less than enthusiastic, however. For some reason he described the *News* as "the greatest nuisance we have in the profession."[44]

The *News* would soon face competition. At first, there was speculation that R.T. Lowery would start a newspaper. He moved a printing press south, but then thought better of it and moved the press to Sandon, where he started the *Paystreak*. Instead, on May 1, 1897, the first issue of the *Slocan Pioneer* appeared. The *Pioneer* was run by Ed Cowen and J.C. McFadden, with Butte's Dick Butler in charge of printing. McFadden was also from Montana, where he had been city circulator and advertising agent for the *Anaconda Recorder*. He left Montana in March but got stuck in Kaslo for more than two weeks with his printing outfit due to snow blockage on the K&S. Cowen, a former Paris correspondent for the *New York Herald*, was something of a legend in western newspaper circles. In 1882, he was working as the capitol correspondent for the *Denver Tribune* when Colorado lawman Bat Masterson walked into his office. A year earlier, Bat's friend Wyatt Earp, along with Earp's brothers and Doc Holliday, had been involved in the infamous gunfight at the O.K. Corral in Tombstone, Arizona.

The Arizona authorities wanted to extradite Holliday from Colorado to face charges for events that took place in the aftermath of the gunfight. Bat Masterson didn't think Holliday would get a fair trial, and, knowing that Cowen had some influence with the governor of Colorado, he asked the newspaperman to intervene on Holliday's behalf. Cowen contacted the governor and claimed success in convincing him to oppose the Arizona extradition request. Cowen and Doc Holliday later became friends in Leadville, Colorado, where Holliday worked the gambling tables and Cowen wrote for the *Leadville Tribune*.

R.T. Lowery was generous in welcoming the new paper: "It is a better paper than most of the camps can boast of. Its columns teem with ancient history and its editor from the big words cropping out all over the sheet must be desirous of showing the trail blazers that he once went to school and swallowed a dictionary."[45] The *Pioneer* promised it would not dwell on "individual iniquity" or mount "crusades."[46] However, typical of most two-newspaper camps, it didn't take long for the *Pioneer* and *Slocan City News* to begin insulting one another. The *Calgary Weekly Herald* couldn't help but comment on the squabble: "The *Slocan News* calls the editor of its contemporary, the *Pioneer*, a member of the swine variety, and the *Pioneer* retaliates by saying it has no desire to enter into a controversy with a 'scavenger of the English Language.' And there you are."[47] Like his competitor at the *Slocan City News*, though, Cowen was quick to boom his new home. Interviewed in early June, he was adamant that Slocan City would be "the commercial and mining center of the Slocan country."[48]

For Slocan mine operators who used the N&S, and for mines closer to Slocan City, the CPR line from Slocan City to the Kootenay River was welcome news. When completed, it would eliminate one significant transshipment bottleneck. No longer would ore have to be unloaded from cars for shipment by steamboat. For the CPR, the new route would provide an alternative should the Arrow Lakes ever be closed to shipping. Once the new line was completed between the lake and Slocan Crossing, mines would have three different portals for shipping ore. The residents of New Denver and Silverton, however, would be left cold on the shoulder once again by the railways. But it was at least some compensation to have the CPR's luxurious new steamboat, the SS *Slocan*, joining the SS *W. Hunter* in service on Slocan Lake.

By April 1, 1897, the value of Slocan ore shipped out over the railways and steamers already equalled half the value of all the output from 1896. The Whitewater, Ruth, Reco, Last Chance, Slocan Star, and Dardanelles were all busy. The Slocan Star alone shipped thirty-two tons of ore a day in January 1897. By the end of that month, it was estimated that fifty mines were being worked in the Slocan and adjoining areas and three thousand dollars was being paid out every day to nine thousand men. During July 1897, more than five times as much ore shipped over the K&S than had shipped in the same month a year earlier.

British capital was on the upsurge. English match king Wilberforce Bryant and other like-minded investors were finally waking up to the Slocan's potential. By June 1897, at least two Scottish investment companies were involved in the Slocan. The Scottish Colonial Goldfields Company, based in Edinburgh, acquired interests in a number of venerable Slocan properties, including the Cumberland Mining Company, the Slocan Mining and Milling Company, and the Idaho Mining Company. Interest was increasing in Canadian investment circles too. The president of the Dardanelles Mining and Milling Company was no less a figure than the Honourable Edgar Dewdney, the sitting lieutenant-governor of BC. He was joined on the board by former prime minister Sir Charles Tupper and a former premier of Prince Edward Island, Fred Peters.

In March 1897, the *Vancouver Daily World* published a list of more than fifty new mining companies incorporated to do business in BC. As R.T. Lowery colourfully put it: "Stock companies continue to spring into life as fast as buzzards fly to a dead buffalo."[49] West Kootenay residents would have sat up and taken notice when they saw "Barnato Gold & Silver Mining Co." on the list.[50]

Barney Barnato was something of a rags-to-riches legend at the time. Barnett Isaacs, a.k.a. Barney Barnato, was born into poverty in London in the early 1850s. He and his brother eked out a living as a vaudeville act, billing themselves as the "Barnato Brothers." In the 1870s, they emigrated from England to South Africa, where Barney built up a fortune as a diamond magnate. He later branched out to silver and gold mines. There was great excitement when it was rumoured he might be investing in the Slocan. Some thought that H. Hirschfield Cohen, an associate of Barnato who was in the Slocan as recently as January 1897, was an agent for the "Diamond King." Cohen denied it, but the issue was soon moot. In May 1897, Barnato either jumped, fell, or was pushed off an ocean liner close to the island of Madeira.

Some sound companies would emerge from the list published in the *World*, but there were others whose sole purpose was to exploit gullible investors through an overabundance of cheap shares. BC's provincial mineralogist, William Carlyle, said some of the capitalization schemes "savoured of the ridiculous."[51] Another account denigrated the "oily-tongued promoters" pushing shares.[52]

An increasing interest in the Slocan from Winnipeg, Vancouver, and other Canadian centres was welcome, but whether this would lead to any kind of return on investment remained to be seen. Sometimes the expectations of Vancouver investors strained credulity. The *Ledge* poked a bit of fun in August 1897: "Most of them want a good shipping mine with a boarding house on it for $500. Some want a concentrator too."[53] In order to deal with the explosion of stock companies, in July 1897, the province enacted a new Companies Act, which required those wishing to register companies to pay licence fees up front. Carlyle felt this would check at least some of the schemes set up solely to fleece investors.

Most British investors knew little of silver mines, and few had the opportunity to visit the Slocan. They relied instead on the word of stock promoters and the various mining experts brought in to testify to the riches thousands of miles away. British investors ate it up. One estimate has British capital investment in BC mines more than doubling between 1890 and 1900. One Canadian historian has noted that many investors were simply "given bad advice by their engineers."[54]

It was a statutory requirement for British stock companies to hold meetings. In early 1897, the first meeting of the Galena Mines Limited, the company that owned the Galena Farm mines south of Silverton, took place at Winchester House, Old Broad Street, London. The chairman explained to the shareholders that it was a statutory meeting and the board of directors had nothing to report. However, the meeting was not a complete waste of time, as the company's consulting engineer, C.W. Callahan, was on a short visit to London and came to describe the Slocan and the Galena Farm. After wandering the western mining frontier, he said, he came across "the famous Slocan" and became convinced that high-grade silver mines could yield more profits than gold mines. He claimed to have come across a huge silver ledge that led to the Galena Farm:

> I traced the ledge over a series of mountains and it brought me to the Galena mines, where I found a shaft had been sunk on the ledge by some inexperienced people who sank at right angles to the course of the lode, resulting in their not finding what they expected. I procured a bond on the best of it, about 200 acres, and pumped out the shaft, crosscut the ledge and found it to be 12 feet wide carrying high-grade galena ore. I then drifted on it 100 feet east and west, sunk a winze an additional 30 feet, which gave me 100 feet from the surface, which was enough to demonstrate that there was a very rich and large mine there, which only required skillful and systematic working to make it a profitable and dividend-paying property.[55]

One can just imagine the bemused but enthusiastic shareholders reaching for their cheque books. In late 1896, the Galena Mines Limited had been placed on the London stock exchange. Very quickly about $2.5 million in stock was subscribed. While the outlook initially looked promising, there was no way the property was worth that much.

16

SONG AND DANCE

WHEN THE HOTEL SLOCAN OPENED in Kaslo in April 1893, there was a grand ball in celebration. Some prospectors and miners walked twenty-five to thirty miles from the mines to take in the occasion. They drank and danced with "undiminished vigor" until three in the morning.[1] Most of the crowd were Americans, but they did their best to conform to the laws of Canada. One observer noted that they were dressed "frontier style," but without their customary belts and six-shooters. "The boys didn't seem to dance as gracefully without them, but after three or four whirls about the grand dining room, they caught on to the step and enjoyed themselves immensely."[2]

It wasn't the first ball at the new hotel. In February 1893, the hotel, though not yet completed, staged a ball and banquet. The hotel was owned by the Kaslo townsite company and was already welcoming travellers. The elite of Kaslo turned out to celebrate, and according to George Hardy, using his descriptive Chinook jargon, everyone had a "hiu skookum" time.[3] He thought the event would long be remembered, not because of the food, the dancing, or the elegance and mining camp finery on display, but because of the good times and sense of occasion.

Music, song, and dance were integral components of BC's late nineteenth century mining rushes. In an era with no television, no internet, and where recorded music was rare and usually unavailable, the importance of dances and concerts cannot be overemphasized. Whether in the mining camps and towns that served the mines, or in the bunkhouses of the mines themselves, music was everywhere. The variety was expansive—from parlour music in the towns to traditional ballads and breakdowns in the bunkhouses—there was music and song for all tastes.

The Comique theatre in Kaslo was filled with music and song in 1892 and early 1893, often with sultry singers like Maud Roselle who worked the circuit between the coast cities, Spokane, and the mining camps. However, the Great Panic of 1893 turned down the volume, and the Comique closed for a few months. But there was still a place for song, even in the depths of the depression. A Vancouver magazine published a parody of the song "Castles in the Air" to mark the downfall of a fictional Kaslo real estate shark, John Joblots:

Poor Joblots is now slinging hash — at least so people say —
On Carrall and Cordova streets, at the noted Oyster Bay,
And, as he lays your order down, he wears a look of care,
He knows his hopes have gone sky-high — like Kaslo — in the air.[4]

The music was not quiet for long. After the initial shock, the Comique reopened, and the recovery began. Song and dance would reignite hopes and dreams.

The mining camps and towns of West Kootenay affected airs of modernity and were quick to adopt popular songs and dances from across North America and Europe. You would be sure to hear the latest songs from New York and London repeated in the dance halls and theatres of the west. Parodies were common. The "Rocky Road to Dublin" was often heard in Sandon's early days and was quickly transformed into the "Rocky Roads in Sandon." In 1895, performers in Revelstoke, north of Nakusp, sang "Dance of the Vegetables," which was a parody of the Webling Sisters' "Dance of the Roses." The Weblings themselves performed in Sandon in 1896, but we don't know if they performed "Dance of the Roses."

New Denver and some of the other mining camps had brass bands, and while they occasionally played for dances and indoor concerts, their focus was on open-air performance and holiday celebrations. With a repertoire that ranged from contemporary songs such as "Hot Town in the Old Town Tonight" to traditional Irish classics like "Brian Boru's March," they were much in demand on Victoria Day and Dominion Day. Indoor dances and concerts often featured "orchestras" comprising local musicians, sometimes including members of the brass bands. There were many talented local musicians and singers to choose from. Mrs. Yates, from Helena, Montana, was an accomplished guitar player who often performed in Sandon and gave lessons there and in Silverton. Peter Carrieri also played guitar at some of the concerts and dances. Concert recitals followed a standard formula, with instrumental pieces interspersed with songs and recitations.

George Spencer, the owner of Spencer's Hall, where many of Sandon's musical events took place, was a fine banjo player who performed often at his own hall and other venues. As a youth in Port Huron, Michigan, he had snuck into a performance by one of the troupes organized by Canada's Colin "Cool" Burgess. The minstrel show likely inspired the young Spencer to take up the banjo. Spencer's wife was a capable pianist and banjoist, and the two occasionally performed duets, but Spencer's regular partner was Thomas Duffy on fiddle. Another duo was composed of Maggie Funk and her daughter Sophie. Maggie did the singing, accompanied by Sophie on banjo.

The popular music of North America in the late nineteenth century was heavily influenced by the minstrel traditions that had emerged in pre–Civil War times. The chief instrument of minstrelsy was the banjo. Adapted by enslaved African Americans from its African antecedents, the banjo and many of the songs and tunes associated with it were taken up by northern white actors, who often performed in blackface. European influences entered the mix too, and mazurkas, polkas, jigs, and reels would have been included in the repertoires of George Spencer, Sophie Funk, and others like them. Dance music would have been essential.

In contrast to recitals, which were usually polite and somewhat reserved, dances, like the high-flying performance of Trenery, Delaney, and Hill at the benefit for New Denver's brass band in 1894, were often rowdy affairs. Newspaper accounts were often misleading. One attendee at a dance in Kaslo reported that everyone had a "rattling good time" kicking up their heels to a fiddle or two. However, when the event was reported in the local newspaper, the dance had become a "function" attended by "elegantly gowned ladies."[5]

Press Woodruff, an American humorist, described an "orchestra" he encountered on one of his trips through rural eastern Washington. The fiddle-led "Sloppy 4" played "good old-time careless music." At the time, they were planning to take their old-time music to Kaslo.[6] String bands were a staple at mining camp dances. Banjos, fiddles, and guitars were the instruments of choice. There was no amplification, so the louder the instrument the better. In October 1893, Curly Robinson and Con Doherty hosted a "Mystic Circle Ball" at their Bon Ton restaurant in Nakusp. There was no mystery to the music, and the dancing would have been lively when couples took to the floor in response to the banjo and fiddle tunes.

In early 1895, Archie Grant hosted a dance at his Sandon Hotel. The *Slocan Prospector* published the following poem to accompany the announcement. It's probably representative of what early dances in the Slocan were like:

Tater's they are bakin' brown;
Jimmy, shet the door;
Dickie, get your fiddle down;
Molly, sand the floor;
Kettle's just a steamin';
An' rosy cheeks is beamin';
We'll dance the night away.[7]

The music for an impromptu dance at Brandon's Victoria Hotel in early 1897 was provided by a string band and caller. The highlight was a particularly energetic highland fling in "true old Scottish style."[8]

There was song and dance in the saloons and brothels too, of course. Pianos were a particular attraction, and hotels that had them were quick to advertise the fact. Finely dressed women belted out popular songs and ballads, backed by rippling piano riffs. Banjos or guitars twanged out from behind the swinging doors of hotels that didn't have pianos. And it wasn't just the hotels and brothels. By the summer of 1897, Sandon's *Paystreak* was boasting of the camp's progress: "The piano and the guitar, and the sweetness of woman's [*sic*] voices are heard from the houses on the hills in the evenings."[9]

Dancing was popular throughout the Slocan but especially in Sandon. In August 1895, Sandon's "Dutch Jake" opened his new building with a very successful dance. Soon there were dances in one or another of the hotels or halls on almost every other night. It was in response to the demand for dancing that George Spencer put up his hall adjacent to his barbershop. He intended to give dancing lessons and have a "hop" at least once a week. As mining camp historian Elliott West has noted, "Few forms of entertainment captured the interest and enthusiasm of mining town dwellers as much as dancing."[10]

By 1896, Sandon was basking in its newfound prominence as the "centre of the Slocan." Hotels and halls outdid themselves, offering grand balls and dances. In the first two months of 1896, there were dances at the newly opened Clifton House, the McDonald brothers' Balmoral Hotel, and a grand ball at Tom Duffy's new Sandon Hall. Well-attended dances took place at the houses of prostitution on most nights too. A glee club sprang up in Sandon, and there were probably clubs in other camps too. The glee club performed at Spencer's Hall in late 1895 but had competition from the latest modern marvel—a gramophone. For only a dollar, attendees could listen to the celebrated musicians of the world.

Competition between the various hotels and halls was keen. Balls, dances, and "pretty waiter girls" were expected, and hotels that could not offer or afford them suffered in patronage. By late 1896, it was clear that the McDonald brothers' Balmoral Hotel could not keep up with newer hotels like the Clifton House. When the Weblings stayed at the Balmoral, Peggy described the waitress as "a very untidy young woman," and complained that "plates were unknown at the Balmoral."[11] However, though hard pressed financially, the McDonald brothers still managed to put on a successful ball and supper in November in celebration of St. Andrew's Day.

Duffy and Spencer were passionate about their music. In early 1895, they formed a quadrille club where they would teach dance lessons. Dance classes were very popular at the time and were offered throughout West Kootenay. "Professor" Lawler ran a dancing school in Nelson and often rented halls in Kaslo and Sandon to offer dance classes after one touring entertainment or another. He accompanied the Weblings to Sandon in 1896. Peggy Webling noted that there was "no nonsense" about his instruction methods, inducing men to dance with each other by "sheer force of will." After one of the Weblings' performances in Sandon, Lawler was giving one of his dance classes when he approached the Weblings, declaring that "a lot of the gentlemen would be tickled to death at having a dance with any one of the famous Sisters Webling."[12] Tired though they were, Lucy Webling obliged by trying a French minuet with one of the eager young gentlemen.

Dancing became something of a cause célèbre in early 1897, when the Presbyterian minister, William Beattie, mounted a vigorous denunciation of the practice. He likely didn't expect the reaction from the multitude of residents who vehemently disagreed with him. The *Paystreak* pointed to the social benefit of dances in a mining camp such as Sandon: "There are very many young people in this camp who would never have the opportunity of meeting with each other, were it not for these dances. Taken moderately it is a most desirable and healthful means of working off superfluous spirits and were it not for these opportunities of meeting with the refining influence of good women, the standard of morality among the men would be much lower than it is."[13] The *Paystreak* had a point. The brothels in Sandon were thriving and certainly had the capacity to take up any excess business from men who did not have the opportunity of courting young ladies at dances or other public events.

As the *Paystreak* noted, music and dance were sometimes catalysts for romance. The dances provided venues for courtship, but there were other settings too. The marriage of William de Ruchie Rose and Nellie Wilson is a good example. De Ruchie was a well-known Slocan mining man who had charge of the St. Keverne and several other mining properties. Born in Portland, Maine, de Ruchie moved to Quebec before heading west. Nellie Wilson was born in Illinois, but then relocated to Olympia, Washington, with her brother C.M. "Milo" Wilson. Milo got work in the Slocan mines, and Nellie followed him there. One day she was practicing on the organ for an upcoming church service. Milo brought de Ruchie to the church. He was enchanted by the music and by Nellie. They were married in Sandon on July 13, 1897.

Arthur St. Claire Brindle and Mabel Estabrooks also had a shared interest in music. Brindle was an early and enthusiastic member of the brass band. Mabel attended the band meetings and provided piano accompaniment. Soon she and Arthur were off on camping trips—chaperoned of course. Brindle did a little prospecting and named one of his claims "Mabel." They were married in September 1897.[14]

Music sometimes became an irritant between the competitive mining camps. With Queen Victoria's birthday fast approaching in 1898, Silverton wanted to celebrate in a big way. They wanted the New Denver brass band to headline. However, New Denver was planning a celebration of its own. In a coup for the Silverton organizing committee, they negotiated a deal with the band. For fifty dollars and expenses, the band would play in Silverton on May 24. Advertisements were printed, but when it came time for the Silverton committee to settle accounts, they were only prepared to pay thirty-five dollars. The band balked. They abruptly cancelled their appearance and accepted a more lucrative offer from Kaslo. They would appear there for $125. Silverton settled for the Slocan City Band instead.

Hard feelings lingered for months. There were likely some in Silverton who sported self-satisfied smiles in September 1898 when a "zealous young preacher" described the band as "emissaries of Hell" for playing on a Sunday.[15] D.R. Young of the *Slocan City News* poked a bit of fun at the controversy:

ABOVE: The New Denver Brass Band, May 23, 1898. Photographer unknown. At Denver Siding, ready to leave for Kaslo's Victoria Day celebration. Charles Smitheringale is standing third from the left. The man standing sixth from the right is likely cornet player and local assayer Howard West. According to the *Kaslo Morning News*, the band that played in Kaslo consisted of J.H. Millward, J. Aylwin, H. West, H.J. Robie, W. Thompson, H. Pyman, A. Brindle, C. Nelson, J. English, W. Coulter, C.E. Smitheringale, C.M. Nesbitt, E.M. Brindle and H. [*sic*] Thomlinson.[16] IMAGE COURTESY OF JANICE WILKIN

BELOW: First Slocan City band, c. 1898–99. Photographer unknown. IMAGE COURTESY OF THE SLOCAN VALLEY HISTORICAL SOCIETY

New Denver has a fine brass band
That knows just how to play;
But Silverton was wise, couldn't stand
Their noise,
And let them at Kaslo Bray.[17]

While the churches may have frowned on secular music or dances performed on Sundays, they had no hesitation in singing and playing sacred music on the Sabbath. The power of hymn was strong. A Presbyterian missionary who gave one of the first services in Nakusp had an audience of about fifteen or twenty to start with. However, after one or two hymns, the numbers swelled to more than eighty.[18]

William Beattie—who was so against dancing—vividly described his first Sunday service in Slocan City, on the banks of the Slocan River:

> At the hour of prayer, no fewer than twenty-four big, stalwart men assemble. Having no hymn books, we announce hymns we all learned at Sunday-school in childhood. Oh! What a service! As we joined in singing "Nearer, my God, to thee," and the strains of that grand old hymn stole out upon the stillness of the night, it seemed as though the very angels caught up the refrain, and brought back to each heart a keen sense of the nearness of the Almighty.[19]

As congregations grew, the music one could hear in the churches became more elaborate. In 1899, the Church of England proudly opened St. Stephen's, its church in New Denver. The new building was full for both morning and evening services. Mrs. Millward and the choir received high praise. Charles Smitheringale was complimented for producing the choral services. Many visitors were surprised by the quality of the choir's performance, some expressing the verdict that "it could not have been surpassed in even the coast cities."[20]

Masquerade balls and other themed dances, like the "pink supper" held in New Denver in 1895, were very popular across Canada during the late nineteenth century. By November 1893, Kaslo was already looking forward to its second masquerade ball. The first was held a month earlier at the Palace Hotel. While judged a success, it was a relatively modest affair with only five masked couples on the dance floor. The Valentine's Day masquerade ball held at Lemon's Hall in Nakusp in 1895 was a grander affair. New Denver's Duffy and Spencer provided the music. The women's costumes were "out of sight," and the whole affair was topped off with a midnight supper.[21]

Sandon hosted its first masquerade ball, in celebration of St. Valentine's Day, on February 14, 1896, in Spencer's new hall. The event was very well received. On February 17, 1896, Lord and Lady Aberdeen hosted a memorable masquerade ball in Ottawa. The theme of the ball was Canada's history. Largely organized by Lady Aberdeen, the ball was a triumph and likely inspired other balls in the Slocan and across Canada. Sandon already had the bug, and the masquerade ball at Spencer's Hall was quickly followed by another at Duffy's Sandon Hall on February 22.

When Peggy Webling visited West Kootenay in 1896, she took note of the masquerade balls and their newspaper announcements, which often stated something to the effect that order would be strictly maintained and questionable characters would not be admitted. This is good evidence that the rowdyism that often accompanied dances sometimes crept into the masquerade balls. Often associated with Valentine's Day and New Year's Eve, masquerade balls also took place on other occasions. The ball held on the evening of St. Patrick's Day in 1897 at Sandon's Spencer Hall was judged one of the best yet. F. Smith was awarded the prize for "ugliest costume," for his portrayal of a Sandon chambermaid.[22]

New Denver's first masquerade ball was held in Clever's Hall on Christmas Eve 1897. More than thirty costumed couples took to the dance floor. Miss Purviance took the honours dressed as a fairy Queen, though the Misses Barclay of Silverton also impressed as a Red Cross nurse and Little Red Riding Hood. Another masquerade followed on New Year's Eve at Spencer's Hall in Sandon. Miss Smith was judged to have the best costume, dressed as "the spirit of Christmas." Fairy costumes were popular at the time, and Miss Genelle, as "Fairy Bells," took away the honours at the 1896 New Year's fancy dress ball at Mrs. Crawford's Nakusp Hotel. However, there were no fairies at the second Knights of Pythias masquerade in New Denver in February 1898, when Mrs. Watson ascended the throne as the Gipsy Queen.

Fraternal societies were instrumental in hosting dancing and recitals. Like the Knights of Pythias and the Oddfellows, the Independent Order of Foresters was keen to showcase musical talent. At a ball in Slocan City in late 1897, attendees were treated to Clara Bennett singing "The Maid of Dundee" and a male quartet singing "Tenting on the Old Campground."

Sophie Funk and Peter Carrieri entertained with a banjo and guitar duet. As might be expected, the evening finished off with "refreshments" and dancing. The various clubs also hosted musical events, and sometimes provided their own entertainment. In late 1896, the members of New Denver's Fat Man's club serenaded their guests with the raucous squawking of their kazoo band.

By the mid-1890s, the populations of Kaslo, New Denver, and particularly Sandon had grown large enough to attract a series of circuit performers. A multitude of entertainers would follow the McKenzie Trio and the Webling Sisters, who had visited Sandon in 1896. The acts ran the gamut of genres and styles. There were Voorhees and Davis on banjo, guitar, and mandolin; Kosminsky on violin—no doubt impressing his audience by mimicking the sounds of a saw and a planing mill; Hyde Gowan, the "wizard of the banjo"; and Signor Patricola on the Italian concertina, accompanied on tour by his daughter Isabella, who also performed.

Music also played at Kaslo's Theatre Comique, which had a house band. The band was modelled after the Spokane Comique's ensemble, which at the time was boasted "the best band in the city."[23] Before the show started, the band would be out on the street playing popular tunes of the day such as "After the Ball," "Sidewalks of New York," "Two Little Girls in Blue," "A Bird in a Gilded Cage," and "Maggie Murphy's Home."

Minstrel shows were particularly well liked at the time. However, a blackface performance by Sandon's "Amateur Minstrels" at Kaslo's May Day celebration in 1896 apparently left much to be desired. According to Nelson's *Miner*, "like the town they come from, they were pretty rocky."[24] Things were much improved by April 1898, when a troupe of actual Black musicians, the Nashville Students, played in Sandon to an appreciative crowd. For two nights, "the audience filled the hall from footlights to box office."[25] One of the highlights was a cakewalk demonstration. Some Black people resided in Sandon at the time, and we can only wonder if any attended the shows.

Before the year was out, the Sandon Drum Band was performing its own version of a cakewalk. Some Black people lived in Kaslo too, including Alfred Perkins, a bartender at the Hotel Slocan, and his wife and daughter Arvell and Lucille. Musical prodigy Minnie Brown and her family were there as well. The residents of Kaslo thought so highly of Minnie that they organized a benefit concert to raise money so that she could receive a musical education in Spokane. More than a hundred people attended and were treated to Minnie's "touching" vocals. Minnie went on to great success, but she never forgot the kindness the people of Kaslo showed her: "The white citizens of Kaslo are excellent people as a whole, many musicians and scholars being found amongst them."[26]

While music in the mining camps, whether played by brass bands, local orchestras, or travelling performers, often focused on popular song, there were occasions when earthier music took the spotlight. Rooted in national and ethnic traditions, these songs and tunes were perhaps less self-conscious and more representative of their performer's origins and lifestyles. A visitor on the steamboat from Rosebery to New Denver was delighted when an Irishman aboard—perhaps inspired by the beauty of Slocan Lake—burst into an impromptu version of a traditional Irish air, "The Lakes of Killarney." A participant in a makeshift concert held at Sanderson's Hot Springs on Arrow Lake in April 1894 reported on the songs delivered by J.G. Devlin and others. We don't know if Devlin, better known as "the Gunner from Galway," sang his signature song at the hot springs, but he did sing a traditional Scottish song, "The Lads That Were Raised Among the Heather." Contributing to the variety of the evening, and representative of the Irish and Highland presence in West Kootenay, a man named Santor sang a song in Gaelic.

The many Irish and Scottish immigrants in West Kootenay in the early 1890s brought their music with them. There were other ethnic groups too, particularly Swedes and Italians. No doubt they had their own songs, but the documentation—at least in English—is lacking.

Irish expatriates were omnipresent in the Slocan in the early years. In September 1893, the Irish contingent in Kaslo celebrated the passage of the Irish Home Rule Bill by the British House of Commons. The bill would eventually be defeated in the House of Lords, but until that happened, Irish nationalists had every reason to be optimistic. The Kaslo band played Irish airs long into the night, Irish jigs were danced, and Irish songs and ballads filled the air. Though the home rule bill would fail, the Irish influence in the Slocan, in both music and politics, would continue.

In 1898, an icon of Irish nationalism, Father McFadden, came to the Slocan looking for money to finance an Irish cathedral. Money aside, he helped finish off a bottle of Irish whisky at the Queen Bess. Journalist P.A. O'Farrell was a staunch Irish nationalist. Writing for the *Freeman's Journal of Dublin*, he lauded the contributions of the Irish and Irish Americans in building up the Slocan. The Hennessy boys, Jack McGuigan, and Billy Lynch received special mention. However, he singled out F.J. Finucane, manager of the Bank of Montreal in New Denver, for the highest praise. Finucane, born in Ireland, was described by O'Farrell as an ardent "dreamer" for the land of his birth.[27]

For their part, the Scots in the Slocan celebrated Robbie Burns Day every year with fiddles, bagpipes, and heathery ballads. Angus McDonald set feet flying with his fiddle playing in 1895, but it's likely there were more than a few capable fiddlers among the Scottish and Irish diaspora.

Bagpipes were early arrivals, and, unsurprisingly, their appearance led to polarized opinions. A bagpiper playing on the streets of Nakusp in late 1893 was followed by a group of keen admirers. The same instrument played a few years later in Kaslo inspired one listener to compare the sounds to that of butcher Pat Burns's pigs being tortured. Most camps had at least one purveyor of the pipes. D.R. Dewar entertained enthusiasts in New Denver, and Kaslo had the eminent Professor Beaton.

Songs from the Scottish and Irish traditions passed down from parent to child. In early 1897, Master Roy Thomas of New Denver, for example, sang a version of "An Irish Gentleman" at a school concert. The song tells the story of an Irishman who left his home to work in a Scottish brickworks. There were other songs from British and American traditions too. At a concert in Slocan City in August 1898, listeners were treated to versions of "Banks of the Clyde" and "Bachelor's Hall," the latter no doubt stirring the heartstrings of the unmarried men in the audience.

There were dozens of railway camps in the Slocan in the 1890s, where songs and tunes, such as "Drill ye Tarriers, Drill," would have been sung and played. Some of these songs would make their way up to the mines, but the miners—many of them Americans—had their own traditions and songs.

There is a good account of Christmas at the Noble Five mine camp in 1894. Ned Durney and Neil Murchison, on duelling harmonicas, provided much of the music. Most of the miners were surprised when Murchison—who had a limp—got up and danced an Irish jig to the syncopated squeals of the mouth organs. Bill McCauliffe, the camp funny man, acted out a piece entitled "The Canadian Fenian Drill." Using a broom as a musket, he sang a song celebrating the Fenian uprising of 1848, when "all Canadians ran away." This was well received by the Irishmen in the crew, who were inspired to get up all together and sing a moving version of the classic Irish song of love and loss, "Shule Agra" (Siúil a Rúin). The evening concluded with three cheers for the cook, Mary Layton, and a rousing rendition of "For They Are Jolly Good Fellows" in tribute to the Noble Five owners.[28]

While perhaps not typical of most Slocan mining camps, Ernest Mansfield's "Camp Mansfield," several miles up Kaslo Creek from Kaslo, illustrates the importance of music in the mining camps. Earlier in his life, Mansfield had given banjo lessons in New Zealand, and clearly, he thought music was an important diversion for the miners when he set up the camp in 1899: "There will be music in the air at Camp Mansfield the coming winter judging from the number of instruments forwarded to that place last week. In the consignment were guitars, banjos, concertinas, accordions, etc."[29] It was essential that mining camp instruments be portable. As far as we know, no one tried to load a piano onto a pack animal.

Music, song, and tall tales were ubiquitous in the bunkhouses of western mines, but much of the tradition in West Kootenay is undocumented. Newspapers rarely carried reports of what went on in the bunkhouses, and few miners recorded their stories. A cryptic note on the back of a photograph of the Slocan Star boarding house, taken by mine manager Bruce White, reads: "'It sounds to me, it sounds to me!' Miner's song to be sung in chorus when anybody told a 'Tall story.'" The notation is signed "E.F.W.," which would be Bruce White's wife, Elise. We don't know the song to which the quote refers, but it provides good evidence of the singing tradition present in the bunkhouses. There were singing traditions underground too, but it's likely that the introduction of noisy air drills put an end to the practice.

Elise White provides additional documentation of music in the mining camps. In 1899, she accompanied Bruce to a mine just across the border in Washington State. There was an old, out of tune fiddle there, and she played a bit for two rows of miners in bunks, but the highlight for the men was probably "Old Pierre," who pulled out a tuned-up fiddle and played "ancient jigs and reels." A few men got up to dance, and the camp washerwoman did a "Red River jig." The evening closed out with songs.[30]

Songs often crossed the border between Canada and the United States, and variations occurred depending on which side of the border they were found. One song sung in West Kootenay by a "grizzled old placer prospector, one of the Cariboo veterans," included the following stanza:

I started in my mining life
By chopping boardwood,
But I was born with an axe in hand,
So I could use it good.

My chum was from the State of Maine,
Somewhere near Tennessee;
But, ah, I was from Canada,
And he could not chop with me.[31]

A tradition of song followed the California gold rush of 1849 to the goldfields of British Columbia, and a few of these songs likely travelled to the silver mines of West Kootenay. Like the parodies of popular songs, most western mining camp songs were based on popular melodies. Folklorist Duncan Emrich, familiar with silver mining districts from his time in Nevada's Virginia City, gives the example of a mining camp song—perhaps sung in the Slocan—based on "Home on the Range":

Oh, give me the hills
And the ring of the drills,
And the rich silver ore in the ground.
Where seldom is heard
A discouraging word,
And many true friends will be found

Oh, give me the camp
Where the prospectors tramp,
And business is always alive
Where dance halls come first
And the faro banks burst
And every saloon is a dive . . .[32]

Whether in the bunkhouses, churches, or concert halls, music was pervasive in the West Kootenay mining camps. Shared songs and tunes raised spirits through everyday challenges and hardships and brought people together if ever a discouraging word was heard.

17

COMMUNITY

EARLY IN 1897, A STRAGGLE of travellers milled about on the Spokane train platform waiting for the train that would carry them across the border to the West Kootenay mining camps. There were hardy prospectors, overalled and blue-jeaned; pink-cheeked Englishmen; an occasional gambler, all dandied up in sporty clothes; serious-looking eastern bankers; and a few others—usually left in the shadows: "The plain faced careworn workwoman, her ticket in her purse, whose flattened sides clearly indicate that the small store of silver dollars has been sadly depleted by the inroads of the ticket. She, clearly, is going north with the longing hope that she may earn a better salary as cook or washerwoman in the north than on this side of the line."[1]

Historians have often written about the circumscribed role of women in the mining camps of western North America. However, while almost always engulfed by a rough and rowdy male majority, the contributions of women were critical. Whether in brothels or boarding houses, restaurants or newspapers, or in schools or telegraph offices, women were there, providing services and support that the camps could not do without. In the early 1890s, women like Sarah Thorburn, Maud Sproat, and Annie Eagan "punched above their weight" in the mining camps they would call home. The women who followed them would continue to play an outsized role in the social evolution of the camps, but they would face more than their share of challenges.

"Chain migration" drew dozens of families from Canada's prairies to Slocan City in 1897 and 1898. Respected townspeople wrote to friends and family back home with glowing accounts of the new district. Sometimes, to reach a wider audience, they would write to local newspapers. Influenced by the "grass is greener" syndrome and fuelled by word of mouth, others from back home joined the trek to the Slocan. The bonds of a shared past would prove themselves in the new home. William White, on his arrival in Slocan City, found comfort in the fact that his neighbour was an old friend from Moosamin. When Regina's James McPherson visited Slocan City in early 1897, he found nearly a dozen refugees from home. He reported that there was "scarcely a spot in the mining country in which one or more Regina men" could not be found.[2] Chain migration likely accounts for the presence of many other national, racial, and ethnic groupings in the Slocan. New Denver, for example, had a large number of French Canadians in the 1890s. Palma Angrignon was one of the first arrivals, but he was soon joined by his brothers Johnny and Ed. Surnames such as Pilon, Jorand, Martin, Sirois, and Gauthier were common.

While the move from the prairies and eastern Canada to the Slocan was seen as an opportunity for men looking to improve their lot in life, it could be hard on the families who often accompanied them. This was the case for twenty-one-year-old Catherine McMillan. She arrived in Slocan City from Calgary on April 24, 1897, with her recently widowed father, Alexander, and her siblings. Alexander McMillan was a drayman who sold milk and produce. Catherine later recalled that she cried every day for months. Some of the tears were for her mother, but she also missed her friends and the flatness of the prairies. She found the mountains surrounding her new home oppressive. In the absence of her mother, Catherine had to take on the responsibility of looking after her younger siblings. Although life was hard, she eventually reconciled herself to Slocan City and the "nice lot of people" who joined her there.[3]

Wherever they came from, people generally adapted quickly to their new homes. However, there were still more bachelors than there were eligible women. In early 1897, two "wealthy young mine owners" placed an ad in the *Vancouver Daily World* seeking wives "between the ages of 17 and 30."[4] Later that year, Seneca G. Ketchum—no stranger to the bachelors or barrooms of West Kootenay—had an inquiry from a "young lady in Vermont" wondering if there was any demand out west for "marriageable girls." Ketchum assured her there was and, tongue firmly in cheek, said that Kootenay characters such as Porcupine Billy, Bughouse Sandy, Cariboo Jack, and Tarantula Ike would make "tender, clinging husbands."[5]

In late 1897, one of the first weddings in Slocan City brought together Thomas Linton and Helen Mar-Bennett. Linton arrived in March 1897 from Calgary. Helen had arrived earlier along with her mother and sister, and they had the distinction of being the camp's first "lady" residents (whether they arrived before the "red curtain" women is unclear). Before coming to the Slocan, Helen had taught elocution in Los Angeles. The wedding took place at the Methodist church in New Denver. Any symbolism attached to the wedding of an American and a Canadian was probably lost on the wedding party.

Wedding bells were ringing in other Slocan camps too. In early 1898, twenty-eight-year-old "Handsome Jack" Souter, first mate on the steamer *Slocan*, married seventeen-year-old Alice Finnie, "the Belle of Rosebery."[6] Weddings in Rosebery, the small camp north of New Denver were few and far between, and the wedding of the "Belle" would have been highly anticipated. Unfortunately, the pastor from Nakusp was a no-show. Undeterred, Handsome Jack loaded Alice into a rowboat and set off for New Denver. There they tracked down a priest, and the knot was quickly tied.

In July, Sandon's Reverend Cleland, who had succeeded Menzies, presided over the marriage of tailor Albert David to Miss Webster. In August, he joined nineteen-year-old Nettie Hoerle, the proprietor of a ladies' furnishing store in Sandon, to Clarence Blackwood of Toronto. The unlikely venue for the wedding was Cody, which didn't often host such events. In September, Cleland officiated at the wedding of Sandon lawyer Martin Grimmett and his fiancée, Maggie Crawford. The wedding took place at six o'clock in the morning so the bride and groom could get an early start on their honeymoon. They intended a rail trip to San Francisco and Los Angeles.

New Denver also had its share of weddings. On February 2, 1898, not long after Handsome Jack's impromptu wedding, Charles Smitheringale married Emma Delilah Alma Kirkwood. Five days later, two other pioneer families were united when George Aylard married Mary Aylwin. Like Martin Grimmett and his bride, George and Mary set off for a honeymoon in Los Angeles. Later in the year, Mary's brother Charles would marry Mary Gathercole—better known in the Slocan as Lily O'Neill.[7]

Marriages and babies proliferated in Sandon as the population there grew. The first baby was a son for Mr. and Mrs. Malloy, born in September 1895. Ownership of the townsite was not yet settled, so it's unlikely that baby Malloy received a town lot. It wasn't until November 1, 1896, that Slocan City's first baby made an appearance. Little Beatrice Edith Robertson's parents were both from the Labrador coast. As expected, there were calls for Beatrice to be given a town lot.

While weddings were publicly celebrated, less traditional and more informal relationships often only came to light through tragedy or when they became the subject of court cases. One case that came before Justice Lilly in Sandon in September 1897 involved Essie Gibbons and John Parks. Formerly a shift boss at Idaho's Bunker Hill, Parks got work at the Reco. Essie claimed to be a widow and admitted that she and Parks had been lovers south of the border and again in Rossland. They quarrelled, and Parks was bound over with a peace bond. They met again in Sandon and resumed their to-and-fro of loving and quarrelling. Essie did not want her lover dealt with harshly but was happy with the peace bond that Lilly issued.

Essie Gibbons clearly had some control over her relationship with Parks, but this was not always the case with other single or widowed women. Immigrant women were particularly vulnerable. In October 1897, a young Finnish woman of nineteen or twenty took Alfred Johnson, the proprietor of the Lakeview Hotel in Kaslo, to court for "seduction under promise of marriage." According to the young woman, Johnson promised to marry her, then, after accomplishing "her ruin," refused to hold up his end of the bargain, offering her $100 instead.[8] The aggrieved woman—who was quickly learning the ways of her new country—thought $1,000 would be more appropriate. Perhaps she had read of a similar case tried in Nelson a few weeks earlier, in which a jury awarded a jilted woman $4,000.

More women were entering the workforce, and the changing demographics in the mining camps were a source of discomfort to some of the men who had been there since the start, when a woman's presence outside the red curtain district was a rarity. In 1897, Kaslo's M.A. Bucke worked in a shared office that could afford to hire a "lady typewriter." He, and likely the other men in the office, weren't entirely comfortable with the situation: "She has quite a modifying effect on the office society, rather too much so, so we are enlarging our offices, and will make a room especially for her."[9]

By 1897, the debate over women's suffrage had moved into the mainstream of provincial politics. A collection of motivated BC women made a concerted effort to win the vote. A petition signed by more than 2,400 settler women and their supporters was submitted to the Speaker of the Legislative Assembly, D.W. Higgins. The petition prayed for the enactment of a law "providing that the rights of citizenship shall not be denied or abridged on account of sex, but that full Franchise shall be granted to the women of this

Province on the same terms as to the men." The first signature on the petition was that of Mrs. D.W. Higgins (nee Mary Jane Pidwell).[10] The petition was introduced by Victoria representative H.D. Helmcken, who also moved second reading of a bill to enfranchise women. In the debate that followed, several members cracked demeaning jokes and made light of the petition. Dr. Walkem got a few laughs when he asked that the petition be read out loud so that he could find out if his wife had signed it.

Though he would oppose the bill, opposition member Colin Sword at least decried those who would treat such a serious matter with levity. The bill was defeated on a vote of sixteen to twelve. The two West Kootenay members split on the issue. J.M. Kellie voted for enfranchisement and Fred Hume voted against. Soon after the vote, Higgins made a trip through the Slocan, where he had some mining properties. Henceforth, he announced, he would side with the opposition when it was appropriate to do so. Coeur d'Aleners in the Slocan must have looked on the suffrage debate in BC with a sense of bemusement. Idaho unanimously approved an amendment to the state's constitution approving women's suffrage in 1895. Colorado had adopted women's suffrage in 1893.

The last decade of the nineteenth century in Europe and North America saw unprecedented debate on women's issues. The emergence of the "new woman" by 1894 challenged social mores. She was sometimes championed, sometimes lampooned, but much talked about. Topics such as marriage, sexuality, and work outside the home were widely discussed. Women in the Slocan were not immune to these discussions, but gender imbalance and frontier geography left them largely on the margins. Bicycles and bloomers proliferated in the 1890s and were taken up by women who revelled in the mobility and independence they offered. Bloomers had arrived in Cody in 1895, but bicycles did not follow. Sandon's *Paystreak* in 1897 offered what was likely the local masculine majority's prevailing view of bicycles and the new woman: "There are twenty-six women in Cody and not one of them rides a bicycle. They occupy their leisure moments in other ways. There are twenty-seven babies in Cody."[11]

Slocan City, with its level ground and wide streets, was one of the few places in the Slocan that could accommodate bicycles. But their arrival was not without controversy. The *Slocan Pioneer* derided the "Mrs. Grundys" who reacted with horror at the first appearance of women on bicycles. Given the slushy streets in winter, the *Pioneer* even accepted the shorter skirts then coming into vogue. However, bloomers were beyond the pale:

> It is fully understood from the start that the ugly, ungainly, flappy things are to be fully and entirely concealed by a skirt, even if the latter contemplates a mud train longer than the story of the advantages of Slocan as a place of residence. Give us mud and slush and sloppy skirts and wet feet and pneumonia and doctor's bills—any old thing—but deliver us from the bloomers.[12]

The "new woman" might have been an inspiration to women bound by convention, but workplace realities left much to be desired. As in earlier years, the great majority of jobs available to women were restricted to traditional roles.

Women continued to have a strong presence in the hospitality sector, operating and working in hotels, dining rooms, and lodging houses. About the same time that Johnny Harris built the Virginia Block, he also put up the Goodenough Hotel. It was "magnificently furnished" and efficiently run by Mrs. M.A. Smith, who advertised the "finest, largest and most elegantly furnished rooms in the Entire Northwest."[13] However, the Goodenough was lacking one feature common to most hotels in Sandon: liquor. It was a temperance hotel.

Teaching was another profession with a female bias. Turnover was high, and most teachers who had pioneered in the early 1890s were gone by the time Sandon and Slocan City exploded onto the scene. Teachers were often assisted by the ladies' aid societies and other members of the community, usually women, who would help organize school functions such as fundraisers or recognition events. The school in Brandon, which also served Slocan City, hosted Annie Rath, and then another Ontario product, Annie Girdwood. Laura Moss, from Whonnock, on the Fraser River, followed her sister to Slocan City and in 1898 succeeded Annie Girdwood at the Brandon school.

Sandon's first public school teacher was likely Miss Moore, who started at the newly completed school in October 1896. Eva Gibbon took over the classes in early 1897, and later that year she was succeeded by Mary Skinner. Sandon also had at the time a private school run by Mrs. W.I. Williams, an experienced teacher from Spokane. By 1898, there were schools in Sandon, Brandon, Slocan City, New Denver, Silverton, and Three Forks. The school in Three Forks, with only half a dozen or so students, suffered with the diminishment of that camp, but the other schools were relatively well attended. Mary McGraw of Victoria, just seventeen, took on teaching duties in Silverton.

Miss McGraw and Silverton school students, June 1899. Photographer unknown.
IMAGE COURTESY OF THE SILVERY SLOCAN HISTORICAL SOCIETY

By 1896, women of property had won the right to both run for office and vote in elections for school trustees in "urban" school districts in BC. However, because of the preponderance of men in the mining camps—particularly the proportion of men who owned property—elected trustees were almost invariably male. In the Slocan City trustee election of 1897, there were ninety-four male voters compared to just twenty females.[14] So, while many teachers were women, school trustees were mostly men.

Several Slocan school trustees and community representatives lobbied hard for male teachers. There was some concern that young, single women would not long remain unmarried in a district largely populated by eager, single men, but it was also argued that women would not be able to control some of the older, rougher boys. Reminiscences of some of the students support this. Fred Vipond and Ray Goodwin both attended school in Kaslo in the late 1890s. Both recalled "unruly" pupils, with some of the older boys being "man-sized" and particularly troublesome. However, if Agnes Deans Cameron of Victoria is anything to go by, there were women every bit as capable as the men in administering schoolroom justice. Cameron, who became the first female principal in the British Columbia school system in

1894, notoriously whipped one of her recalcitrant male students, something her male colleagues would also have done in similar circumstances. But Cameron's use of the whip was something that drew attention to the role of women in the school system.

Drawing less attention was the fact that female teachers were regularly paid less than their male counterparts. There's no evidence that any of the female teachers working in the Slocan in the 1890s were particularly aggrieved by any salary disparity, but the *Vancouver Daily World* took note of the discrepancy and championed the rights of female teachers to equal pay. The paper published an opinion that would be oft repeated in succeeding years: "If ladies do the same work as performed by gentlemen, they are most assuredly entitled to the same remuneration."[15]

The issue of marriage was perhaps more problematic. Married women were rarely hired as teachers, the common belief at the time being that it was more appropriate for them to stay at home and raise children. This philosophy had its drawbacks. In the summer of 1899, school inspector William Burns worriedly reported that up to 50 percent of the unmarried female teachers working in BC took to marriage in the latter days of the 1898/99 school year. Not long before, Nakusp's pioneer teacher, Eleanor Caldwell, had married John Dawson and moved to New Denver. Eliza Livingstone married a Slocan City man in 1898. Her predecessor in New Denver, Martha McDowell, had married Revelstoke's Thomas Graham in 1896. Silverton struggled to find a teacher to replace Mary McGraw, who left her teaching position to marry mine owner Noah McNaught's son, Bert, in July 1899.

The Slocan's female teachers were greatly respected and appreciated in the communities they served. And while some were satisfied with marriage over and above their teaching duties, others, like Mary Skinner and Annie Girdwood, had ambitions beyond a wedding ring. When Mary Skinner left her teaching position in Sandon to pursue a career in medicine, her pupils surprised her with a gift and an address, read by star student Ada McDougall:

> Dear Miss Skinner—it is with regret that we, the pupils of both divisions of the Sandon Public school, learn that you are leaving us and your post as a teacher of this school. We should like you to carry with you the assurance that the patient, faithful work you have done among us has not been unappreciated. We wish that you may enjoy success and happiness in your new sphere of work and that your services may be appreciated by others as they have been by us.[16]

No doubt some tears were shed when the students sang a verse of "Land of the Maple."

•

BY 1897, THE LADIES' AID societies and church-sponsored clubs that were still active in New Denver and Three Forks, had spread to Sandon and Slocan City. The Christian Endeavor Society, an interdenominational organization, was active in Sandon by late 1897. Like the Epworth Club, it offered opportunities for women and men to debate and discuss topical subjects. In early 1896, Dora Kerr presided over a debate in New Denver on whether the press or the compass was more beneficial to humankind. Much to the chagrin of R.T. Lowery and other newspapermen, the compass came out on top.

Despite the results of the debate, however, newspapers in the Slocan were thriving as the population grew. R.T. Lowery noted in 1897 that the woods of West Kootenay were "full of newspaper men." One of those men was Sam de Rackin. De Rackin had run newspapers in Sprague, Washington, in the early 1890s, before taking up the position of sheriff of Lincoln County. He was dismissed for drunkenness in 1895. He briefly edited an early iteration of the *Rossland Miner* and started the *British Columbia News* in Kaslo in 1897.

It seems there was some commonality between tramp printers, booze, and law enforcement. In addition to de Rackin's stint as a sheriff in Washington State, Seneca Ketchum briefly held the post of chief constable in Nelson after leaving Sandon. R.E. Seysler, once of the *Kaslo-Slocan Examiner*, also took a job policing. After managing the *Idaho State Tribune*, he was appointed deputy sheriff in Wallace, Idaho.

In the summer of 1897, Lowery got some help at the *Paystreak* when he hired Weston Coyney. Coyney first showed up in West Kootenay in June as a travelling correspondent for the *Slocan Pioneer*. On one of his travels, he met up with C.E. Smitheringale and J. Langstaff, who were prospecting at Ten Mile Creek, south of New Denver. Coyney was impressed with the two newspapermen. Within days, Coyney was working for their boss, R.T. Lowery. Coyney was a man of considerable experience, both in the newspaper world and in international relations. British-born, he had served the Prince of Wales on a tour of South Africa's Zululand. After immigrating to the United States, he had been plucked from the staff of the *New York Herald* to assist as private secretary to American politician Levi Morton, who served as vice president under President Benjamin Harrison (1889–1893).

YOU NEVER KNEW WHO YOU might meet in the Slocan woods. Though they might have been late to the game, there were still prospectors hopeful of finding their fortunes. A correspondent for de Rackin's *British Columbia News*, passing through the outskirts of Three Forks one morning, came across a roughly hewn cabin within which an older man was cooking up flapjacks for himself and his sons. The man was Ezra Meeker, widely known in the Pacific Northwest as the "Hop King" and founder of the Washington State town of Puyallup. He made a fortune growing hops in the fertile western Washington soil but lost most of it when his crops were wiped out by a hop aphid infestation. Then came the depression of 1893. Four years later, he was eating his breakfast in the Slocan woods off a board balanced on his knees. Still, he was hopeful about the claims he and his sons had staked and confident he would regain his fortune.

While Lowery said the woods of West Kootenay in 1897 were "full of newspaper men," there were aspiring newspaperwomen too. Before accepting her teaching assignment in the Slocan, Annie Girdwood had written articles for the *Guelph Daily Mercury*, a newspaper run by her father. After leaving her teaching position in November 1897, Annie was soon back in Guelph, again writing columns for the *Mercury*. Before she left the Slocan, she wrote a column describing the final stages in the evolution of a mining camp: "The school teacher and the missionary make their appearance after a while, and then the town may consider itself equipped."[17]

Like Annie Girdwood, May Bertram—described by a contemporary as "a very intelligent lady"—pursued newspaper work.[18] The daughter of a Nanaimo newspaper pioneer and married but likely widowed, separated, or divorced, she had some success as a press correspondent in Whitewater in 1897. However, her passion for writing and her family background weren't enough to sustain her. By early 1898 Bertram was running Charlie Borene's dining room at the Victoria Hotel in Whitewater, which was a more typical role for women at the time.

While most working women in the mining camps were restricted to traditional roles, a few seized the opportunities provided by emerging technologies. Telegraph offices were standard fixtures in most mining camps, and telephone exchanges began appearing in the late nineteenth century. Author Tom Standage has described the North American telegraph system as "the Victorian internet," and women were very much involved in operating that system. Some believed that women were better suited than men to be telegraphers. Whether true or not, certainly many women were attracted to the profession. Earlier in her career, Sara Anne McLagan had earned a reputation as an expert telegrapher. There were several male telegraphers in the Slocan, but Miss McQueen, who came from Vancouver in 1896 to take charge of New Denver's telegraph office, was accorded an especially warm welcome on her arrival.

Telephones started appearing in the Slocan in the early 1890s but mostly served the mines. However, later in the decade, they became more common in the camps below. Like the telegraph offices, the telephone exchanges that started popping up attracted many women looking for employment. Mary Aylwin had charge of the New Denver exchange, Maggie Crawford managed the Sandon exchange, and a Miss Cooney ran the Kaslo exchange.

IN SPOKANE, THE SILVER WEALTH of the Slocan was a popular topic in sitting rooms and at church socials. In June 1896, Jennie Hunter, a recent arrival from Illinois to Spokane, wrote glowingly of the investment opportunities to her family and friends in Illinois: "Some formerly very poor people have become, within a few months, very rich from their ventures in mining enterprises." Seeing an opportunity to cash in, a group of Spokane women formed the Woman's Northwest Mining and Investment Company.

Some of the most successful investors in West Kootenay mines were women. In early 1897, Rosa Leigh Spencer, an insurance agent from Nanaimo who had visited West Kootenay in 1893, became something of a sensation in Canadian mining circles when she opened a mining office in Toronto. She was reportedly the first woman to enter the field in all of Canada, though Mrs. Jennie L. Stone, described as a "hustler," was operating in Rossland about the same time. Mrs. Jennie E. Harris, who had lived in Kaslo since 1892, was another woman who profited from her mining ventures.

But it was Rosa Leigh Spencer who got the press. Her interview in the *Canadian Home Journal* was full of practical advice for women who wanted to invest in the western mines: "A clear headed business woman is perfectly capable of going into mining in any department."[19] Miss Spencer had hundreds of women coming to her looking for investment opportunities. She usually advised them to invest in developed properties rather than prospects, which were a greater risk. She also warned against companies that were heavily advertised. She had several examples of women who had successfully invested in Slocan mines. One of them was possibly pioneer West Kootenay hotel woman Sarah Manuel, who was known as a savvy investor.

Another woman who profited from Slocan mines was Mary Layton. While working as a cook at the Noble Five mine, she befriended Ned Durney. In May 1896, Durney transferred to Mary a one-fifth interest in the Noble Five group, all for the nominal fee of one dollar. In June 1896, the Nelson *Miner* reported a tentative agreement between "Mary Saden" and capitalist R.M. Sherman. Mary would "deed out" of her stake in the Noble Five on payment of $10,000.[20] It seems likely that Mary "Saden" and Mary Layton were the same person. If so, it was unlikely that Mary would ever go back to work as a mining camp cook.

WHILE "RESPECTABLE" WOMEN IN THE Slocan were more or less restricted to church socials, school matters, literary societies, and community events for social interaction, men could turn to fraternal organizations like the Masons and Oddfellows. More than secret handshakes and special knowledge, these groups played a similar role in the community to the ladies' aid societies. They sponsored or helped to organize suppers and dances, and in times of need, they rallied to support their members, sometimes paying for health costs and funerals.

There were a number of Masons in the Slocan and Kaslo, but no lodges until one was formed in Kaslo in late 1894. Unlike the pioneering lodges in Victoria, where many of the Masons had English backgrounds, the Kaslo lodge—reflecting local demographics—was largely made up of Canadians from Ontario, Manitoba, and BC, with a sizeable minority of Americans and a couple of Scots.

Several chapters of the Knights of Pythias and Oddfellows opened in the Slocan in succeeding years. The Knights of Pythias was established in New Denver by early 1897 and boasted fifty members by summer. A lodge was established in Sandon too, but when the grand chancellor visited the Slocan, he was particularly complimentary to the New Denver lodge. He thought the members "excellent material" to carry on the secret work of the fraternity and thought New Denver could become the banner lodge of BC. For the residents of New Denver, the Knights were appreciated for their dances and masquerade balls.

Already established in Kaslo, the first meeting in the Slocan of prospective Oddfellows was held in Sandon's Crawford Hall on December 30, 1896. It was decided to form a lodge. By the summer of 1897, the Oddfellows were operating in Slocan City too. Like the Pythians, they were known for their dances. Pioneer prospector Paul Hauck was elected "Vice-Grand" in Slocan City, and Martin Grimmett was involved as recording secretary for Sandon's "Silver City" Oddfellows lodge. By 1898 there was also a Rebekah lodge for Oddfellow women.

Established in Kaslo as early as 1893, the Independent Order of Foresters set up a court in New Denver in early 1897. By the end of the year, the Foresters had added courts in Sandon, Silverton, and Slocan City. There were almost a hundred paid-up members in these courts and the one in Kaslo. Many women in Slocan City signed up to become "companions" of the Foresters. With other societies setting up in Sandon, there was demand for a Masonic lodge too, but when the district deputy grand master visited in June 1897, he found the proposed hall too small, and was dismayed to find that it was being used by three other societies. He recommended that action be delayed until the prospective members could secure a better hall. By 1899, they had secured a roomy hall, and in August, Alta Lodge No. 29, with all "the necessary paraphernalia" was opened for business.

A general belief in a supreme being was a prerequisite for most fraternities, but beyond that, many orders—in theory at least—were accepting of all religious affiliation. Jews and Christians joined together, and among the Christians there were both Catholics (who were technically forbidden to join fraternities) and Protestants. Kaslo's Slocan Tent No. 6 of the Knights of the Maccabees attracted a few men and women of Jewish heritage but was open to other "whites" too, including a large number of women. Mose Holland had a key role as keeper of records. Unfortunately, even in Canada a "colour bar" often kept Black people—where they were allowed—segregated.

Most of the established churches frowned upon the secret societies. One Christian academic objected to their inclusivity: "They link together Christian and un-Christian people and work positive evil to the religion of Jesus Christ."[21] But Methodists and Presbyterians, in the Slocan at least, had no qualms about the fraternal organizations. Martin Grimmett, who would later ascend to the post of grand master of the Masons in BC, was a devout Christian. He was of the view that "freemasonry is not designed to make men good—that is the function of the Church, we only hope to make good men better."[22]

Above and beyond the social amenities that fraternal organizations offered, there were other practical benefits. Chief among them were the de facto insurance services most offered. Death or incapacitation could be expensive. For a small monthly stipend, most fraternal societies would help with those costs.

A variety of locally organized clubs also sprang up in the late 1890s. There were bachelors' clubs, political clubs, dinner clubs, literary societies, and social clubs. One of the most popular—because of the quality of the suppers it put on—was the New Denver Fat Man's Club. The Fat Men were noted for their New Year's Eve suppers, but they also sponsored balls and dances throughout the year. The New Year's Eve supper to close out 1897 was particularly memorable, with songs, speeches, and performances by a makeshift orchestra, as well as a bagpipe player. Between the forty guests, it was estimated that sixty bottles of beer were consumed, eighteen of Seagram's whisky, about the same of stout, and a dozen or so bottles of wine. Despite this, all the Fat Men were able to maintain their sea legs. For the Owl Club of Slocan City, bottled Calgary beer was the drink of choice. The Owls, composed of "a lot of worldlings from various climes and countries" shared common purpose in bachelorhood and a love of practical jokes.

The Virginia Coterie was a "made in Sandon" club that planned to have parties every two weeks on Thursdays in Sandon's Virginia Hall. The first party was held on November 4, 1897. Dancing was the main attraction, with music provided by the Sandon orchestra, but the organizers promised other events and social games for those who didn't like to dance. However, we don't know how far the organizers' initial enthusiasm carried, as there are no references to any parties in subsequent editions of local newspapers. Like a few fraternal organizations, some clubs, including Kaslo's Missouri Club, embraced members of different colours or creeds. Alfred Perkins, who was Black, was a member in good standing, and the club's president was a Black Missourian.

The Orange Lodge was less welcoming. It occupied territory somewhere between a fraternity and a club. Dedicated to the supremacy of Protestantism, particularly in Northern Ireland, members celebrated the victory of William of Orange over the British Catholic King James II in the seventeenth century. There were lots of Irish men with Catholic backgrounds in the Slocan in the early days, but as more eastern Canadians arrived, the Orange Lodge grew in membership and influence. Intolerance between Irish Catholics and Orange Lodge members was certainly present in the Slocan, though staunch Orangeman Joseph Irwin of New Denver, publicly at least, preached tolerance, explaining that to be a good Orangeman, "one had to be a good citizen who would be respected by all classes, Roman Catholic as well as Protestant."[23] However, only those accepting the creed of Protestantism as approved by the Orange Lodge could join.

WHILE WOMEN WERE GENERALLY WELCOMED in the mining camps, though often restricted to traditional roles, and Black and Irish people—outside the restrictions of the Orange Lodge or the fraternities—were "tolerated," people of Chinese heritage were subject to rampant prejudice. In November 1898, the Sandon *Mining Review* reprinted an article written by an eastern Canadian correspondent detailing life in West Kootenay. He described Sandon, with its tennis club and fine hotels, as "just as cosmopolitan as was Venice in its later days. Here Wales and Scotland and Cornwall and Munster and Ulster are fully represented."[24] There were Germans, Swedes, and Frenchmen too. Elsewhere in the newspaper, the local escapades of a travelling Jewish peddler were detailed. The correspondent was amazed at this pocket of civilization and apparent international harmony in the middle of the wilderness. He noted that in Sandon one could dine in fine restaurants, sip French wine, and discuss the latest in politics. Certainly, the Slocan, and Sandon in particular, hosted a mixed bag of men and women of northern European origin. They all had one thing in common—the colour of their skin.

The same edition of the *Mining Review* that described Sandon's "cosmopolitan" outlook carried an overtly racist story about a group of miners who chased four Chinese cooks out of Sandon. All were satisfactory workers. It didn't help. In early 1899, Edward Odlum, a prolific travel correspondent for the *Vancouver Daily World*, visited Sandon. He described it as a "white man's paradise." He was particularly impressed with the absence of any Chinese residents in the camp: "Information comes to hand that it is not a healthy climate for the Mongolian."[25] What did Odlum mean by "white man"? It's clear from his writings and ingrained prejudices that the "non-whites" in his worldview were individuals of Chinese origin. There were Black men and women in the Slocan too, and while this may have raised the eyebrows of some Americans from southern states, Black people were generally accepted by "white" Canadians. Unlike the Chinese, they shared many of the cultural traits of other mining camp residents. They often went to the same churches, ate the same foods, spent their money locally, and participated in the same social milieu.[26]

As noted by historian Dr. Patricia Roy, the concept of "whiteness" seems at times to have had more to do with class, nationality, and/or economic interests than it did with skin colour. Ernest Rammelmeyer, the manager at Silverton's Emily Edith mine, was German born and clearly "white." However, when a labour dispute broke out in 1899, he was criticized because he was not a citizen of Canada. Rammelmeyer pointed out that the Silverton miners' union leader was not a Canadian either, to which his critic replied: "Well, he is a white man," implying that Rammelmeyer was not. New Denver's Black madam, Ella Brown, who came in on horseback from Nakusp in 1893, was reported to have claimed that she was the first "white woman" in the Carpenter Creek camp. And when George Joy first arrived in New Denver in April 1893, his Jewish companion convinced him to head to Nelson, where "every person was white . . . even the colored ladies and gentlemen."[27]

WHILE THE SLOCAN MINING CAMPS were generally doing well through 1897, trouble was brewing below the surface—of both the mines and the mining camps. In July 1897—not that long after his enthusiastic address to the Galena Mines Limited shareholders in London—C.W. Callahan abruptly left his position. There were rumours the mines were not doing well. Shares were being unloaded for next to nothing through insider trading. The true state of affairs was revealed at a meeting held in London in the fall. The *British Columbia Mining Critic* reported that the company's chairman, Mr. P. Comiskey, was applauded in some quarters for laying out the "naked truth." Comiskey was frank. In faltering words, he addressed the meeting: "The lode is . . . somehow broken or twisted, and a deuce and all of a lot of zinc is found to be intermingled with the galena, which is by no means so rich as it first seemed or was stated to be in the prospectus."[28] The trouble at the Galena Farm, compounded by low silver prices, was sobering news for mine owners and investors alike. For the first time since 1893, the future was uncertain.

18

DISTRACTIONS

THE OUTLOOK WAS BRIGHT AND full of promise in February 1897. It looked to be a bonanza year in the Slocan. People crowded the dance floors and shared the thrills at sporting events. New Denver mining man John Vallance could boast that the Slocan had forty-five shipping mines—all making a profit. The Slocan Star alone issued dividends of $350,000 in 1896. As the year progressed, however, the clouds of uncertainty that had been building in the background crept over the horizon. Then, in July, the price of silver plummeted to $0.55 an ounce on the New York market—the lowest price on record. Provincial mineralogist William Carlyle noted that the sudden drop in silver "checked all speculation." Slocan mine owners were not panicking, but they were worried. According to Carlyle, the silver boom was "over."[1]

Later in 1897, Agnes Fraser, an English author who wrote under the pseudonym Frances Macnab, made a whistle-stop tour of the Slocan. She was doing background research for a book she was writing for British citizens thinking of settling in BC. She had only two hours in Sandon but made the most of it. She went straight to Johnny Harris's office, where she found him in conversation with several other gentlemen. She later recalled that "forthwith we plunged into the silver question. The 'slump' in the value of silver had caused a panic, and Sandon was paralyzed. Only the richest mines were working. The fall had been a heavy one and the fear was that it might continue indefinitely."[2]

Agnes Fraser thought that while Harris and the others would quite naturally be concerned by any drop in silver prices, perhaps they were overreacting. Her opinion was based on a conversation she had with Scott McDonald of the Payne, who declared that the best mines in the

Slocan would still pay even if the price of silver dropped to $0.25 an ounce. This might have been fine for the Payne, Slocan Star, and Reco, but it was cold comfort to the other Slocan mines where the silver was of a lower grade. In another prescient observation, Fraser noted that Johnny Harris and the other mine owners were nervous about developments in the far-off Klondike region. The clouds crossing the horizon weren't silver lined.

It had always been a challenge luring British investors to silver. One American capitalist in 1896 felt that English and Canadian investors were equally apathetic when it came to West Kootenay silver mines. It was his view that English capitalists only had eyes for gold, an opinion shared by Fred Kelly: "You tell an Englishman that you have a splendid silver property running 200 ounces to the ton and he will admire the surrounding beauties of nature, but you tell him that you have a gold claim which runs $15 to the ton and he will start as if he was hit on the head and want to know all about it."[3]

The outlook in the Slocan was clouded too by the rise of Rossland. The camp had a population of more than three thousand by early 1897, where there had been only two log cabins in 1894. Perhaps not as rich as those in the Slocan, the Rossland mines had the advantage of producing gold, which had more lustre for investors than silver. Jealousies between the two West Kootenay districts grew, with the *Rossland Record* complaining, "When a prospector goes to the Slocan, the Slocanites surround him and poison his mind against the gold district."[4] It would be an uphill battle for the Slocanites. "Men make a mad rush for the yellow metal, forgetting sometimes that silver mines are even as profitable, if not more profitable."[5]

Vancouver World reporter "Wings" Wilkinson acknowledged the "magic" of gold and the "slur upon silver" from investors who cried "We only want gold mines!" But he pointed out that he would sooner get one hundred dollars for a ton of silver ore than forty-five dollars for a ton of gold ore. However, the sharp drop in the value of silver boosted the attraction of gold. There was gold in Rossland, and while a ton of Rossland ore paid far less than a ton of Slocan ore, the magic of gold attracted British investment in a way which the Slocan mines had never done. But Rossland gold was small potatoes compared to the riches reported from the north. In September 1897, the *Revelstoke Herald* noted that "gold is the cry just now," and for gold, all eyes turned to the Klondike.[6]

IN RETROSPECT, AN EARLY MENTION of the "Klondyke" in the July 29, 1897, issue of New Denver's *Ledge* was full of foreboding: "The new Eldorado lies just across the Alaska boundary in British territory. It is of recent discovery, but already there are at least three thousand people on the ground, and more are flocking in that direction as fast as transportation can be secured." Dozens of Slocan residents would set out for the Klondike later in 1897. For many veteran prospectors, the temptation was simply too great to resist. Wiry old prospector Toughnut Jack explained: "I've waited many years—now my chance has come, and I must take it. Yes! Its [*sic*] me last struggle."[7] The Klondike's lure was enhanced by concurrent events in the Slocan, including the falling silver prices, and troubles afflicting some of the mines that teetered on the edge of profit. Mines that months earlier had been coveted by investors started to falter.

Blame did not rest entirely on falling silver prices or the lure of gold. The increasing attention of British and Canadian investors in late 1896 and early 1897 led to a flood of joint stock companies. Some proved too much of a good thing. William Carlyle had provided a warning, but not all gullible investors listened. The London correspondent for the *Engineering and Mining Journal of New York* also had a warning: "Never sell a mine or a prospect to a London company for anything else but cash, and never deal with a London promoter unless you know his record."[8] Another critic, echoing this advice, urged English and eastern Canadian "suckers" to beware the "horde of sharks, snides, bums, brokers and played out traders" hawking Kootenay mines.[9]

There was trouble at the Galena Farm, which was overstocked and overvalued, and hard hit by low silver prices. For years, naïve British investors had ploughed money into dubious mining ventures in Nevada, Colorado, and Montana. It stood to reason that the pattern would be repeated in BC. In his study of British investments along the western American mining frontier, Clark Spence described the typical British investor: "At times it appeared that, dazzled by promotional literature, sensational promises, and the use of titled guinea pigs, he simply closed his eyes and poured his funds blindly into whatever scheme was placed before him."[10] Between 1890 and 1914, it is estimated that British investors lost more than $150 million on Canadian mining schemes.

The Galena Farm problems and low silver prices were bad news for mine owners and operators, particularly those like Vancouver's Edward Mahon, who owned claims near the Galena Farm. Mahon was in the Slocan late in the summer of 1897 to inspect his mines. The optimism he felt a year earlier, when Callahan's Galena Farm promised its riches, was now tempered. Fortunately, he had his "titled guinea pig." Sir Henry Cunningham, knighted in 1889, was well known for his administrative work on the Indian subcontinent and authored several works dealing with the British experience in India. Cunningham forwarded a cheque for £106 for a hundred shares in Mahon's mining company.

The difficulties at the Ibex were of a similar order to those of the Galena Farm. High up in the Whitewater basin, the Ibex had been capitalized in late 1896 by Major Sam Steele of the North West Mounted Police. The company raised $300,000 in capital stock and put some of that stock on the market at $0.26 per share. A mixed bag of Steele's police colleagues invested in the mine. R.T. Lowery wasn't convinced of the investment potential. He noted that Major Steele and his police colleagues may have been "experts on Indians and bad men" but their knowledge of mines was limited.[11]

One of Major Steele's colleagues, Superintendent Burton Deane of Lethbridge, later recalled: "We had faith." Deane felt that with Steele at the helm, they had a guarantee that "the conduct of the business was at least honest."[12] Major Steele might have been honest, but the promoter of the mine, Fred Steele (no relation) was not. Fred Steele took advantage of his relationship with the major and at one point visited the police barracks in Fort McLeod to solicit investments. This came to the attention of Major Steele's superiors. The matter went all the way to the prime minister's office. Asked to explain his actions, Major Steele was adamant: "I have never asked any N.C.O. or Constable in the Force to join me in any speculation whatever . . . I had pointed out to one or two officers in the Forces that the group of claims were for sale but only on account of their having previously asked me to let them know if any good opportunities presented themselves."[13] The explanation did not satisfy the prime minister. Major Steele was urged to retire from the board of the Ibex mining company. He declined.

When Major Steele visited the Ibex in July 1897, he fired Fred Steele and then signed a contract with the Bartlett brothers to ship out eighty tons of ore. As it turned out, much of the Ibex ore was worthless. The men working the mine could not get paid either. By the end of 1897, a sheriff had been appointed to sell the company's assets to satisfy outstanding debts. When news of the troubles first surfaced, one account reported that Fred Steele had "entirely lost his reason."[14] Superintendent Deane and friends lost $1,000 between them. As he put it, "we backed our faith with good dollar bills, which we had far better have kept in our pockets."[15] Presumably

"Ibex mine; Whitewater," c. 1897. Photographer: Fred Steele. A visit to the Ibex mine. The man second from the right is possibly Major Sam Steele. IMAGE COURTESY OF THE ROYAL BC MUSEUM AND ARCHIVES

humbled, Major Steele went back to doing what he knew best—policing. Soon he would be off to the Yukon to police the Klondike gold rush.

The drop in silver and the crowded field of overstocked investments led to trouble. A rash of mines closed due to one setback or another. Some were in difficulty even before the slide in silver. In January 1897, the Vancouver syndicate operating the Two Friends, located down Slocan Lake on Springer Creek, threw up the bond on the mine. This puzzled some investors, as the mine was still producing quality ore in paying quantities. The mine had shipped forty tons in January. It appears the operators had a cash shortage.

The Two Friends directors offered the mine owners a share offering instead of the cash payment of $37,500 that was due, but the offer was refused. The company then decided to pull out of the Two Friends altogether and instead invest in the Great Western, a mine up the lake and closer to the heart of the Slocan. The annual meeting of the Two Friends Company—which now had no interest in the Two Friends mine—was held in Vancouver in June. The company defended its actions, insisting it had been supported by shareholders "in the east." The directors issued a conciliatory statement that read in part: "It is of course to be expected that the individuals who anticipated so large a sum of money feel chagrined at the turn events have taken, and doubtless have inspired the adverse criticism, which was apparent in one of the Kootenay papers, but the directors felt their first duty was to protect the interest of the shareholders."[16]

The bad news continued with more setbacks for mines down Slocan Lake. In a shocking development, J.A. Finch's mighty Enterprise mine on Ten Mile Creek shut down in September. The *Ledge* reflected local opinion: "The unexpected had happened."[17] Just three months earlier, superintendent George Aylard was planning to more than double his workforce. Instead, all the miners were paid off. The mine's future looked uncertain. Another Slocan casualty in 1897 was the Noble Five. Like the Enterprise, its difficulties caught everyone by surprise. There had been some trouble earlier in the year, but things had seemed to be going well during the summer of 1897. Ore was shipping continuously, and there were about sixty men at work. There were few complaints about working conditions or wages, and certainly no indication that jobs or the mine itself might be in jeopardy. However, trouble was brewing in the board room.

In early October, it was rumoured that the mine had closed and the entire crew discharged. The rumours proved only half true. The day shift was laid off, purportedly to allow for repairs on the flume. There wasn't "the remotest possibility" of the mine closing.[18] Something was up, though. Two of the mine's managers headed to Spokane to meet with shareholders. A few weeks later the mine was shut down with no explanation. Miners were given their cheques, but when they went to cash them, they were told there were no funds available.

Speculation ran rampant. Some thought the mine had simply run out of ore. Others thought it was a ruse to manipulate stock prices, since shares had fallen from just over $0.50 to $0.17 in the space of a year. The truth was more straightforward. William Carlyle was blunt in his assessment: "The Noble Five was forced to suspend work on account of the lack of funds, and indebtedness."[19] Carlyle and others attributed the problems to mismanagement and the mine's inability to pay off a $35,000 debt to the Sandon branch of the Bank of British North America. The bank issued a summons to the local management of the Noble Five. All work stopped.

The future of the mine was left in the hands of its directors and shareholders. The mine's directors wanted to borrow $150,000 to continue working the mine. However, this was opposed by some shareholders, who wanted to put the mine into the hands of a liquidator. A shareholders' meeting was scheduled for late October in Cody. Before the "official" meeting, Kaslo shareholders had a meeting of their own. W.A. Hendryx presided. The Kaslo shareholders decided they would try to raise enough stock to defeat the loan plan. As it turned out, there weren't enough votes for a quorum. The meeting had to be adjourned without a decision.

Frustrated creditors opposed to the loan came up with their own plan. The Bank of British North America, along with several other creditors, started taking steps to have a liquidator appointed. There was a scramble of creditors in November, all eager to stake their claim for a share of the Noble Five's assets. However, the Noble Five directors were not going down without a fight. The adjourned shareholders' meeting was reconvened in Cody in late November, and the directors were able to get a resolution passed authorizing them to borrow the $150,000. The plan was to apply $53,000 to retire the debts owed to the bank and the other creditors and to put the remaining money into development work. The money would come from Victoria investors, headed by coal baron James Dunsmuir. The faction representing disgruntled creditors raised numerous procedural objections to the majority decision. The objections were overruled. The Noble Five was back in business.

As part of the liquidation proceedings, the Noble Five directors issued a trial balance outlining the assets and liabilities of the company. It shows how close to the margin many Slocan mines operated. The gross value of the ore shipped since the incorporation of the stock company was $119,781.08. The total operating costs, excluding management fees and interest, amounted to $117,833.05. One of the storied mines of the Slocan had a net profit of less than $2,000.

There was still money to be made in silver mining, but as the Klondike garnered headlines around the world, it became ever harder to combat the lust for gold. While dozens of miners were coming to the Slocan from eastern Canada, just as many Slocan veterans were leaving for the Klondike. The Bartlett brothers—Al, Ed, and Mike—who ran the biggest packing outfit in the Slocan during the later 1890s, decided to close up their Sandon operation in November 1897 and move all their stock to the Klondike. Their departure was a blow to Sandon. The brothers had been fixtures in

Bartlett's pack train, Reco Avenue, c. 1897. Photographer: R.H. Trueman.
IMAGE COURTESY OF THE ROYAL BC MUSEUM AND ARCHIVES

the Slocan since 1892—when Sandon was no more than a few tents and log shacks. In December, the brothers wrote a heartfelt letter of thanks to their friends in the Slocan: "While the rush of travel to Alaska has opened up for us a promising business enterprise, necessitating our removal to the scene of activity, we wish to reiterate our faith in the future of Sandon and to join with our farewell a hearty expression of goodwill to those we leave behind."[20] The brothers arrived safely in Skagway and were soon tapping into the freight market. For the first few months they wrote faithfully to friends in the Slocan detailing their adventures in the north. They did very well.

By the end of 1897, the lure of the north was almost irresistible. In a troubling development, a number of miners, desperate for money to outfit themselves for the Klondike, started advertising their Slocan claims for sale at discount prices. Some miners simply quit their claims and headed north. In one week alone, in January 1898, some eighty people left Sandon for the Klondike. The Sandon *Mining Review* reported at the time that scarcely a train left the Slocan without carrying from six to twenty miners out. Local businesses suffered, as miners weren't spending their money. Instead of cashing their cheques, they hoarded them, hoping to save enough to outfit for the north.

The trek to the Klondike required a major investment. George LeDuke sold his interest in Sandon's Palace Hotel to finance his trip. He had his ticket on the steamer *Cleveland*, freight paid on a thousand pounds of supplies, and $300 in cash. According to Sandon's *Paystreak*, before setting out, LeDuke decided to have one last fling in Seattle's red-light district. We can't be sure how reliable the *Paystreak*'s sources were, but the intimation was that LeDuke had been "rolled" by one of the good time girls. The truth was more mundane and likely embarrassing to LeDuke. He was drinking at Seattle's Hoffman House when he visited the bathroom. There he absent-mindedly left his wallet, with his ticket, letters of credit, and cash. When he returned, all were gone. He thought to postpone his trip indefinitely but fortunately, he had friends willing to advance him the funds he needed to continue. Less than a week later, he was aboard the *Willamette* bound for the Klondike. It couldn't have been easy. The *Willamette* was an old coal ship. First class passengers were directly below the horse's quarters, and the animals' excrement slid through the deck panels, drizzling down on the travellers.

In September 1897, Agnes Fraser (a.k.a. Frances Macnab) had noted that Slocan mine owners were nervous about developments in the Klondike. Within weeks, Slocan business owners—at least those who had not already left for the north—were nervous too. Several businesses failed in early 1898. Local newspapers—looking to save their skins—did what they could to discourage people from leaving for greener pastures. They took every available opportunity to extol the virtues of West Kootenay and regularly published accounts that either denigrated the Klondike or described expeditions gone horribly wrong. In December 1897, for example, the *Ledge* published a letter sent from the north by prospector Owen Jackson to a friend in the Coeur d'Alenes: "This is the most over-rated country under the sun."[21] Some prospectors, like Billy Will and George LeDuke, returned to the Slocan with tales of failed fortune. Then, news was received that Billy McKinnon had drowned in the Stikine River. Still, people left.[22]

In the 1897 annual report for the Minister of Mines, William Carlyle tried to put a positive spin on the situation: "Many prospectors and miners are preparing to join the great rush northward to the gold fields, and their unusual economy is being felt in all the towns, but this hegira will not be an unmixed evil, as the prices asked for prospects are already falling rapidly, and in all probability in spite of quieter times, more and better development work will be done, as it will be found that many, if not more purchasers will be now in search of good properties."[23] Carlyle was searching for a silver lining and his words were meant to be encouraging, but they weren't always taken that way.

Despite the newspaper efforts, attempts to discourage the "northern gold cure" failed. Crowds in the Slocan, as elsewhere, continued to pack out for the Klondike. Some business owners—resigned to reality—adopted an "if you can't beat 'em, join 'em" attitude. Hotels and restaurants that had thrived just months earlier now struggled to stay afloat. Some businessmen resorted to desperate measures. The owners of Sandon's Filbert sold the hotel for $4,500. Their debts totalled more than $3,000, but by the time warrants were sworn out, they had skipped across the border to Northport and would soon be on their way to the Klondike with a troupe of dancing girls.

THE EXODUS WAS HARD ON local newspapers. Many Slocan and Kaslo newspaper editors and employees were Americans. It was perhaps inevitable that there would occasionally be tensions between Americans and Canadians. Those tensions were high enough in Kaslo in 1897 to induce W.C. Nichol, the Canadian co-owner and editor of the *Kaslo Kootenaian*, to sell his interest in the paper. The *Ottawa Journal* sympathized: "He explains that he had to go because he was too much of a Canadian. His writing in the *Kootenaian* was from a Canadian point of view, in connection with the Klondyke country, the alien labour law and such matters, but a large number of the paper's readers in Kaslo were citizens of the United States; they didn't like Mr. Nichol's style, and kicked, and his business partner, also an American, represented to him that the paper was being hurt, so Nichol got out."[24] Perhaps he was speaking metaphorically, but Nichol claimed that a loaded pistol was "put to his head" to convince him to "renounce his regard for this country [Canada] and cater to American interests."[25] By May 1897, Arthur B. Keeler, an American newspaperman with experience in Washington and Montana, had joined the *Kootenaian*. We don't know exactly when Nichol left the paper, but it was likely shortly after Keeler's arrival.

Dave King, Nichol's erstwhile partner at the *Kootenaian*, vehemently disagreed with Nichol's description of his departure. According to King, it was "purely a business proposition." King was unhappy with the way Nichol was running the paper. He made Nichol an offer on his interest in the paper and Nichol accepted. It was as simple as that. However, lest anyone doubt his allegiance to Canada, King added: "The *Kootenaian* is as loyal to the interests of Canadians in Kootenay as any paper published in the province, but it is not a ranting, blustering jingo seeking to stir up strife and discord in a community which to its everlasting credit has always stood as one man."[26] M.A. Bucke, a Canadian friendly with both King and Nichol, expressed his disappointment with Nichol, who dwelt too much on the "Canadian versus American sentiment" and was "not smart enough to get along in the west."[27]

Controversy followed Nichol to his next assignment as editor of the *Province* newspaper, then located in Victoria. The *Province* was an opposition paper and often railed against the government of Premier Turner. On December 11, 1897, an article written by Nichol appeared, accusing Premier Turner and C.E. Pooley, president of the Executive Council, of passing on secret government information to a British investment company with interests in the Klondike. Both Turner and Pooley were shareholders. Nichol wrote of the two politicians: "They have become mere political strumpets and are not entitled to recognition as honorable men."[28] Nichol soon found himself at the centre of a criminal libel suit brought by Turner and Pooley.

AS IF THE FALL IN silver prices, the failure of British and Canadian stock companies, and the lure of the Klondike weren't enough, labour unrest was looming. With thousands of miners working high in the mountains, it's not surprising that working conditions, which varied widely from mine to mine, would become an irritant. Hardrock mining was dangerous work. While Slocan miners didn't have to worry about the deadly gases that could kill coal miners, there were more than enough hazards to contend with. Broken bones, typhoid, and pneumonia were common. Primitive working conditions and solitary living did not help. William Hanna, in his fifties, suffered for two days in his tent before he was discovered and taken to Sandon. He died in the Balmoral Hotel before he could get to the hospital. Another troubling trend saw a rash of patients from the Payne mine being treated for lead poisoning. And then there were snow slides.

In the fall of 1897, Joe McGibbons was working at the Red Fox mine when he was swept away and carried to the bottom of the Queen Bess ore dump. His partner, William Dixon, survived but spent twenty-four terrified hours trapped in the mine's tunnel. McGibbons's body was not recovered. The Red Fox mine closed down, but the Queen Bess continued to operate. Joe McGibbons's broken-hearted brother wrote to Superintendent Hussey to ask if there were legal means to prevent the Queen Bess from dumping ore before the corpse could be recovered: "I intend to take the body to where he was born [and] raised in Nevada Co. California for burial & I do not want the remains covered by any company."[29] Joe McGibbons was just twenty-six.

IN MARCH 1897, BEFORE THINGS turned sour, representatives from Kaslo, Rossland, Nelson, Sandon, and Spokane got together to discuss the organization of an international baseball league. Despite general enthusiasm and the support of Johnny Harris, Sandon didn't join. Nelson did but soon withdrew when a suitable ball field could not be secured. Kaslo was fully committed, however, and the Kaslo *Kootenaian* put up a league trophy.

George "Chief" Borchers managed the Kaslo team, played first base, and sometimes pitched. Borchers once played for the Chicago White Stockings—later to become the Chicago Cubs of the National League—and then played for Portland in the Pacific Northwest League. He had a reputation as a loose cannon, having once entered a baseball diamond drunk and on horseback. He seemed like a good fit for Kaslo. He opened a newsstand there in 1897, presumably to supplement his baseball income—or vice versa. His wife joined him, along with his St. Bernard show dog, "Smudge." Ed Rankin, another member of the Kaslo team, had played for the Boston Red Stockings—another charter National League team like the White Stockings, later to become the Atlanta Braves. Borchers and Rankin were part of an impressive lineup. There were negotiations for star player Owney Patton too, but he ended up playing for Spokane.

In preparation for Kaslo's participation in the international circuit, the city spruced up their baseball field, adding a grandstand and bleachers. Admission was fifty cents, plus another fifty cents for the grandstand. Kaslo was competitive, usually holding its own against a strong Spokane team. Despite losing the first two games of the season to the Americans, Kaslo had a winning record up until mid-July, when the international league came to a crashing and scandalous end. Rossland had a losing record and was experiencing financial challenges. In mid-July, they hosted the powerful Spokane team. Two of the Rossland players, pitcher George Baker and second baseman Eddie Marshall, were talked into throwing the game. The score was close to start with, but in the later innings the Rossland pitcher started throwing wild. Marshall got into the act too, deliberately flubbing plays. He later admitted: "Had I fielded the ball that let in two runs in the eighth I would have thrown it over the fence."[30] The Kaslo *Kootenaian*, with a touch of hyperbole, called the actions of the pitcher and second baseman "the most disgusting exhibition ever seen on a ball field."[31] The Rossland team disbanded, followed shortly afterwards by the league itself.

ONE MAN WHO DIDN'T SEEM concerned with the fall in the price of silver or the other troubles afflicting the Slocan was Robert E. Lee Brown, better known as "Barbarian" Brown. Brown earned his sobriquet during the early Coeur d'Alene troubles when he published a newspaper—the *Barbarian*—that generally supported the Coeur d'Alene mine owners. After the Coeur d'Alenes, Brown travelled to South Africa where he had worked for Barney Barnato. In late 1897, he invested heavily in Whitewater. This included the purchase of the prospering Whitewater Deep mine, Jim and the entire townsite of Whitewater. As its name implied, the Whitewater Deep, which adjoined the Whitewater, was intended to tap the vein deeper down where it crossed over from the Whitewater. Fellow Coeur d'Alener John Hayes Hammond, an advocate for deep mining, had also worked for Barnato and likely influenced Brown.

The big mines like the Payne, Noble Five, Slocan Star, and Whitewater would still produce profits during 1898, but new money dried up. Investors looked elsewhere, to the Klondike, or Atlin, or Rossland. Copper and gold—even coal—proved more attractive than silver. BC's provincial mineralogist, William Carlyle, had declared the silver boom was over. But as long as the mines could be worked for profit, the Slocan mines would continue to support the mining camps they had given life to. Mine owners like Johnny Harris were still making money, but miners and camp followers were likely examining their options. Sadly, some felt they were out of options.

Edward P. Suydam, a Colorado miner who had boomed the Slocan in earlier years, had by 1897 soured on Canada. His suicide note, written in Rossland, made it clear he wanted to be buried in the United States. A few months later, an Englishman, E. Weeks, who had worked at several Slocan mines, ended his life in a McGuigan hotel by slashing his throat with a straight razor. The circumstances were clear enough that Dr. Brouse decided the death did not warrant an inquest or coroner's jury. Weeks was quickly and quietly buried, and life carried on as before. But suicides were not always private affairs. Sam Wharton was aboard a train in 1897 when one of the passengers suddenly stood up and put a bullet into his brain.

19

BAD BEHAVIOUR

IN THE SUMMER OF 1897, an American lawman was in the Slocan looking for a suspected murderer. The crime had been committed in 1892, in Gassville, Arkansas. It began with a feud between two cattle-ranching families: the Dentons and the Twiggses. When brothers Eng and Lee Denton were acquitted after killing John Twiggs in a hail of gunfire, Twiggs's father sought vengeance. He hired a gunslinger named Jesse Roper. Fearing for public safety, Baxter County Sheriff Abraham Byler rounded up a posse and headed to Twiggs's ranch. When he got there, Roper came out of the house, his Winchester blazing. Byler was killed and Roper escaped.

The American authorities had been looking for Roper ever since the shooting. In August 1897, they believed they had found him—working as a cook in the Selkirk mine just outside Sandon. "John Taylor" had been in the Slocan for a few months. It seems he kept mostly to himself. According to one account: "He put in his time the same as other men of his class, and said but little about himself, but generally gave out he was the owner of a ranch in Idaho, and on one occasion said he had been in Arkansas."[1] Back in Arkansas, the authorities were monitoring Roper's brother's mail when they intercepted a letter written by Taylor on Selkirk mine letterhead. This was the clue they had been waiting for.

Early in September, armed with a warrant, Constable Fred Mountain went up to the Selkirk mine along with Sheriff Smith from Arkansas. They worked an elaborate charade, rounding up Taylor and others to question them on whether they had paid their poll tax. When Mountain put this to Taylor, Smith grabbed his suspect by the arm. Taylor was soon in shackles. "John Taylor" (a.k.a. "James Taylor," a.k.a. "James Hardy," a.k.a. "Jesse Roper") offered no resistance. As he was led away, he admitted he had expected to be arrested at some point, but not for murder.

Unidentified cook house, Sandon, c. 1897. Photographer unknown. For anyone in the 1890s looking for anonymity with a paycheque, a Slocan mine was a good place to start. Aliases were common, and the mine superintendents usually didn't care so long as the work got done. ORIGINAL IMAGE COURTESY OF THE VANCOUVER PUBLIC LIBRARY

Though there may still have been gunslingers like Jesse Roper hiding out in the Slocan or in other camps, their time had passed. Even former badman Frank James recognized this. Taking a job in 1896, as a special express messenger in Kansas City, he sadly concluded that business wasn't "what it used to be."[2] For Americans on the lam, however, the transient nature of work in the Slocan mines offered income and anonymity for those with secrets to keep. Indeed, the *Ledge* noted that it was customary in the Slocan not to ask questions.[3] Visitors carried their secrets with them and in some cases took them to their graves.

Despite the drop in the price of silver and the exodus to the Klondike, hundreds of miners were still working in the Slocan mines. Come payday, they would spend freely in the Slocan mining camps. Saloons still did good business and the brothels thrived. It was harder to get work in the mines though, and men who couldn't get jobs often looked to other means to make money. Petty crime had always existed in the Slocan, but the hard economic times likely increased the temptation to skirt the law.

There were no murders that we know of with certainty—whether by gun or by other means—in the Slocan during the 1890s, but men and women capable or guilty of such crimes did pass through the mining camps. Joe

Michaels, for one, the owner of a Slocan mine, had in July 1892 gunned down a man in the Oregon gold mining camp of Cracker City. Whether murder or "justifiable homicide," Johnny Harris and a companion had killed a man in Idaho before coming to the Slocan. In early 1896, Charles E. Plunkett (a.k.a. Charles Miller) was arrested in Idaho for murder, just after finishing his Canadian jail term for a Kaslo theft. James Woods travelled through the Slocan in 1897 before he was convicted and hanged in Nelson for the murder in that place of Samuel "Paddy" Woods (no relation).

There was also a puzzling death in Silverton in 1894. Peter Jackson was reported to be in good health on the afternoon of Wednesday August 29. The next day he was suffering "considerably" and soon died. The coroner's jury suspected poisoning. Was he murdered? We don't know.[4]

At least two women who had pioneered or passed through Kaslo and the Slocan met their demise on the "outside." We don't know if Charles Plunkett was the same "Charles Miller" who married Caroline "Fool Hen" Anderson in New Denver in 1893, but if he wasn't, they were at least both familiar with the wrong side of the law.

Taking up the life of a sailor after leaving the Slocan, Miller returned to the Washington State lumber port of Port Blakely—where he and Caroline had relocated—to find that Caroline no longer wanted his company. He shot her in the head then turned the gun on himself. She died, he didn't. Miller narrowly avoided being lynched by the citizens of Port Blakely. He was found guilty of manslaughter and sent to the state penitentiary.

Maud Roselle, "well known to the sporting fraternity of Victoria" in the early 1890s, was one of the "good time girls" who livened things up at Kaslo's Comique Theatre in its early incarnation.[5] By 1899, she was in Dawson City, making money with every smile. Her lover was a man named Davis. When she decided to part ways with Davis, he put a .32 calibre pistol to her head and blew her brains out before turning the gun on himself. The sporting life could be dangerous.

THE RED CURTAIN DISTRICTS IN the Slocan were often associated with crime, sometimes exacerbated by excessive liquor and raging libido. The rise of Sandon in 1896 and 1897 moved the hot spot for prostitution from Kaslo to the "sunless city." At one time, at least 115 prostitutes were said to have been plying their trade in Sandon. Within an hour of his arrival there in January 1896, future constable Harold Christie was assured there were "about two whores to every man."[6] The prostitutes thrived during the busy summer of 1897. Business was good and competition fierce. In addition to Rose Cramer's place—known as "the Nook"—other establishments included "the Castle," run by Grace Hill; "the Woods," probably operated by Sadie Woods; and "the Crown." One of the most popular venues, "54," was run by Nellie Howard. Nellie hosted dances every Saturday night.

On most Saturday nights, one could find an assortment of Sandon's leading citizens kicking up their heels at 54 with Kitty Squires or one of the other women. Johnny Harris was a regular, as were former constable E.M. Sandilands and lawyer F.L. Christie. According to Harris, most, if not all Sandon's leading citizens, frequented the red curtain establishments from time to time. It was even rumoured that Harris's partner, Fred Kelly, ran one of the operations.

The red curtain area in Sandon was located at the lower end of town on the way to Three Forks. The dead line, more figurative than physical, marked the divide between "respectable" society and the demi-monde. In the late 1890s, there were dozens of women operating out of lodgings strung along Carpenter Creek below the dead line. Some business was also being carried out in Kate Barger's Waldorf and a few of the other hotels. A church-going eastern visitor was shocked and surprised with Reco Avenue: "One end of the street is entirely devoted to the fallen women, who have very tasty houses, each with a name on the fanlight over the front door, denoting the trade of the inmates."[7]

Liquor sales were a lucrative sideline for most of the red curtain houses. There were some wild times, as reported in early 1896: "Money must be flush in Sandon. One of the Red Curtain Sisters in that burg gave a dance last week, and realized $250.50 from the sale of 2½ gallons of whisky, 36 bottles of beer, 57 cigars, and 8 packages of coffin nails (cigarettes)."[8]

While most prostitutes in the Slocan in the later 1890s operated out of Sandon, they were also doing business in Silverton, New Denver, Three Forks, Whitewater, and Slocan City. We know, for example, that in 1897, Hazel Attwood and her "band of Cyprians" were in business in New Denver.[9] They left hurriedly in early 1898, leaving behind debts and perhaps a few bruised hearts. Annie Law, who had run a house of "ill fame" in Sandon in 1897, moved her operation to Whitewater, where there would have been less competition.

In August 1897, the Silverton *Silvertonian* ran a piece critical of the "red-light brigade" in Sandon. The *Mining Review* was quick to come to

Whitewater Hotel, c. 1897–98. Photographer unknown. IMAGE COURTESY OF THE KOOTENAY LAKE ARCHIVES, KASLO, BC

the defence of both Sandon and the red-light brigade. While conceding that Sandon had more red lights than perhaps any other camp in the district, the *Review* wrote: "There is in Sandon a population resident with as keen a sense of the rights and wrongs from a morality line as can be found in Canada; but we are glad to say most of them have judgment and discretion."[10] The *Silvertonian* should have been more careful when casting stones. A month later, the proprietors of the Lakeview House in Silverton were charged with keeping a "disorderly house." Three members of the "tenderloin district" were charged, each receiving a five-dollar fine.[11]

Fines for prostitution were generally low but were not infrequent. Women were occasionally rounded up and fined in what was generally viewed as an informal means of taxation. The police were chronically underfunded, and fining the prostitutes was seen as a quick way to raise funds for much-needed supplies. The practice was common in western mining centres. Of 1,705 documented arrests in Spokane in 1894, the monthly visits of prostitutes paying their fines accounted for 544 of them.

In February 1897, Three Forks Constable Fred Mountain wrote to Police Superintendent Fred Hussey to complain about the bills he was unable to pay and the prisoners he could not look after. However, he was expecting some relief: "We are having a round up tomorrow night of all ladies of easy virtue in both Sandon & Cody & should get about $500 out of them."[12] Among those rounded up was Sandon madam Rose Cramer, fined twenty dollars for keeping a house of ill fame. Three of her inmates, Babe Hale, Dick Tremaine, and Benita Collis, were fined ten dollars each. It was all part of doing business. The fines didn't deter Rose or several others, including Nellie Howard, Grace Hill, Sadie Woods, and Mabel Smith, from contributing to the fund for Sandon's celebration of Queen Victoria's Diamond Jubilee.

Sadly, Mrs. Mabel Hayward—better known as Dick Tremaine—wouldn't live to enjoy the celebrations. Having once survived a knife to the face in Wallace, Idaho, she died in a bathtub at an Arrow Lakes hot spring in early 1897, likely by suicide. One of Mabel's colleagues in Sandon, a woman known as "Wildcat," survived a suicide attempt when a doctor pumped a belladonna overdose from her stomach. Another woman a few months later tried iodine with three quarts of whisky as a chaser.

Prostitutes were usually restricted to specific areas of the mining camps, like the rough shacks below the dead line in Sandon. Slocan City had its own red curtain district. After finishing off a jug of whisky there one day in the summer of 1897, Lotta Robertson decided to "run the town." She made a pretty fair success of it until she was corralled by Constable Rankin and locked up in a second-floor room on Main Street. She immediately opened the window and gave an assembled crowd a drunken serenade. Rankin moved her to a room on the river front. The next day she received a five-dollar fine for "giving an open air concert without a license."[13] A similar event in Sandon a couple of years later resulted in a twenty-dollar fine for "Big Lou."

Despite the antics of Lotta Robertson and Big Lou, Slocan prostitutes were often discreet. However, they sometimes suffered from the violent, drunken behaviour of their customers. Two of the Black women in Slocan City could attest to this. In October 1897, Frank Provost was fined five dollars for a "difficulty" with a lady named Jessie. The difficulty suffered by Mamie was perhaps more serious. A drunken Swede named Sam Samson went to a house kept by Mamie and started breaking up the furniture and throwing things about. Arrested, he ended up with sixty days in the Kamloops lock-up.

While madams could run their brothels as businesses and sometimes reap considerable profit, this was not often the case for their inmates or for the women that operated independently out of hotel rooms or solitary cribs. The inmates of well-run brothels could rely on a certain amount of protection offered by their madams, who sometimes even provided health care. However, they had to live according to the madam's rules and were sometimes subjected to corporal punishment if they misbehaved. "High class" brothels often received police protection—one of the benefits of the fines they regularly paid. Women who operated outside of the brothels usually had no such protection. Their lives were often marked by hardship and tragedy. Suicides, while likely no more common than in the general population, did occur and were often sensationalized in local newspapers.

The life and death of Caroline Bertrand provides a glimpse into the desperation that a life of prostitution on the mining frontier could bring. The French-Canadian woman travelled west, marrying a farmer in Fort McLeod, Alberta, territory. They had a daughter, but the marriage didn't last. Caroline travelled from Fort McLeod to Fort Steele, and from there to Kaslo, where she plied her new-found trade on A Avenue. With her daughter in a convent in Colville, Washington, and her brother in Sandon, she was separated from family and loved ones. One evening in March 1897, intending to end it all, she drank a strong dose of laudanum. She was rescued that night but found dead the next morning. She had written to her brother to tell him he would never again see her alive. She was about thirty-five.

Because of the women's transient lifestyle, we have little detailed information about the Slocan's red-light brigade. A disproportionate number of Slocan prostitutes were Black women, perhaps more comfortable under Canadian law than with the wild west below the border. By the end of the 1890s, the *Paystreak* took to calling the rude dirt tracks leading off of Reco Avenue below the dead line African Avenue and Kaffir Street. Many prostitutes were accompanied by husbands or lovers. A few names slip in and out of the record, sometimes in court appearances or obituaries, but often these women are anonymous to us. This is no doubt how many would have wanted it. Regardless of their defenders—and there were many—a significant proportion of the prostitutes who travelled through the western mining camps were happy to maintain their anonymity. Many took on aliases, perhaps to spare family or friends back home.

Anonymous or not, prostitutes played an integral role in the fabric of the mining camps. The red-light women were quick to give back to their communities by contributing to social events and funds and pitching in to help where they could. More than sex-trade workers, they contributed in many other ways to mining camp life. Brothels often offered lodging, laundry, and meals in addition to their core services. More important than sex, many contemporary sources, particularly in the early days, lauded the simple presence and "refining influence" of a female element in the mining camps.

One of the greatest defenders of the Slocan's prostitutes was New Denver lawyer R.B. Kerr. Given his liberal views, it's not surprising that Kerr often took up the causes of the downtrodden, disadvantaged, or oppressed. He laid out his defence of prostitutes and the men who consorted with them in a letter written in 1895:

> Would West Kootenay be better off without these women than it is with them? Here is the situation. Every new mining camp is first discovered and opened by a number of hardy pioneers. These men are nearly all of one class. They are not married men, for married men do not leave their wives and families, and throw up good jobs to try their chances in a new camp hundreds of miles away. In most cases their livelihood is so precarious that they would be fools to marry, and criminals to have children. Even if they did wish to marry, they preponderate so much in numbers that the country would have to be scoured for a thousand miles around to find a sufficient number of wives. And now, what do these men do for society? They go into the mountains, endure the greatest hardships, and often suffer disappointment. But their work as pioneers enables a large class of married men to bring in their wives and children, and make a living and a comfortable home. Then these people, having all the pleasures they want by their own firesides, turn round and try to deprive the men to whom they owe everything of the few pleasures which it is possible for them to obtain.[14]

The red curtain girls saw a decline in trade from the economic downturn in the late 1890s, but their fines continued to supplement the finances of Sandon and other Slocan camps. In addition to fines routinely issued for prostitution, other fines were levied for behaviour that did not meet contemporary moral standards. Cross-dressing was considered a serious assault on those standards. A prostitute known as "Annie Rooney" was fined fifty dollars for wearing men's clothing and passing herself off as "Jack Gordon."

The money would be useful to the Sandon city administration, which was struggling to stay afloat. Annie Rooney was born Lillian Storey, into a well-off New England family. She claimed to have written the song "Little Annie Rooney," popular at the time. But if she did, it did not keep her from a troubled and dissolute life.

While prostitutes and other women in the Slocan were generally treated with respect, they didn't have the equality with men that they deserved. But certainly, they had more rights and were treated better than the Chinese. When Edward Odlum visited the Slocan in 1899, he was pleased to report of the Chinese people: "They have come and gone, and vanished." He shared his view of the economic impact:

> Strangely enough, the stoves are supplied with wood, the dinners are cooked, floors scrubbed, dishes washed, clothes laundried and the people generally alive and happy. And all the money earned by cooks, laundries, woodsmen and others is spent with the butchers, bakers, grocers, clothiers, hotels, restaurants, shoemakers and others who in turn spend it in the country.[15]

With no Chinese workers to cook, sweep, and scrub, there was a great demand for "white" female domestics. Some Kaslo and Slocan residents wrote to American newspapers looking for help. Most of the work would be menial and align with contemporary stereotypes. However, there was room for advancement, and there was no shortage of ambitious women ready to make their mark. The pay was relatively good too. One West Kootenay woman wrote that while it was difficult to find competent help, she was willing to pay twenty to thirty dollars per month plus room and board.

In a curious irony, while miners were eager to run Chinese workers out of the Slocan, for married women with households to run, employing Chinese help was a symbol of status. About a month after the miners ran the Chinese cooks out of Sandon, Bruce White and his new bride, Elise, returned there from her family home in Maine. They stayed at the Reco Hotel but planned to take up permanent residence in Nelson. Elise was ever-conscious of maintaining her social standing, and this would be easier in Nelson than in Sandon, with its antipathy to Chinese workers. On December 22, 1898, Elise sat down in the Reco Hotel to record some of the priorities for her new life in Nelson: "We hope to be in our house and all started in housekeeping by New Year's. The main thing is to find a good

Chinaman. They tell me a good one does everything in the world that one wants. All the Ladies have them."[16]

Things could have been so different. In the summer of 1897, the *San Francisco Chronicle* carried the remarkable tale of Sing Lee, a cook at the Montezuma mine on the Kaslo slope. He was deeply interested in the science of mining, and every night after he finished cooking and cleaning, he put on miner's clothes and walked through the mine studying the workings. The operators of the Montezuma had lost the vein and were struggling to find it again. After several failed test bores, Sing Lee pointed to a spot where he believed they would find rich ore. With nothing to lose, they opened a tunnel and were quickly back in the thick of things. Other than some recognition from the mine's owners, Sing Lee reaped no great reward for his contribution, but that wasn't what was important to him. His ambition was to learn as much as he could about mining and take that knowledge back to China.

Sing Lee may have been a "one-off," but it was clear that despite the general antipathy to Chinese in the Slocan, there were some who could see an upside. Slocan mine owners yearned for the increased profits that cheap Chinese labour could bring. The *Mining Review*—generally sympathetic to mine owners—carried a relatively thoughtful and reasoned piece on Chinese labour that stood in marked contrast to the racist vitriol that often appeared in Lowery's papers: "When a Chinaman pays the necessary fee to enter this country, he is entitled to a full and impartial administration of the law protecting citizens."[17]

The *Mining Review* opinion piece went on to implicitly recognize a growing divergence between the interests of mine owners and the interests of the miners in their employ. By 1898, with few exceptions, mines run by the prospectors who first discovered them, or by small-scale owner/operators, who often worked alongside the miners, were a thing of the past. Most of the big producing mines were now owned by syndicates or corporations controlled from London, Chicago, or other faraway places. Profit was the byword, and the interests of the miners were sidestepped wherever possible if they didn't coincide with the interests of the owners. In 1898, many Slocan miners were wary of James Dunsmuir's interest in the Noble Five mine. Dunsmuir was notorious for hiring cheap Chinese labour in his Vancouver Island coal mines. It was feared that he would import the practice to the Slocan.

As the *Mining Review* noted, Chinese men and women who were legally in Canada were entitled to the "full and impartial" protection of the law. This was a challenge for constables in the Slocan. To his credit, New Denver's Alex Sproat arrested two of the miners who had run the Chinese cooks out of Sandon in 1898. They were both charged with being members "of an unlawful assembly to carry out a common purpose so as to cause persons in the neighborhood to fear they would disturb the peace tumultuously, or without reasonable excuse, cause others to disturb the peace."[18] The charges would not have been popular in New Denver or anywhere else in the Slocan.

Petty crime was prevalent in Kaslo and the Slocan during the late 1890s, likely exacerbated by the deteriorating economic conditions. Silverton was hit by a rash of burglaries, some of which, including a theft from the Thistle Hotel's till, were likely the work of Dan Forbes, who was well known in the Slocan as a regular church-goer and member of the Knights of Pythias. When confronted by one of his victims, however, he confessed to fraud. There were other bad actors too. Mrs. Mary Gleim, a woman with "rather a shady record," was arrested in Kaslo in September 1897, for possession of stolen property. But before she could be tried, she fled the city. "Mother" Gleim was a criminal mastermind headquartered in Missoula, Montana. She presided over the brothels there, ran a vast smuggling ring, and had once been convicted of murder. Kaslo was well rid of her.

There were a few gun crimes in Kaslo and the Slocan too, but one in particular didn't fit the usual pattern. Arthur Clague was rifling through a suitcase belonging to the Last Chance's E.H. Tomlinson when he came upon a pistol. Clague took the pistol, but in doing so, accidentally shot a hole through his hand. The court showed no sympathy and sentenced him to three months. Not long after his release, he was arrested again for the theft of a suit from Kaslo's Lakeview Hotel and was sent to the lock-up in Nelson. Like Mrs. Gleim, he escaped before he could be tried.

The constables and police officers who served West Kootenay in the 1890s lack the name recognition of Wyatt Earp and other famous American lawmen, but they deserve our respect and remembrance. Kaslo's first constable, J.D. Graham, set the bar high, but at the time, Big Jack Kirkup, who worked through the 1890s in Revelstoke and Rossland, was considered the epitome of a lawman. Big, bold, and brash, he commanded respect wherever he appeared. One man said he would rather take sixty days in jail than suffer a beating from Kirkup. However, there were some who considered his counterpart in Slocan City to be equally effective. Compared to Kirkup, Harold Christie was a study in contrast. The British-born, college-educated

Christie was of no great physical stature, but whatever he lacked in size, he made up for in grit. He arrived in the Slocan in early 1896, and at first found policing work in New Denver before being reassigned to Slocan City. There, the "British dude," as some called him, warned all the saloon keepers that "fighting and quarrelsome men must not be countenanced."[19] What followed was reported in a Chicago newspaper:

> One night a big saloon bully beat a couple of half drunken miners savagely in Jim Wilson's place, and was preparing to clear out the barroom when Christie arrived. Christie sized him up in an instant, and then asked him if he knew how to fight fair. The constable gave no intimation of his authority to the stranger, and he wore nothing to indicate he was an officer. A string of oaths in the affirmative answered him. "Well; take off your coat" said he, calmly, "and let's have a go."[20]

Needless to say, Christie subdued his bully and earned the enduring respect of the camp. The writer for the *Chicago Daily Tribune* concluded that Christie, with the "mental fitness to govern, the pluck of a game cock, the skill of a scientific boxer and wrestler, and the hardened elastic frame of a lifelong athlete," was "simply ideal" to administer law in the Slocan.[21]

Like Christie, Alex Sproat in New Denver was another official praised for his ability to defuse potentially deadly situations. Sproat was not prone to fisticuffs but was adept in other ways. J.C. Harris recalled a situation where the mining recorder was confronted by an old-school American prospector who was adamant that he wasn't going to give up his guns. He would carry them anywhere he wanted in this "goddamned country" and "no bloody policeman would stop him."[22] Calmly and quietly, Sproat talked the tough down: "What is the use of your carrying all that extra weight, no one here is allowed to carry weapons openly, so we shall be glad to take care of them for you and give you a receipt for them, they will be returned to you when you want to leave the country."[23]

Sproat never had it easy. In 1896, Jim Skerret—also known as Popcorn Jim—rolled into New Denver with several of his rowdy companions. They raised trouble at the Windsor, Newmarket, and Central hotels. Making their way back to the Newmarket, they had to be forcibly removed by a group of patrons. Once outside, Popcorn, in a case of mistaken identity, viciously attacked Bob Sutherland, a New Denver contractor, who received a deep knife wound to his arm. Popcorn disappeared into the bush but was later apprehended near Three Forks by Sproat. When Popcorn appeared before a magistrate, he was given six months hard labour for his antics. The *Ledge* predicted that "if another batch like this should drop into New Denver in the future it is almost dead certain that they will be the chief but silent actors in a hurried and unceremonious funeral."[24]

As far as we know, New Denver was spared the likes of Popcorn for the rest of the 1890s, but in 1897, Charlie Borene's Victoria Hotel in Whitewater emerged as a notorious hangout for badmen, including some of "Soapy" Smith's gang: the Mexican Kid, Skunk-Face, Black Dan, the Silent Kid, and Laughing Jack. They all cleared out when Soapy relocated to Skagway during the Klondike Gold Rush. But while Soapy's men left, Borene soon found himself in trouble of his own making. First, his live-in woman ran off with a travelling salesman (though Borene claimed he kicked her out when he learned she was a prostitute), then he cracked a whisky bottle over the head of a non-paying customer, who later died. Borene was charged with manslaughter. The charges were later dismissed, but Borene's reputation was in tatters.

The rise of Sandon in the mid 1890s, before 1897's drop in silver, significantly increased the workload of local law enforcement officers. With two international railways penetrating the heart of the Slocan, crowds—including some men and women familiar with the wrong side of the law—flocked in. BC Police Superintendent Fred Hussey, who visited Sandon in the summer of 1896, was having a hard time finding a constable for Sandon. Fred Mountain certainly didn't want the job. Harold Christie, at the time serving in New Denver, was assigned to Sandon. He didn't want the position either. In February 1897, he wrote a heartfelt letter to Hussey: "In the event of your appointing a constable at 'Slocan City,' I should be glad if you would give me the appointment in exchange for the one I have at present. Sandon is a most undesirable place of residence for a woman or children & as I am a married man I should like to be stationed at Slocan City as I could then live with my family, which I cannot do here. Hoping this application meets with your approval."[25] Hussey noted that he had no objections.

Crime thrived in Sandon during the policing vacuum of late 1896. When Peggy Webling arrived with her sisters and their troupe, she was advised by her agent not to stay at the "best" hotel in Sandon, because of troubles there. The agent said he had narrowly escaped being shot when a gunfight broke out between one of the camp's doctors and one of its Black inhabitants. The doctor would attend the Weblings' show, while his badly wounded adversary was consigned to the lock-up.

BACK AT SANDON, HUSSEY EVENTUALLY found a man willing to serve as constable: Alexander Hamilton. Like Harold Christie, Hamilton was from Moosamin. He joined the BC police force in January 1897 and was assigned to Sandon in April. Hamilton took to his new role immediately. Within weeks he had uncovered a bomb plot, arrested a man and woman for robbery, and written a letter to Superintendent Hussey with advice as to how the superintendent should do his job. If Hussey wasn't having second thoughts about Hamilton, he should have been.

Policing the "houses of ill fame" in Sandon seems to have taken up much of Hamilton's time. Indeed, there were citizens who felt he was spending far too much time tending to these duties. This all came to surface in the summer of 1897 in a story that broke in the *Slocan Pioneer*:

> Charges are openly made by the most reputable citizens that bribery and extortion are of daily occurrence; that the red-curtained houses are subject to a system of blackmail levy practiced by collusion between the magistrates and police; that individual freedom is under constant restraint and menace after nightfall; that the constabulary is made with the use of money, the instrument of private revenge and of schemes of personal prosecution; and that the whole management of government affairs has become so venal, so shameless that bribes have been demanded and paid for the mere perfunctory work of attending legally to the advancement of public house licenses. A recent instance is cited of an applicant being required to pay $25 in addition to the $250 government fee.[26]

The *Pioneer's* exposé was picked up by other newspapers. The *Spokesman-Review* of Spokane added salacious details: not only was Hamilton accused of trying to extort money from some of Sandon's leading citizens, but it was also suggested that he was in league with some of the prostitutes. One account had him at the opening of a new brothel where he was alleged to have celebrated "after the playful manner of Satyr and the nymphs."[27] Apparently, he had "conceived a jealous passion for a Thais of the mountains whose coquetry and indifference inspired him to commit many acts of extravagance."[28] More serious to some, it was said that Alex Sproat had found "discrepancies" in Hamilton's government accounts.

The evidence unearthed during the investigation suggested a relationship between Hamilton and prostitute Grace Hill, and with another woman known as "Dutch Zora." The charges were considered serious enough that

Hamilton was relieved of duty pending a "court of investigation." The court was conducted by acting gold commissioner Goepel and attended by Police Superintendent Hussey. Hamilton represented himself, with Sandon lawyer Martin Grimmett as backup.

The evidence was ambiguous at best and mostly of the "he said, she said" variety. Hamilton was reinstated by Superintendent Hussey, and the evidence against him was forwarded to the Attorney General. The government decided, however, not to send Hamilton back to Sandon. Instead, he was transferred to Silverton. On the back of a letter written by Deputy Attorney General Smith to Hussey, Smith wrote: "Say that Constable H. has been removed from Sandon to Silverton at his own request."[29]

Hamilton's brief tenure at Silverton was marked by much of the same controversy that had dogged him in Sandon. Several Silverton residents signed a petition asking for his removal. Once again, Hamilton found himself under investigation, this time by O.G. Dennis, the new gold commissioner. The hearing was held in New Denver. While the evidence was deemed insufficient to hold Hamilton, Dennis felt it appropriate to suspend the constable pending further instructions from Victoria. This wasn't well received by Hamilton, leading to the following exchange between Dennis and the accused:

> "Sir, you will be suspended awaiting actions from headquarters."
> "I don't want to be suspended."
> "Then you are discharged."
> "I would rather resign than be discharged."
> "Very well, you may resign. I accept your resignation."[30]

The resignation of Hamilton was not the end of the police story in Sandon. With incorporation as a city scheduled for January 1898, Sandon was still in need of provincial police protection until then. When Hamilton was reassigned to Silverton, Constable Fred Mountain became responsible for police operations in Sandon. Much to his relief, however, Constable Callin, formerly of the North West Mounted Police, was assigned to active duty. D.L. Lloyd, who had been on duty with Hamilton as a special constable, retained his position.

After Hamilton's resignation and about the time that Sandon was incorporated in January 1898, a "comique" type theatre made its first appearance in the new metropolis. The Central Music Hall, run by the Pearson brothers, was an offshoot of the Kaslo Comique. As with the Kaslo Comique, R.T. Lowery took every opportunity to blast the venue in his newspapers.

The *Paystreak* described the typical comique as "generally a dirty dive, with a bar in front, boxes around the walls, and a stage upon which fine art is murdered every evening."[31] Like Kaslo, the community was divided on the theatre, with saloon keepers and the Church joining Lowery in opposition. In October 1898, the city council decided to hold a plebiscite on its continued operation. Lowery was sure it would be closed, but most voters disagreed. However, the results were close and indicated a polarized community: 52 for continued operation and 48 for closure.

Police Superintendent Hussey was likely relieved when Sandon was designated a "city" in January 1898. The BC police would no longer have jurisdiction, and it would be left to city officials to police the new "comique." After the Hamilton debacle, it seems that Hussey was more careful with his appointments. Like Christie and Sproat, Lestock R. Forbes, the man chosen to replace Hamilton in Silverton, was a British expatriate. Born in India in 1866, he was the son of a Welsh civil servant serving in Bengal. Perhaps Hussey was counting on Forbes's civil service upbringing to bring order and discipline and restore the reputation of the police force in the Slocan. Forbes was just settling in when he faced an early challenge. He was attending court in Silverton when it was discovered there was no bible available. Forbes was sent out to fetch one. He returned half an hour later, dejected. He had been unable to locate a single bible from surrounding establishments.

"Jake Pearson, Harry Nash, and Ike Pearson sitting outside log cabin at Sandon," 1898. Photographer: R.H. Trueman. The Pearson brothers were the proprietors of Sandon's "comique" style theatre. IMAGE COURTESY OF THE ROYAL BC MUSEUM AND ARCHIVES

20

A POOR SHOWING

BY 1898, SANDON HAD BECOME something of an urban oasis in the mountains. In a few short years, it had come all the way from mining camp to city. It owed its existence to the rich mines that encircled it, but it also had an illusory existence independent of the mines. There were many Sandon residents in the cluttered buildings that clung close to Carpenter and Sandon Creeks who took the mines for granted. They were largely oblivious to the network of tunnels and stopes threading through the mountains above them and likely didn't pay too much attention to the price of silver. Instead, they were preoccupied with the urban life that surrounded them more closely. As in any other urban enclave, they complained about public services, argued about taxes and rents, and gossiped about their neighbours.

Sandon still attracted visitors eager for a taste of the mining frontier, even in the thick of the Klondike excitement. Entertainers, authors, and "personalities" still trekked through the Slocan, though they often played to diminished crowds or muted receptions. Sandon hosted E. Pauline Johnson in 1897, and author Julia Henshaw paid a visit in 1898. Just before her trip to the Slocan, Henshaw had her first novel published, under the pen name Julian Durham: *Hypnotized? or, The Experiment of Sir Hugh Galbraith.* The novel was a potboiler, but no matter, it lent her the distinction—in company with an earlier visitor to the Slocan, Clive Phillipps-Wolley—of being one of BC's first novelists.

Henshaw was captivated by Sandon. She was generally impressed with the Reco Hotel, where she stayed, but found the butter a little "old fashioned" and the meat a "trifle advanced." She also concluded that those who went to Sandon for rest and change might find "that the hotel keepers get your change and the express drivers all the rest."[1] Nevertheless, Henshaw was impressed enough with Sandon to include some references to the dizzying heights of the Payne Bluff in her next novel, *Why Not Sweetheart?* Alice Harriman—perhaps the first woman publisher in the United States—may also have visited. Her story, "Lost in the Silvery Slocan," published in 1899, accurately captured the country: "Rough, steep, broken, and covered with underbrush and fallen timber."[2]

Curiosity lured author Julian Price to the Slocan. Although he was only in Sandon for a few days on his journey to the Klondike, he managed to get an audience with Johnny Harris, who shared some stories of the early days. Harris had come a long way since then. By the summer of 1898, he was flush with success and good fortune. He had a bonanza in the Reco, a mine that could easily withstand the assault on silver; he owned most of the real estate in Sandon; and he was in control of both the electricity and water supply systems, which provided him with a tidy income.

Harris was also on the receiving end of many of the complaints about public services, taxes, and rents. Given his stake in Sandon, it's no wonder that some residents and visitors had started calling him the "king" of Sandon. The Spokane *Spokesman-Review* celebrated Harris's success: "Fortune has favored him from the time he acquired an interest in the Reco until now when his many carefully planned investments are returning to him a comfortable income as a reward for his enterprise and business sagacity."[3] He had no need or desire to leave Sandon for the Klondike, but he could not prevent others from doing so.

The dimming prospects in the Slocan were hard on newspapers. Readership diminished as populations shrank, and advertising faded as businesses closed their doors. Then, in early 1898, war between Spain and the United States broke out. Many American readers left for their home country, but at least the newspapers had something other than the Klondike to write about. Sam de Rackin's *British Columbia News* briefly ran as a daily—The *Kaslo Morning News*—with expanded coverage of the war. The *Kootenaian* printed daily editions too. De Rackin stuck with the *News* until the summer of 1898, but then succumbed to wanderlust, leaving for Puerto Rico—soon to be ceded by Spain to the United States.

While the Spanish-American War attracted patriots from West Kootenay back to their homeland, the American influence at the *Kootenaian* continued. In 1898, the paper was sold to another American company, and Harold Bolce, formerly of the *New York Journal*, took over as news editor.

Bolce had served several years on the staff of the *Spokane Spokesman*, and prior to his arrival at the *Kootenaian*, he had been delivering sermons at his "Cosmopolitan Church of San Francisco," where he did his best to discredit the tenets of the establish western churches. Dave King stayed on for a time as business manager, but by the end of 1898 he had given up on journalism and taken on a job as ore-buyer for a smelter in Great Falls, Montana. The *Cranbrook Herald* recognized King's newspapering talents and lamented Kaslo's loss:

> It will seem strange to the people of Kaslo to see other men in Dave King's place on the *Kootenaian*. He made it one of the best weekly newspapers in Canada, and through its columns spread the fame and name of Kaslo and West Kootenay over two continents.[4]

There was another provincial election in 1898, and the various newspapers all picked sides. Most favoured the incumbent government, but there were opposition partisans too. A new paper emerged in Kaslo, the *Slocan Sun*, run by S.P. Tuck, Robert Nisbet, and Billy Sanders. The *Sun* was specifically devoted to the defeat of the government. Tuck had edited a few editions of the *Kaslo Times* prior to the election of 1894, but he was a surveyor by trade. Nisbet had printing experience with the *Calgary Herald* and de Rackin's *British Columbia News*. Tuck, Nisbet, and Sanders also had the capable help of Peck McSwain (alias "the lunatic") to get the paper out. McSwain was a tramp printer well known in the west. He had worked with Nisbet on the *Calgary Herald* and would also do some work for R.T. Lowery.

In the first issue of the *Sun*, Tuck promised that during the election campaign the paper would not indulge in the lurid language of the "fishwife and the brothel" and would instead express its views "decently." In the same issue, he accused one of his rival newspapers of carrying "the smell of the sewer into every house it enters."[5]

Premier Turner's criminal libel case against W.C. Nichol was ongoing at the time, and any hopes of resolving it before the election were dashed when Nichol's defence secured an adjournment. This meant that Turner would be going into the election with open charges that he had prostituted himself and betrayed the voters of BC in the name of capital gain. The charges were unproven, just like the countercharges against Nichol. However, the whiff of scandal could not stand in Turner's favour. Nichol stuck to his story, offering no apologies whatsoever.

The election results across the province were close, but when the votes were counted, the oppositionists carried the day. Turner would be replaced by Charles Semlin and a ragtag assortment of oppositionists—some with close ties to labour activists.

The ascendency of the new government was not without controversy. The election results were largely inconclusive. Premier Turner's government suffered significant losses. However, the oppositionists were disorganized and could not at first decide on a leader. In an unexpected turn of events, Lieutenant-Governor Thomas McInnes decided to intervene.

It began with a routine order-in-council on a purely administrative matter. The Turner government sent McInnes an order-in-council recommending confirmation of the jurisdictions and responsibilities of West Kootenay mining recorders Alex Sproat and Jack Kirkup, and the appointment of the Nakusp mining recorder, Fred Fauquier, to the position of gold commissioner for his district. McInnes approved the confirmations of Sproat and Kirkup on the basis that this simply maintained the status quo, but he refused to approve the appointment of Fauquier. He believed Turner had lost the confidence of the people. Even though the final election ballots had not yet been counted, McInnes told Turner he would not approve any new appointments or expenditures unless and until the premier could form a majority from the slate of elected members. If he could not, McInnes would dismiss his government.

Such actions were almost unheard of. Turner was furious. He set about trying to form a new government but was flabbergasted when McInnes's son, T.R.E. McInnes, who acted as the Lieutenant-Governor's private secretary, approached him with an offer. According to Turner, the younger McInnes promised to assist him to form a government on condition that the beleaguered premier offer a cabinet seat to another of the Lieutenant-Governor's sons, W.W.B. McInnes, who was holding down a seat in the federal Parliament. Turner met with W.W.B. McInnes, but there was no agreement. Then, in another surprising and unprecedented decision, the Lieutenant-Governor dismissed Turner and his government and instead asked former premier Robert Beaven to try to form a government.

Beaven did not hold a seat in the Legislative Assembly, and he couldn't rally sufficient support from the elected members. The senior McInnes finally turned to Semlin, the tentative leader of the opposition. Where Turner and Beaven failed, Semlin succeeded. He pulled together a hodgepodge team of political spirits who had little in common other than ambition, ego, and a willingness to govern. Semlin appointed two of his rivals for leadership, Joseph "Joe" Martin, and Francis Carter-Cotton, to the posts of Attorney General and Finance Minister, respectively. In an appointment of more interest to Slocan residents, Semlin chose Fred Hume to be his Minister of Mines and provincial secretary. On the other side of the aisle, a humbled Turner settled into the uncomfortable role of leader of the opposition. The task was made somewhat easier by the ineptitude of his successor's administration. Former Slocan newspaperman B.R. Atkins, likely as a reward for his support during the election, was pegged as the new premier's private secretary.

With the election over and the incumbent government defeated, S.P. Tuck started his new job as sheriff of South Kootenay. The *Slocan Sun* sank below the horizon and Peck McSwain departed for Manila.

BY THE END OF THE nineteenth century, the glory days of the Slocan were coming to an end. Both the *Slocan City News* and the *Slocan Pioneer* were "extinct," and other newspapers were struggling. In 1898, the editor of the Sandon *Paystreak* spoke from experience when he noted that "the Slocan is hard upon newspaper men."[6] New Denver's *Ledge* and Sandon's *Paystreak* were still printing, but their days were numbered. In 1899, William "Billy" McAdams joined Lowery's *Paystreak* and soon took over publishing the paper as well as editing it.

When R.E. Gosnell visited the Slocan in 1899, he offered his assessment of the district's newspapers and their editors. He found the *Kootenaian*'s Dave King "clever," and Harold Bolce "gifted," but he saved his highest praise for R.T. Lowery: "The Ledge is a bit irreverent at times, but is decidedly original and humorous."[7]

For Lowery, the days of the Slocan as the last bastion of "white" BC, were coming to an end. He could sense the winds of change. In early 1898, he noted the appearance of a Chinese man in Slocan City. Chinese men had made appearances in Slocan City in 1897, but in those instances, they had been "encouraged" to leave. However, on a visit to Slocan City in 1899, Lowery's colleague in anti-Chinese sentiment, Edward Odlum, noted: "Already I see signs of the Chinamen carrying round their baskets of vegetables." Looking into the future, Lowery had a frightening vision of "when the cheap Celestial will be domesticated and permanently installed in every town in the Slocan."[8] He feared that the pursuit of profits would overrule his prejudices.

Lowery had warned incomers about boozereno, gambling, and the red curtain women, but he had no warnings or solution for unrequited love. Ben Rankin came to BC from Calgary. He had earned his living in Alberta as a cowboy, once working for the Bar U Ranch, perhaps crossing paths with the Sundance Kid. Married in 1896, Rankin left for the Slocan when the union foundered after less than two years. After a brief stint as a special constable and night watchman in Slocan City, he moved to Sandon. He befriended Jack Lowes—our adventurer from the Three Forks fire of 1894. Four years later Lowes was still in the hotel business, at least the part of it that involved gambling and drinking.

One night in May 1898, Lowes and Rankin played blackjack at the Bartlett House. They met up again at 1:00 AM for a meal at the Palace Hotel. Back at the Bartlett an hour later, Rankin turned to Lowes: "Jack, lend me a lead pencil." Rankin took it and went upstairs to his room. Lowes and a few others remained below. All were feeling drowsy when they were startled by a loud "crack" from the rooms above. Some thought it was a champagne bottle, and others joked about an invasion by the Spaniards. Smiles and jokes evaporated when they heard groans from above. Lowes rushed upstairs and found Rankin in a pool of blood with a .44 calibre pistol lying nearby.

Rankin died within minutes without speaking. Among his possessions, there was a letter written in bold pencil strokes to a friend in Slocan City; a note to Jack Lowes; letters from his wife, Jane; and a "photo of a woman with an unmistakable stamp of the wanton."[9] The most recent letter was from the object of his affection, announcing her intentions to break off all relations with him. After deliberating for a few minutes, a coroner's jury ruled that Rankin had killed himself in a "temporary fit of insanity."[10]

The Slocan's social and sporting life suffered during 1898 and 1899. Many Americans left to fight in the Spanish-American War, and dozens of prospectors and miners of all nationalities joined the exodus to the Klondike. In 1899, the Boer War broke out in South Africa, and many miners of British background signed up to serve overseas. Among them was Ben Lee, who had been a cog in the wheels of Slocan business and politics in the early years.

The church was still an important influence, and by early August 1898, a Methodist church—Sandon's first house of worship—was finished. The Sandon *Paystreak* waxed lyrical on the sense of occasion marked by its completion:

> The days of Sandon as a mere mining camp are passed and gone. The stranger who two years ago saw down the gulch two or three hotels, a few stores, and a number of scattered shacks, now alights from the railroad car to look down upon a bustling town, with nearly a score of hotels, with a long street flanked on each side by stores of all kinds, with pretty homes dotting the mountain sides. And rising from among these cottages his gaze is held by the graceful spire of a church. This conveys more to his mind of the rapid progress Sandon has made than would ten pages of the Paystreak devoted to her mineral wealth and output. At a glance upward he grasps the fact that the mining camp has emerged from its protoplasmic condition; that gentle women and children have followed the trails cut for them by the hardy pioneer, and brought hither their grace to sweeten his life.[11]

Maybe so, but Sandon still had more grit than sweetness. Yes, there was now a church in town, and its lofty spire looked down on the camp below. However, one couldn't ignore the reality that it was just one building among the hotels, saloons, and brothels spread out along Carpenter and Sandon Creeks.

"Sandon, Reco Avenue," c. 1897. Photographer unknown. Showing the Methodist church above Reco Avenue, Albert David's tailor shop, and a shoe shop—likely Nick Palorcia's. IMAGE COURTESY OF THE ROYAL BC MUSEUM AND ARCHIVES

THERE WERE NO MINERS' UNIONS in the Slocan in the early 1890s, and while many mines required ten-hour shifts, there was enough work to go around, and the wages were reasonable. However, complaints about working conditions became more common as production increased. By 1897, nearly all the Slocan mines were on the subscription scheme started by Dr. Brouse, but he found it hard to keep up. Hospital staff treated more than eight hundred patients from the beginning of 1896 to September 1897. Most of these would have been miners suffering from illness or injury.

In January 1897, Thomas Cherry, president of the Rossland miners' union, visited Silverton to organize a union. The twenty charter members expected to recruit another fifty to eighty members by the end of the month. The new union was affiliated with of the Western Federation of Miners (WFM). Slocan mine owners would surely have been concerned.

In July, the Silverton union hosted Ed Boyce, president of the WFM. Boyce was a radical firebrand who had been a leader in the Coeur d'Alene mining strikes of 1892. In 1894, he was elected to the Idaho state senate as a Populist. Frustrated that he could not effect real change through the political process, he quit the senate after one term. He was elected president of the WFM in 1896 and worked hard to expand its reach and influence. An advocate of industrial unionism, he promoted class warfare and advised all union members to arm themselves and form rifle clubs.

Boyce's address in Silverton seems to have been relatively tame. There is no indication that he encouraged Slocan miners to arm themselves. Instead, he was "full of advice and common sense . . . He pointed out that lack of harmony amongst themselves was the curse of the working class and asked why it was that miners who are daily creating wealth for others cannot create it for themselves."[12] He inspired miners to think of others besides themselves and encouraged them to become more involved in labour matters. They seem to have got the message. In October 1897, a pair of Queen Bess miners placed a notice in the Sandon *Mining Review.* The new owners of the Queen Bess had vowed to work the mine hard. It appears they meant business:

> SANDON, OCTOBER 7, 1897
> This is to warn each and every man who don't wish to make a slave of himself and have a pauper's pocket to keep away from the Queen Bess mine, as they are working the men 10 hours both night and day shifts, and no short shift on Saturday and no work on Sunday, and $1 a day board for Sunday. The total amount a man can receive for his

month's work is $51.25. This is the smallest wages ever paid at a mining camp in the west.

Gentlemen and fellow miners, this is what makes tramps out of working men.

J.W. Smith

Frank McArthur[13]

R.T. Lowery was sympathetic. At about the same time, he included an editorial in the *Ledge* commenting on the recent massacre of coal miners in Hazleton, Pennsylvania. The miners, mostly immigrants from Eastern Europe, were on strike for better wages and fairer treatment. On September 10, 1897, about three or four hundred unarmed and peaceful miners marched on a coal mine. They were met by a sheriff and an armed posse of about 150. The posse opened fire and nineteen strikers were killed. Most were shot in the back as they retreated. Lowery called the actions of the sheriff and posse "wholesale butchery": "When a body of miners marching peacefully along a public road, unarmed, molesting no one, threatening violence to no one, are set upon by the legalised hirelings of the coal trust, the alleged guardians of the peace and are shot down like mad dogs or marauding brigands, the indolent stupid public conscience is roused long enough to ask if this sort of thing is to become common."[14]

While Silverton miners unionized early in 1897, it would be almost another two years before Sandon miners took the same path. In November 1898, about 250 miners crowded into Crawford's Hall to discuss the pros and cons of unionizing. The tone of the meeting was one of moderation. The principal speaker, D.W. Dawson, while emphasizing the benefits of a union, noted that miners, for the most part, were treated well in the Slocan. There were no feelings of anger against any class of people—presumably referring to mine owners. Nevertheless, the assembled miners decided to go ahead with a union. They set up a committee to get the ball rolling.

One of the less publicized campaign commitments of at least some of the oppositionists elected to government was the introduction of an eight-hour law for the benefit of underground workers in hardrock mines, who typically worked ten-hour shifts. The responsibility for this in Semlin's Cabinet fell to the Slocan's former representative, Minister of Mines J. Fred Hume. As far as we know, Hume did not press for eight-hour legislation during the 1898 election campaign. However, it was revealed that he later met with James Wilks, an influential labour organizer and vice president of the Trades and Labor Congress of Canada. Wilks offered to support Hume in return for an assurance that Hume would back an eight-hour law. In February 1899, Hume introduced the eight-hour provision as an amendment to the Metalliferous Mines Inspection Act.

The Sandon miners' union, formed in December 1898, was strongly supportive of the eight-hour law—provided that their members continued to be paid what they made working ten-hour shifts. Loosely affiliated with the WFM, the Sandon union was not as radical as its American counterparts were generally perceived to be. Members seemed more interested in running a union hospital and looking after the social needs of their members than they were in seeking confrontation. The hospital, which opened March 1, 1899, was welcomed, but it arrived at a most inopportune time. Slocan mine owners, incensed by passage of the eight-hour law, lobbied hard for repeal or relief. On March 14, 1899, Johnny Harris and other prominent Slocan mine owners wrote to Minister Hume protesting that the implementation of the eight-hour law would lead to disaster. Hume promised to bring the matter to the Executive Council, but given Cabinet's dependence on labour support, chances of the legislation being repealed were slim.

On March 31, Silverton's William Hunter also wrote to Hume, his old partner, worried about the effect the eight-hour law would have on commerce in the Slocan. On April 6, 1899, Slocan mine owners met in Sandon's Reco Hotel. They agreed to form an association to protect their interests. In May 1899, most joined the Silver Lead Mine Owners Association. Its principal goals were to fight the new law and counter the unions. Johnny Harris was instrumental in both forming and guiding the association. The Slocan Star was one of the few large mines that did not join.

When Slocan mine owners failed to have the eight-hour legislation repealed, they instead decided to reduce wages from $3.50 to $3.00 for an eight-hour underground shift. The miners insisted on keeping the $3.50 wage. It was an impasse. When the eight-hour law finally came into effect on June 12, 1899, most mines closed. However, there were a few that kept operating. The Whitewater Deep, run by Barbarian Brown, decided to pay the union rate of $3.50 per day. This raised the ire of the Mine Owners Association, who put "great pressure" on the mine to shut down and align its interests with those of the association.[15] The pressure tactics didn't work, and the Whitewater Deep joined a few other mines that kept working.

Whether the mines shut due to a strike or lockout didn't really matter, given the end result. Fearing violence, mine owners hired the Thiel

Detective Service to gather intelligence on the miners and their unions. While the WFM unions had a violent history in Idaho, by almost all accounts the miners involved in the Slocan strike/lockout went out of their way to avoid violence. However, there was no doubt that agitators were in the ranks. One correspondent for a Scottish newspaper claimed that some of the Americans were "trying to excite [*sic*] a riot," while the Canadian miners remained "quiet."[16]

The dispute turned into a waiting game. The standoff staggered awkwardly between threats and demands through the dog days of summer. By September 1899, both sides were getting restless. A series of high-profile visitors appeared. Ralph Smith, the Labour representative for Nanaimo, showed up with Wilks in tow. It must have been satisfying for Smith to know that he was causing grief to James Dunsmuir, his nemesis from the coalfields of Vancouver Island who was now in control of the Slocan's Noble Five mine.

Some mine owners began bringing in "contract" labour from the United States to work the mines. The Silverton miners' union decided to make a show of force at the Emily Edith mine, which was being worked by non-union miners. Union members went up to the mine in late October 1899. Mine manager Ernest Rammelmeyer ordered them to leave. They did, but shortly thereafter, about forty returned. Some were carrying axe handles and other implements that could be used as weapons. Rammelmeyer phoned down to New Denver to summon Police Constable Lestock Forbes, but Forbes couldn't get hold of a horse and didn't show.

Officials in Victoria didn't quite know what to do. The labour dispute was unfamiliar territory. On one hand, they had pleas from mine owners and managers asking for extra protection. On the other, they had reports from their own officers downplaying threats of violence and generally concluding that things were under control. The Attorney General asked Police Superintendent Hussey to dig a little deeper. Hussey sent Constable Christie from Slocan City, and Chief Constable Bullock-Webster from Nelson, to investigate. Both felt that matters were in hand. This wasn't good enough for Rammelmeyer. He wanted arrests.

The government tried to match the cloak-and-dagger propensities of the mine owners. The Attorney General hired Pinkerton agent W.B. Sayers to go undercover. Known for their union-busting ways south of the border, the hiring of Pinkerton's Detective Agency would have raised union hackles. The police officers on the ground felt the Pinkerton hiring was unnecessary. Indeed, Sayers felt the same way. After arriving in the Slocan, he reported:

"Had I known one half of what I now do I should have strongly objected to coming at all . . . there is no necessity for a secret man in the 'Slocan' and no place for one at either New Denver, Silverton or Sandon."[17]

The escalating labour troubles came to the attention of the federal government, which took the issue seriously, and appointed a Royal Commission to investigate. It would be headed by respected Toronto lawyer Roger Clute. Slocan miners wanted the government to invoke the Alien Labour Act, legislation intended to restrict the importation of workers from outside Canada. By the close of December, however, it was clear that Clute would not recommend application of the Alien Labour Act and would not be able to find enough common ground to reach a settlement. Slocan businessmen were demoralized. A visitor in late 1899 noted: "The merchants are howling blue ruin, and the camps are dead. When union men are around the merchants try to smile and say, 'We hope for better times'; when the unionists are not near they say bitter things."[18] But they were bitter with the mine owners too. Johnny Harris felt the businessmen of Sandon were "almost to a unit against the mine owners."[19]

In September 1899, the *Calgary Weekly Herald* printed a humorous anecdote that highlighted how things had changed in Sandon since the gravy days of 1897:

> A mining man from Victoria dropped into Sandon the other day, after an absence of many months. He, thinking that the Sandon club was still in bloom, dropped into the old quarters and sat down. He thought things had changed, and after reading a magazine for a short time, he called for Ed. No one replied, and the mining man commenced to search for the decoction room. He ran up against a sign for nurses and immediately fled the scene, realizing that evolution had changed the haunt of congenial spirits into a haven of rest for those wounded by accident or disease.[20]

We don't know who "Ed" was, but it's likely that by the summer of 1899, he had joined the steady stream of workers abandoning the Slocan because of the labour troubles.

A West Kootenay capitalist who travelled to Victoria in early December 1899 reported—with some exaggeration—that there were a few "foreigners" hanging around Sandon "but no miners, they have left in disgust."[21] Lane Gilliam, now something of a mining "expert," had already moved on from the Slocan. He and John Hardee took a look at Baker City, Oregon, before Gilliam and Billy Hireen decided to try their luck in Idaho at the Buffalo

Hump camp. M.A. Bucke was managing a mine in Bear Gulch, Montana. He may have hoped to return to the Slocan one day, but it was not to be. In December he jumped from a runaway wagon, hit his head on landing, and was instantly killed. His death would weigh heavily on his father, Dr. R.M. Bucke, who dedicated his groundbreaking work on cosmic consciousness to his recently deceased son.

M.A. Bucke had looked forward to reading his father's magnum opus, but he would not get the opportunity—at least not in this life. We do know, however, that he read and enjoyed *The Story of the Mine*, an 1896 history of the Comstock Lode that detailed the critical role played by his father in the great silver discovery. M.A. Bucke wouldn't return to the Slocan, but Scots visitor and aspiring novelist Frederick Niven stopped in New Denver in 1899, young and eager to "see the west." Landing in the dull times at the tail end of the labour troubles, he soon relocated to Nelson.

Tensions in the Slocan mines during the summer of 1899 were mirrored by tensions in Sandon. The long-simmering dispute between Johnny Harris and squatters such as Nick Palorcia finally came to a head. Palorcia was by no means alone against Harris. The divisions between the "leading citizens" of Sandon and the renters and squatters further down the social pecking order had not abated. George Spencer, the owner of Spencer's Hall, sued Harris in 1899 over a rent issue. Like Palorcia, he lost his case. In May, Harris seized Spencer's Hall—the home of so many dances in happier times. In early 1899, others rose up against the "king" of Sandon. Forty-four Sandon residents signed a petition and sent it to Victoria. They again tried to make the case that as Harris's Loudoun mineral claim had never been used as a mine or exploited for minerals, despite the tunnel work done in 1897, the Crown grant that Harris and his partners received on their "mineral claim" was based on false information and should, therefore, be considered defective.

Sandon pioneer Mike Kerlin was the first name on the petition, followed by Nick Palorcia. There were other prominent names too, including George Spencer, and Moore, of the Ivanhoe hotel, who had had earlier issues with Harris and G.M. Sproat after his liquor licence was denied. The forty-four names on the petition exceeded by thirteen the number on the petition to incorporate Sandon, but the signatures of miners, labourers, carpenters, hotel keepers, and bakers—no matter how respected in the community—did not carry the same weight as the mine owners and capitalists who had signed the incorporation petition. Harris was furious. The petition was published in the Sandon *Mining Review*, along with Harris's analysis of the signatories.

According to Harris, only eight of the petitioners actually resided on the Loudoun claim; five of them had ground leases from Harris or Sproat; three rented from squatters; two of the petitioners were currently in jail on vagrancy charges; fifteen were located outside the Loudoun claim; and the other nineteen were generally not known and therefore could not have an interest in the matter. As if in apology, at the conclusion of Harris's analysis, the *Mining Review* noted: "Mr. Harris requested us to publish the foregoing."[22]

Unfortunately for Kerlin, Palorcia, Spencer, and the others, the petition failed. They were left to deal with Harris. Spencer licked his wounds and paid Harris his rent money. Palorcia wasn't so inclined. He had already lost one building to Harris and would now lose another. Harris also again seized Palorcia's tools. Despite this, Palorcia somehow managed to be back "pegging away" at shoemaking for a while in September. A self-admitted "poor man," Palorcia was likely rich in pride. He was the son of a Polish general and had

The sun not quite falling on Sunnyside, Sandon, c. August/September 1898. Photographer: William Bauer. William A. Bauer Photo Album. Uno Langmann Family Collection of British Columbia Photographs. IMAGE COURTESY OF THE UNIVERSITY OF BRITISH COLUMBIA LIBRARY DIGITIZATION CENTRE AND ITS GENEROUS DONORS

been a soldier in the Balkan wars. In October 1899, faced with the inevitable, Palorcia packed it in and moved to the new mining town of Phoenix, in the Boundary district. He stayed there for years and became a valued and highly respected member of the community. Residents would have been glad to have Spencer's Hall back in business, but with the departure of Palorcia, they lost one of their mainstays, and Sandon lost a small part of its ethnic and cultural diversity. Mike Kerlin would stay in Sandon. His dispute with Harris would continue.

The hard times were by no means restricted to Sandon. Barbarian Brown had invested heavily in Whitewater. He made major improvements to the Whitewater Hotel, but it was all for naught. Shortly after the improvements were complete, a "tramp" invaded the hotel and proceeded to smash all the hotel's windows on the ground floor. Within weeks, the hotel closed permanently. Kaslo businesses were suffering too. The significant downturn in ore shipments going out over the K&S was a major concern. Francis Carter-Cotton visited the Kootenay Lake City in September. He defended the eight-hour law, confirming that it was "here to stay," and the people of West Kootenay would have to "make the best of it."[23]

The first snow of the season fell on Sandon in November, one layer of a thick blanket that would pile up over the next few months. When Clute left in late December, the sun had retreated behind the snow-covered mountains. Those left in the mining camp were literally in the dark because of an ongoing dispute between Johnny Harris and the city council that resulted in the streetlights being turned off. As the days fell tediously one after another, the dark winter cast a pall over the idle mines. Still, the dispute dragged on. For those who intended to stay through the winter, Harris issued a dire warning: "The Slocan country will undoubtedly be dead, in a business way this coming winter."[24] No one felt this more than Harris himself. As a result of the exodus out of Sandon, he had numerous businesses and vacant buildings up for rent. The list was a telling testament to the hard times and included the Reco and Goodenough hotels, three stores, the Sandon steam laundry, a stable ("for 12 horses—cheap"), a two-storey barn, a plumbing shop, and several offices and cottages.[25] Harris decided to spend the winter at his estate in Virginia. When he returned to Sandon, he would find the city—his "kingdom"—in ruins.

IN EARLY 1900, THE MINE owners decided to go all out to break the strike by bringing in non-union miners. On January 14, Sandon union leader

W.L. “Billy” Hagler and a clutch of men had a tense standoff with manager Hand of the Payne mine. Fearing the worst, Hand had armed himself, but there was no evidence that any of the men threatened violence (though Hagler kept his hand on his hip pocket throughout the incident). Nevertheless—though he would later be acquitted—Hagler was arrested for “unlawful assembly.”[26] Four days later, twenty union miners, without Hagler, made a second visit to the Payne. Hand telegraphed the magistrate, who read the riot act. The men stood down and tramped back down the mountain.

Public opinion in West Kootenay generally supported the miners. The “eight-hour law” was popular across the province. One newspaper estimated that not one voter in ten would oppose it. However, the mine owners had the power and money. The union realized that without enforcement of the Alien Labour Act, they could not hope to win the battle. The strike/lockout ended with a whimper on February 16, 1900. A day earlier, the Slocan unions had voted to lower the union scale of wages to $3.25 a shift. This was a figure offered by the owners of the Slocan Star mine at the start of the troubles, and the mine owners’ association several months later. It represented a raise of about six cents an hour for the miners but hardly seemed like something worth celebrating—either by the miners or by the owners. It was about three cents an hour more than the mine owners had originally offered and three cents less than the miners had demanded. The damage done to the mining industry in the Slocan for pennies was incalculable.

People in the Slocan were just starting to feel a small spark of optimism with the opening of the mines and the coming of spring when disaster struck once again. On the evening of May 3, 1900, a local amateur theatre company gave a performance in Sandon of *A Bitter Atonement* at Spencer’s Hall. Long after the performance had finished—sometime after midnight—fire was spotted burning in the lot behind the hall. It spread rapidly, first consuming Spencer’s Hall and then racing down Reco Avenue. The fire brigade was called out, but due to the late hour, it took them precious minutes to get organized. By the time they got their hoses out, the fire was well under way. The fire brigade worked feverishly, but they couldn’t control the flames. Steady streams of water seemed to have no effect. Then the hoses burned and had to be replaced by bucket brigades. In less than three hours, nearly every building on Reco Avenue and Sunnyside was reduced to charcoal. Only just completed, the new Presbyterian church joined the Methodist church in the ashes.

The cause of the fire was never determined, but with the hard times and hard feelings, arson could not be ruled out. Given the extent of the devastation, there were surprisingly few casualties and only one death. Though the fire was in the middle of the night, there had been enough time to rouse most inhabitants. George Spencer was in bed when he saw the blaze from his window. He just had time to wake his wife, put on some clothes, and rush out of the building. Some hotel residents stayed in their rooms at first, believing that the fire brigade would be able to bring things under control, but when fire burst through the roof of one hotel, the residents decided to get out and head up the gulch.

The play that had preceded the fire, *A Bitter Atonement*, was adapted from *Married for Her Beauty; or, A Bitter Atonement*, a novel written by English author Charlotte M. Brame (writing as Bertha M. Clay). In the novel, the heroine sins and suffers but ultimately redeems herself: "She sinned, but she suffered; she did wrong, but she made, as she remembers well, a bitter atonement." In its brief existence, Sandon had seen its share of sin. It had suffered too. It was too young to have felt the immediate impact of the Great Panic of 1893, but it had been witness to the fall of silver in 1897, the exodus to the Klondike, the lengthy strike, the deadly snow slides, and now the cruel visitation by fire. Things would never be the same. Unlike the novel, there would be no atonement and no happy ending for Sandon. While experts determined that the nineteenth century would not officially end until December 31, 1900, the glory days of the Slocan were certainly over before then. As the century wound down, the curtain closed on the greatest silver act BC had ever seen.

Sandon after the fire, May 4, 1900. Photographer: R.H. Trueman. IMAGE COURTESY OF THE VANCOUVER CITY ARCHIVES

EPILOGUE

JOHNNY HARRIS RETURNED TO SANDON two weeks after the fire. When he first heard news of the devastation, he immediately vowed to rebuild. And indeed, much of the city was rebuilt, but a visitor more than a year later noted the "charred remains" of burnt homes everywhere.[1] All the king's horses and all the king's men could not restore Sandon to its former glory. Times had changed since Harris first paddled up Slocan Lake to Eldorado in 1892. Most of the pioneers who had camped on the shores of the lake in those early days, impatiently waiting for the snow to melt so they could scramble up the mountainsides to find their fortunes, had long gone. Only a few stalwarts like Harris and Silverton's William Hunter remained. By 1900, pioneers from the gravy days were routinely referred to as "old-timers."

The death of Queen Victoria in January 1901 concluded the nineteenth century with an emphatic full stop. Less heralded, sometime in 1900, young Christina Kane passed away, severing one of the few links to Kaslo and the Slocan's Indigenous past. In July 1891, the price of silver on the New York stock exchange was reported at a dollar an ounce. By 1900, the price hovered around $0.60. Silver was no longer a strong attraction for fortune-seeking prospectors. The long-term prospects for the white metal did not look good. The last lingering dreams of bimetallism died with the defeat of William Jennings Bryan in the American presidential election of 1900. Gold became the standard for the twentieth century, and prospectors abandoned silver in droves to stake their futures on gold.

The population mix had changed drastically during Harris's years in the Slocan. When he first arrived at Eldorado, most of his camp mates were Americans—many from Idaho's Coeur d'Alene district. As the years passed by, the demographics gradually shifted. American prospectors and capitalists extracted what they could from the Slocan, but most eventually returned to the United States. In their place came British capitalists and hundreds of workers from eastern Canada willing and able—before the labour troubles of 1899 and 1900—to go underground for $3.50 a day. The increasing number of Canadians was a good thing for nation-building, but the drive, determination, and, most of all, the willingness to take risks that the early crowds of American prospectors and entrepreneurs had, would be sorely missed.

In addition to Americans, the Slocan in the 1890s hosted a medley of nationalities, races, and ethnicities. In December 1897, Welshman Elias Owen wrote home to his family in Wales from New Denver: "Here I met some other Welshmen, including a man from Dowlais and another from Flint. We live here in a log house, and, as there is no woman about the place, do all our own housework."[2] While people far away from their homes—and this would have been almost everyone in the Slocan—would have found common comfort in others with whom they shared interests, it would have been almost impossible not to mix into the broader community. Social events such as the dances in Sandon or the much-anticipated celebrations on the Queen's birthday or Dominion Day drew attendees from across racial, national, religious, and ethnic lines. Orangemen from Ontario mixed—admittedly sometimes uncomfortably—with Irish nationalists; Catholics worked alongside Presbyterians; Swedes drank and brawled with Germans, Finns, and Scots.

In 1900, some Slocan residents, like Johnny Harris, still believed in the future of the silver mines. Over the next half century, there would be brief spells when the mines rebounded. But the mining camps would never return to the heady days of the 1890s. Gone were the days when premiers and cabinet ministers would come calling with promises of railways and roads. Instead, the Slocan gradually receded from newspaper headlines and slipped into the decaying and forgotten backwater it would eventually become.

In 1903, the Slocan was attracting butterfly collectors from Washington, DC, but fewer and fewer miners. The collectors—on the trail of exotic and unique insects—were encouraged by Kaslo's own butterfly expert, J.W. Cockle. Once he had been "Black Jack" Cockle, the discoverer of the famous big boulder. Now he was J.W. Cockle of scientific journals and the discoverer of a local butterfly variation: *Colias kootenai*. Cockle arranged for the experts from Washington, DC, to visit the Slocan mines. They made a couple of trips to McGuigan basin with mixed success. Then they tried the slopes above Bear Lake. One of them later described the scarred and largely deserted landscape:

> Mr. Cockle, Mr. Claudell and I climbed the mountain north of Bear Lake on the morning of July 21 and, as the day was warm and sunny, spent a few hours collecting at the summit near the abandoned London Hill Mine. The forests on the mountains about Bear Lake have been completely destroyed by fires and only the charred and dead tree trunks remain standing. There was little collecting, therefore, on the way up.[3]

Their fortunes changed when they reached the summit. They managed to scoop a number of Bombyliidae, Tachinidae, and Syrphidae (commonly known as "flies"). They came back a week later, but despite having sugared the undergrowth to attract insects, they only managed to bag "a crane fly, a slug, and a mouse." A decade earlier, the "Silvery Slocan" had attracted fortune seekers like flies to sugar. Now the attraction on a wet day in July 1903 was not silver, but sugar for flies.

What of the Slocan's pioneers? What became of the men and women responsible for turning a wild and largely uninhabited pocket of wilderness into a thriving, industrialized urban outpost? Most ended up with little to show for the years invested in the Silvery Slocan. Despite the many claims he staked in 1891 and 1892, including the mighty Payne, Eli Carpenter never realized any great profit from his exploits. In 1895, before he got a second wind in Slocan City, he was viewed as something of a tragic figure:

> Eli Carpenter is living in New Denver today. He is getting old and has a very limited bank account. Probably, if he visited many of the mines in the district the owners would not give him a job. Yet, he was the man who found the Slocan, and opened a way for many to make fortunes. Eli does not yet receive a pension but may in time if he has good fortune.[4]

Indeed, a story was later told of Eli trying for a job at the Payne—the claim he had discovered—but he was denied.

As far as we know, after heading out for the Klondike in 1897, Eli Carpenter never returned to the Slocan. At first, it was rumoured that he had died on the way north—perhaps in the Peace River Country, or maybe Atlin. Then a report came back that no, he was still alive and still en route to the Klondike. The longer Carpenter was gone, the more people assumed he had died. In truth, he made it to the Klondike. He made some money there too, but it wasn't a fortune. After toiling in the Klondike, he turned up in 1911, squatting on some school land east of Calgary. He tried his hand at ranching, but he wasn't cut out for it. After breaking a leg when a horse threw him, he decided to take up prospecting again and took the train west to Kamloops. He lingered about Sicamous and Salmon Arm for a while but had no better luck than he had as a rancher.

Carpenter reportedly set out for Australia, but after two weeks there, he decided to come back to Canada. Another report had him off to Bolivia in 1914. He later took up a homestead on Shuswap Lake and lived out his remaining days there. An old man now, he struggled to make ends meet and depended in large measure on the kindness of his neighbours and friends. He was a proud man and didn't want to go to the home for the elderly in Kamloops—though he had subscribed to it for a time. In January 1917, aged seventy-five, he fell asleep in his cabin and never woke up.

Eli Carpenter, the "discoverer" of the Slocan, could have been the archetype for the "lonely prospector." In an insightful essay on old age in BC, Megan J. Davies quotes from a 1947 Old-Age Pension Board report: "The mining prospector doesn't stake a claim and proceed in due course to find himself a wife and establish a family in the fastness of the mountains. He keeps on chasing the elusive pot of gold, often until he is an old man."[5] After the great mining rushes in the late nineteenth and early twentieth centuries, there were hundreds of these "lonely prospectors" in BC, quietly living out their lives of ever-diminishing returns. Gene Petersen, who grew up in Sandon during the 1920s and '30s, recalled "many lonely bachelors living in cabins scattered around the hills."[6] Perhaps Ben Coombs, a grizzled old Colorado prospector, had it right. Interviewed in 1895, he had this to say: "Every one of us old fools who spend our time in the hills looking for something we never find is crazy—yes, incurably insane."[7] Bill Springer might have agreed. The Slocan pioneer died in Arizona in 1930, at age 87, after collapsing outside his mine.

Lonely they may have been, and perhaps crazy, but at least Eli Carpenter and Bill Springer lived to relatively ripe old age. Many of their younger contemporaries never made it so far. Carpenter's one-time partner Jack Seaton lived little more than a year after the famous discoveries of the Payne and Noble Five mines. Like the mythology that grew about Carpenter, within years the reason for Seaton's death was transformed from chronic illness and alcoholism to a shoot-out in an Idaho saloon. It wasn't true. But if people wanted lurid tales riddled with violence and tragedy, they didn't have to make them up. There was the sad murder of Caroline "Fool Hen" Miller, one of the first women to prospect in the Slocan, and other tragedies too.

Eli Carpenter's old prospecting partner, E.A. Bielenberg, despondent, drinking heavily, and due to be married in weeks, while "laboring under a fit of temporary insanity," died by suicide in 1901 after cutting his own throat.[8] It was said that Bielenberg had made and lost two fortunes since his prospecting days in the Slocan. Jack McGuigan, after a few prosperous years in the Slocan, bought a gold mine in Oregon. Soon after he purchased it, he fell from a fourth-storey window at the Imperial Hotel in Portland. He suffered a fractured skull, but being a tough old prospector, he managed to last nine days before succumbing. These tragic endings—both real and imagined—gave some credence to a notion popular in the Slocan and other mining districts that "the finders of bonanza mines always come to violent ends."[9]

Even those who managed to make a bit of money in the Slocan often had their success tempered by disappointment or death. After selling his interest in the Payne, Scott McDonald travelled to California in a bid to restore his health. Unfortunately, it didn't work out. He died of tuberculosis soon afterwards, leaving an estate worth almost a million. G.W. Hughes was one of the exceptions. He made money off both the Mountain Chief and, in later years, the Lucky Jim. He made a fortune when zinc, a much neglected component of galena ore, rose in value, which allowed him to spend time in New York City indulging his passion for sailing. When he died in Portland, Oregon, in June 1910, after a lengthy illness, some accounts said he left an estate of somewhere from $100,000 to $2.5 million. However, others said the lifelong bachelor had given most of his fortune away to his lady friends.

After leaving the Slocan, E.C. Carpenter, founder of Three Forks, settled down in Rugby, England. He took a job at the Wolston Silk Mills. One day in October 1898, he was on the high street in Coventry and began walking into shops asking for goods. He was disinclined to pay for them and became agitated when asked to do so. He eventually punched a man in the head, and a police constable took charge of him. He was declared insane and sent to the workhouse. It turned out he had some kind of pressure on his brain. He died less than two years later.

Of the crowds of Slocan prospectors who packed out for Alaska and the Klondike in 1897 and 1898, there was a mixed bag of winners and losers. Among the winners was Toughnut Jack Clunan. There were rumours, at first, that he had lost both legs in the frozen north. The stories were false. Instead, news followed that Toughnut had struck it rich in Nome, Alaska. Toughnut gave up drinking for a while and focused on gold. Now partnered with Jim Wardner, they made a fortune from the sands at Cape Nome. In late August 1900, Toughnut was on a steamer travelling from Nome to Seattle. There was two million dollars' worth of gold on board, and a good portion of it belonged to Toughnut. He was back in the Slocan in late 1900, but he didn't stay long. Dave King, former editor of the Kaslo *Kootenaian*, cashed in on the Klondike too by collaborating with author Rex Beach on Beach's novel *The Spoilers*.

Grant Thorburn saw some success too. After resisting the call of the Klondike in 1898—when he expressed his confidence in the Slocan—by 1901, he was ready to try the northern cure. In that year he set out for Dawson City. His wife Sarah followed him, and the two were reunited in October. Sarah's departure from Silverton marked the end of an era. The dock in Silverton was crowded with well-wishers to see her off. The *Silvertonian*'s account of the occasion is elegiac in tone:

> In losing Mrs. Thorburn Silverton says good-bye to one of her earliest citizens, she being one of the first women in the Slocan, having come in in '92 over the trail from Nakusp. In '94, with her husband, she came to Silverton, then Four Mile City, and has watched this town change from a hamlet of log shacks to a town with substantial stores, hotels and residences. To all the old timers in the Slocan, she is known for her kindness in the sick room, when "the touch of a woman's hand" was welcomed at its true worth, and for her unfailing cheerfulness during the trying pioneer days.[10]

Grant Thorburn stayed in the north for at least the next five years before heading south to Hazelton in BC. Grant and Sarah separated sometime after her arrival in the north. We don't know what became of her. She left the Yukon and in 1905 stopped briefly in Vancouver on her way "south." By 1908, after a brief stint in Alaska, Grant had remarried and had an infant daughter. He eventually landed in the Cowichan Valley on Vancouver Island. For several years he managed the Tzouhalem Hotel in Duncan. He passed away in 1930 at Resthaven Hospital in Sidney.

Jim Startsman was sentenced to five years imprisonment in 1893 for fraud. He missed most of the 1890s in the Slocan but got out of prison in time for the Klondike rush. There's no evidence that he found his fortune in the north, but he did find one thing that earned him a bit of fame: a frozen and well-preserved woolly mammoth.

E.E. Coy struggled for years in Alaska—never giving up on the prospector's dream. Bad luck continued to dog him. In 1902, he accused two men of trying to defraud him out of as much as $100,000. However, they counterclaimed that it was not them, but Coy who was running some kind of crooked scheme. Coy gradually began to lose his mind. One Alaska judge who encountered him in 1903 referred to him in his private notebook as a "crazy old idiot."[11] In failing health and unable to make a living in Alaska, Coy moved south to Washington State. In the spring of 1906, nearly destitute and no longer with Belle, Coy applied for admission to the state soldiers' home in Orting, just south of Tacoma. Not yet sixty, he was a broken man. However, he never surrendered his soldier's pride. The soldiers' home couldn't take in men of "unsound mind" or those afflicted with "loathsome diseases," but Civil War veteran Coy was warmly welcomed, his earlier transgressions either forgiven or forgotten, though one of the administrators described him as "mentally weak."[12]

Mike Bartlett was another veteran of both the Slocan and Klondike rushes who settled down in Washington State. Mike was the youngest of the Bartlett brothers. The brothers did great business packing out of Skagway and Bennett, making money hand over fist. It was in Bennett that Mike met red-headed Mollie Walsh, who was running a restaurant at a place called Log Cabin. She soon took a job bookkeeping for the Bartlett brothers.

Mollie was a beautiful woman with more than enough personality to win over even the most hardened miners with her kindness and generosity. She was soon known far and wide as the "angel of the Klondike trail"—though one contemporary writer uncharitably referred to her as "Few Clothes Molly."[13] She had several suitors, including Jack Newman, a smitten packer who claimed to have fought a duel over her. He hoped she would marry him, but Mollie fell for Mike Bartlett. She married him and moved to Dawson City. Unfortunately, they did not live happily ever after. With the money they made in the Klondike, they moved to Seattle and subsequently separated. In 1902, Mike shot his red-headed angel dead. He was acquitted on grounds of insanity and later took his own life. It might have run in the family. Mike's brothers Ed and Al both landed in insane asylums in the early 1900s.

Will Bennett stubbornly stuck with the Slocan when many of his contemporaries moved on. He kept chipping away at ore croppings, looking for the mother lode. He had survived the sixty-foot fall in the Slocan Star mine, but he wouldn't survive the snow slide that carried him away in November 1918.

There were few hazards more dangerous or unpredictable than snow slides, but war was one of them. In July 1900, Corporal Ben Lee was on a scouting mission in Natal Province, South Africa. He was just sitting down to light up his pipe when he was hit by an exploding bullet fired by a Boer sniper. Lee was hit by two more rounds and died in a land far from his home. He was thirty-five years old.

In the early years of the new century, Lane Gilliam landed in Los Angeles, where he opened a mining brokerage office. He had a silver mine in Arizona's Sonora Mountains and by 1909, was spending much of his time in Mexico, where he also had mining interests. Lane's brother, Marc, who had been with him in the Slocan, also relocated to California. His granddaughter, Michelle Phillips, achieved fame in the 1960s when, as a member of the Mamas and the Papas, she sang a paean to her grandfather's adopted state—"California Dreaming."

HISTORIAN GREG NESTEROFF HAS NOTED that it did not bode well for a mining camp if the local newspaper went broke. This certainly rings true of the Slocan as the camps followed their newspapers into the shadowy recesses of local history. Running a mining camp newspaper was no picnic, and credit is due to those who stuck with them.

In 1902, the Sandon *Paystreak*'s Billy McAdams got into trouble for criticizing BC's Supreme Court. This led to a prison sentence, which was reduced following McAdams's abject apology. Chief Justice Hunter reviewed several issues of the *Paystreak* and concluded that he had never seen "a more disreputable and atrocious paper."[14]

R.T. Lowery returned to edit the *Paystreak* while McAdams was in jail, but it was clear that the end was near. However, Lowery was not one to be easily deterred. He even tried to expand his influence. To fill the vacuum in Slocan City left by the demise of the *Pioneer* and the *Slocan City News*, he financed the *Slocan City Drill*. C.E. Smitheringale moved down the lake from New Denver to run the new paper. It was a bold, but ultimately futile move. In September 1901, the Silverton *Silvertonian* shut down when it reached the end of its "string." The *Silvertonian* was followed down the drain by the *Paystreak* (1902), the *Mining Review* (1903), and the *Ledge* (1904). The *Drill* succumbed in 1905.

In the dispute between Dave King and W.C. Nichol, and between Nichol and former Premier John Turner, Nichol came out on top. He was found not guilty on the allegations levelled by the former premier and was appointed Lieutenant-Governor of BC in 1920. In the early twentieth century, after the West Kootenay boom was over, many American newspaper workers returned to their homes south of the border. Most Canadian newspaper editors stayed in the business, moving from town to town to ply their trade. John Houston, after several years in BC's Legislative Assembly, ended up in Prince Rupert. David Bogle, after leaving Rossland, briefly edited the *Victoria Daily Colonist* before moving on to Manitoba, where he would spend his time championing the aspirations of working class Canadians.

No veteran of the Slocan newspaper scene achieved the lasting recognition of R.T. Lowery. He left the Slocan in 1904 to edit newspapers in Fernie, Poplar, and Greenwood, with brief forays into the rough-and-tumble of Vancouver. Before leaving New Denver, he listed many of those who had worked for him: Charles Smitheringale, Harry Walker, Johnny Cole, George Miers, Seneca Ketchum, Tom Tobin, Billy Evans, Ric Fraser, Johnny Langstaff, Peck McSwain, Billy McAdams, Weston Coyney, E.C. Bissell, Dave King, Jim Grier, Edwin Mertens, "Edi," "Long Primer Jack," and printer's devil Harry Pyman. It was an impressive list with many names familiar in newspaper circles across North America.[15]

Lowery edited the *Ledge* in Greenwood from 1906 to 1920—a longer tenure than any of his Slocan or Kaslo newspapers. He died in Grand Forks in 1921. Pioneers from across the Kootenays paid their respects at his funeral. There were several tributes, including one in the Sarnia *Canadian Observer*, a paper once run by Lowery's brother, William. The most poignant tribute, however, appeared in Enderby's *Okanagan Commoner*, run by Harry Walker. Walker had worked with Lowery on the New Denver iteration of the *Ledge*:

> We look back on those days as a time never to be forgotten. It was in the boom days of the Silvery Slocan, the heyday of poker and blackjack, of wine and scotch, and the strenuous life in the oldest profession on earth . . . If "wine and women" mean sin, and "noise and frolic" mean hell, then hell "broke loose" in the Lowery days of the Silvery Slocan, and the Lord must have loved it because we had so much of it.[16]

Other Slocan pioneers led quieter, less celebrated lives than Colonel Lowery. Nick Palorcia faithfully served the shoe-wearing public in Phoenix for nearly twenty years. His shoe shop in later years became a favoured stopping spot for old prospectors. After a stay in the Boundary district, R.B. and Dora Kerr relocated to the Okanagan, where they took up the mantle of women's suffrage. Retiring from a successful career in law, Kerr returned to Britain and continued his interests in socialism. Late in life he took up the population theories of the Reverend Thomas Robert Malthus.

Sandon's demographic mix changed after the fire. Jim Kee, of Chinese descent, relocated from Whitewater to Sandon to set up a market garden. The *Paystreak*, taking its cue from earlier remarks by R.T. Lowery, could read the future: "[He] will no doubt be followed by many others."[17] However, the *Paystreak* could not see far enough into the future to divine Sandon's role as an internment camp for Japanese Canadians during the Second World War.

Unlike Palorcia and the Kerrs, Johnny Harris kept his faith in the Slocan. He put a lot of his own money into rebuilding Sandon and was consistently charitable to churches and old friends. Things were changing, however. He had to deal with a city council that wasn't always willing to do his bidding. This was evident when he started to reassert his property rights. In July 1900, he wrote to the city council to demand that they not issue liquor licences to operators on lots that he claimed as his own. Council referred the matter to the city inspectors. Harris would keep pushing. Ever the entrepreneur, he even saw an opportunity to capitalize on the fire. He campaigned for a re-survey of Sandon, which he felt would be of benefit to everyone. Not coincidentally, it would allow him to realign property lines and reclaim more lots from the creek.

Harris would not stop fighting for his interests. Like Harris, Bruce White was a Slocan pioneer. Indeed, White prospected the mountains above Carpenter Creek months before Harris arrived on the scene. After Sandon's great fire, Harris, White, and Bruce's brother Byron became bitter adversaries. They and their partners fought a celebrated and long-running legal battle over extra-lateral rights all the way to the Privy Council in London. After a few setbacks in the lower courts, Harris came out on top—as he usually did. After losing the court case, Bruce White and his wife settled down to life in Nelson. Bruce spent a few years travelling around the western mining frontier, even going as far as Mexico. He kept some interests in the Slocan but put his money into other districts too. Sadly, though, he and Elise separated in 1907. Bruce died a broken man in 1918, a victim of the great influenza pandemic—sometimes referred to as the Spanish flu.

Johnny Harris stayed on in Sandon. A newspaperman who visited in 1937 painted a bittersweet portrait of the man who was still "king" of Sandon, though most of his subjects had long since moved on:

> Living alone in this large hotel, he keeps a little store where once was the hotel office, to sell a little tea, butter, sugar to the few that need it. He looks after his plants and experiments with the large radio he has installed. With great pride he shows visitors the lemon and orange trees that he is growing in the dining room of his hotel. This year two trees are bearing fruit. One has two oranges on it and the other several small lemons in spite of the fact that neither tree has been in the sunlight. On a quiet night, as the light of the day fades Mr. Harris sits in his cosy chair in front of the "Reco" and lives again the days when the town was a blaze of light, hundreds milling up and down the street, 23 hotels filled with happy-go-lucky men and women, when everybody had money and spent it as they earned it.[18]

Harris was still there in 1950, "loath to leave the familiar ghosts" that inhabited his "silent city." Even at eighty-nine years old, his confidence in the Slocan was undiminished: "There's still plenty of ore here," he said. "It's a little hard to find but when big money starts rolling again, Sandon will come to life with a bang."[19]

Johnny Harris lived out his life in the mining camp he had largely created. He died in 1953. Two short years later, debris plugging the old Carpenter Creek flume led to a flood that destroyed it and carried away much of what was left of Sandon. At the time of the flood, no more than thirty people were left living in the town that had once been the silver capital of BC.

The lakeside towns of New Denver and Silverton fared better and became peaceful refuges for many Slocan pioneers. William Hunter was another survivor from the early days. After his long experience as a merchant, he took up politics in the early years of the new century and served as the Slocan's representative in the BC Legislative Assembly from 1907 to 1916, and then again from 1920 to 1924. After retiring from politics, he spent the rest of his life in Silverton, dying there in 1939, at the age of eighty-one.

THEY SAY THAT MILITARY HISTORY is written by the victors. It is equally true that local history is shaped by those who stayed and those who survived. Johnny Harris and William Hunter were both blessed with long life and the good fortune to live and die in the Slocan. They are remembered fondly and loom large in local history. When a succeeding generation of Slocan pioneers was interviewed in the 1970s, they had many stories to tell about Johnny Harris and a few about William Hunter. They had also heard the stories of Eli Carpenter, Jack Seaton, and a few other pioneers. It seems, though, that the stories of men and women like Nick Palorcia, Curly Robinson, Alex Sproat, Jim Delaney, "Fool Hen," Alfred and Arvell Perkins, Sarah Thorburn, and others unnamed and unknown, had slipped into an abyss. They led transitory lives in an ephemeral frontier community that seems to shimmer just beyond our awareness. So close—but just out of reach. That community would not have been the same without them.

Slocan City, c. 1897. Artist: Lindley Crease. IMAGE COURTESY OF THE ROYAL BC MUSEUM AND ARCHIVES

ACKNOWLEDGEMENTS

IN AN EARLIER BOOK, *Silver Rush: British Columbia's Silvery Slocan, 1891–1900*, I acknowledged the many friends, archivists, and enthusiasts who helped me get that book to print, which built the foundation for this book. For *Mining Camp Tales*, I would particularly like to acknowledge the late Cole Harris for his support and encouragement. While he recognized the work that went into *Silver Rush*, it was he who thought that its "mass of information" would likely overwhelm a more casual audience, which started me thinking about this book. I am grateful to the local history societies that have helped and encouraged me at every step of the way. In particular, I would like to thank Elizabeth Scarlett of the Kootenay Lake Archives, Joyce Johnson of the Slocan Valley Historical Society, and Henning von Krogh of the Silvery Slocan Historical Society. I appreciated Hal Wright and Vida Turok's kind words, and all the work that Hal has done in the service of Sandon. I must also thank *British Columbia History* magazine for allowing me to use an article that formed the basis for chapter twenty of the present work. Greg Nesteroff has been a constant source of encouragement and assistance. There's not much about West Kootenay history that he doesn't know. I would also like to thank Stan Sherstobitoff, Mabel Collins, and others for the use of photos, and Ian McKay for the map that appears on page 11. Last and by no means least, I would like to thank Alexis Anderson for her meticulous copyediting, and Lara Kordic, Kimiko Fraser, Nandini Thaker, Monica Miller, and all the staff at Heritage House Publishing.

NOTES

INTRODUCTION

1 William Carlyle, "Report on the Slocan, Nelson and Ainsworth Mining Districts in West Kootenay, British Columbia: Bureau of Mines Bulletin No. 3," British Columbia Sessional Papers (Victoria, BC: Government Printer, 1898).

2 Patrick Donan, *The New Bonanzaland: With a Brief Dissertation on Booms* (Portland, OR: Passenger Department of the Oregon Railroad and Navigation Company, 1897), 7.

3 Cole Harris, *Newspapers & the Slocan in the 1890s*, 1.

4 *Rossland Weekly Miner*, September 22, 1898.

5 *Vancouver Daily World,* May 6, 1892.

6 *Inland Sentinel* (Kamloops), February 11, 1893.

7 *Guelph Evening Mercury*, September 25, 1897.

8 *Inland Sentinel* (Kamloops), June 18, 1892.

9 Gowen, *Pioneer Church Work in British Columbia*, 199–200.

10 *The Tribune* (Nelson), September 15, 1894.

11 Kipling, *Letters of Travel*, 187–88.

12 Some today, as others did at the time, would cast doubt on Sproule's guilt. For an account of early Kootenay Mines—in both fact and fiction—see Elsie Turnbull, "Old Mines in the West Kootenay," *British Columbia Historical Quarterly* 20, nos. 3 & 4 (July–October 1956).

13 British Columbia Legislative Assembly, "Return to an Order of the House for a Copy of Instructions to Messrs. Farwell and Sproat, Before Leaving for Kootenay, and a Copy of Their Report on the Mining, Agricultural and Timber Resources of That District," *British Columbia Sessional Papers* (Victoria, BC: Government Printer, 1884); The Daily News (Nelson), March 31, 1919.

14 Scholefield and Howay, *British Columbia from the Earliest Times to the Present*, vol. 2:475.

15 Belshaw, *Becoming British Columbia*, 49.

16 Tuchman, *The Proud Tower*, 235.

17 *Slocan Prospector*, January 19, 1895.

18 *Montreal Gazette*, February 16, 1897.

19 Vipond to B.A. Little, April 8, 1973. Author's collection.

20 Cole Harris, "Industry and the Good Life around Idaho Peak," *Canadian Historical Review* 66, no. 3 (September 1985): 315–343.

1—DISCOVERIES

1 Affleck, *Kootenay Lake Chronicles* ("Early Days in Kootenay," from British Columbia Mining Record, February 1897).

2 *Spokane Review*, January 9, 1892.

3 The identification of specific Indigenous Peoples has changed over time and varies on either side of the Canada–US border. For the Ktunaxa Nation, variations have included the Kootenay, Kootenai, Kutenai, and Ksanka Peoples. For the Sinixt Nation, variations have included the Colville, Lakes, and Arrow Lakes Peoples.

4 *Spokane Review*, November 4, 1891.
5 Fraser, *Wheeler*, 52.
6 Roosevelt, *The Wilderness Hunter*, 134. For a (possibly apocryphal) account of Roosevelt's shooting of a grizzly bear in BC, see *Muscatine News-Tribune* (Iowa), January 20, 1899.
7 *Spokane Review*, November 4, 1891.
8 Harold Sands, "Bonanzas of the Slocan," *Canadian Magazine of Politics, Art and Science* 35, no. 5 (September 1910).
9 *Spokane Review*, November 4, 1891.
10 *The Miner* (Nelson), September 26, 1891.
11 *The Tribune* (Nelson), September 22, 1894.
12 *Hot Springs News* (Ainsworth), October 10, 1891.
13 *Hot Springs News* (Ainsworth), October 3, 1891.
14 *Hot Springs News* (Ainsworth), October 3, 1891.
15 Hot Springs News (Ainsworth), October 24, 1891.
16 Spokane Falls Review, October 8, 1891.
17 The Miner (Nelson), October 3, 1891.
18 Daily Independent (Helena, Montana), October 12, 1891.
19 *Hot Springs News* (Ainsworth), October 10, 1891.
20 *Spokane Review*, October 8, 1891. The word "Siwash" comes from the Chinook jargon and was used in a derogatory manner to describe the Indigenous inhabitants of the Pacific Northwest of North America.
21 *Victoria Daily Colonist*, October 13, 1891.
22 *The Miner* (Nelson), October 31, 1891.
23 *The Miner* (Nelson, from the Chicago Herald), January 2, 1892.
24 Kanes, *A Maine Prodigy*, 198.
25 *New York Evening Post*, October 27, 1896.
26 *Spokane Review*, November 5, 1891.
27 *Spokane Review*, November 6, 1891.
28 *The Daily News* (Nelson), April 19, 1924.
29 Wardner, *Jim Wardner of Wardner*, Idaho, 110.
30 *The Tribune* (Nelson), December 1, 1894.
31 *Spokane Daily Chronicle*, November 5, 1891.
32 J.C. Gwillim, "Eli Carpenter, Discoverer of the Slocan," *Canadian Mining Journal* 40, no. 16 (April 23, 1919).
33 *The Daily Independent* (Helena, Montana), December 16, 1891.
34 *The Mining Review* (Sandon), January 1, 1898.

2—THE RUSH

1 *Seattle Post-Intelligencer*, June 2, 1892.
2 *The Miner* (Nelson), December 5, 1891.
3 *Hot Springs News* (Ainsworth), December 26, 1891.
4 *Spokane Review*, January 6, 1892.
5 *Spokane Spokesman-Review*, October 5, 1895.
6 *The Daily News* (Nelson), April 19, 1924.
7 *Hot Springs News* (Ainsworth), March 16, 1892.
8 Keenan, *The Life of Yellowstone Kelly*, 53.
9 Though Alonzo S. Reed did move to California later in life.

10 *Dalles Daily Chronicle* (Oregon), August 31, 1892.
11 Angier, We Like it Wild. According to Neil Gething's son, King Gething, 120.
12 *Victoria Daily Colonist*, August 6, 1892.
13 *The Ledge* (New Denver), June 6, 1895.
14 *Spokane Review*, October 29, 1892.
15 *Spokane Review*, August 10, 1892.
16 *Chicago Inter Ocean*, August 28, 1894. Letter from A.T. Leith.
17 *The Ledge* (New Denver), October 27, 1910.
18 *Inland Sentinel* (Kamloops), June 25, 1892.
19 *Inland Sentinel* (Kamloops), June 25, 1892.
20 *Hot Springs News* (Ainsworth), October 24, 1891.
21 *Hot Springs News* (Ainsworth), October 24, 1891.
22 *Coeur d'Alene Miner* (Wallace, Idaho), December 5, 1891.
23 *The Tribune* (Nelson), December 1, 1892.
24 *The Miner* (Nelson), October 22, 1892.
25 *The Miner* (Nelson), October 22, 1892.
26 *Canadian Mining Review* 13, no. 10 (October 1894).
27 *Spokane Chronicle*, December 19, 1892.

3—CAPITAL

1 *Victoria Daily Colonist*, February 7, 1893.
2 *Spokane Review*, November 5, 1891.
3 *Inland Sentinel* (Kamloops), December 3, 1892.
4 *Spokane Review*, February 25, 1892.
5 *Hot Springs News* (Ainsworth), June 29, 1892.
6 Jim Wardner, *Jim Wardner, of Wardner*, Idaho (New York: Anglo-American Publishing, 1900), 106.
7 MacGowan, *The Hard Road to Klondike*, 60.
8 Crampton, *Deep Enough*, 42.
9 *Canadian Mining and Mechanical Review* 2, no. 8 (August 1892).
10 *Tacoma Daily Ledger* (Washington), August 8, 1892.
11 *Kootenai Herald* (Bonner's Ferry), September 16, 1892.
12 *Seattle Post-Intelligencer*, November 13, 1897.
13 *The Tribune* (Nelson), December 14, 1893.
14 Ibid.
15 *The Paystreak* (Sandon), October 7, 1899.
16 *Calgary Herald* (from the *Ledge*), September 12, 1896.
17 *The Miner* (Nelson), February 18, 1893.
18 *The Spokane Review*, July 29, 1892.
19 *Victoria Daily Colonist*, September 24, 1892.
20 *Western Advocate* (Mankato, Kansas), March 31, 1893.
21 *Walkerville Telegraph* (Montana), March 31, 1893.
22 *Spokane Review*, December 19, 1892.
23 *Spokane Review*, November 8, 1892.
24 *Victoria Daily Times*, November 29, 1892.
25 *Spokane Review*, November 26, 1892.
26 Ibid.
27 Clive Phillips-Wolley, "Mining Development in British Columbia," *Canadian Magazine of Politics, Science, Art and Literature* 8, no. 4 (February 1897).

28 *London Advertiser* (Ontario), July 3, 1893.
29 Pocock, *Following the Frontier*, 216–17.
30 Lees and Clutterbuck, *A Ramble in British Columbia*, 332.

4—BOOM TOWNS

1 *Spokane Review* (from The Miner [Nelson]), March 29, 1892.
2 E.P. Whalley, "The Eldorado Rush," *Wide World Magazine* 14, no. 84 (March 1905).
3 *Victoria Daily Colonist*, June 13, 1893.
4 *The Field: The Country Gentleman's Newspaper* 82, no. 2127 (September 30, 1893).
5 *Anaconda Standard* (Montana), August 25, 1890.
6 *The Daily News* (Nelson), February 19, 1919.
7 E.P. Whalley, "The Eldorado Rush," *Wide World Magazine* 14, no. 84 (March 1905).
8 A.P. Coleman Field Notebooks, series 3, box 1, notebook 14, Victoria University.
9 *The Miner* (Nelson), June 11, 1892.
10 *Victoria Daily Times*, July 8, 1892.
11 *The Miner* (Nelson), July 23, 1892.
12 *Victoria Daily Colonist*, August 23, 1892.
13 *The Miner* (Nelson), October 22, 1892.
14 *Vancouver Daily World*, October 29, 1892.
15 Church and Affleck, *A Young Scotsman's Adventures in Canada*, 34.
16 *The Tribune* (Nelson), December 1, 1892.
17 *The Miner* (Nelson), December 10, 1892.
18 *Seattle Post-Intelligencer*, January 2, 1893.
19 *The Tribune* (Nelson), March 16, 1893.
20 F.W. Laing, "Life in West Kootenay," *Knox College Monthly and Presbyterian Magazine*, September 1893.
21 *The Miner* (Nelson), May 7, 1892.
22 *The Ledge* (New Denver), August 29, 1895.
23 *Spokane Review*, November 4, 1891.
24 *Spokane Daily Chronicle*, April 27, 1893.
25 *The Independent Record* (Helena, Montana), January 21, 1893.
26 Smith, *The Trail of Gold and Silver*, 132–33.
27 E.P. Whalley, "How We Ran the Miner," *Wide World Magazine* 12, no. 67 (November 1903).
28 *The Miner* (Nelson), October 29, 1892.
29 *Victoria Daily Times*, December 2, 1892.
30 An alternate account has the printing press coming from Oregon.
31 *The Miner* (Nelson), July 8, 1893.
32 *Victoria Daily Times*, October 2, 1893.
33 *The Tribune* (Nelson), September 29, 1894.

5—BY WAGON ROAD AND STEAMBOAT

1 Affleck, *Kootenay Yesterdays*. As recalled by Ed Picard. There were a lot of Madden brothers in West Kootenay at the time, including Hugh and Thomas, who ran a hotel in Nelson. The pack train on the Slocan trail was likely run by Jack and Anthony Madden.
2 *Kaslo Claim*, June 2, 1893.

3 E. Molson Spragge, "The Eldorado of British Columbia," *Canadian Magazine of Politics, Science, Art and Literature* 2, no. 4 (February 1894).
4 *The Tribune* (Nelson), April 6, 1893.
5 *Vancouver Daily World*, January 10, 1896.
6 *The Miner* (Nelson), April 2, 1892.
7 *Nelson Daily Miner*, June 30, 1899.
8 *The Canadian Mining and Mechanical Review* 11, no. 1 (January 1892).
9 Captain Otto Estabrooks, interview by Imbert Orchard, November 4, 1964, Imbert Orchard fonds, PR-0374, accession T1076, BC Archives.
10 *The Tribune* (Nelson), December 15, 1892.
11 *The Week* (Victoria), June 8, 1907.
12 *The Miner* (Nelson), October 29, 1892.
13 *Kootenay Star* (Revelstoke), June 18, 1892.
14 *Hot Springs News* (Ainsworth), September 7, 1892.
15 *Markdale Standard* (Ontario, from the Montreal Star), November 3, 1892.
16 G.O. Buchanan (chair of wagon road committee) to Lane & Marks, December 6, 1892; Lane to Buchanan, December 8, 1892. Kaslo Wagon Road File, Kootenay Lake Archives.
17 *The Tribune* (Nelson) January 5, 1893.
18 *The Miner* (Nelson), November 12, 1892. In fact, there had been a civil engineer involved in picking out the route—John Keen of the Kaslo townsite company. He wouldn't have engineered anything in detail though.
19 *The Miner* (Nelson), December 31, 1892.
20 *The Miner* (Nelson), December 3, 1892.
21 *Kootenai Herald* (Bonner's Ferry, Idaho), April 1, 1893.
22 *The Miner* (Nelson), January 14, 1893.
23 *The Miner* (Nelson), March 25, 1893.

6—SIN CITY

1 *San Francisco Chronicle*, December 12, 1892.
2 Magnuson, *Coeur d'Alene Diary*, 193.
3 "Diary written while Provincial Police constable at Nelson, 1892–93," Joseph Dee Graham fonds, MS-0443, BC Archives (hereinafter "Graham Diary"), February 11, 1893.
4 *Kootenay Star* (Revelstoke), October 7, 1893.
5 *Spokane Review*, December 19, 1892.
6 *The Commercial* (Winnipeg), July 15, 1892.
7 *The Miner* (Nelson), September 23, 1893.
8 *The Miner* (Nelson), January 7, 1893.
9 *Coeur d'Alene Miner* (Wallace), April 8, 1893.
10 Graham Diary, January 9, 1893.
11 *The Tribune* (Nelson), January 5, 1893.
12 Faro—a popular card game associated with gambling.
13 *Boston Evening Transcript*, July 24, 1893.
14 *The Tribune* (Nelson), February 9, 1893.
15 *The Tribune* (Nelson), April 6, 1893.
16 *The Miner* (Nelson), February 11, 1893.
17 *West Virginia Argus*, March 23, 1893.

18 E.P. Whalley, "On the Grade." *Wide West Magazine* 13, no.77 (September 1904).

19 Graham Diary, March 30, 1893.

20 *The Tribune* (Nelson), March 23, 1893.

21 *The Owl* (Vancouver), vol. 1, no. 1 (May 4, 1893).

22 *London Advertiser* (Ontario), July 8, 1893.

23 *Anaconda Standard* (Montana), June 19, 1893.

24 *Northwest Mining Review* (Spokane), April 15, 1893.

25 Graham Diary, January 10, 1893.

26 *Victoria Daily Times* (from Kaslo-Slocan Examiner), March 18, 1893.

27 *The Tribune* (Nelson), February 9, 1893.

28 *Victoria Daily Colonist*, May 10, 1893.

29 *Butte Weekly Miner* (Montana), May 11, 1893.

30 *Coeur d'Alene Press* (Wallace, Idaho), May 13, 1893.

31 *Vancouver Province*, August 25, 1934.

32 Dyar, *News for an Empire*, 56–57.

33 Graham Diary, September 7, 1893.

34 Graham Diary, September 4, 1893.

35 *Spokane Review*, January 7, 1893.

36 "Bowes v. Hughes," GR-0419, box 59, file 51, Attorney General Correspondence, BC Archives.

37 *Kaslo Claim*, June 2, 1893.

38 *Kaslo Claim*, June 9, 1893.

39 *The Tribune* (Nelson), June 8, 1893.

40 "Ewin v. Coy," GR-0419, box 49, file 43, Attorney General Correspondence, BC Archives.

41 Chief Justice Walkem's Bench Books, GR-1727, vol. 20, Bench Books, BC Archives (hereinafter "Chief Justice Walkem's Bench Books").

42 Ibid.

43 *Kaslo Claim*, June 2, 1893.

44 Chief Justice Walkem's Bench Books.

45 *Spokane Review*, April 15, 1894.

46 Chief Justice Walkem's Bench Books.

47 *Vancouver Weekly News-Advertiser*, August 9, 1893.The newspaper felt that the reason given for wanting a pardon was an unintended comment on "social life in West Kootenay."

48 *The Tribune* (Nelson), June 8, 1893.

49 *Nakusp Ledge*, March 29, 1894.

50 "Hesketh v. Thomas," GR-419, box 54, file 50, Attorney General Correspondence, BC Archives.

51 *Nakusp Ledge*, April 5 and September 30, 1894.

7—CHURCH AND COMIQUE

1 F.W. Laing, "Life in West Kootenay," *Knox College Monthly and Presbyterian Magazine*, September 1893.

2 *The Tribune* (Nelson), January 26, 1893.

3 *The Presbyterian Record*, January 1893.

4 *The Miner* (Nelson), April 23, 1892.

5 *Victoria Daily Colonist*, November 23, 1892.

6 *The Miner* (Nelson), November 2, 1892.

7 Violet E. Sillitoe, *Early Days in British Columbia: With a Foreword by the Bishop of New Westminster* (Vancouver: Evans & Hastings, 1922).
8 *Victoria Daily Times*, June 9, 1893.
9 *Tillamook Headlight* (Oregon, from the Kaslo-Slocan Examiner), January 23, 1893.
10 Wardner, *Jim Wardner of Wardner*, Idaho.
11 Kathryn Bridge, *Henry & Self: The Private Life of Sarah Crease, 1826–1922* (Victoria, BC: Sono Nis, 1996).
12 Turner to Robson, November 24, 1893, Ebenezer Robson fonds, PR-1654, BC Archives (hereinafter "Robson fonds").
13 Turner to Robson, June 6, 1892. Robson fonds.
14 Runnalls, *It's God's Country*.
15 *Knox College Monthly and Presbyterian Magazine* 17, no. 8 (December 1893).
16 *Kootenay Star* (Revelstoke), August 13, 1892.
17 *The Miner* (Nelson), September 23, 1893.
18 *Victoria Daily Times*, July 14, 1893.
19 *Victoria Daily Times*, July 14, 1893,
20 *The Miner* (Nelson), January 7, 1893.
21 Diary of Ebenezer Robson, September 14, 1893. Robson fonds.
22 Ibid.
23 Diary of Ebenezer Robson, September 16, 1893. Robson fonds.
24 *The Miner* (Nelson), May 27, 1893.
25 *Vancouver Weekly World*, July 20, 1893.
26 *Boston Evening Transcript*, July 24, 1893.
27 Canada's two principal holidays in the 1890s were May 24 and July 1. May 24 celebrates Queen Victoria's birthday. Victoria Day is sometimes referred to as May Day in Canada. July 1 celebrates Canada's formation as an independent nation in 1867, and was originally called Dominion Day, but is today known as Canada Day.
28 *The Ledge* (Greenwood), March 4, 1915.
29 *Spokane Chronicle*, July 22, 1893.
30 *Spokane Review*, May 14, 1893.
31 *Daily News-Advertiser* (Vancouver, from the *Kaslo-Slocan Examiner*), March 11, 1893.

8—THE GREAT PANIC

1 *The Daily News* (Nelson, from the *Miner's Truth*), March 31, 1919.
2 *Lethbridge News* (from the *Inland Sentinel*), June 22, 1893.
3 *Coeur d'Alene Press* (Wallace, Idaho), May 13, 1893.
4 *The Miner* (Nelson), June 10, 1893.
5 *Kaslo Claim*, June 8, 1893.
6 *The Tribune* (Nelson), June 29,1893.
7 *The Miner* (Nelson), June 29, 1893.
8 *Spokane Review*, August 21, 1893.
9 D.C. Corbin, "Recollections of a Pioneer Railroad Builder," *Washington Historical Quarterly* 1, no. 2 (January 1907).
10 *Anacortes American* (Washington), April 20, 1893.
11 *The Black Hills Daily Times* (Deadwood, South Dakota), May 24, 1893.
12 *Kaslo Claim*, June 23, 1893.

13 Black, *My Seventy Years*, 73.
14 Church and Affleck, *A Young Scotsman's Adventures in Canada, 36. Watson to "Aunt" Sara*, October 16, 1893.
15 *The Miner* (Nelson), September 9, 1893.
16 *Spokane Review*, June 23, 1893.
17 *Victoria Daily Colonist*, July 18, 1893.
18 *Minneapolis Journal*, May 10, 1895.
19 Interview quoted from *The Tribune* (Nelson), September 21, 1893.
20 *Butte Miner* (Montana), August 13, 1893.
21 *The Columbian* (Columbia City, Montana), June 29, 1893.
22 *Philipsburg Mail* (Montana), August 3, 1893,
23 *Philipsburg Mail* (Montana) August 24, 1893.
24 *The Inter Lake* (Kalispell, Montana), June 16, 1893.
25 *The Columbian* (Columbia City, Montana), June 29, 1893.
26 *The Miner* (Nelson), October 28, 1893.
27 *Hosmer Times* (from the Los Angeles Mining Review), July 21, 1910..
28 *Victoria Daily Times*, August 18, 1893.
29 *The Tribune* (Nelson), June 22, 1893
30 *Kaslo-Slocan Examiner*, October 28, 1893.
31 *The Miner* (Nelson), September 23, 1893.
32 *The Tribune* (Nelson), September 21, 1893.
33 *Vancouver Daily World*, September 29, 1893.
34 *Preston Journal* (Scotland), July 22, 1893.
35 *Northwest Mining Review* (Spokane), June 15, 1893.
36 *The Miner* (Nelson), July 22, 1893.
37 Twain, *Roughing It*.
38 *Victoria Daily Colonist* (from the *Slocan Times*), October 12, 1894
39 British Columbia Legislative Assembly, "Annual Report of the Minister of Mines for the Year Ending 31st December, 1893," *British Columbia Sessional Papers* (Victoria: Government Printer, 1894).
40 *Seattle Post-Intelligencer*, August 4, 1893.
41 Turner to Robson, November 24, 1893, Robson Fonds.

9—HARD TIMES

1 Black, *You Can't Win*, 140.
2 *The Miner* (Nelson), November 25, 1893.
3 *Kaslo Times*, March 3, 1894.
4 *Nakusp Ledge*, March 15, 1894.
5 Ibid.
6 *The Miner* (Nelson), March 10, 1894.
7 "Queen v. Paul Savage," GR-0419, box 54, file 53, Attorney General Correspondence, BC Archives.
8 Ibid.
9 *Spokane Review*, February 26, 1894.
10 *The Miner* (Nelson), September 23, 1893
11 Ibid.
12 *Nakusp Ledge*, October 26, 1893.
13 *Vancouver Weekly World*, January 18, 1894.

14 *Nakusp Ledge*, October 26, 1893.
15 *Victoria Daily Colonist*, March 23, 1894.
16 *Nakusp Ledge*, April 26, 1894.
17 *The Tribune* (Nelson), January 27, 1894.
18 *Pacific Canadian* (New Westminster), February 24, 1894.
19 *The Tribune* (Nelson), February 24, 1894.
20 *The Miner* (Nelson), May 19,1894.
21 *The Miner* (Nelson), May 12, 1894.
22 *The Tribune* (Nelson), July 7, 1894.
23 *Nakusp Ledge*, July 19, 1894.
24 *The Province* (Victoria), April 6, 1894.
25 *Nakusp Ledge*, August 16, 1894.
26 Ibid.
27 *Nakusp Ledge*, August 30, 1894.
28 *The Tribune* (Nelson), September 1, 1894.
29 *Kootenay Mail* (Revelstoke), October 6, 1894.
30 *The Tribune* (Nelson), October 13, 1894.
31 *Slocan Prospector* (Three Forks), January 26, 1895.
32 *Slocan Times* (New Denver), December 27, 1894.
33 *Slocan Prospector* (Three Forks), January 11, 1895.
34 *The Miner* (Nelson), February 9, 1895.
35 *The Prospector* (Kaslo), July 25, 1895.
36 *The Ledge* (New Denver), April 4, 1895.
37 *The Weekly World* (Vancouver), January 18, 1894.
38 *The Oregonian* (Portland), November 3, 1893.

10—NATURE'S WRATH

1 D. Septer, *Flooding and Landslide Events Southern British Columbia, 1808–2006* (Victoria, BC: Ministry of Environment, Government of British Columbia, 2007).
2 *The Tribune* (Nelson), May 26, 1894.
3 *Nakusp Ledge*, June 7, 1894.
4 *The Miner* (Nelson), June 23, 1894.
5 *Nakusp Ledge*, December 6, 1894.
6 *Kaslo Times* (extra edition) June 9, 1894.
7 *Vancouver Daily World*, June 16, 1894.
8 *The Miner* (Nelson), June 9, 1984.
9 *Nakusp Ledge*, June 9, 1894.
10 *Nakusp Ledge*, August 2, 1894.
11 Ibid.
12 *Weiser Signal* (Idaho), August 2, 1894.
13 *Kootenay Mail* (Revelstoke), August 4, 1894.
14 *The Tribune* (Nelson), August 4, 1894
15 Ibid.
16 *Nakusp Ledge*, August 2, 1894.
17 Ibid.
18 *British Columbia Mining Record* 2, no. 1 (January 1895).
19 Church and Affleck, *A Young Scotsman's Adventures in Canada*, 43. Watson to Alice Clarke, August 27, 1894.

20 *Slocan Times* (New Denver), August 25, 1894.
21 *Chicago Inter Ocean*, August 26, 1894.
22 W.S. Drewry, "Report on Photo-Topographical Work in West Kootenay," *British Columbia Sessional Papers* (Victoria, BC: Government Printer, 1894).
23 Ibid.
24 *Inland Sentinel* (Kamloops), August 24, 1894.
25 *Nakusp Ledge*, September 13, 1894.
26 *The Tribune* (Nelson), July 27, 1893.
27 *The Tribune* (Nelson), October 6, 1894.

11—RAILWAYS

1 *Nakusp Ledge*, November 1, 1894.
2 *Slocan Times* (New Denver), November 3, 1894.
3 *The Miner* (Nelson), October 22, 1892
4 *Victoria Daily Colonist*, February 12, 1892.
5 *Tacoma Daily Ledger* (Washington), November 17, 1892.
6 *Victoria Daily Colonist*, May 4, 1892.
7 Affleck, *Kootenay Pathfinders*.
8 *Victoria Daily Colonist*, August 25, 1893.
9 *Nakusp Ledge*, March 1, 1894.
10 Julian Ralph, "Dan Dunn's Outfit," *Harper's Monthly Magazine* (November 1891).
11 Ferdinand, *Tagebuch meiner Reise um die Erde*. Translation by author.
12 *Dundee Courier* (Scotland), January 17, 1895.
13 Ibid.
14 *Kaslo Claim*, May 12, 1893.
15 *Kaslo-Slocan Examiner*, May 13, 1893.
16 Munn to Hill, April 12, 1893 (2), Great Northern Railway Company, President's records, Kaslo & Slocan Railway . . . 1892–1895, folder 1490, Minnesota Historical Society (hereinafter "GNR President's records").
17 *Helena Independent* (Montana), April 27, 1893.
18 *Nanaimo Free Press*, April 17, 1893.
19 Hill to Munn, April 13, 1893. GNR President's records.
20 Munn to Hill, May 22,1893, GNR President's records.
21 Parks to William Baillie, August 2, 1893, GNR President's records.
22 Stevens to Hill, September 8, 1893, GNR President's records.
23 *The Tribune* (Nelson), May 5, 1894.
24 Mrs. Leola Leon to Postmaster, Vernon, Kentucky, March 15, 1901, *Kirtley Family Genealogy Notes*.
25 *Nakusp Ledge*, July 5, 1894.
26 *Slocan Times* (New Denver), September 1, 1894.
27 *Kootenay Mail* (Revelstoke), December 1, 1894.
28 *The Ledge* (New Denver), January 3, 1895.
29 *Nakusp Ledge*, February 29, 1895.
30 British Columbia Legislative Assembly, "Annual Report of the Minister of Mines for the Year Ending 31st December, 1894," *British Columbia Sessional Papers* (Victoria: Government Printer, 1895).
31 Ibid.
32 *Spokane Spokesman-Review*; November 12, 1894.
33 *Kootenay Mail* (Revelstoke), December 15, 1894.

12—SETTLING IN

1 *Nakusp Ledge*, October 26, 1893.
2 *The New York Times*, October 27, 1896.
3 *The Miner* (Nelson), October 21, 1896.
4 *Slocan Prospector* (Three Forks), January 4, 1894.
5 *The Ledge* (New Denver), April 18, 1895.
6 Ibid.
7 *The Paystreak* (Sandon), April 3, 1897; Kaslo Morning News, June 1, 1898.
8 *The Miner* (Nelson), September 2, 1893.
9 *The Ledge* (New Denver), July 29, 1897.
10 Mary Lee Spence, "Waitresses in the Trans-Mississippi West: 'Pretty Waiter Girls,' Harvey Girls, and Union Maids," in *The Women's West, eds. Susan Armitage and Elizabeth Jameson* (Norman, OK: University of Oklahoma, 1987).
11 Frederic Niven, *The Lost Cabin Mine* (John Lane, The Bodley Head), 69.
12 Birth record for Katherine Ivy Sproat, Birth Registration 1895-09-907608, GR-2965, Birth registrations, BC Archives.
13 *The Ledge* (New Denver), May 14, 1896.
14 Middleton, *The Journal of Lady Aberdeen*.
15 *Slocan Times* (New Denver), December 27, 1894.
16 *The Ledge* (New Denver). December 27, 1894.
17 Rafferty to Brouse, July 26, 1896, in John Brighton, *J.E. "Doc" Brouse* (New Denver, BC: printed by author, 1978).
18 *The Ledge* (New Denver), December 5, 1895.
19 *Nakusp Ledge*, October 12, 1893.
20 *Butte Weekly Miner* (Montana), May 11, 1893.
21 *The Tribune* (Nelson), June 22, 1893.
22 *Slocan Times* (New Denver), September 1, 1894.
23 *Kootenay Mail* (Revelstoke), September 29, 1894.
24 *Kootenay Mail* (Revelstoke), December 8, 1894.
25 *The Ledge* (New Denver) April 25, 1895.

13—TRACKS TO SANDON

1 *Spokane Review*, February 12, 1894.
2 *Spokane Chronicle*, May 16, 1895.
3 *Victoria Daily Colonist*, July 14, 1895.
4 *Victoria Daily Colonist*, July 13, 1895.
5 M.A. Bucke to R.M. Bucke, July 4, 1896. Bucke Family Correspondence.
6 *The Paystreak* (Sandon), September 26, 1896.
7 *The Ledge* (New Denver), August 18, 1898.
8 *The Tribune* (Nelson), May 12, 1894.
9 *The Province* (Victoria), May 11, 1895.
10 *The Ledge* (New Denver), August 29, 1895.
11 Ibid.
12 *Kootenay Mail* (Revelstoke), August 10, 1895.
13 *The Ledge* (New Denver), August 22, 1895.
14 *The Ledge* (New Denver), January 9, 1896.
15 Ibid.
16 *Spokane Spokesman-Review*, December 24, 1894.

17 Middleton, *The Journal of Lady Aberdeen*.
18 *The Ledge* (New Denver) July 7, 1898.
19 British Columbia Legislative Assembly, "Report of the Chief Commissioner of Lands and Works of the Province of British Columbia for the year ending 31st December 1895," *British Columbia Sessional Papers (Victoria, Government Printer*, 1896).
20 Abbott to Premier Turner, December 9, 1895, Premier's Records, GR-0441, box 3, vol. 1, 46/96, BC Archives.
21 Joseph Harris, *Boom Days in the Slocan*.
22 *Woman's Signal*, May 7, 1896.
23 *Slocan Times* (New Denver), September 8, 1894.
24 Ibid.
25 *Nakusp Ledge*, October 18, 1894.
26 *The Ledge* (New Denver), June 6, 1895.
27 Campbell Sweeny Diary, April 2, 1896 and May 20, 1896, Campbell Sweeny fonds (AM22), City of Vancouver Archives.
28 *Victoria Daily Times*, August 14, 1897.
29 *The Ledge* (New Denver), February 18, 1897.
30 *Victoria Daily Colonist*, January 4, 1896.
31 *Rossland Miner*, December 3, 1896.
32 McDonald, *Making Vancouver*.
33 *Daily News-Advertiser* (Vancouver), September 12, 1896.
34 *Seattle Post-Intelligencer*, June 23, 1896.
35 Albert Frederick Sproule, "The Role of Patrick Burns in the Development of Western Canada" (MA thesis, University of Alberta, 1962).
36 *The Miner* (Nelson), April 25, 1896.
37 Kanes, *A Maine Prodigy*.
38 Ibid.
39 Webling, Peggy.
40 *Vancouver Semi-Weekly World*, September 1, 1896.
41 *San Francisco Call*, June 27, 1896.
42 *San Francisco Call*, May 29, 1896.
43 Ibid.
44 *Vancouver Semi-Weekly World*, September 1, 1896.

14—BATTER UP!

1 *Nakusp Ledge*, May 30, 1895.
2 *The Ledge* (New Denver), June 5, 1895.
3 British Columbia Legislative Assembly, "Third Report of the Provincial Board of Health of British Columbia Being for the year Ending 31st December 1897," *British Columbia Sessional Papers* (Victoria: Government Printer, 1898).
4 *The Province* (Victoria), May 12, 1894.
5 Barman, *Constance Lindsay Skinner*.
6 *Nakusp Ledge*, April 12, 1894.
7 *The Tribune* (Nelson), July 21, 1894.
8 *The Ledge* (New Denver), July 4, 1895.
9 Ibid.
10 *The Miner* (Nelson), July 13, 1895.

11 *The Ledge* (New Denver), August 1, 1895.
12 *Kaslo Claim*, August 10, 1895.
13 Ibid.
14 *The Miner* (Nelson), August 24, 1895.
15 Ibid.
16 *Kaslo Claim*, August 24, 1895.
17 White to Fellows, April 29, 1896, coll. 2504, box 14, folder 14, Maine Historical Society.
18 Dr. A. M. Sanford, "Notes and Comments," *British Columbia Historical Quarterly*, vol. 9 no. 1, (January 1945).
19 Dr. A.M. Sanford, "Notes and Comments," *British Columbia Historical Quarterly* 9, no. 1 (January 1945).
20 *Rossland Weekly Miner*, March 25, 1897.
21 *The Paystreak* (Sandon), January 29, 1898.
22 *Slocan City News*, May 29, 1897.
23 *The Ledge* (New Denver, from the Chicago Chronicle, August 28, 1898), September 22, 1898

15—GOOD TIMES

1 *Evening Mail* (Halifax), August 12, 1897.
2 *British Columbia Mining Record*, August 1896.
3 *Vancouver Daily World*, January 15, 1896.
4 Ibid.
5 *Chilliwack Progress*, March 18, 1896.
6 *Vancouver Daily World*, February 15, 1896.
7 *Vancouver Daily World*, November 7, 1896.
8 *Vancouver Daily World*, December 11, 1896.
9 H.P. Christie to A.J. McLorg, January 9, 1896. In Larry Jacobsen, *Walhachin: Birth of a Legend* (Port Coquitlam, BC: printed by the author, 2014).
10 *The Ledge* (New Denver), April 22, 1897.
11 *Rossland Miner*, March 11, 1897.
12 Porter to Harris, April 17, 1897, Bill Barlee Fonds, University of British Columbia Library Rare Books and Special Collections.
13 *The Tribune* (Nelson), October 6, 1894.
14 *The Inquirer* (Lancaster, Pennsylvania), August 16, 1913.
15 *Vancouver Daily World*, October 8, 1897.
16 *The Paystreak* (Sandon), July 17, 1897.
17 The term "Mrs. Grundy" refers to an extremely conventional or priggish person.
18 *The Province* (Victoria), November 14, 1896.
19 Ibid.
20 British Columbia Legislative Assembly, "Third Report of the Provincial Board of Health of British Columbia, being for the year ending 31st December, 1897." *British Columbia Sessional Papers* (Victoria: Government Printer, 1898).
21 *Victoria Daily Colonist* (from the New York Tribune), April 25, 1897.
22 British Columbia Legislative Assembly, "Second Report of the Provincial Board of Health of British Columbia, Being for the year ending December 31st, 1896." *British Columbia Sessional Papers* (Victoria: Government Printer, 1897).
23 *Spokane Spokesman-Review*, April 8, 1897.

24 *Spokane Spokesman-Review*, February 19, 1897.
25 *Morning Review* (Decatur, Illinois), July 8, 1897.
26 Ibid.
27 *The Mining Review* (Sandon), June 26, 1897.
28 A.S. Monro, "The Medical History of British Columbia," *The Canadian Medical Association Journal 1931–1932*.
29 *The Paystreak* (Sandon), May 1, 1897.
30 *The Paystreak* (Sandon and Cody), March 13, 1897.
31 *The Ledge* (New Denver), March 8, 1897
32 *The Ledge* (New Denver), June 3, 1897.
33 *Anaconda Standard* (Montana), May 3, 1897.
34 *Revelstoke Herald*, June 19, 1897.
35 British Columbia Legislative Assembly. "Third Report of the Provincial Board of Health of British Columbia, being for the year ending 31st, December, 1897."
36 *The Mining Review* (Sandon), September 11, 1897.
37 *San Francisco Examiner*, September 3, 1897; Sandon Mining Review, September 11, 1897.
38 British Columbia Legislative Assembly. "Third Report of the Provincial Board of Health of British Columbia, being for the year ending 31st, December, 1897."
39 *The San Francisco Call*, October 2, 1897.
40 *Tacoma Daily Ledger*, April 4, 1897.
41 *Spokane Spokesman-Review*, April 22, 1897.
42 Smyth, *Tales of the Kootenays*.
43 *Vancouver Daily World*, November 27, 1896.
44 *The Ledge* (New Denver), April 22, 1897.
45 *The Ledge* (New Denver), May 6, 1897.
46 *Slocan Pioneer* (Slocan City), May 1, 1897.
47 *Calgary Weekly Herald*, October 7, 1897.
48 *Spokane Spokesman-Review*, June 8, 1897.
49 *The Ledge* (New Denver), March 4, 1897.
50 *Vancouver Daily World*, March 5, 1897.
51 British Columbia Legislative Assembly, "Annual Report of the Minister of Mines for the Year Ending 31st December, 1897: Being an Account of Mining Operations for Gold, Coal, Etc., in the Province of British Columbia," *British Columbia Sessional Papers* (Victoria: Government Printer, 1898).
52 *New York Evening Post*, October 27, 1896.
53 *The Miner* (Nelson), August 29, 1896.
54 Robert Kubicek, "Economic Power at the Periphery: Canada, Australia and South Africa," in *Gentlemanly Capitalism and British Imperialism, ed. Raymond E. Dumett* (London: Longman, 1999).
55 *The Ledge* (New Denver), April 29, 1897.

16—SONG AND DANCE

1 *Spokane Daily Chronicle*, May 3, 1893.
2 *Butte Weekly Miner* (Montana), May 11, 1893
3 *Spokane Review*, March 1, 1893.
4 *Ye Hornet* (Vancouver) 1, no. 2, (July 8, 1893). "Castles in the Air" was a popular Scots song attributed to James Ballentine but based on a traditional tune. Cariboo gold rush poet James Anderson based his song "Rough but Honest Miner"

on "Castles in the Air." See Richard Thomas Wright and Kathryn Wellner, Castles in the Air: Music & Stories of British Columbia's 1860s Gold Rush (Kelowna, BC: Winter Quarters Press, 2000).

5 *British Columbia News* (Kaslo), September 3, 1897.
6 *Spokane Chronicle*, December 28, 1892.
7 *Slocan Prospector* (Three Forks), January 19, 1895.
8 *Slocan City News*, January 23, 1897.
9 *The Paystreak* (Sandon), July 31, 1897.
10 West, *The Saloon on the Rocky Mountain Frontier*.
11 Webling, Peggy.
12 Ibid.
13 *The Paystreak* (Sandon), January 16, 1897.
14 *The Tribune* (Nelson), September 25, 1897.
15 *The Tribune* (Nelson), September 10, 1898.
16 *Kaslo Morning News*, May 26, 1898; Canada Census 1901.
17 *Victoria Daily Times* (D.R. Young, from Slocan City News), June 2, 1898.
18 *Knox College Monthly and Presbyterian Magazine* 17, no. 8 (December 1893).
19 William Beattie, "West Kootenay Mission Field," *Knox College Monthly and Presbyterian Magazine* 20, no. 2 (June/July 1896).
20 *The Church Record* 3, no. 6 (June 1899).
21 *The Ledge* (New Denver), February 21, 1895.
22 *The Paystreak* (Sandon), March 20, 1897.
23 Ralph E. Dyar, *News for an Empire: The Story of the Spokesman-Review* (Caxton Printers, 1952), 54.
24 *The Miner* (Nelson), May 30, 1896.
25 *The Paystreak* (Sandon), April 16, 1898.
26 Greg Nesteroff, "Educating Hester: A Black Pioneer Family in Nelson," *Nelson Star*, March 6, 2016.
27 *The Freeman's Journal* (Dublin), December 5, 1898.
28 *Slocan Prospector* (Three Forks), February 2, 1895.
29 Susan Barr, David Newman, and Greg Nesteroff, *Ernest Mansfield: Gold, or I'm a Dutchman* (Trondheim, Norway: Akademika, 2012).
30 Kanes, *A Maine Prodigy*.
31 *The Miner* (Nelson, from the Daily Mail—London, March 26, 1897), May 1, 1897.
32 Duncan Emrich, "Songs of the Western Miners," *California Folklore Quarterly* 1, no. 3 (July 1942).

17—COMMUNITY

1 *Spokane Spokesman-Review*, May 22,1897.
2 *The Leader* (Regina), April 15, 1897.
3 Catherine O'Neail, interview by Imbert Orchard, October 1, 1964, AAAB0528, BC Archives.
4 *Vancouver Daily World*, April 9, 1897.
5 *Washington Standard* (Olympia), December 10, 1897.
6 *The Ledge* (New Denver), January 13, 1898.
7 *The Paystreak* (Sandon), November 26, 1898.
8 *Spokane Spokesman-Review*, October 23, 1897

9 M.A. Bucke to R.M. Bucke, April 5, 1897, Bucke Family Correspondence.

10 Petition, Women's Franchise, 1897, Journals of the Legislative Assembly of British Columbia, (Victoria: Government Printer, 1897).

11 *The Ledge* (New Denver), December 12, 1895; The Paystreak (Sandon), July 31, 1897.

12 *Slocan Pioneer*, November 27, 1897.

13 *The Paystreak* (Sandon), January 23, 1897.

14 *Slocan Pioneer*, August 14, 1897.

15 *Vancouver Daily World*, January 11, 1898; *The Mining Review* (Sandon), October 1, 1898. New Denver seems to have been anomalous, with the starting salary for a teacher at fifty dollars per month, regardless of gender.

16 *The Mining Review* (Sandon), September 30, 1899.

17 *Guelph Daily Mercury and Advertiser*, September 25, 1897.

18 *The Mining Review* (Sandon), July 24, 1897.

19 "Women Miners," *Canadian Home Journal*, vol. 2 no. 11 (March 1897).

20 Nelson *Miner*, June 27, 1896

21 *Kappa Alpha Theta* 8, no. 1 (October 1893).

22 Robie L. Reid, Historical Notes and Biographical Sketches: 1848–1935 (Vancouver: Chapman & Warwick, 1945).

23 *Mining Review* (Sandon), July 17, 1897.

24 *The Mining Review* (Sandon), November 5, 1898.

25 *Vancouver Daily World*, February 25, 1899.

26 *Vancouver Daily World*, March 2, 1899.

27 *The Daily News* (Nelson), May 22, 1922; Bullock-Webster to Hussey, November 7, 1899, GR-0353, BC Archives.

28 *British Columbia Mining Critic*, November 1897.

18—DISTRACTIONS

1 British Columbia Legislative Assembly, "Annual Report of the Minister of Mines for the Year Ending 31st December, 1897: Being an Account of Mining Operations for Gold, Coal, Etc., in the Province of British Columbia," *British Columbia Sessional Papers* (Victoria: Government Printer, 1898).

2 Fraser, *British Columbia for Settlers*.

3 *Vancouver Daily World*, September 17, 1896.

4 *The Evening Star* (Toronto), February 15, 1897.

5 *Vancouver Daily World*, February 25, 1896.

6 *Revelstoke Herald*, September 8, 1897.

7 Warren Bell, "Seven Years in Kootenay" (unpublished manuscript, 1945–51?), Gold Trails and Ghost Towns Facebook site.

8 *The Ledge* (New Denver), October 1, 1896.

9 *Canadian Mining Review*, December 1896.

10 Spence, *British Investments and the American Mining Frontier*.

11 *The Ledge* (New Denver), September 23, 1897.

12 Deane, *Mounted Police Life in Canada*.

13 Samuel B. Steele to Commissioner, December 14, 1896, RCMP Papers, RG-18, vol. 132, Library and Archives Canada (referenced in Dempsey, *Charcoal's World*).

14 *The Ledge* (New Denver), September 23, 1897.

15 Deane, *Mounted Police Life in Canada*.
16 *The Weekly News-Advertiser* (Vancouver), June 9, 1897.
17 *The Ledge* (New Denver), September 16, 1897.
18 *Kaslo Kootenaian*, October 6, 1897.
19 British Columbia Legislative Assembly, "Annual Report of the Minister of Mines for the Year Ending 31st December, 1897: Being an Account of Mining Operations for Gold, Coal, Etc., in the Province of British Columbia," *British Columbia Sessional Papers* (Victoria: Government Printer, 1898).
20 *The Paystreak* (Sandon), December 18, 1898.
21 *The Ledge* (New Denver), December 16, 1897.
22 *The Silvertonian* (Silverton), May 28, 1898.
23 Annual Report of the Minister of Mines for the Year Ending 31st December 1897.
24 *Ottawa Journal*, September 11, 1897.
25 *Victoria Daily Colonist*, August, 24, 1897.
26 *Kaslo Kootenaian*, August 25, 1897.
27 M.A. Bucke to R.M. Bucke, August 31, 1897, Bucke Family Correspondence.
28 *The Province* (Victoria), December 11, 1897.
29 McGibbons to Hussey, February 12, 1898, GR-0353, box 17, BC Archives.
30 *Spokane Daily Chronicle*, July 14, 1897.
31 *Kaslo Kootenaian*, July 17, 1897.

19—BAD BEHAVIOUR

1 *The Mining Review* (Sandon), September 4, 1897.
2 *Arizona Republican*, September 19, 1896.
3 *The Ledge* (New Denver), January 28, 1897.
4 *Slocan Times* (New Denver), September 1, 1894.
5 *Vancouver Daily World*, August 28, 1899.
6 H.P. Christie to A.J. McLorg, January 9, 1896. In Larry Jacobsen, *Walhachin: Birth of a Legend* (Port Coquitlam, BC: printed by the author, 2014).
7 *St. John's Evening Telegram*, June 4, 1897.
8 *Kaslo Claim Relocated*, February 1, 1896.
9 *Sandon Paystreak*, February 12, 1898.
10 *Mining Review* (Sandon), August 21, 1897.
11 *The Ledge* (New Denver), September 30, 1897.
12 Mountain to Hussey, February 20, 1897, GR-055, box 13, file M, BC Archives.
13 *Slocan Pioneer* (Slocan City), September 4, 1897.
14 *The Prospector* (Kaslo), August 1, 1895.
15 *Vancouver Semi-Weekly World*, March 3, 1899.
16 Kanes, *A Maine Prodigy*.
17 *The Mining Review* (Sandon), November 19, 1898.
18 *The Miner* (Nelson), November18, 1898.
19 *Chicago Daily Tribune*, March 26, 1899.
20 Ibid.
21 Ibid.
22 Joseph Harris, *Boom Days in the Slocan*.
23 Ibid.
24 *The Ledge* (New Denver), December 10, 1896.
25 Christie to Hussey, February 8, 1897, GR-055, box 13, file C, BC Archives.

26 *Slocan Pioneer* (Slocan City), July 31, 1897.
27 *Spokane Spokesman-Review*, August 6, 1897.
28 Ibid.
29 Smith to Hussey, August 6, 1897, GR-055, box 16, file S, BC Archives.
30 *The Ledge* (New Denver), September 30, 1897.
31 *The Paystreak* (Sandon), July 30, 1898.

20—A POOR SHOWING

1 *The Ledge* (New Denver), December 29, 1898.
2 *The Commercial* (Bangor, Maine), May 6, 1899.
3 *Victoria Daily Colonist* (from the Spokane Spokesman-Review), August 25, 1898.
4 *Cranbrook Herald*, December 15, 1898.
5 *Kaslo Morning News*, June 24, 1898.
6 *The Paystreak* (Sandon), October 8, 1898.
7 *Victoria Globe*, May 4, 1899.
8 *The Ledge* (New Denver), January 13, 1898
9 *The Paystreak* (Sandon), May 21, 1898.
10 *The Mining Review* (Sandon), May 21, 1898.
11 *The Paystreak* (Sandon), August 14, 1897.
12 *The Paystreak* (Sandon), July 31, 1897.
13 *The Mining Review* (Sandon), October 9, 1897.
14 *The Ledge* (New Denver), October 7, 1897.
15 *The Province* (Vancouver), July 5, 1899.
16 *Daily Record (Glasgow), November 14, 1899.*
17 Sayers to Hussey, November 19, 1899, GR-0353, BC Archives.
18 *The Daily Colonist* (Victoria), December 8, 1899.
19 *Nelson Weekly Miner*, October 13, 1899.
20 *Calgary Weekly Herald*, September 28, 1899.
21 *Victoria Daily Colonist*, December 8, 1899.
22 *The Mining Review* (Sandon) March 18, 1899.
23 *Victoria Daily Colonist* (from the Kaslo Kootenaian), September 30, 1899.
24 *The Mining Review* (Sandon), October 14, 1899.
25 *The Mining Review* (Sandon), September 23, 1899.
26 *The Paystreak* (Sandon), January 20,1900.

EPILOGUE

1 Stocks, *Journal of a Six Months' Tour by a Lady Octogenarian*.
2 *The Ledge*, February, 3 1898. The man from Flint was likely Thomas Jones Lloyd. See von Krogh, *Early Stories from Slocan Lake*; *Rossland Weekly Miner*, December 10, 1896.
3 Rolla P. Currie, "An Insect-Collecting Trip to British Columbia," *Proceedings of the Entomological Society of Washington*, vol. 6 (1904).
4 *The Ledge* (New Denver), October 17, 1895.
5 Megan J. Davies, "Old Age in British Columbia: The Case of the 'Lonesome Prospector,'" *BC Studies*, no. 118 (1998).
6 Petersen, *Window in the Rock*.
7 *DeLamar Nugget* (Idaho), March 2, 1895.
8 *Cascade Record*, January 12, 1901.

9 *The Paystreak* (Sandon), March 20, 1897.
10 *The Silvertonian* (Silverton), September 14, 1901.
11 Diary of James Wickersham, November 22, 1904, Alaska State Library, MS 107, Diary 8.
12 E.E. Coy military records, Washington State Digital Archives.
13 R.N. DeArmond, "Stroller" White, *Tales of a Klondike Newsman* (Vancouver: Mitchell Press, 1969).
14 *Rossland Weekly Miner*, April 20, 1899; Victoria Daily Times, August 1, 1902.
15 *The Ledge* (New Denver), September 9, 1904.
16 *The Okanagan Commoner*, June 2, 1921; Canada Census 1901.
17 *The Paystreak*, October 20, 1900.
18 *Lethbridge Herald*, September 2, 1937.
19 Jim Hazelwood, "British Columbia's Lost City," *Vancouver Sun Magazine Supplement*, September 16, 1950..

BIBLIOGRAPHY

A select bibliography is included below. Sources not listed in the bibliography will be found in the endnotes.

PUBLICATIONS

Affleck, E.L. *Kootenay Lake Chronicles*. Vol. 4 of *The Kootenays in Retrospect*. Vancouver: Alexander Nicolls Press, 1978.

Affleck, E.L. *Kootenay Pathfinders: Settlement in the West Kootenay District 1885–1920*. Vol. 2 of *The Kootenays in Retrospect*. Vancouver: Alexander Nicolls Press, 1976.

Affleck, E.L. *Kootenay Yesterdays*. Vol. 3 of *The Kootenays in Retrospect*. Vancouver: Alexander Nicolls Press, 1976.

Angier, Bradford. *We Like it Wild*. Toronto: Stackpole Books, 1963.

Barman, Jean. *Constance Lindsay Skinner: Writing on the Frontier*. Toronto: University of Toronto Press, 2002.

Barman, Jean. *Sojourning Sisters: The Lives and Letters of Jessie and Annie McQueen*. Toronto: University of Toronto Press, 2003.

Barman, Jean. *The West Beyond the West: A History of British Columbia*. 3rd ed. Toronto: University of Toronto Press, 2007.

Barrington, H., ed. *The L.S. Group: British Columbia's First Land Surveyors*. Altona, MB: Friesens/Association of British Columbia Land Surveyors, 2007.

Basque, Garnet. *West Kootenay: The Pioneer Years*. Langley, BC: Sunfire Publications, 1990.

Belshaw, John Douglas. *Becoming British Columbia: A Population History*. Vancouver: University of British Columbia Press, 2009.

Black, Jack. *You Can't Win*. New York: Macmillan, 1926.

Black, Mrs. George [Martha]. *My Seventy Years*. As told to Elizabeth Bailey Price. London: Thomas Nelson & Sons, 1938.

Blake, Don. *The Valley of the Ghosts: The History along Highway 31A, B.C.* Vernon, BC: Wayside Press, 1988.

Bowlsby, Craig H. *The Knights of Winter: Hockey in British Columbia 1895–1911*. Vancouver: printed by the author, 2006.

Cail, Robert E. *Land, Man, and the Law: The Disposal of Crown Lands in British Columbia, 1871–1913*. Vancouver: University of British Columbia Press, 1974.

Casorso, Victor. *The Casorso Story: A Century of Social History in the Okanagan Valley*. Okanagan Falls, BC: Rima Books, 1983.

Church, John S., and Edward L. Affleck. *A Young Scotsman's Adventures in Canada: The Letters of John Adam Watson*. Vancouver: Alexander Nicholls Press, 2002.

Connor, Ralph [Charles Gordon]. *Black Rock: A Tale of the Selkirks*. New York: Grosett & Dunlop, 1903.

Crampton, Frank A. *Deep Enough: A Working Stiff in the Western Mining Camps*. Norman, OK: University of Oklahoma Press, 1982. First published 1956.

Deane, R. Burton. *Mounted Police Life in Canada: A Record of Thirty-One Years' Service, 1883–1914*. Toronto: Cassell and Company, 1916.

Dempsey, Hugh A. *Charcoal's World*. Saskatoon, SK: Western Producer Prairie Books, 1978.

Dunae, Patrick A. *Gentlemen Emigrants: From the British Public Schools to the Canadian Frontier*. Vancouver: Douglas & McIntyre, 1981.

Dyar, Ralph E. *News for an Empire: The Story of the Spokesman-Review*. Caldwell, ID: Caxton Printers, 1952.

Fahey, John. *Inland Empire: D.C. Corbin and Spokane*. Seattle: University of Washington Press, 1965.

Ferdinand, Franz. *Tagebuch meiner Reise um die Erde, 1892–1893*. 2 vols. Vienna: A. Holder, 1895.

Fetherling, George. *River of Gold: The Fraser & Cariboo Gold Rushes*. Vancouver: Subway, 2009.

Findley, J.M., and K.S. Coates. *Parallel Destinies: Canadian-American Relations West of the Rockies*. Seattle: University of Washington Press, 2002.

Fraser, Agnes [Frances Macnab]. *British Columbia for Settlers: Its Mines, Trade and Agriculture*. London: Chapman & Hall, 1898.

Fraser, Esther. *Wheeler*. Banff, AB: Summerthought, 1978.

Galloway, C.F.J. *The Call of the West: Letters From British Columbia*. London: T. Fisher Unwin, 1916.

Gordon, Katherine. *The Slocan: Portrait of a Valley*. Winlaw, BC: Sono Nis Press, 2004.

Gosnell, R.E. *A History of British Columbia*. Victoria, BC: Lewis Publishing Company, 1906.

Gowen, Herbert. *Pioneer Church Work in British Columbia: Being a Memoir of the Episcopate of Acton Windeyer Sillitoe, First Bishop of New Westminster*. London: A.R. Mowbray, 1899.

Graham, Clara. *Kootenay Mosaic*. Vancouver: Evergreen Press, 1971.

Grove, Lyndon. *Pacific Pilgrims*. Vancouver: Fforbez Publications, 1979.

Harris, Cole. *Newspapers & the Slocan in the 1890s*. New Denver, BC: Chameleon Fire, 2016.

Harris, Cole. *Ranch in the Slocan: A Biography of a Kootenay Farm, 1896–2017*. Madeira Park, BC: Harbour Publishing, 2018.

Harris, Cole. *The Resettlement of British Columbia: Essays on Colonialism and Geographical Change*. Vancouver: University of British Columbia Press, 1997.

Harris, Joseph Colebrook. *Beginnings of the Bosun Ranch*. New Denver, BC: Chameleon Fire, 2015.

Harris, Joseph Colebrook. *Boom Days in the Slocan*. New Denver, BC: Chameleon Fire, 2014.

Harris, Joseph Colebrook. *Martin Fry, Frontiersman*. New Denver, BC: Chameleon Fire, 2018.

Johnson, Kate. *Pioneer Days of Nakusp and the Arrow Lakes*. Nakusp, BC: n.p., 1964. First published 1951.

Jones, Jo Fraser, ed. *Hobnobbing with a Countess and Other Okanagan Adventures: The Diaries of Alice Barrett Parke, 1891–1900*. Vancouver: University of British Columbia Press, 2001.

Jonnes, Jill. *Empires of Light: Edison, Tesla, Westinghouse, and the Race to Electrify the World*. New York: Random House, 2003.

Kanes, Candace A., ed. *A Maine Prodigy: The Life & Adventures of Elise Fellows White*. Compiled by her grandson, Houghton M. White. Portland: Maine Historical Society, 2011.

Keenan, Jerry. *The Life of Yellowstone Kelly*. Albuquerque: University of New Mexico Press, 2006.

Kingsmill, Harold. *First History of Rossland, B.C.: With Sketches of Some of Its Prominent Citizens, Firms and Corporations*. Rossland, BC: Stunden and Perrine, 1897.

Kipling, Rudyard. *Letters of Travel (1892–1913)*. London: Macmillan, 1920.

Knapfla, Louis A., ed. *Law & Justice in a New Land: Essays in Western Canadian Legal History*. Calgary: Carswell, 1985.

Lees, J.A., and W.J. Clutterbuck. *A Ramble in British Columbia*. London: Longman, Green and Co., 1888.

MacEwan, Grant. *Pat Burns: Cattle King*. Saskatoon, SK: Western Producer Prairie Books, 1981.

MacGowan, Michael. *The Hard Road to Klondike*. London: Routledge and Kegan Paul, 1962.

Macnab, Frances. *See* Fraser, Agnes.

Magnuson, Richard G. *Coeur d'Alene Diary: The First Ten Years of Hardrock Mining in North Idaho*. Portland: Binford & Mort, 1968.

Marks, Lynne. *Infidels and the Damn Churches: Irreligion and Religion in Settler British Columbia*. Vancouver: University of British Columbia Press, 2017.

Marshall, D. *Sawdust Caesars and Family Ties in the Southern Interior Forests*. Salmon Arm, BC: Okanagan Historical Society, 2003.

May, Dave. *Sandon: The Mining Centre of the Silvery Slocan*. Kaslo, BC: printed by the author, 1986.

McCuaig, George. *Kaslo: The First 100 Years.* Kaslo, BC: Semco Press, 1993.

McDonald, Robert A.J. *Making Vancouver: Class, Status, and Social Boundaries, 1863–1913*. Vancouver: University of British Columbia Press, 1996.

Middleton, R.M., ed. *The Journal of Lady Aberdeen: The Okanagan Valley in the Nineties*. Victoria, BC: Morriss Publishing, 1986.

Mills, George G., ed. A *Half Century of Random Reminiscences of Captain William White, K.C.* Sainte-Anne-de-Bellevue, QC: Shoreline, 2010.

Minister of the Interior. *Summary Report of the Geological Branch for the Year 1894*. Ottawa: S.E. Dawson, Printer to the Queen's Most Excellent Majesty, 1895.

Moir, Rita. *The Third Crop*. Winlaw, BC: Sono Nis Press, 2011.

Morgan, Murray. *Skid Road: An Informal Portrait of Seattle*. New York: Viking Press, 1951.

Morrissey, Katherine G. *Mental Territories: Mapping the Inland Empire*. Ithaca, NY: Cornell University Press, 1997.

Mouat, Jeremy. *The Business of Power: Hydro-Electricity in Southeastern British Columbia 1897–1997*. Victoria, BC: Sono Nis Press, 1997.

Mouat, Jeremy. *Roaring Days: Rossland's Mines and the History of British Columbia*. Vancouver: University of British Columbia Press, 1995.

Murray, Peter. *Home From the Hill: Three Gentlemen Adventurers*. Victoria, BC: Horsdal & Schubart, 1994.

Myers, Clark. *The Bennett Letters*. Kitchener, ON: Clark Myers, 2016.

Niven, Frederick. *The Lost Cabin Mine*. London: John Lane, The Bodley Head, 1908.

Nobbs, Ruby M. *Revelstoke: History and Heritage*. Altona, MB: Friesens, 1998.

Norris, John. *Historic Nelson: The Early Years*. Lantzville, BC: Oolichan Books, 1995.

Norris, John. *Old Silverton*. Silverton, BC: Silverton Historical Society, 1985.

Ormsby, Margaret A. *British Columbia: A History*. Vancouver: Macmillan, 1958.

Parent, Milton, ed. *Port of Nakusp*. Vol. 2, *Centennial Series*. Nakusp, BC: Arrow Lakes Historical Society, 1992.

Payne, Don, ed. *Life and Experiences of Dan Alton, in Western and Eastern Canada: An Autobiography*. USA, printed by the editor, 2007.

Pearkes, Eileen Delehanty. *The Geography of Memory: Recovering Stories of a Landscape's First People*. Winlaw, BC: Kutenai House Press, 2002.

Pellowski, Veronika. *Silver, Lead & Hell*. Sandon, BC: Prospectors Pick, 1992.

Petersen, Eugene (Pelle). *Window in the Rock*. Fairfield, WA: Ye Galleon Press, 1993.

Phillipps-Wolley, Clive. *Songs from a Young Man's Land*. Toronto: Thomas Allen, 1917.

Pocock, G. *Outrider of Empire: The Life & Adventures of Roger Pocock*. Edmonton: University of Alberta Press, 2007.

Pocock, Roger. *Following the Frontier*. New York: McClure, Phillips & Co., 1903.

Pryce, Paula. *Keeping the Lakes' Way: Reburial and the Re-Creation of a Moral World among an Invisible People*. Toronto: University of Toronto Press, 1999.

Ralph, Julian. *On Canada's Frontier: Sketches of History, Sport, and Adventure, and of the Indians, Missionaries, Fur-Traders, and Newer Settlers of Canada*. New York: Harper & Brothers, 1892.

Reksten, Terry. *The Dunsmuir Saga*. Vancouver: Douglas & McIntyre, 1991.

Ringheim, Margery. *Historical Kaslo: British Columbia*. Kaslo, BC: Kaslo Historical Society, 1959[?].

Roosevelt, Theodore. *The Wilderness Hunter: An Account of the Big Game of the United States and Its Chase with Horse Hound, and Rifle*. New York: G.P. Putnam's Sons, 1909.

Roy, Patricia E. A *White Man's Province: British Columbia Politicians and Chinese and Japanese Immigrants, 1858–1914*. Vancouver: University of British Columbia Press, 1989.

Runnalls, F.E. *It's God's Country: A Review of the United Church and Its Founding Partners, the Congregational, Methodist, and Presbyterian Churches in British Columbia*. Ocean Park, BC: published by the author, 1974.

Sands, Harold. *The Dashing Sally Duel and Other Tales*. New York: Broadway Publishing, 1905.

Scholefield, E.O.S., and F.W. Howay. *British Columbia from the Earliest Times to the Present*. Vol. 2. Vancouver: S.J. Clarke Publishing, 1914.

Sinclair, J. *The Refiners: A Century of B.C. Sugar*. Vancouver: Douglas &McIntyre, 2009.

Smith, Duane A. *Rocky Mountain Mining Camps: The Urban Frontier*. Lincoln, NE: University of Nebraska Press, 1975. First published 1967.

Smith, Duane A. *Silver Saga: The Story of Caribou, Colorado*. Boulder: Pruett Publishing, 1974.

Smith, Duane A. *The Trail of Gold and Silver: Mining in Colorado, 1859–2009*. Boulder: University Press of Colorado, 2009.

Smith, Peter J. "Eight Hours Underground." *British Columbia History* 56, no. 4 (Winter 2023): 13–14.

Smith, Peter J. *Silver Rush: British Columbia's Silvery Slocan, 1891–1900*. 2nd ed. Ladysmith, BC: Two Daughters, 2022.

Smyth, Fred J. *Tales of the Kootenays*. Vancouver: J.J. Douglas, 1972. First published 1942.

Spence, Clark C. *British Investments and the American Mining Frontier, 1860–1901*. Moscow, ID: University of Idaho Press, 1958.

Spence, Clark C. *Mining Engineers and the American West: The Lace-Boot Brigade, 1849–1933*. London: Yale University Press, 1970.

Spinks, William Ward. *Tales of the British Columbia Frontier*. Toronto: Ryerson Press, 1933.

Stainton, Shirley D. *Children of the Kootenays: Memories of Mining Towns*. Victoria, BC: Heritage House, 2018.

Standage, Tom. *The Victorian Internet: The Remarkable Story of the Telegraph and the Nineteenth Century's On-Line Pioneers*. New York: Walker and Company, 1998.

Steele, Samuel B. *Forty Years in Canada*. Vancouver: Prospero, 2000. First published 1916.

Stocks, Anne J. *Journal of a Six Months' Tour by a Lady Octogenarian from Scotland to British Columbia and Back: With Views and Portraits*. Kirkcaldy, Scotland: Fifeshire Advertiser, 1901.

Stonier-Newman, L. *The Lawman: Adventures of a Frontier Diplomat*. Victoria, BC: Touchwood Editions, 2006.

Stovel, Laura. *Swift River: Stories of the First People and First Travellers on the Columbia River around Revelstoke*. Oregon Grape Press, 2019.

Thomas, Philip J. *Songs of the Pacific Northwest*. Saanichton, BC: Hancock House, 1979.

Tolton, G.E. *The Cowboy Cavalry: The Story of the Rocky Mountain Rangers*. Victoria, BC: Heritage House, 2011.

Trennert, Robert A. *Riding the High Wire: Aerial Mine Tramways in the West*. Boulder: University Press of Colorado, 2001.

Tuchman, Barbara. *The Proud Tower: A Portrait of the World Before the War, 1890–1914*. London: Hamish Hamilton, 1966.

Turner, A.T. *Bluebell Memories: A Pictorial History of the Bluebell Mine, Riondel, B.C.* Riondel, BC: Riondel Historical Society, 1997.

Turner, R.D. *Sternwheelers and Steam Tugs: An Illustrated History of the Canadian Pacific River*. Victoria, BC: Sono Nis Press, 1984.

Turner, R.D., and D. Wilkie. *The Skyline Limited: The Kaslo and Slocan Railway*. Victoria, BC: Sono Nis Press, 1994.

Twain, Mark. *Roughing It*. Hartford, CT: American Publishing Company, 1872.

Volovsek, Walter O. *The Green Necklace: The Vision Quest of Edward Mahon*. Castlegar, BC: Otmar Publishing, 2012.

von Krogh, G.H. *Early Boats on Slocan Lake*. New Denver, BC: printed by the author, 2018.

von Krogh, G.H. *Early New Denver 1891–1904: A Selection of Data on People, Places & Things*. New Denver, BC: printed by the author, 2016.

von Krogh, G.H. *Early Stories from Slocan Lake*. New Denver, BC: printed by the author, 2021.

von Krogh, G.H. *Early Years: Dr. J.E. Brouse & His Slocan Hospital*. New Denver, BC: printed by the author, 2023.

von Krogh, G.H., and Cole Harris. *Early New Denver*. New Denver, BC: Chameleon Fire, 2017.

Wardner, Jim. *Jim Wardner of Wardner, Idaho*. New York: Anglo-American Publishing, 1900.

Webling, Peggy. *Peggy: The Story of One Score Years and Ten*. London: Hutchinson, n.d., c. 1924.

Wells, M.J. *Tramway Titan*. Victoria, BC: Trafford Publishing, 2005.

West, Elliot. *The Saloon on the Rocky Mountain Frontier*. Lincoln, NE: University of Nebraska Press, 1979.

Williams, D.R. *Call in Pinkerton's: American Detectives at Work for Canada*. Toronto: Dundurn Press, 1998.

Williams, D.R. "... *The Man for a New Country": Sir Matthew Baillie Begbie*. Sidney, BC: Gray's Publishing, 1977.

Willis, B. et al., eds. *Pioneer Families of Kaslo*. Kaslo, BC: Kootenay Lake Historical Society, 1980.

Woodhouse, Philip R. *Monte Cristo*. Seattle: Mountaineers, 1979.

UNPUBLISHED SOURCES

Cottingham, Mollie. "A History of the West Kootenay District in British Columbia." MA thesis, University of British Columbia, 1947.

Meyer, Ronald Howard. "The Evolution of Railways in the Kootenays." MA thesis, University of British Columbia, 1970.

Mouat, Jeremy. "Mining in the Settler Dominions: A Comparative Study of the Industry in Three Communities from the 1880s to the First World War." PhD thesis, University of British Columbia, May 1988.

PRINCIPAL NEWSPAPERS

Many historic newspapers can now be found online. Sources include:

- British Colonist Online Edition, 1858–1980: britishcolonist.ca
- University of British Columbia Open Collections, BC Historical Newspapers: open.library.ubc.ca/collections/bcnewspapers
- Chronicling America: chroniclingamerica.loc.gov/newspapers
- Newspapers.com: newspapers.com
- Proquest Historical B.C. Newspapers: discover.clarivate.com/ProQuest_BCHistoricalNewspapers

British Columbia News (Kaslo, BC)
The Coeur d'Alene Miner (Wallace, ID)
Guelph Evening Mercury (Guelph, ON)
Hot Springs News (Ainsworth, BC)
Inland Sentinel (Kamloops, BC)
The Kaslo Claim (Kaslo, BC)
The Kaslo Claim Relocated (Kaslo, BC)
The Kaslo Times (Kaslo, BC)
The Kaslo-Slocan Examiner (Kaslo, BC)
The Kootenai Herald (Bonner's Ferry, ID)
The Kootenaian (Kaslo, BC)
The Ledge (Greenwood, BC)
The Ledge (New Denver, BC)
The Miner (Nelson, BC)
The Mining Review (Sandon, BC)
Nakusp Ledge (Nakusp, BC)
The News-Advertiser (Vancouver, BC)
The Paystreak (Sandon, BC)
The Prospector (Kaslo, BC)
The Province (Victoria and Vancouver, BC)
Rossland Miner (Rossland, BC)
Rossland Weekly Miner (Rossland, BC)
The Silvertonian (Silverton, BC)
The Slocan City News (Slocan City, zBC)
The Slocan Pioneer (Slocan City, BC)
Slocan Prospector (Three Forks, BC)

The Slocan Sun (Kaslo, BC)
The Slocan Times (New Denver, BC)
The Spokane Daily Chronicle (Spokane, WA)
The Spokane Review (Spokane, WA)
The Spokesman-Review (Spokane, WA)
The Tribune (Nelson, BC)
Vancouver Daily World (Vancouver, BC)
Victoria Daily Colonist (Victoria, BC)
Victoria Daily Times (Victoria, BC)

JOURNALS AND MAGAZINES

BC Studies
British Columbia Gazette
British Columbia Historical News
British Columbia History
British Columbia Mining Record
The Canadian Magazine of Politics, Science, Art and Literature
Canadian Mining Journal
Canadian Mining and Mechanical Review
Canadian Rail
Engineering and Mining Journal
The Illustrated London News
Harper's Monthly Magazine
Knox College Monthly
Pacific Northwesterner
Wide World Magazine

ARCHIVES, MUSEUMS, AND LIBRARIES

Arrow Lakes Historical Society
British Columbia Archives
British Columbia Legislative Library
City of Vancouver Archives
Cowichan Valley Archives
Glenbow Archives
Kootenay Lake Archives (Kaslow)
Library and Archives Canada
Maine Historical Society
Minnesota Historical Society
Silver Slocan Historical Society (New Denver)
Slocan Valley Historical Society (Slocan)
Touchstones Museum and Archives (Nelson)
University of British Columbia Library, Rare Books and Special Collections
University of Western Ontario, Archives and Special Collections
Vancouver Public Library
Washington State Digital Archives

MISCELLANEOUS

Canada Census
British Columbia Orders-in-Council
British Columbia Sessional Papers
Journals of the Legislative Assembly of British Columbia
United Kingdom Census
United States Census

INDEX

Note: Page numbers in *italics* refer to photographs or maps.

PETER SMITH is a lifelong history buff, award-winning author, and retired civil servant. He holds a post-graduate degree in Folklife Studies from the University of Leeds (UK), and has published articles in *British Columbia Magazine* and the *Silvery Slocan Historical Society* newsletter. In 2020, he won the BC Historical Federation's Community History Award for his extensively researched first book on BC's silver rush.